MY DEAR
PEOPLE

BY

Monsignor Joseph Ferraro

the PeppertreePress, LLC
Sarasota, Florida

ISBN: 978-1-61493-791-3

Library of Congress Number: 2021920563

Printed October 2021

In loving memory of

Monsignor Joseph Ferraro,

who often said,

*"I have no doubt in my mind that in some way
God will touch you during this Mass."*

We will always remember how beautifully
he sang the Doxology:

*O through Him, with Him, and in Him in the unity
of the Holy Spirit. All glory and honor is yours,
oh Father, forever more. Amen.*

We will always remember
His love for us.

Monsignor Joseph Ferraro

BLESSING FOR THE BOOK

May all of you be blessed by reading the homilies and stories in the book from Monsignor Joseph Ferraro. He came from a great Italian family where many of his values and beliefs were shaped at the dinner table. Monsignor is also known for his book, "Evening Prayers at Sea", with prayers of precious sailors of the USS Carl Vinson. May he continue his ministry of faith, duty, and love for all of you through this book. I thank God for Monsignor's years of ministry here at Holy Cross Church.

FATHER MARCIN KOZIOLA

Father Joe was known to every sailor, coast guardsman and marine as more than a priest, but as a friend as well. His pastoral acumen transcended every relationship and friendship he made during his military and civilian ministry.

Father Joe and I were friends over fifty years in and out of the military. On many occasions I attended his Masses. Father Joe always met his parishioners where they lived and what they were experiencing. As Navy Chaplains, we both understood how important it was to deliver real homilies to reach the heart and soul of the believer. Father Joe did this in a most spiritual and personal way.

We can now enjoy these homilies and stories again and again in this format. In our long history and friendship, I am honored to open this dialogue with Father Joe's most important thoughts and works.

REV. VINCE CARROLL,
CAPTAIN, U.S. NAVY CHAPLAIN (RETIRED)

Saint Pope John Paul II and Monsignor Ferraro

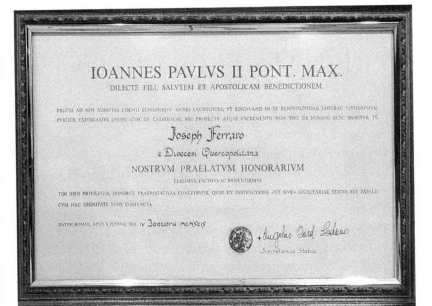

Recognition as Monsignor, January 4, 1999

POPE JOHN PAUL II

TO OUR DEAR SON

OF THE DIOCESE Of OAKLAND

OUR GREETINGS AND BLESSINGS

WE HAVE RECEIVED VARIOUS COMMENDATIONS OF YOU, WHICH BRING JOY TO OUR HEART AND PROMPT US TO SHOW PUBLICLY A SIGN OF OUR HIGH REGARD FOR YOU. THEREFORE, IN LIGHT OF YOUR SPECIAL MERITS, WE CHOSE TO NAME YOU

MONSIGNOR JOSEPH FERRARO

OUR PRELATE OF HONOR

AND WE GRANT YOU ALL THE RIGHTS AND PRIVILEGES AND HONORS WHICH ARE ATTACHED TO THIS TITLE, AS THEY ARE ENUMERATED IN THE DOCUMENT "UT SIVE" OF THE PAPAL SECRETARIAT OF STATE.

ISSUED AT SAINT PETER'S IN ROME

ON THE 4TH DAY OF JANUARY 1999

NOTARIZED BY

CARDINAL ANGELO SODANO
SECRETARY OF STATE

TRIBUTES FROM PRIESTS

I had the privilege of meeting then Brother Joseph Ferraro in July 1963 when I entered the Trinitarian Seminary in Baltimore. Brother Joseph was already a member of the religious order, and we became fast friends. Later in his life when he chose the Navy Chaplaincy as a way of expressing his priestly vocation, I was able to visit him in several of his assignments: California, Rota, Spain, Florida. My time with Joseph was filled with trips, culture, conversation and a lot of fun.

In my own priesthood, I was eventually assigned to St. Ann Church, Bristol, PA as its pastor, and this was the home parish of Monsignor Ferraro. I got to know his parents, his sister, Maryanne and her family, and I spent 18 years with them reconnecting with the Ferraro Family and with Monsignor. It was always an exciting time to be together.

One of the gifts that Monsignor gave to all of us was his ability to focus on us and to help us feel that he believed in us and wanted us to be happy and healthy. In the midst of his humor and his sometime acerbic dialogue, beneath it all was his desire to connect with others and to help us realize our potential. That is a gift which all of us need today in our daily lives.

His installation as a Monsignor by the Vatican and his retirement from the Navy ceremony were held at St. Ann Parish, Bristol, and it was a thrill for his family and parishioners to be present for one of their "own boys" when he was recognized for all that he had achieved and all that he did for others. He is missed by all, and we are grateful for him.

Fr. James R. Day, O.SS.T,
President, DeMatha Catholic High School

I had the great fortune to meet Monsignor Joe Ferraro in the 1980s while I was living in Hawaii. I was a Navy Reserve Chaplain and was assigned to several active duty units while living in Hawaii. I was the Parochial Vicar at St Anthony of Padua Parish in Kailua, Hawaii and later as the Administrator of Our Lady of Sorrows Parish in Wahiawa, Hawaii. As a reserve Chaplain I had the great honor of serving temporary duty at the Submarine Base at Pearl Harbor. This was my first encounter with Msgr Joe. From the beginning I was impressed with Joe. His love of God, the military and the people he ministered to were always his first love. He loved life and was well respected by his peers.

When I left Hawaii, we had no contact until I came to Florida for a visit with a priest friend of mine. My friend had mentioned several times that he had a retired Navy Chaplain helping him at times in his parish. It was then that I came in contact with Msgr Joe after many years. Joe, several Retired Chaplains living in Bradenton and Sarasota area would get together once a month for priestly fraternity. It was always a joy for me to be with Joe and to hear of the countless stories that he shared with us. I was present at his 50th anniversary of Priesthood at Holy Cross Church in Palmetto, Florida.

One thing that stands out for me about Msgr Joe was his love for people. I would see him at restaurants and movies with his beloved friends. I heard of his great homilies that he delivered and heard him sing – what a beautiful gift of voice he had and he shared it with so many.

I was saddened to hear that he came down with COVID and that he died alone, without family and friends beside him. He who was at the side of so many dying people, found himself alone. No, he was not alone. The Lord was with him and he has a special place now in the Kingdom. May he rest in the peace of the Risen Lord.

Fr. Salvator M. Stefula, TOR,
St. Patrick Church, Tampa, Florida

I knew MSGR Ferraro for several decades as a U.S. Navy Chaplain and later into his retirement here in Florida. He was not pretentious but a very down to earth guy regardless of his various titles. The priesthood was the center of his life but there was much more in this world that he enjoyed to the fullest. Msgr. came from humble beginning, the son of blue collar Italian parents. He loved art, the opera and took his voice lessons seriously. Getting a chance to speak in Italian or Spanish were enjoyable moments for Joe. Preaching and celebrating the Eucharist were very special times for Joe as well as just being a simple pastor to anyone in need regardless of their age and background. Only a few days before he died Joe texted me and said: "I have so much more to give." I have no doubt he was speaking the truth but while he was with us he gave us his all. I will let Joe's words that follow in this book speak for themselves.

RESPECTFULLY SUBMITTED BY A FRIEND OF
MSGR. FERRARO, FR. PAUL MCLAUGHLIN

My first encounter with Monsignor Joseph Ferraro occurred soon after I came to Florida to work as a priest in the year 2001. I was assigned to St. Bernard Parish in Holmes Beach when Monsignor Joe called me after he heard that there was a new priest assigned to St. Bernard Parish. He invited me to have lunch with him, and we talked over lunch for close to two hours. He immediately impressed me as a man who was sincere and had a great love for the priesthood. I knew that I had a new friend with whom I could be comfortable in sharing my experiences of priesthood and who would be at ease in sharing his own experiences.

When I was assigned to San Marco Parish at the other end of our diocese, we had lost contact for some years, but I never forgot the warmth and kindness he always showed me in our times together. I was very pleasantly surprised to learn upon my assignment to Holy Cross Parish in Palmetto that Monsignor Joe was working there as well. We soon rekindled our friendship and shared many happy and many challenging times together. Monsignor Joe was always there when we needed him and gave one hundred percent of his effort to every person and every situation with which he was faced. I truly admired his love for people and his willingness to give of himself whatever the cost. He truly lived the Priesthood of Jesus Christ and was an inspiration to all who knew him. He delighted in sharing his experiences as a Chaplain in the Navy, and we were always eager to hear about them. Not only were we entertained, but more importantly, we were challenged to grow in our call to be the Presence of Jesus in our own lives.

Monsignor Joe has touched my life in ways that I will always remember. He has been a blessing for me, and I thank God that I was privileged to know him as a fellow priest and a great friend.

FATHER BERNIE EVANOFSKI

During the four years of conflict in the civil war, around 50 Priests ministered to the Union's soldiers. These Chaplains were often called "Holy Joes." During the time of Vietnam, Chaplain Joseph Ferraro (who would later be called "Monsignor Joe") began his ministry being a modern day "Holy Joe" to the thousands of men and women who he was called to serve.

I had the privilege of getting to know Monsignor Joe for most of my life. I recall always looking forward to being an altar boy and serving the Masses where Msgr. Joe would celebrate. He had a unique way of capturing the faithful by preaching the Word of God while including stories from his decades of experience ministering to our sailors. Msgr. Joe helped to inspire me not only to answer my call to become a Catholic priest but also to pursue my vocation as a U.S. Navy Chaplain. Every time I would return home on break from the seminary, Msgr. Joe and I would always meet over a meal where he would continue to mentor me and share some of his fascinating sea stories and experiences as a priest.

Msgr. Joe lived out his commission every day not only as a Chaplain in the Navy, but he lived out the Great Commission given to us by Christ: "Go, therefore, and make disciples of all nations ..." (Mt. 28:19). At the beginning of every Mass, Msgr. Joe would say how it was his prayer that in some way, God would speak to you. The immortal memories of Msgr. Joe continue to live on today through his homilies and inspire many, just as they did for me, my family, and the thousands of lucky sailors and parishioners. As it was Msgr. Joe's prayer, I am confident that God will speak to you in some way through the homilies contained herein.

JACOB C. GWYNN, SEMINARIAN

Tisa and Kent Walker's Grandsons with Monsignor

Kelley and Tracy

Monsignor and Kent

TRIBUTES FROM SECOND FAMILY

Dear Father Joe,

I can't even begin to tell you how much you are missed! Our history began in Iwakuni, Japan in 1975 and rode for 45 years! We met at Mass and became instant friends starting with dinners at our home including Mass around our dining room table. You gave our sons Keith and Todd their First Communion and we celebrated many holidays and special occasions together, becoming family!

There was plenty of antique shopping at Laughing Lady and dinners at The Blue Bird practicing our Japanese language as we shared so much of the Japanese culture.

Fast forward to Naples, Italy in 1980 where you gave our twins, Kelly and Tracy their First Communion and once again shared holidays and special events that included the Giaimes, Vinnie, Nina, Mike and Frank. Your Masses in Parco Azzuro, our Thanksgiving trip to Assisi, our private audience with the Pope, (us and 10,000 other guests!). Plenty of shopping at Shoe Alley, and so many restaurants.

Back in the States we loved all of your visits wherever we were and then you married our four children and baptized our grandchildren. Each one has special memories with you and are so thankful you were such a big part of us. We cherish your beautiful Masses and sermons, your sense of humor and your ability to immediately connect with our families and friends you met along our journey.

You will never be forgotten, you will always be missed, and as the Japanese people would say, we all have a hole in our heart.

In our hearts forever,
Tisa Walker

My history began with Father Joe during the summer of 1975 in Iwakuni, Japan where he was the Catholic Chaplain at the Marine Corps Base. We became instant friends and shared so many wonderful times together. Our four children Keith, Todd, and twins, Kelly and Tracy were all under seven years old. He was part of our family. The twins always called him "Wadu" which he said was twin talk for Father!

In 1980 we were stationed together in Naples, Italy where Father was the Catholic Chaplain at the Navy Base. Our relationship grew, including with another close family, the Giaimes. We were all so fortunate to have each other for so many events and experiences. Father Joe was the kindest, genuine person. His sense of humor and love of life was a perfect example for everyone. He comforted so many people and his smile was infectious and would warm the coldest heart.

Father's move to Florida was an added bonus and so we continued our friendship almost 50 years. Father referred to me as the brother he never had! I felt privileged to be so close to him. We miss "Wadu" so much that the tears will never end. When he was sick, we prayed for him but now we pray to him. For there is no heaven without Father Joe.

Kent Walker

Kent Walker, Monsignor and Jim Krich

Walker Home Gathering

Max's Baptism

Monsignor Joseph Ferraro — Consecration

PREFACE

PRAYER OF BLESSING

Bow your heads, and within the moments of silence that I will take to offer my prayerful reflection, let's let our hearts swell with pride at the great heritage that God has given us Italian Americans. Let us pray:

Heavenly Father, You who know and bless the work and spirit of generations, hear our prayer of gratitude this evening, gratitude for the rich, precious heritage of a wonderful Italian culture and spirit. We think of our grandfathers, grandmothers, our fathers and mothers, who gave us their suffering and their joy of what it meant to be Italian in America. At this moment, o God, I think of my own Grandfather, Antonio Guigno, like so many grandfathers of those present here, who once said to me, when I was a young boy, that when he came here from Italy, he found out three things: that the streets were not paved with gold; that most of the streets were not even paved; that he had to help pave them! A spirit of hard work, a spirit of family devotion, a love for our religion, a humble faith in You, o God, enormous talent and energy, a willingness to fight in America's wards, to make America better, a genuine pride in being an Italian American, is what we bring before You this evening as we remember our heritage, as we see ourselves in this multi-colored and diverse tapestry of our Italian backgrounds. For this we thank you, o Lord. And now we ask you to bless our evening with fun, bless the food we are to receive from Your goodness. Amen.

Navy Medals

Hat and Chalice

U.S. Memory Box

MONSIGNOR JOSEPH FERRARO

MARCH 19, 1941 – DECEMBER 17, 2020

Monsignor Joseph Ferraro passed away Thursday, December 17, 2020 after a nine-day battle with Covid-19. Although the Monsignor's life was cut short by this deadly virus, he lived a life in which most people could only dream of. His lifelong dedication to God and his country created a vast amount of opportunities all over the world, which also lead to a laundry list of accomplishments and accolades.

Born and raised on Lafayette Street in Bristol Borough, Pennsylvania, Joseph Ferraro received a calling to God at a very young age. After graduating from St. Ann Elementary School in 1954, Joseph Ferraro entered St. John DeMatha High School in Hyattsville, Maryland. It was here that he would go on to graduate Valedictorian in his class and immediately enter the Order of the Most Holy Trinity Seminary University in Baltimore. His ordination to the priesthood took place at the Cathedral of Mary Our Queen in Baltimore on May 20, 1967. A major influence to Joseph's vocational call were the countless visits by the Trinitarian priests and nuns at his family home on Lafayette Street.

For most men a calling to the priesthood and God would have been enough to fulfill life's journey, but that wasn't the case for Joseph Ferraro. Just over two years into being a priest, the United States would have their peak involvement in the Vietnam War and with the permission of the Trinitarian's superior, Joseph was commissioned as an officer in the US Navy and began what would be a 30-year career as a Naval Chaplain. Immediately following Chaplains School in Newport, Rhode Island, he would serve our country in Vietnam and then Okinawa Japan. After returning stateside in 1971, Joseph Ferraro would spend a few years in California serving as the Chaplain to the US Coast Gard Training Center before returning to Japan where he would spend the next three years as a Chaplain to the Marine Corps Air Station in Iwakuni. The remainder of this decade would bring him back to California where he served as a Chaplain to the Construction Battalion Center before beginning postgraduate studies at the University of California Berkley.

One of Joseph Ferraro's career highlights occurred in 1979 when he was credited with peacefully disarming a Philippine woman who held three of her own family members hostage and barricaded inside their home. "It was with God's help" according to the Monsignor that this woman and her family were saved.

The 1980s would end with a promotion to Captain in the Navy, but began with an assignment in Naples, Italy for two years. In 1982 Joseph returned from Italy as the Chaplain of the US Pacific Submarine Force in Pearl Harbor Hawaii and his official promotion to Captain came in 1989. Captain Ferraro would often share stories about switching submarines in the darkest of night out in the middle of the ocean with hardly any idea of location or whereabouts. It was unaccountable moments like this where Joseph Ferraro's calling to God and commitment to his country became one.

The 1990s would start out with Joseph serving as Chaplain for the Marine Corps Recruit Depot in San Diego and then Air Station in El

CDR J. Ferraro

U.S.S. Carl Vinson CVN70

JOSEPH A. FERRARO

(CAPTAIN, USN-RET)
2909 Captains Court
Palmetto, FL 34221

Home: (941) 722-5050
Cell: (941) 266-0041
Email: ferrarojoseph@hotmail.com

U.S.S. Carl Vinson

U.S.S. Carl Vinson

Flight deck of the U.S.S. Carl Vinson

Mass on U.S.S. Carl Vinson

Scrapbook

CDR J. Ferraro   LT O. Mozon   RPC G. Hite

Hawaiian photo

Worship on Ship

Toro, before heading off to his last assignment in Rota Spain where he would act as the Chaplain for the US Naval Forces. 1999 would mark one of Captain Joseph Ferraro's lifelong accomplishments as he was granted the title of Monsignor by St. Pope John Paul II. Monsignor Ferraro would retire from the US Navy in 1999 after 30 years of dedicated service to his country where he received numerous medals, badges and commendations.

The remaining 20 years of his life would be spent in retirement at Sts. Peter and Paul the Apostles Church at Bradenton, Our Lady of the Angels Parish, at Lakewood Ranch, and at Holy Cross Catholic Church in Palmetto, Florida where he was loved and adored by the parishioners. He would regularly be requested for weddings, baptisms and funerals. On a personal level the Monsignor would speak highly of the individuals who he would brunch with on Sundays after Mass at the world renown Don Cesar in St. Pete Beach, FL. A large celebration of the 50th anniversary of his ordination was held at Holy Cross Church in Palmetto on April 30, 2017. A dinner was served, and a book provided of his accomplishments. Even with his incredible circle of friends in Florida, Monsignor Ferraro returned to his roots at St. Ann Church in Bristol Borough on May 21, 2017 to celebrate his 50th Anniversary of becoming a Priest. This was a true testament to how much he valued the people of Bristol Borough, and how despite his numerous travels all over the world, he still viewed himself as a Bristolian. Those who had the pleasure of growing up with Monsignor Ferraro or visiting Lafayette Street over the years, can attest to the fact that the Ferraro (and then Lorenzo) household was always a place for friends to gather. This was especially true when Joseph was coming home to Bristol Borough. For days, if not weeks, his mother, Mary Ferraro and sister, Maryann would prepare for Joseph's arrival cooking and baking a vast amount of food for Joseph and everyone who would be coming to visit. Despite living the majority of his life all over the world, Monsignor Ferraro was a Bristolian, and whenever he returned the stories would go on for hours on end, and the laughs around the kitchen were endless.

Joseph was preceded in death by his loving parents, (Mary and Nick) and his beloved sister, Maryann (Lorenzo). Maryann and Joseph shared an unbreakable bond that most siblings would begrudge. The sun would rise and set on her brother. This was never more evident than in her own passing when she waited for him to be by her bedside before moving on to God. Joseph is survived by his only nephew, Gary Lorenzo Jr., his brother-in-law, Gary Lorenzo Sr., along with numerous cousins and dear friends from his days on Lafayette Street. "The Unc", as his nephew typically referenced, was the most influential figure outside of his parents. Always emphasizing that Gary Jr., knew right from wrong, and that he had a more positive outlook on life by trying to instill in him Joseph's soothing nature.

Monsignor Ferraro would always begin his masses by letting the congregation know that before the Mass ended, "God will touch you in some way!" Monsignor Joseph Ferraro, Captain Joseph Ferraro, or as his closest friends and family knew him, simply Joseph, you were the one who touched many lives in ways no one ever imagined when you left Lafayette Street as a 13 year old boy and for that the country and Catholic Church will forever be grateful.

Monsignor with his Mother and sister Maryann

Don't grieve for me for now I'm free!
I follow the plan God made for me.
I saw His face, I heard His call,
I took His hand and left it all.
I could not stay another day,
To love, to laugh, to work or play;
Tasks left undone must stay that way.
And if my parting has left a void,
Then fill it with remembered joy.
A friendship shared, a laugh, a kiss
Ah yes, these things I too shall miss.
My life's been full, I've savored much;
Good times, good friends, a loved one's touch.
Perhaps my time seemed all too brief -
Don't shorten yours with undue grief.
Be not burdened with tears of sorrow,
Enjoy the sunshine of the morrow.

Monica and Ralph, Monsignor's cousin

Mass

Monsignor with Knight

Marcia, Monsignor and Sue

*Monsignor and
Father Bernie*

Max's Baptism

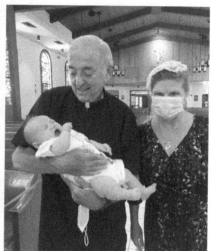

Richard with his mother

Savea Sundberg's Baptism with family

Chrissy and Gary's wedding

Baptism of Summer Gentry

Jane Shambour and Monsignor

Baptism of Carson Barnett

Thanksgiving with Jim and Lynn Barnett

Monsignor and a friend having fun

Jack Shambour and Monsignor
Jack was adopted from the Marshall Islands.

Monsignor and Alicia Shambour. Alicia was adopted
from Guatemala and just celebrated her Quinceanera.

Monsignor Joseph Ferraro, Memorial Mass
January 16th 2021

MEMORIAL MASS HOMILY

Fr. Paul McLaughlin, Celebrant

This morning we gather at this Eucharist to thank our loving Creator for the gift of Monsignor Joe Ferraro, and in spite of our sadness to also remind ourselves of the blessing of life given to all of us.

We thank the Lord for having given Joe the gift of his Catholic faith: the sacraments of Baptism, Communion, Confirmation, the anointing of the sick, and especially the gift of the Priesthood. For giving Joe the opportunity to gather together people like yourselves and so many others around the world to share the Eucharist and to preach God's Holy Word. There is much we can be thankful for!!!

I will not make Joe more in death than he was in life but he was an unforgettable guy. I remember meeting Joe over 30 years ago in Naples, Italy. He served there as a Navy Chaplain, but how lucky for him to be in a city with such an opera history. Not surprisingly he took voice lessons there and enjoyed the opera as much as he could. Later we met up in San Diego. He tried to scheme to get me to take his place on the Carl Vinson, but that didn't quite work. Years later in Spain I went up to Madrid with Joe to get him measured for his Monsignor robes. We

stopped in the plaza major where I purchased an inexpensive painting that Joe pushed me into buying. It hangs in my living room – a picture of Don Quijote and Sancho from the story "The Man from La Mancha."

Eventually I replaced him in Rota where he had served and I think fell in love with all of Spanish culture. I found Joe loving, funny, serious and dedicated to the people he served as a Priest, a Navy Chaplain and friend. He was an ordinary guy but he was special. I just don't want to overlook his love of opera, music and the Spanish community.

Joe was a blessing to all of us, especially to all of you here at Holy Cross Church. He showed us the best of the Priesthood and the humility of being a follower of our Lord Jesus Christ. The Gospel today was Joe's own choice for his funeral Mass. The Beatitudes were the center of his life. They characterized how he cared for his friends and how he tried to touch both the stranger as well as so many of the people of God. God will be good to him, may he rest in peace.

Polished shoes

SELECT HOMILIES AND DEVOTIONALS

BY MONSIGNOR JOSEPH FERRARO

SECOND SUNDAY OF ADVENT
MARK 11:1-8

Every Advent, John the Baptist calls us to shut down the past, to begin again. He calls us to embrace the meaning of our own baptism and to straighten any crooked roads in our lives.

Some of us might remember the little ditty we would sing as kids. It went like this: "Ring around the rosy, pocket full of posies. Ashes, ashes, all fall down!" I am sure that only a few of us knew then that there was a dark side to this little tune. The "ring around the rosy" referred to the death caused by the Black Plague in the fourteenth century. The sign of the dreaded disease was a black ring around a red spot. And so we have "ring around the rosy." "Pocket full of posies" referred to the people's use of carrying flowers with them to try to cover over the terrible stench of decaying bodies. Finally, "ashes, ashes, all fall down" referred to the fact that the Black Plague killed a fourth of the population of Europe. People trying to cover up the despair they had to live with, so they sang, "Ring around the rosy!"

Advent is just the opposite of this song's intent. It covers up nothing. On the contrary, Advent insistently remembers. It wants us to remember that before we should die, things that should change in our lives; it wants us to know that we can rise anew. It invites us to return to basics. It says we must take the time to ask ourselves what is really important to us. What are our priorities! But above all, it demands that we ask if Jesus Christ is the number one priority in our lives?

All three readings the Church gives us today talk about the need to prepare the way for the coming of the Lord. All three readings tell us that if our lives are not what they should be, then we must do something about it. If we have strayed from the basics, then the Second Sunday of Advent invites us to return to them. "Ring around the rosy, pocket full of posies." If we have placed our work ahead of our families, then we must take a good look at this. If we have placed success ahead of our personal relationship with God, we are to change this. If we have brought into our lives, the strange values of this world so that we are always politically correct, always playing it safe, refusing to stand firm on our Gospel values, then we must do something about this. "Ring around the rosy, pocket full of posies."

John the Baptist has the answer: "change," "straighten the crooked roads of our lives," transform the "barren desert," and proclaim the coming of Christ in the way we live our lives.

THE FEAST OF THE IMMACULATE CONCEPTION; — DECEMBER 8
LUKE 1:26-38

It is especially fitting that we should celebrate the Feast of the Immaculate Conception during the season of Advent. For just as Mary prepared herself for the coming of Jesus by prayer, so should we prepare ourselves to celebrate His coming by prayers. Mary is a model of our own Advent preparation for Jesus' coming. She is one to whom we can turn to in our own Advent preparation and ask her for her help and her grace.

An American soldier tells this story. He had been taken prisoner by the Nazis during World War II. One day he found himself in a long columns of prisoners marching across the countryside. After several hours walking, the guards halted the column next to a woods. They then gave the prisoners permission to take care of nature. The American soldier decided to take a chance and hide. It worked. The column marched off without him.

That night, the soldier left the woods and began to work his way through enemy territory to the American lines. When dawn came, he went back into hiding, taking shelter between two huge rocks.

Then came a frightening experience. On a hill, not far away, stood a group of German villagers, staring at him and the 'POW' on his uniform. The soldier knew he had to take a big risk. He walked toward the villagers, making signs that he was unarmed. When he reached them, he began to recite the Mass prayers in Latin. He figured they might be Catholic, like himself. But they didn't seem to understand. Then the soldier reached into his pocket and pulled out a tiny prayer book. The inside cover contained a picture of the Rosary of Our Lady. Pointing to it, he made the sign of the cross. This time the villagers understood perfectly.

The soldier then returned to his hiding place, hoping he would now be safe. An hour later, however, his hopes were dashed. A rifle shot rang out, hitting the rock. But then he noticed an old villager motioning for him to return to the hill. The villagers had arranged to smuggle him back to the American lines.

American servicemen in World War II, like Americans in general, had a special devotion to Mary, the Mother of Jesus. They were particularly devoted to Mary under the Title of the Immaculate Conception for it was under this title that we dedicated our country to Mary in the earlier days of our history. The Doctrine of the Immaculate Conception was defined by Pope Pius IX on December 8, 1854.

Belief in this doctrine dates back to the earliest days of Christianity. It holds that Mary was untouched by sin from the moment of conception. In other words, Mary was born free of original sin and remained free of all sin throughout her life.

THIRD SUNDAY OF ADVENT
A – MATTHEW 11:2-11

The great English writer G.K. Chesterton was once playing a quiz game with some of his friends. One of the questions was, "If you were shipwrecked alone on a deserted island, what one book, above all others, would you wish to have with you?" One of the players immediately said, "The Bible," and gave a very pious reason for his selection. Another said, "A volume of Shakespeare," and gave a very learned reason for wanting Shakespeare. Chesterton said, "Well, if I were allowed just one book on that deserted island, I would choose a one-volume manual of instruction for amateur boat-builders." Chesterton was a very practical person; and 'practical' is the word that came to me as I meditated on the Gospel for this Sunday.

As we move deeper into the season of Advent, the real preparation for Christmas must come not so much in putting the spirit of Christmas into flimsy, pious words, but putting it into our everyday, practical, life experience. In other words, if we tell people that we have faith, we can't expect them to believe us unless we demonstrate our faith through the kind of life we live.

Psychologist Dr. Karl Menninger once asked a very wealthy patient, "What are you going to do with all of your money?" The patient replied, "Just worry about it, I guess." "In that case," Dr. Menninger said, "Do you experience pleasure from worrying about your money?" With a deep sigh, the patient said, "No, but I feel such terror when I think of giving any of it away." And, commenting on what he termed his patient's money sickness, Dr. Menninger said, "Generous people are rarely mentally ill."

We can safely say, "A truly generous person rarely lacks for anything." I know a person who says, "My hobby is giving something away every day—something tangible—so that I will be reminded to give away the vastly more important intangible: a smile, a word of encouragement, a healing touch, the promise of a prayer. And he goes on to say, "I may not be a person of great wisdom, but this I know: The more I give to others, the more I have."

MDP, no amount of pious words about Christmas can serve as an easy substitute for this kind of practical experience of Christmas. You see, we need to remember that the truth of Christmas for each one of us is that we experience God's presence through the things we do, the life we live. We experience God's presence in this material world, which God has created and in which we are living.

The experience of Christmas is the best evidence of how God's love comes to us in specific, concrete, tangible, practical ways. This is what Jesus is doing in the Gospel this morning. He is reminding us that Christianity is very practical and a highly particularized lifestyle. John is in prison, yet he manages to dispatch messengers to ask Jesus if He is the real Messiah. And Jesus makes it clear that He intended to be recognized not as some political, warrior Messiah, but as the Messiah of healing and reconciliation. "The blind see, the cripples walk, the lepers are cured, the deaf hear..." by these real, tangible, practical, down-to-earth signs, the people would be able to recognize the true Messiah.

Perhaps some of you will remember a ditty kids would sing years ago when they were skipping rope. It went like this:

> *Oh, you can't get to Heaven in a rocking chair*
> *...'cause that clumsy old thing won't get you there!*
> *Oh, you can't get to Heaven on roller skates*
> *...'cause you'll roll right past those pearly gates!*

Put up with me for just a minute. I added a few lines which go like this:

> *Oh, you can't get to Heaven on United TWA (Trans World Airlines)*
> *...'cause that big old jet won't find the way!*
> *Oh, you can't get to Heaven in a Cadillac car*
> *...'cause the gas and oil won't go that far!*

A thirteen-year-old girl said to her mother, "I feel so nervous." Her mother replied, "What do you mean by 'nervous'?" "Well," said the young girl, "I feel in a hurry all over. It's like I'm not quite sure where I'm going, but I can't wait to get started."

The Advent season seems tailor-made for "We're not quite sure where we're going, but we can't wait to get there" persons. The word 'Advent' and the word 'adventure' have a common root. Advent is a season of adventure. In the midst of lost hopes and fading dreams, we celebrate the coming of Christmas in an atmosphere of renewed hope and renewed expectation. And our fading dreams are transformed into bright new visions of things to come.

B – JOHN 1:6-8, 19-28

"He came as a witness...to speak for the light so that everyone might believe through him..."

There are times when it isn't easy to say the right thing in a given situation. I feel we can sympathize with the man who met an old friend whom he hadn't seen in years. "How is your wife?" he asked. His friend answered, "Haven't you heard, she's in Heaven." "I'm so sorry," the poor fellow stammered. Then he realized that this may not have been the right thing to say, so he added, "I mean, I'm glad!" But that didn't seem quite right either, so he quickly said, "I mean to say, I'm surprised."

John the Baptist had no trouble saying the right thing. He is telling us that we must be witnesses to Christ in this world; we must communicate His presence. He reminds us on this third Sunday of Advent, that a simple act of love can be more effective than thousands of words in thousands of books. We can talk, talk, talk about Jesus, but a simple act of love can convince where words have failed.

Like John the Baptist, we are not the light, but we are followers of Christ to be witnesses to the light. All of us here are good, church-going people, and our presence here around the world and Eucharist is so necessary in our quest for spirituality. But also important to our quest for holiness and a solid spirituality is our commission to serve one another's needs.

As followers of Christ, "we must give some food, when we see hunger; we must give something to drink, when we see somebody thirsty. We must give some kind of clothing, when we see a person without clothes. We must give comfort, when we see somebody sick. We must give friendship, when we see somebody lonely.

MDP, it is not just what we do here in Church that matters, it's what we do when we leave this Church; it's what we do in our relationships with other people. This is the mark of a true witness to the light of Christ, as John the Baptist says.

Life is continually unfolding in the big, wide world outside the beautiful walls of a church. Life unfolds for us in our kitchens when we cook for our loved ones. At our dinner tables where we sit with our family and friends, in our shopping malls, on the streets of our neighborhood, in our fire and police stations, on our highways, in our factories, in our work places. God is here in our Parish Church, but He is also out there. And both here and there, we are constantly being called to be witness to this reality. When you think about it, like John the Baptist and the first Disciples, we are being called to turn the world "upside down."

MDP, the same God who reveals himself at this Mass, reveals Himself to the world out there. The same God, who gives us His Holy Spirit, requires us to breathe out that Holy Spirit to others. As Disciples of Jesus Christ, our mission is never to break hearts, but to go out from here and melt hearts.

I read this not long ago by Judith Viorst, an author.

"Even if I were collapsing from thirst and hunger, even if I were reduced to the darkest gloom; even if I observed between sobs that we should have arrived three hours ago and the inn was going to give away our rooms, I still would be incapable of persuading my husband, then lost, to stop—just stop—the car and ask for directions.

"Even if I were to throw a full-scale temper tantrum, even if I were to call him an uncouth name, even if I were to not-so-gently remind him that, should we wind up but himself to blame. And even if I, in

a tone I concede is called screaming, I still would be incapable of persuading my husband, when lost, to stop the car and ask for directions."

Directions on how to light up our lives; it is because we are not taking the time to stop..., look..., and listen!

C – LUKE 3:10-15

J ohn the Baptist sets the tone of our third week of Advent: "Whoever has two coats should share with the person who has none...and whoever has food should do likewise..."

I went to Wal-Mart and other stores in the area and saw, in this season, the dedicated people of the Salvation Army ringing their bells for donations. When William Booth founded the Salvation Army in the London slums in 1865, Victorian England was not very kind to its poor people. William Booth was even arrested for his charitable work. But he persevered, and by 1880, Booth was ready to send his troops to America, where today his Salvation Army now numbers thousands of members in all fifty states. One Christmas, William Booth wished to send a cable to Salvation Army posts all over the world. A long cable was out of the question—money was tight, so he chose to cable one word that Christmas. Booth greeted his coworkers around the world with the word: "Others!"

MDP, I believe that single word—'others'—is the essence of today's Gospel. It is doing for others that we come to know the presence of God in our midst, a presence that we are often too busy or too overwhelmed to realize. John the Baptist was trying to tell us when he spoke at the River Jordan, that we can only celebrate the Messiah in our lives when we step beyond ourselves to embrace the needs and hopes and pains and tears and joys of others.

I just read a story about a shopping mall Santa Claus. It was his first day on the job. He needed the job because money had become scarce. So he stuffed his shirt front into the baggy pants, pulled on the red Santa Claus jacket and carefully applied the white whiskers. Well, he was ready! He took his place in Santa's chair right in the middle of the shopping mall. At ten A.M., the rush began as children with their parents in tow raced into his lap to tell him their hopes and their wants.

The requests for "PlayStations" and other computer games got old pretty fast—until a pretty seven-year-old girl approached Santa. He bent to listen to her request. She whispered, "Santa, would you please bring me a small chest for my doll clothes and, would you please, please, bring my grandfather back? He was very sick. This will be my first Christmas without him…"

Now, they didn't tell him how to answer that in Santa training school; but something within the tender Santa told him what to say. He said, "Your grandfather is still with you—right there," and he pointed to her heart. "He's not sick anymore. And can you imagine what kind of Christmas he is having up in Heaven?" Well, the little girl's face lit up and she gave Santa a big hug before scrambling off his lap. The little girl's mother, with tears in her eyes, leaned over and whispered in Santa's ear, "Thank you and God bless you." The shopping mall Santa slouched back into his chair. He never would have believed it. The shopping mall Santa heard the message of John, the Baptizer.

MDP, scripture tells us that the word of God came to John the Baptist "in the wilderness." I wonder if we have ever thought of what 'wilderness' means to us. We have so many opportunities—every day—like our shopping mall Santa, like William Booth, to bring God's love and word into so many of the wilderness experiences that comfort us. There is, for example, a wilderness of **grief** when we lose someone we love. There is a wilderness of **pain** when we are sick or hurt. There is a wilderness of **fear** when the doctor says, "it is terminal." There is a wilderness of **disappointment** when plans for financial security come apart. There is a wilderness of **despair** when a son or daughter goes off the deep end into drugs, into immoral behavior and suffers destructive consequences. There is a wilderness of **sadness** when a person discovers that his or her spouse has been unfaithful. There is a wilderness of **hurt** when we, Catholics, live through the cover-ups and excuses of immoral behavior in the clergy. There is a wilderness of **violence** which keeps one looking over his or her shoulder wondering, "Will I be next?"

MDP, the Gospel of the third Sunday of Advent is about **others**. John the Baptist is telling us that we are called to be witnesses of God's love by the love we extend to others; we are called to be heralds of His justice by our unfailing commitment to be with others in the wilderness of their lives. We are called to imitate the example of Christ, the Servant, in our humble, joy-filled service to one another. On this third Sunday of Advent, we are called to transform and re-create our lives and our world in the life and love of God.

FOURTH SUNDAY OF ADVENT
A – MATTHEW 1:18-24

St. Joseph is the real hero in this beautiful Gospel of St. Matthew. It is hard to imagine the greatness of Joseph's sacrifice. He will wed the young girl, and raise a child that is not his. It will be an act of heroism, planned by God, who will use Mary and Jesus to make of Joseph far more than a Jewish man who followed the law. Joseph, upright and humble, will be the foster father of Jesus, Emmanuel, who is "God with us."

Several years ago, I saw a movie named "Simon Birch", which always comes back to me when I read about the heroism of Joseph in Matthew's Gospel. "Simon Birch" is the story of a twelve-year-old boy who is suffering from the bone-stunting disorder known as Morquio syndrome. Simon may have been the smallest body in his New England town, but he definitely possesses the largest heart. In spite of the cruel treatment of his classmates and the callous ostracism of his parents, Simon believes that God "made me the way I am for a reason." Taunted by the people in his town, neglected by his mother and father, rejected by his phony priest, Simon remains absolutely convinced that "things will be different once God has helped me be a hero."

Simon's faith is rewarded. Because of his small size and obsession with being able to hold his breath underwater for a long time, Simon becomes a hero when he is able to save the life of a little boy trapped in a bus that has plunged into a raging, icy river. Because of his persistence, Simon is able to help his best friend discover the identity of his father. In his all, too-brief life, Simon Birch discovers what too few of us ever realize: that God has planned great things for us.

MDP, in Matthew's account of the birth of Jesus, Joseph wonders how he should handle the embarrassing situation regarding his fiancée, Mary. But he has the faith to carry on, trusting in the angel's word that God has planned great things for Mary's Child. If we are the men and women of faith that we believe we are, then we, too, must believe that God has great things planned for us; that God intends for us to be 'heroes' in our own time and place, in wherever we find ourselves. On this last Sunday of Advent, may we possess the faith of a Simon Birch and Joseph, that we enable us to fulfill the great things God has planned for us and become the beautiful persons He created us to be.

B – LUKE 1:26-28

The Russia novelist Ivan Turgenev once received a letter from a friend who summoned up his philosophy of life in these words: "I have decided that the real problem in life is learning to put oneself in second place." To which Turgenev replied, "I have decided that the real problem in life is learning what to put in first place." And for those of us who follow Jesus Christ, the real problem in life is learning who to put in first place. Today's beautiful Gospel takes us back to the time when Mary learns she is with Child and will give birth to the Savior of all mankind.

In a Catholic school just a few days before Christmas, the curtain was about to go up on the annual Christmas play. In the center of the stage was a Christmas crib, complete with statues of Joseph, Mary, the wise men, the shepherds. All of the nuns were busy making last minute adjustments to the children's costumes. The school principal was standing by, keeping an eye on the preparations. Suddenly in a panic, one of the nuns rushed up to her and said, "Mother Superior, we forgot the Child Jesus." With a pensive look, the mother superior replied, "That's exactly the trouble with this world."

Christmas is almost upon us, and even though we may have forgotten a thing or two in our Christmas preparations, we must not forget the Child Jesus. It's time to think about what Christmas means to us, to those whom we love—and those whom we don't love. And as we ponder the meaning of Christmas, we discover the good news that in Jesus Christ, God broke into our human history. And we see that it's not simply a matter of Christ having come a long time ago; it's a matter of Christ continuing to come in every act of kindness, in every victory of goodness, in every instance of one putting the needs of another above his or her own.

There is a story of a business executive who was running late for a meeting—and the traffic was helping neither his schedule nor his mood. Stopping for a red light at a business intersection, he thought to himself, "All right, I can beat the next light if I can get ahead of the pack."

He was ready to take off the instant the light turned green, but then he saw a young couple—both blind—crossing the street. The woman was carrying a baby and the man was using his white cane to navigate them all across the street. To the executive's horror, the couple was not walking in the crosswalk but was instead veering diagonally, directly into the intersection and traffic. Without knowing the danger they were in, the couple began to walk right into the path of oncoming cars. But the executive's annoyance and fear gave way to a sense of wonder as a miracle unfolded before his eyes: every car in every direction came to a simultaneous stop. There was no angry honking and beeping of horns, no screeching of breaks, no shouts of "Are you crazy:" or "Get out of the way!" The traffic just stopped. In that moment, time seemed to stand still for this family as they made their way safely across the busy intersection.

It was as if, for a moment, God had broken into the executive's world, telling him to look around and discover God's presence in his midst.

In Today's beautiful Gospel, the mother-to-be, Mary, is greeted by the angel, "Do not be afraid, you have found favor with God." Perhaps she could not intellectually grasp the angel's message, but in her "Let it be done to me as you say," Mary put God first in her life! When she did this, she helps us learn Who to put first in our lives! So this is the challenge of today's Gospel of Christmas itself: to put the Christ Child first in the hectic commerce of our lives, to look for Him in the quiet desperation of our pain and anguish. To see Him—in our kitchens; on our soccer fields; in our hobbies; in our offices; in our patients or clients; in our music; in the places where we just hang out. To see Him—in our calendar; in our day planners; and to place Him first in our homes and our hearts.

C – Luke 1:39

In a few days, we will celebrate Christmas. And, with this reading of this beautiful Gospel in mind through the week, I feel that the question we need to ask ourselves is "Do we believe in the Christmas message?" I had lunch with friends from the parish yesterday and was telling them about some of the sadness the last months has been with the death of several of our good parishioners. I had the chance to speak to a wife whose husband died recently. She said that she had begun to write her Christmas cards and some of her friends would say to her, "This first Christmas without your husband will be hard for you."

And then she said, "It will be, of course. But without Christmas, my life would be impossible." At the time of her husband's death, my friend thought that God had turned out the light. But then came the Christmas message to remind her that with Christmas God had reached out and really turned on the light—for all the time, and for all of us. That light touches all of us on so many levels. One of those levels the Lord Jesus shows us that we are capable of loving in the midst of chaos, fear, terrorist violence, confusion, and on another level the light of the Lord Jesus challenges you and me to stand before the 'light of the crib' and ask what is the personal message being addressed to you and me. Each of us, in the midst of our weakness and humanity, is capable of loving and of being loved in whatever circumstances, we find ourselves. The level of our love is always capable of growing and triumphing over all.

CHRISTMAS SERVICES

CHRISTMAS VIGIL
MATTHEW 1:1-25

If you are interested in sports, I am going to tell you a story which I'm sure none of you will have trouble visualizing. It's about a young American Indian girl, who looked into the Christmas crib on her reservation, as she told it, and transformed the lives of others. Her name was SuAnne Big Crow, and SuAnne Big Crow played basketball on her Pine Ridge Indian reservation in South Dakota in 1989. She was a great player on a great team where high school basketball was as big as college football in Nebraska or baseball in New York and Boston. But what people remember most about SuAnne Big Crow was not only her great skill on the court, but the spirit in which she played and lived her life. She was a follower of Christ, a star human being; a star athlete. Because she was so kind and generous, she inspired hope.

It was Christmas on Pine Ridge and SuAnne Big Crow and her team were going to play at a game in a town not far from the reservation. As they passed by the Christmas crib set up outside the gym, they stopped for a moment to look in, said a prayer, and ran onto the court for their pre-game warm-ups.

Well, as soon as they hit the court, they were greeted by ugly and loud racist shouts and jeers from the crowd. SuAnne Big Crow and her team were humiliated and scared, and nervously they circuited the court. And by herself, SuAnne Big Crow ran to the dead center of the court. She unbuttoned her warm-up jacket, draped it over her shoulders. While the crowd continued to shout ugly and brutal words, SuAnne Big Crow began to perform the traditional

Lakota Indian shawl dance. She spun and stepped gracefully, her warm-up jacket extending behind her like the wings of a bird. As she moved, she chanted a traditional song in the strange, other-worldly tones of her Indian people. As she continued to dance and sing in a world all her own, the voices in the crowd grew silent. And when she finished, she took the ball, ran a lap around the court dribbling expertly all the way, sprinted to the basket and executed a perfect lay-up. The crowd that had jeered her moments before were on their feet cheering. An American Indian teenager's simple dance and song had transformed hearts.

We need to put aside self-centeredness, and to dance, like SuAnne Big Crow, to light up the world with our love for God and one another.

MDP, today God is one of us and the light coming from the crib becomes a love story. May that light for all of us, fill us with a confidence to dance, fill us with peace. And when Christmas is over and we go to bed, we can be assured that "We are living the greatest love story ever told!"

[SuAnne Big Crow was killed in a terrible car accident; she was seventeen years old.]

CHRISTMAS MIDNIGHT
LUKE 2:1-14

Today, when each of us looks into the Christmas crib, we are attracted to the light in that crib, Christ the Lord. MDP, in giving His Son "as the Light of the world," God's purpose is to transform the dark and the unhappy of this world, to transform us into people of light—giving us the power to radiate His love, moment-to-moment, for a lifetime. As we look into the crib, we must ask ourselves where, Christ, the Light of the World, is leading us. Maybe He is telling some of us today to begin simply with a holy hug of your wife, your husband, your children, even that someone from whom you have been withholding your forgiveness. As we look into the crib, maybe we can hear Him say that today we must drop our egotism, self-centeredness, and to light up the world with our love for God and for one another.

In a book called, "The Rabbi's Gift", there is a story of a once great monastery that had fallen on hard times. Once—it had been filled to capacity with hundreds of dedicated monks. But, for various reasons, the monastery's population had dwindled to the extent that only the abbot and four monks remained, and all five were in their seventies. Clearly, it looked like the great monastery would soon no longer exist. In the woods nearby, there was a small hut which a wise old rabbi used as a hermitage. The abbot decided to visit the rabbi to see what advice he could offer that might restore the monastery to its former glory. After the rabbi had listened to the abbot's woes, he said, "I know how it is. The spirit has gone out of the people. Almost no one even comes to the synagogue anymore." Well, as the abbot prepared to leave, he said to the rabbi, "I have failed in my purpose for coming. Have you no piece of advice that might save the monastery?" The rabbi said, "The only thing I can tell you is that the Messiah is one of you."

When the abbot returned to the monastery and told the others what the rabbi had said, they were filled with wonder: "The Messiah is one of us? One of us? Do you suppose he meant the abbot? Of course—it must be the abbot, the one who has been our leader for so long. On the other hand, he might have meant Brother Thomas, who certainly is a holy man. He could not have meant Brother Elrod; he is so crotchety. Surely, he could not have meant Brother Philip—he's too passive. But, then, he is always there when you need him. Of course, he didn't mean me—yet suppose he did? O God, not me!"

With their thoughts concentrated in this way on what the rabbi said, they began to treat each other with greater and greater respect. After all, any one of them might be the Messiah! And when the townspeople, as was their custom, walked along the monastery paths or picnicked on the edge of the woods, they began to sense a whole new spirit permeating the area. They could literally feel the aura of extraordinary respect and love with which the five monks treated one another. Consequently, the people began to come to the monastery! They brought their friends. Their friends brought others. Young men and women from the town began to talk more and more with the old monks. And soon many of the young men began to enroll in the order. And within a few years, the monastery had once again come alive as a community of light and love for all to see.

On this Christmas Day, when there is so much darkness in the world, maybe we can remember this little story.

MDP, at the first Christmas, in the little town just down the hill from Jerusalem, God became Man, and light entered the world. God became one of us with our history. At the first Christmas, the light coming from the crib became a love story.

As we look into the crib today, may the light of that love story fill us with confidence—fill us with peace. And when today is over and we're ready for bed, we can be assured that "we bought the happy ending."

CHRISTMAS MASS AT DAWN
LUKE 2:15-20

Mary gave birth to her firstborn Son and wrapped Him in bands of cloth, and laid Him in a manger, because there was no place for them in the inn...

The shepherds said to one another, "Let us go now to Bethlehem to see this thing that has taken place, which the Lord has made known to us." (Luke 2:1-20)

No celebration for the year appeals more to our different senses than Christmas: the sights of glittering lights, the taste of the many delicacies of yuletide feasting, the smell of freshly cut evergreen branches, the feel of the crisp winter air and first winter snow, the sounds of the magnificent music of Christmas.

But that first Christmas had none of those things. Consider the real sights and sounds; and feel and tastes; and smells experienced by the family of Joseph, Mary, and the Child on that night centuries ago:

- The damp, aching cold of a cave in the Bethlehem hillside;

- The burning in the eyes and throat from days of traveling on foot along hard, dusty roads;

- The panic of having no place to stay, the paralyzing fear that robbers and wild animals could strike from out of nowhere.

What are you giving for Christmas this year? Oh, I know the usual question is, "What are you getting for Christmas?" but tonight I would like to raise the question, "What are you giving for Christmas this year?"

As we get older, we learn that giving is more fun than receiving during the holiday season. I mean, after so many years of getting presents, what's left? What's new? You may be glad to get a new sweater or new shirt for Christmas, but you've got older clothes in the closet, some you hardly wear. In my case, I would be happy to get the new "Garth Brooks" album, but I've got so many other albums and cassettes. And if eight-track tapes ever come back, I'll be set!

No, it's the giving that makes Christmas fun. It's seeing the shock on someone's face when you really surprise her, or give her something that she dearly wanted. It's also the humor of silly gifts: one of the other chaplains here on station, for example, whose hairline is very similar to mine, gets a hairbrush and a bottle of shampoo every Christmas! When it comes to Christmas presents, most folks grow up to learn that, not only is it more blessed to give, than it is to receive, it's also more fun!

I noticed this last weekend at the mall. Even though it was crowded and hectic, it seemed that most people were having fun talking about what to buy: "Do you think so-and-so would like this?" "I don't know; she told me once that blue was her favorite color..." Most people enjoyed stopping to talk about someone else, and to decide what would be best to give him or her.

It's the giving that really makes Christmas fun. Did you happen to see the newspaper article about the woman who was standing in the supermarket checkout line and noticed a very poor, raggedy looking man up ahead of her? He looked like he was homeless and he smelled like he hadn't been close to soap and water in a month. He was reaching into his pocket for some dimes and nickels so he could buy a loaf of day-old bread and a jar of sale-priced peanut butter.

She quickly went up to him and gave him twenty dollars-worth of food. It really wasn't much by this lady's way of thinking, but it was all she could think of in a moment's notice. But the raggedy man, "you would have thought he had just won the lottery!" said one witness. He was filled with a gratitude he could not express. And the woman felt pretty good herself. She said it was the high point of her Christmas—the feeling she got from giving. She noted that many people who get so much each year seem to appreciate so little.

Giving really is much more fun, so... what are you giving this year? Think back to the things you've bought, things that are hidden in closets or lying under the tree right now. What are you giving for Christmas this year? What presents are you most anxious to see opened tomorrow morning? The one's you want opened just so you can see the expression on your loved one's face.

Well, if we have this much fun giving material gifts to one another...How much more fun would we have giving spiritual gifts? Considering all the time and money we spend giving worldly gifts that wither or fade or get sold in a garage sale a couple of years from now, how much more rewarding would it be to give spiritual gifts that last forever because they come from God.

Will we give a gift of, say, forgiveness this year? It's certainly something we all need. I don't think any family, any marriage; any friendship can do without it. When it's so easy to hurt the one's love, and sometimes so hard to forgive the ones we love most, who will be the peacemaker when one is needed? Who will give the gift that heals old wounds and stops new wounds from bleeding?

Jesus Christ is born tonight to give us forgiveness that we may give it to one another. He tells us to forgive the people who wrong us "seven times seventy." He teaches us to pray saying, "Forgive us our trespasses, as we forgive those who trespass against us." And, finally, He says from the cross, "Father, forgive them, for they know not what they do." I hope we have forgiveness on our Christmas list this year. We've all seen a lot of fine homes with fine dishes and fancy clothes. And perhaps we've even thought that there was too much fine stuff. But who has ever seen a home with too much forgiveness?

Will we give the gift of encouragement this year? Everybody needs it. We all need to know that someone is pulling for us, rooting for us, and wishing the best for us. We all need some help along life's way. When it's so easy to take the people we love for granted, who will offer a word of praise for a job well done or a word of thanks for a thoughtful gesture? Who will give the gift of being a positive and uplifting influence on someone else's life?

Jesus Christ is born tonight to give us encouragement, that we may give it to one another. He is born to say, as He said so long ago, "Rise up and walk. Open your eyes and see. Come unto me all who are weary and heavy laden, and I will give you rest."

I hope we have encouragement on our Christmas list this year. We've all seen homes with too many toys and too many gadgets for grown-up boys and girls. But have you ever seen a home with too much encouragement?

Will we give the gift of love this year? Everybody needs love, and I'm not talking about love or lust. I'm not talking about the romantic "good feeling" love they sing about on the radio. I'm talking about deep abiding Christian love—the kind that reminds you that a mountain top is waiting for you even though you're walking ankle deep in the valley of the shadow of death. When it's so easy to think about yourself in this world, who will give the gift of love this year?

Jesus Christ is born tonight to give us God's love that we may give it to one another. He said, "As the Father has loved Me, so

I have loved you; continue in My love." Who will say to a parent, a child, a husband, or a wife, 'You can count on me today and always, for better or for worse, in sickness and in health; I'll be here for you as Christ is here for me... because I love you!'

I hope we have love on our Christmas list this year. We've seen a lot of homes with too many material things of every description. But who has ever seen a home with too much love?

Spiritual gifts like forgiveness and encouragement and love are given to us on this silent, Holy Night. They cannot be purchased at any price. They can only be given to others, as God in Christ gives them to each of us.

Take a look at the people you are sitting with tonight. Think about other friends and loved ones who are close to your heart. There are worldly gifts and spiritual gifts. What are you giving for Christmas this year?

CHRISTMAS DAY
JOHN 1:1-18

"And the Word became flesh and dwelt among us." (John 1:14) There is something about the sights, sounds, and rituals of the season that make it possible for us to experience God's presence in a special way. This is the day of the year when we give our full attention to God's Christmas presence.

I think about how easy it is to become nostalgic at Christmas time, and the way in which we experience God's presence through the memories of our past. I think about material things—the trees, the lights, the gifts, and all the things that are a part of Christmas—and I realize that God's presence becomes real to us in and through those material things.

I think about the way in which we celebrate with family and friends, and even strangers, and how God becomes real to us in these relationships.

I think about the special music of Christmas and how, over-and-over again, through the gift of music, God becomes real to us in a special way.

I think about the Nativity Scene as the most exciting place of all to be with God in this season, the most exciting place of all to experience God's real Christmas presence.

If we're paying close attention to the Nativity story, we realize how much activity was centered around Jesus' Birth. There was Joseph, with difficult decisions to make before the Birth of the Child, and with heavy responsibilities to meet after the Birth. There was Mary, so vulnerable after the Birth of her Child. She and her husband—both refugees—unable to go home again. There were the wise men, clomping over the desert with heavy thoughts of their astrological readings about a new king and having to deal with the murderous jealousy of King Herod. There were the shepherds, running from the fields to the stable, then back to the fields, then into the town. There were the angels, singing their song of praise and then disappearing into the heavens. There was the old couple, Simeon and Anna, waiting with great expectation in the temple. Soon their long years of longing and waiting would come to an end, and they would hold and be able to bless the Messiah. All of this was going on, but in the midst of it all was a newborn Baby. This Child, Mary's Child, was the reason for all of that activity, and the reason for all of our activity during this season of the year.

MDP, the Holy God, Creator of the Heaven and the earth, the Almighty God who sustains all of life, comes to us in this tiny, fragile Baby. In order for us to experience the fullness of His power and love, God comes to us in this human way:

In the beginning was the Word, and the Word was with God... and the Word became flesh and dwelt among us. (John 1:1, 14)

During the year, as we listen to the Gospels, we give our attention to a Man that the Child became. We talk about the teachings of Jesus, the parables of Jesus, the miracles of Jesus. We focus on the death of Jesus and the resurrection of Jesus. But rarely do we spend time with the Child.

Let me suggest that on this Christmas Day we focus our attention on the Child. What is God saying to you through this Baby? What is God saying to you about Himself? What is God saying to you about your life? What is God saying to you about our world through this Child? Give this Child your full attention, and the answer will come; and you'll know... you'll know.

There is an old Chinese custom whereby all debts are settled on New Year's Day. One reason they're able to do this, of course, is that they don't have Christmas the week before.

Did you have the usual problems with your gift selections this year? Perhaps some of you used the Internet to help you in this situation. If so, you may have noticed such items as 'his-and-her' airplanes, 'his-and-her' live ostriches. Then there was a robot, a pair of matched camels. While you were browsing through the Internet sites, perhaps the idea crossed your mind that if a gift-giving contest were to be held, you would have no chance of winning. But that's not a good idea. It's a wrong idea. Price tags are not the measure of the value of a gift. The greatest gift you can give doesn't come with a price tag. What is the greatest gift a husband can give his wife; a wife can give her husband; parents can give their children? No diamonds! Not a new BMW! Not an around-the-world vacation. Not even a pair of matched camels! The greatest gift one can give to another is sincere, loving attention.

As we focus our attention on Mary's Child of poverty, born in a stable to refugee parents, we are reminded of millions of children who are hurting in our world. As we take the Child into our hearts and carry Him around with us, we experience a new sensitivity for children, a new desire to be an instrument of God's love for children.

I want to suggest that the coming year be for you your own very special "Year of the Child." I want to suggest that you find something special to do through the year for children—especially children who are hurting. I won't presume to tell you what to do or how to do it. But I can tell you that if you lovingly embrace Mary's Child, you will be empowered to discern what you are to do in your "Year of the Child."

Many years ago, a woman was visiting a great cathedral in Italy. Just inside the great cathedral door she saw an enormous mosaic which, when completed, would extend across the entire width of the building. The mosaic represented the scene of the Last Judgment, containing hundreds of figures. A mind-boggling number of tiny pieces of different colored marble went into the design. Then the woman saw a man on his knees painstakingly setting the tiny pieces into place, one-by-one. The woman, who spoke Italian, said to the artisan, "What a tremendous task you have. I would never be able undertake such an enormous project." The man replied, "Oh, it doesn't seem like that to me at all. You see, I know how much I can do in one day. So, each morning, when I come to work, I mark out the area that I can cover in a day. But I never bother to think of the space outside that area. Before I know where I am, the job will be finished."

Undertaking your own personal "Year of the Child" may seem to cover too much ground. It may even boggle your mind at first. It may cause you to be anxious over where to begin, and where it will all end. If so, why not think of your "Year of the Child" in terms of one-day-at-a-time?

Starting today, do something special for a child, especially a child who is hurting—it may be your own child—and 365 days hence, you will rejoice as never before on a Christmas Day. And you'll be ready to begin your "Year of the Child II."

What is God saying to you in and through Mary's Child? God is saying, "Now do you see how much I love you!"

HOLY FAMILY SUNDAY
A (1) – MATTHEW 2:13-15

On this Sunday after Christmas, we read the beautiful Gospel of how Joseph showed his love for his family, Jesus and Mary, by fleeing to Egypt to protect them from the wicked Herod.

I would like to tell you a little story that took place at Riverside Church in the heart of New York City. It was Christmas Eve and the church was putting on a Christmas pageant. The pageant had come to the point where the innkeeper was to say that there was no room at the inn for Joseph and Mary, who was pregnant with Jesus. The part seemed perfect for little Tim, an earnest and faithful kid who had Downs Syndrome. Only one line to memorize and he had practiced it again and again with his parents and with the pageant director. Tim seemed to have mastered it. So there he was standing at the altar, a bathrobe over his clothes, as Mary and Joseph made their way down the center aisle. They approached him, said their lines, and waited for Tim to reply. Tim boomed out, just as he rehearsed, "There's no room at the inn." But then, as Mary and Joseph turned to travel further, Tim suddenly yelled, "Wait!" Mary and Joseph turned back, startled, with tears in his eyes, Tim called, "You can stay at my house." Thinking quickly, the minister went to the pulpit and said, "Amen!" ... He had the congregation repeat the Amen – and both the pageant and the planned sermon came to an unexpected but perfect completion with the singing of Joy to the World.

My dear people, Tim's "twist" to the Christmas pageant underscores the true miracle of Christmas: In the child of Bethlehem, God makes His dwelling in our home, in our families, and in our hearts. In Matthew's account, Joseph is the saintly head of the Holy Family and accepts the challenge. In our lives as husbands and wives, as sons and daughters, in our lives as relatives and friends, we often are called to "flee" to our own Egypts! As is clear from the Gospel, Mary, Joseph and the Child's struggle as a Family was filled with heartaches, fears, anxieties and doubts ' just like we experience; but in our faith we know that the love of God enables us to accept the challenge to make our way through family life in all of its complexities and disappointments. As we gather as a family around the Christmas tree, may we take on hard but diligent work to make our family a place of love and peace.

A (2) – MATTHEW 2:13-15

The story is told of a certain pastor whose congregation tended toward sleep whenever he preached. One Sunday he came prepared with a solution to this problem. When he went to the pulpit, the very first thing he said was, "I feel I must confess to you, as your pastor, that I spent several years of my life in the arms of another man's wife." Immediately, everybody was hanging on his every word. Then, he said, "My mother!" The congregation had a good laugh and the pastor had accomplished his purpose.

But, it didn't work out that well for another pastor who tried the same technique. The trouble was that he was one of those persons who just couldn't tell a joke. He could never remember the punch line. One Sunday, he went to the pulpit and soon noticed that half the congregation was drifting off to slumber land. Now was the time to try the 'shocker' on them, he decided. Whereupon he said, "I feel I must confess to you, as your pastor, that I have spent several years of my life in the arms of another man's wife." Immediately he had everyone's attention. There were no more sleepers; everybody was hanging on his every word. Then, he paused and said, "But, for the life of me, I can't remember who she was."

Unfortunately, we have a tendency to tell the Christmas Story with equally sorry results. We tend to tell only the sweet parts and leave out the hard parts. We tend to forget the punch-line, which is that God loves us down in the depths of all of life – the sweet side and the bitter side, both.

The kind of joy and renewal that should literally sweep us into the months ahead in lively hope and expectation will be absent to those who have forgotten the Christmas story's "punch line".

There are some of us who are not hurting very much at this moment (although we know that sooner or later the deep hurt will come). And there are some of us who are hurting very deeply right now. Part of being a Christian family is to know that those who are not hurting can give strength and support to those who are.

Christmas is a time when we want to be home. We want members of our family who are not home to come home. But is not Christmas also for those who have no home or family to go to?

Christmas is a time for strong reaffirmations of faith and beautiful expressions of hope, as we no doubt have noticed from the inscriptions on our greeting cards. But is not Christmas also for those whose hearts are heavy with doubt and anxiety about the meaning of their existence and the worthwhileness of life?

Christmas is a time for giving our loved ones gifts that symbolize all the good things that occur in close, warm relationships. But is not Christmas also for those who still mourn for the loss of a loved one to whom they can no longer give in this way? We thank God that we are not abandoned ever, even in our deepest hurt.

MDP, within our families we experience heights of joy and depths of pain. Our belonging to a family means that each one of us—parent and child—reflects for the other the selfless, unconditional love of Christ in good times and in bad.

A friend of mine, the Navy mother of two young teenage sons made an agreement with her boys. Whenever the boys find themselves in an uncomfortable situation—say at a party where drugs are being passed, where there's an abuse of alcohol, anything the boys didn't want to be a part of, they call home and then casually and nonchalantly start whistling into the phone. The mom would ask them where they are and how long it is going to be before she gets there. No questions are asked so that their friends won't realize the boys are calling their mother. Mom just picks them up. Once returned to her love and care, mom congratulates them on their good judgment.

B (1)– Luke 2:22-40

This beautiful Feast of the Holy Family reminds me of a story about Mother Theresa. Mother Theresa of Calcutta was a living legend of love for the poor and oppressed and the homeless and people dying in the streets. Not only was she involved directly with people in need, but also managed to find time to travel all over the world to find support for her ministry. On one such trip she gave a talk at a Presbyterian church. An author who was there said she was so deeply moved by Mother Theresa's talk that she would have done anything for her. The author asked Mother Theresa, "What can we do to help you?" Mother Theresa turned to the author and quietly said, "Love your family!" Mother Theresa knew that "anyone who aspires to greatness must serve the needs of all. Mother Theresa knew that it all begins in our family and in our close relationships.

In World War II a soldier was on duty on Christmas morning. It had been his custom to go to church every Christmas morning with his family, but now, being in the outlying districts of London, this was impossible. So as dawn was breaking, with some of his buddies he walked down the road that led to the city. Soon they came to an old, gray stone building over whose main door were carved the words, "Queen Ann's Orphanage." So they decided to knock and see what kind of celebration was taking place inside. In response to their knock, a matron came and explained that the children were orphans whose parents had been killed in one of the many bombings that took place in London. The soldiers went inside just as the children were tumbling out of bed. There was no Christmas tree in the corner. There were no presents. The soldiers moved around the room wishing the children "Merry Christmas" and giving them whatever they had in their pockets: a stick of chewing gum, a life saver, a nickel, a dime, a pencil, a pocket knife, a good luck charm.

The soldier who had gotten his buddies together noticed a little fellow alone in the corner and that little fellow looked an awful lot like the kids in his family back home. So he approached him and said, "And you, little guy, what do you want for Christmas?" The lad replied, "Will you hold me?" The soldier, with tears brimming in his eyes, picked up the little boy and held him in his arms very close. This, MDP, is what family, a holy family, is all about: holding each other very tight. This is truly one of the greatest blessings we can have. This is why the church wants us to focus on family love with this feast day.

As a priest I am often party to troubles that happen within a family. I often see each member of a family refusing to hold on tightly to the other, refusing to see that there are differences in personality, in attitudes, in values, expectations, fears, hopes. It is always difficult to respect and love someone who is different from us. But it might be a little easier if we understand that God created diversity among us. God himself holds on tightly to each one of us; God loves each one of us as we are with all of our peculiarities, and strangenesses, and differences. He sent His Son, Jesus, into the world at Bethlehem not to make every human being like every other human being, but to give us the strength and the faith and the hope and the patience to hold on tightly to the one who is different from us in our families. It's all part of the wonder of God's universe; it's all part of the glory we celebrate at Christmas. This is what the church wants us to focus on today. None of us is a saint. We have to struggle with our successes and our failures. We must realize that the one thing worse than having a family is not having one.

B (2) – LUKE 2:22-40

MDP, we are still very much in the Christmas season, and the church gives us the scene of the Holy Family.

There's a story about a Catholic school, where just a few days before Christmas, the nuns were getting everything ready for the Christmas play. At the center of the stage, of course, was the crib, statues of Joseph and Mary, the shepherds, the three kings, the animals. The nuns were busy fixing the children's costumes and tending to last minute preparations. And just before the curtain was to go up, one of the nuns noticed that the baby Jesus was not in the crib. And in a panic, she rushed up to the Mother Superior, who was standing at the door watching the preparations. "Mother Superior," she said, "We forgot the child Jesus." And with a deep look on her face, the Mother Superior replied, "That's exactly the trouble with the world."

The church gives us, just a few days after Christmas, the Feast of the Holy Family to again tell us, "Don't forget the child Jesus" we still have this beautiful time to ponder what He means to our lives and to the lives of those who we love – and those who we don't love, to discover that in Jesus, God broke into our history, not a long time ago, but right now – in every act of kindness, in every victory of goodness, in the times we are compassionate and caring, every time we put the needs of another above our own; yes, to show us that we can't get along without God.

C –Luke 2:4-53

Among the works of the great artist, Raphael, is a beautiful painting of "The Holy Family." Because of the warm feeling the painting evokes, one can look at it and suddenly realize, as never before, that God Almighty who created us in love, chose to come to us in a family setting. It was in this family setting that Jesus first experienced the presence of God. It was in this family setting that our Lord first knew the joy of being loved. It was in this family setting that He learned His first lessons in how to love. It was in this family that Jesus began to develop His deep sense of self-integrity.

So, we have this beautiful Gospel this morning: Jesus is 12 years old. Mary and Joseph believe he is lost. They search for Him. On finding Him they learn that He simply had gone His own way. Mary reacts as any mother would: "My Child, why have you done this to us. See how worried your father and I have been, looking for You" ... and with some frankness, Jesus answers, "Why were you looking for Me? Did you not know that I must be busy with My Father's affairs?"

I bet that answer hurt Mary and Joseph, but having said what needed to be said, Jesus went back home with them and "lived under their authority," as Luke says. Here we have all the reality of a family situation. When God decided to come to us and to focus His love for us, He did it in a family setting. He penetrated our human situation in a family context. You know, my dear people, we are living in a time of deep pessimism and cynicism about marriage and the family. So it is very important for us, as Christians, to affirm the value of the family; to do all we can to strengthen it; to use it as God intends it to be used. As a people, we are only as intact as our families. But we have been allowing our families to disintegrate. Perhaps without realizing it, we're all too busy, too busy to take time to be with our family.

In a CCD school class, a teacher was talking about God as Father. In very serious tones, one little boy said, "I hope he's not like my father. He's always too busy." You see, we should be concerned with the quality of family life. There are fathers and mothers who are at home most of the time but they are not really there at all. It is a certain quality of caring, of being involved that needs to be there to sustain the family.

There are some statistics out today which say more twins are being born. When a teacher mentioned this to her third grade class, one little student said, "I guess more twins are being born because little children are afraid to come into the world alone." Yes, little children are afraid to come into the world alone – so God gives them a family. It is within the family that we are really ourselves. You can't hide the real you in the family. Day after day, week after week, who you really are inevitably comes out.

There was a young man who left his home and family when it seemed to most everyone that his family life was really ideal. His father was a judge and the pillar of the community. But when the young man was asked why he left, he said about his father, "I've seen him at home with his judge's robes off. I know who he is."

So our family, my dear people, is the first and best place for the love of God to come alive. Today's Feast of the Holy Family calls us to discover and celebrate our own families as a place for forgiveness and understanding, a place of unconditional love.

Sometimes the family often is the context in which cruel and unloving things happen, even in families where there is some measure of warmth and affection. It's so strange how members in the family begin to take each other for granted! We know that often the words "I love you" spoken by a husband or wife really mean "I want to exploit you; I want to use you." We know that often the words "I love you" spoken by a parent to a child really mean, "I want you to do as I say. I want you to turn out as I say so that you won't embarrass me." And we know that as a consequence, when a child says "I love you" to a parent it means "I want something."

MDP, Today's beautiful Feast of the Holy Family tells us that the very light of God shines in our families, that we must nurture each other to goodness, to holiness, and that when we say, "I love you," we must mean it honestly and sincerely, without conditions. The challenge of Christmas with its Holy family is to make the love of God alive in our families, in or own lives and in the loves of those we love.

THE BLESSED VIRGIN MARY;
JANUARY 1

A, B, C – Matthew 5:1-12

One would think that the Church should force on us this morning all kinds of warnings about the New Year—what to do, what not to do. But, instead, the Church is about another business. She reassures us, encourages us; tells us about peace and joy; instead of presenting for us a picture of hell. The Church, through her liturgy, lays out the charming scene of Mary, the Mother of God, with her Child, Jesus, and the humble shepherds visiting the manger. Instead of telling us how bad we are; the Church gives us a glimpse of Mary, our great Mother, as our Model.

With Mary as our Mother by our side, we are being urged today to look ahead to the opportunities of the future. With Mary by our side, we should not look back to the frustrations and failures of the past, but, like Mary, we should rejoice in our dignity as sons and daughters of almighty God. With this simple Gospel scene, the Church begins the new year by making us feel good about ourselves, building our confidence and our hope. The past is gone. Hope is the name of the game. We are given this Gospel of Mary and the Child and we are asked to meditate, think about the decisive change that occurred in the human race at Bethlehem. Because this change has occurred, it is never too late for any of us to change, and so we can face the new year with a hopeful view of ourselves and our lives. Things may go wrong, but because there is a Mary and Jesus, we can keep going ahead without ever giving up the fight.

EPHIPHANY SUNDAY; JANUARY 2-8

A, B, C – MATTHEW 2:1-12

Like the magi's search for the newborn King, our lives are a constant search for meaning, for purpose, for love, for God and the things of God.

This was brought home to me yesterday as I returned from a Christmas holiday in Philadelphia with my family. The flight from Philly to Tampa was crowded, and when we arrived, everyone seemed to be in a hurry to reach the baggage claim. I was walking next to a gentleman who was hurrying to meet his family waiting for him in the baggage claim area. As soon as he saw his young son, he picked him up and gave him a hug. I heard him say, "You have become quite the man, son. I missed you so much." The little guy smiled and said, "Me, too, Dad." And while all this was happening, a baby girl was squirming in her mother's arms, never once taking her eyes off her father. He said, "Hi, sweetheart!" as he took her from her mother's arms. He kissed her and held her close to his chest while he rocked her from side to side. After several moments, the man handed the little girl to his son and said, "I've saved the best for last," and proceeded to give his wife a tender kiss. I heard him say, "I love you!"

For that minute, I felt that I was witnessing something sacred. I stood beside him as we were waiting for our bags, and struck up a conversation. I asked him how long had he been married. "Fourteen years," he said. Then referring to the beautiful reunion I had just witnessed, I asked, "How long have you been away?" He said, "Two whole days!" I thought there is something here for my Epiphany homily. MDP, it's not so much the length of time it takes to find the Lord in our lives, not so much the length of time apart that determines the passion in a relationship. It's what we do when we have found the star of our love. It's really staying in love with the people we love.

More and more we read that the business of loving another human being is the most challenging of all human enterprises because of the demands it makes on us. And because of these demands there are many of us who have never loved another person deeply; or, perhaps, we have loved someone deeply and have been hurt in some way. And so we retreated from the passion of living life and love to the fullest.

One of the greatest needs of the human heart is to move in and love another person at the deepest level. There's a real sadness in some families where husbands and wives, mothers and fathers have lived together for years, yet have never gotten to know each other as persons. It's sometimes baffling to know that even the most intimate lovers can really be strangers to one another. And it's common for men and women to miss the fantastic opportunity which marriage, friendship, present, that is, to share life at the deepest level. We go places; we do things together, but the real thing never gets said.

This is what St. Paul is all excited about in his letter today to the Ephesians. He is telling them – and us- that because God loves us so much, it is possible for us to love at a deeper level, where we can say the real thing. When we begin to realize how much God loves us, we have a new sense of our worth, our own integrity. As St. Paul sees it, when we, like Magi, search and find God's love in our lives, we then sense our own worth, and have a new appreciation for the worth of the other person. We begin to listen to the other person; we begin to be present to the other person in new ways; we begin to see how the light of Christ can shatter the darkness.

There was a repeat Christmas episode of the West Wing which was aired a few days ago. You might remember it: A few days before Christmas, Toby Ziegler, the president's communications director, receives a call from the D.C. police asking if he knew a homeless man who had died in the cold the night before. Toby has no idea who the man is. The police found Toby's card in the coat the man was wearing. Toby had given the coat to a shelter long ago. Toby discovers that the man was a decorated Vietnam veteran; his only survivor is a brother, who also lives on the streets. Toby uses his presidential connections to arrange for the man's burial with full military honors at Arlington National Cemetery on Christmas Eve.

During the last five minutes of the episode, the scene switches back and forth between a children's choir – surrounded by beautiful poinsettas and candles, performing for the President and the White House staff, and the austere Arlington honor guard laying the homeless veteran to rest, attended only by Toby, the man's brother, and the president's secretary. At first, you only see the children's choir singing The Carol of the Drums; but as the scene cuts to the hearse pulling up to the grave site at Arlington, the orchestra begins the relentless base rum-a-tum tum, rum-a tum tum of the carol. You see, in those last few moments of the program, the same drum beat that celebrates the birth of the Christ Child accompanies a homeless veteran on his last journey.

Magi from the East arrived in Jerusalem saying, "Where is the newborn King of the Jews" We saw His star at its rising and have come to do Him homage."

MDP, with the three magi we too must look for the star, Jesus, the Lord, and chart the course of our lives. With the Magi, we must walk with Jesus from the manger in Bethlehem all the way to the hill of Calvary outside of Jerusalem. We too must follow not only the beautiful star of Christmas, with the Magi we look into the face of the Son of God and move to share on the deepest level His love and life, and know we are looking at the light that shatters the darkness.

Whether or not you and I can help God in the building of His Kingdom of love depends on whether or not we reflect the light and the love of God. And it all begins when, like the 'three Wise Men from the East," we fall to our knees and pay homage to the dazzling image of God who was born in a stable and lay on a bed of straw – and whose powerful bright light continues to shine on us today and every day.

Let's begin with myrrh

One of the kings brought myrrh. Among ancient peoples, myrrh was used to prepare the dead for burial. For example, the women brought myrrh to the tomb of Jesus. Because of myrrh's relationship with death, it made an ideal symbol of human vulnerability. The gift of myrrh; therefore, is symbolic of the Humanity of Jesus. It speaks to us of Jesus' Human vulnerability. Like us, He experienced the whole range of human emotions: joy, sorrow, fear, frustration, loneliness. He was like us in everything but sin.

The next king brought frankincense. Ancient peoples used incense in their religious worship. The aroma and smoke, spiraling upward to Heaven, spoke to them of gods and divinity. The gift of incense; therefore, is symbolic of the Divinity of Jesus.

The third king brought gold. Among ancient peoples, gold was regarded as the king of metals. It was, therefore the ideal gift for a King.

MONSIGNOR HAD A SPECIAL DEVOTION TO MARY

Our Blessed Lady says, "My soul proclaims the greatness of the Lord and my spirit exults in god my savior." That's what Mary is all about. She is there to point us to God!

Through her unconditional surrender to God, she proclaims His Greatness and she became a model of fruitful living for all ages to come. She gives us the secret to living a beautiful life when, pointing to the Lord, she says, "Let it be done according to your will."

Ephphatha must become our word of healing; it must become our prayer that we may be 'open' to the presence of God in our own lives and in the lives of those we are privileged to touch.

BAPTISM OF THE LORD
A – Matthew 3:13-27

In today's beautiful Gospel, the voice of God identifies Jesus as "My beloved Son, with Whom I am well pleased." The Feast the Church gives us should remind us of our own baptism, when we were baptized we were given a name by which we will be addressed for the rest of our lives: We were given the name "Christ," and so we are called "Christian".

Not so long ago a friend told me the story of how one Christmas he scolded his three year old daughter for wasting a roll of gold wrapping paper. He didn't want her to waste money and so he became angry when his little girl tried to decorate a box to put under the Christmas tree. Nevertheless, the little girl brought the gift to her father the next morning and said, "This is for you, Daddy." He said to me that he was embarrassed by his earlier over-reaction, but his anger flared up again when he opened the box and found it was empty. He yelled at his daughter, "Don't you know that when you give someone a present, there's supposed to be something inside the box?" The little girl looked up at him with tears in her eyes and said, "Oh Daddy, it's not empty. I blew kisses in the box. I filled it with my love. All for you, Daddy."

Well, he was crushed. He put his arms around his little daughter, and asked her to forgive him. My friend told me that he kept that gold box by his bed for years. And whenever he was discouraged or wondered where his life was going, he would take out an imaginary kiss and remember the love of the child who had put it there.

MDP, in a very real sense, this is what God does at our baptism. He gives each of us a gold box filled with unconditional love; He tells us we have been marked with the sign of faith in His Son, Jesus; He says we are never to be afraid or discouraged because we now bear the name "Christian," that we are to take on the mission of His unconditional love and be willing and eager to mirror that love in the lives of others.

This is the meaning of our baptism. And today on the Feast of the baptism of the Lord, we must hear Him say to us, "You are My beloved sons and daughters with whom I am well pleased."

B – MARK 1:7-11

There's a story I like to tell about how, at the end of our Revolutionary War, the newly formed nation almost came to disaster. The government, which was short of funds, owed back pay to the military officers who had fought long and hard for the nation's independence. There was talk that the Army officers would not disband until they were paid, and, perhaps they would march on the Capital. Mutiny was at hand.

Hurriedly, George Washington assembled the officers and urged them to be patient. He produced a letter from Congress explaining the problems the government faced. But when he began to read, he continually stumbled over the words until he finally stopped. He seemed lost. Then Washington pulled from his pocket something his army had never seen him use before: a pair of eyeglasses, and speaking softly he said: "Gentlemen, you must pardon me. I have grown gray in your service, and now find myself growing blind."

Suddenly, the anger that had permeated the officers began to subside. They were touched by their leader's willingness to appear before them as an ordinary, humble human being with ordinary human problems. The soldiers voted to do as he asked, and gave Congress more time to sort things out.

It is, perhaps, a bit of a stretch, but writers who comment on this story say that Washington's humility and vulnerability spared the young Republic the agony of armed rebellion.

Abraham Lincoln would often quote a verse from a poem which began, "Oh why should the spirit of mortal man be proud?" Lincoln knew how flimsy pride is in the face of human mortality. Life is short.

We come and we go, and yet, there are times we get so puffed up over our achievements and our powers.

Shakespeare put it this way: "What a piece of work is man!" And the Psalmist put it another way: "Who is man that God should be mindful of him? He has made him a little less than the angels and crowned him with glory and honor."

MDP, sometimes it is so easy for us to forget that everything we have comes from God, and we lose sight of what God expects from us.

In today's Gospel, St. Mark writes, "The Spirit, a dove descended on Him" and a voice from heaven said, "You are My Son and My favor rests on You."

We who are followers of Jesus, share in this favor to the extent that we strive to be the salt of the earth, a light to others, the yeast in our community, the servant to others.

You know, MDP, that in Philadelphia, here, all over the world, violence is on the rise. The holiness of marriage is under attack, governments are losing credibility. Our world, our nation, our homes need a spirit of humble redeeming. False values need to be challenged. And it begins with little old us!

If we are serious about following Christ, we must think about what it means to be a "light to the world", to be the "salt of the earth." It takes humility! Jesus never minced words about this: "The person who serves is the greater. The person who is humble is the one who is exalted." It is not our position in life which counts, but what we do with it. It is not the exercise of power and authority that counts, but how we exercise power and authority. Our status in life does not really explain who we are. But humbly, ever so humbly, we must acknowledge that everything we have is a gift from God.

St. Mark in the Gospel today tells us that Jesus came from Nazareth in Galilee and was baptized by John. Matthew tells us that John tried to dissuade him, saying, "it is I who needs baptism from You, and yet You come to me Jesus." God, the Messiah, replies, "Leave it like this." And John gave in to Him. "Everyone who humbles himself will be exalted."

C – Luke 3:15-16, 21-22

The Church gives us this beautiful Feast so that we can reflect on our own baptism and so to ask ourselves if we have mirrored Christ since the waters of the baptism have been poured on us.

In 1982, the Navy gave me a set of orders to the Naval Hospital in Oakland, California. It was a pretty good-sized Naval hospital and I was the only Priest/Chaplain. It was probably one of the busiest and tiring assignments I had in my Navy career. But there were so many joys, so many miracles.

I want to reconstruct an incident. I was making my rounds in the maternity ward, and a baby had just been born. The family was there to welcome little Elizabeth. I began to congratulate the young sailor-father, who was a man of few words. I said, "Beautiful baby" as we looked through the nursery window. Little Elizabeth was squirming. I remember she was red-faced and screaming. I though the father might be concerned, so I said, (like I really knew) "She's not sick; I think it's good for babies to scream. It clears out the lungs and gets their voices going. So don't worry; it's all right."

The young sailor-father answered, "Oh, I know that she's not sick, but she's mad as hell." Then he caught himself and apologized. So I said, "Tell me, why is she mad". He answered, "Well, wouldn't you be mad, Father? One minute you're with God in heaven and the next minute you're in California?"

"Wow," I thought this guy has been reading one of the old philosophers. So I remember asking him, "you believe she was with God before she came here?" "Oh yeah." Then I said, "Do you think she'll remember?" He answered with words that have stuck with me all these years: "Well, that's up to her mother and me. It's up to the church. We've got to see that she remembers, cause if she forgets, she's a goner."

MDP, this young sailor understood that little Elizabeth is part of the story of God, and that it is her mother and dad's job to make sure she understands that story and her place in it.

And that is why the church gives us this beautiful Feast: so that we understand that with our baptism we become part of a family that tells the story of a God who created us out of love and who recreates us again in the gift of His Son. In our baptism we take our place in that story and are entrusted by God with the holy task of re-telling the story of God's love "so we don't forget." Because if we forget, in the words of the young sailor, "we are all goners."

LENT BEGINS

The season of Lent is a time of creative waiting. It is a time of prayer and fasting and self-examination, as we go deep within ourselves in order to come to terms with whatever it is in our life that is blocking out God's rule. It is a time for acknowledging, from the depths of our being, the need for change in our life. This is truly a creative effort because now we are cooperating with God in the re-making of our life. More and more we begin to put a higher value on our own worthwhileness and on the worthwhileness of other people. More and more we begin to see ourselves and others as having been created in the image and likeness of God. More and more we begin to transform our vague hope in God's promise of our ultimate fulfillment into outright expectancy. More and more we begin to see that the more we prepare for Good Friday and Easter Sunday in this creative way, the more we have to wait for.

ASH WEDNESDAY
MATTHEW 6:1-6, 16-18

Before we receive the Blessed Ashes, I thought we might reflect – just for a minute – on the idea of ashes. The ashes we will receive should remind us of our relative insignificance in the big picture of things. We all are ashes in waiting, that is, we are all going to die. So Ash Wednesday reminds us of our mortality. All of our big plans and great ideas will eventually be ashes. All the energy we spend on mundane things – collecting things, cars, clothes, computers, stocks, gold, will one day be ashes. All of our thoughts and worries about issues – political, domestic, nuclear, will one day be ashes.

At first thought this reflection can seem pretty depressing, but if we think a little more about the idea of ashes, we can be peacefully joyful. All the things that stress us, everything we worry about, these too will be ashes. All those things that threaten us, one day, ashes. All the expectations of others – ashes. The financial pressures, ashes. The words from others that hurt and bruise us – ashes. Everything that weighs us down, will, in the end, be ashes.

Thomas A Kempis wrote that our problem as Christians is that we are not fully alive to God. The old habits in us still kick us around too much. May the ashes we receive today begin our Lent with the resolve to be fully and joyfully alive to Almighty God.

FIRST SUNDAY OF LENT
A - MATTHEW 4:1-11

MDP, it is so interesting that the Church begins Lent with the story of Jesus confronting Satan in the desert. The desert is a place where light exposes all things. The desert is a place where truth can be faced in a kind of light we can experience in no other place. We need our moments in the desert. We need to stop procrastinating, to take stock of how we use our Christian time. It is not so much pride or power that tempts us, but it is apathy, routine, indifference; it is putting things off, putting off the challenge to live a solid, balanced, holy life. So many of us get stuck in monotony, in routine, that we think we have plenty of time, and so we put off the things we must do to live fervently the Gospel of Jesus Christ.

So the Church gives us Lent to stand still for a moment, so that we can move ahead. Lent is our six week push, our desert, where we go from ashes to fire and discover again who the real Treasure within us is.

It has been said by some wise person that "there is nothing noble in being superior to other persons. Our true nobility is in being superior to our previous self."

These forty days of Lent should remind us of this need to become superior to our previous self: the need to be kinder, the need to be more compassionate, the need to be more forgiving, the need to be more giving of ourselves.

A young voice student rushed up to one of today's great tenors after a concert and blurted, "I'd give up my life to sing as beautifully as you do." To which he replied: "I did."

MDP, if we wish to become the beautiful persons God made us to be, we must place God at the very center of our lives. There is no other way.

B – MARK 1:12-15

During one of my tours in Europe, I had to spend some time in England. On one of my free days, I visited Yorkminster Cathedral. This Cathedral was built in the 13th century and for 700 years it stood tall and true. But some years ago, people began to notice cracks in some of the walls of this Grand Cathedral. A contractor, an architect, and a building inspector were brought in and they traced some of those cracks back to severe faults in the foundation. The mighty and ancient Yorkminster Cathedral was closed. It had to be structurally repaired because of those cracks. It looked so great on the outside, but inside there was structural damage.

As I stood before this Cathedral, I thought there is a Gospel message in all of this, that it just might represent the age we live in. Here and everywhere, some of us resemble the Yorkminster Cathedral. We look great on the outside, but inside there is structural damage. There are cracks in our hearts, our spirits, our souls. When we are asked how we are doing, we say, "Fine, thank you." But deep inside we know there is anxiety, worry, restlessness, fear, emptiness. Deep inside, like the Cathedral, there is something wrong with the structure of our soul. And if any of this is going to change, we need to listen to the one word that sums up this Gospel of the first Sunday of Lent: Jesus says, "Repent!" "Change your way of living!" "Turn your life around; forget the shabby old life you have been living."

It might mean giving up the pleasure of blaming others, and looking deep into our own souls for a clue to what ails us. It might mean that pursuing the fullness of life Jesus offers will put us at odds with much that is going on in today's world. It might mean that as a follower of Christ we will be accused of being out of step with things as they are. This is all part of Jesus' call to reform.

In a Charlie Brown comic strip, Linus comes to Charlie and says, "Charlie Brown, do you want to know what's the trouble with you?" Charlie says, "No." They just stare at each other. Then Linus says, "The trouble with you, Charlie Brown, is that you don't want to know what is the trouble with you." That's the problem so many of us have. We feel threatened at the prospect of having to admit our imperfections.

In another cartoon, a husband and wife are lying in bed, about to go to sleep. The husband has a smug look on his face. The wife has rolled over on her side and is not facing him. She is overheard praying, "Dear God," she prays, "please give Mr. Perfect one tiny flaw." Again, that's the problem with so many of us. We think we are Mr. and Mrs. Perfect. But the call of the Gospel means admitting that we are not, which is why the word, "repent" is one of the hardest words Jesus ever spoke. But we are not left alone to accomplish change in our lives. God never withdraws His love and mercy and help. It is a matter of changing our own minds and hearts.

All of us, without exception, are called to repentance, called to change, called to reverse our values, called to a better way of life. Think about it: we multiply our possessions, our money, but reduce our values. We have conquered outer space but not inner space. We've added years to life, but not life to years. We've learned to make a living, but not a life. These are the days of two income households but more divorces. These are the days of disposable diapers and disposable babies. These are the days of fancier houses, but broken homes. These are the days when we have more experts on everything, but more problems; more medicine but less genuine wellness. More nuclear power and more nuclear weapons to destroy us.

So, the Church gives us the season of Lent, as the Gospel suggests, a time to think about temptation. It is a time for our community to test its fidelity to God. It is a time for deep decision making. It challenges us to rise above the ashes of last Wednesday to the joy of Easter.

In medieval times a knight of old, when full-dressed, needed a strong, large horse to bear the weight of his armor-clad body. When hunting, however, he used a small horse. But when parading through a village in full regalia, he was on a high horse. He was looked up to as being superior to the lowly peasant who was forced to travel on his own two feet.

And so we have the expression, "Get down off your high horse" which came to mean, "Quit acting as if you are above us." For the "high-horse" set of our time, Jesus has but one word: "Dismount; Get down off your high horse."

None of us is perfect, there are no Mr. or Mrs. Perfect among us. That includes me, that includes you. Lent is our season to dismount, to get off our high horse.

C – LUKE 4:1-13

"MAN DOES NOT LIVE ON BREAD ALONE.: (LUKE 4:4)

There is a "Peanuts" comic strip in which little Linus meets Charlie Brown on the street. "Where have you been?" Charlie asks. "Church school," Linus replies. "We've been studying the Letters of the Apostle Paul." "That should be interesting." Charlie offers. "It is," says Linus, "although I must admit it makes me feel a little guilty. I always feel like I'm reading someone else's mail."

During this Lenten season, we must concentrate on the need to renew our family life. We must concentrate on the need to have our lives protected by the only security system in which we can place our full confidence and trust: the security of the Lord's abiding love.

Paul says it all: "If your lips confess that Jesus is Lord and if you believe in your heart that God raised Him from the dead, then you will be saved." During this Lenten season, let us concentrate on reading that certain someone's mail!

An older couple was driving down the road on a Sunday afternoon. He was driving; she was leaning against the door on the passenger's side. They caught up to a very slow moving car. A young man was driving; a young woman was cuddled up to him. Seeing this, the older woman looked across to her husband, then looked ahead toward the young couple and said, "Why don't we sit together like that anymore?" Quick as a flash, the husband replied, "I haven't moved!"

Perhaps some of us have come to this first Sunday of Lent feeling just a little distant, a little apart from God; perhaps we might feel we aren't as close to the Lord as we once were. But if we listen closely, I am sure we will hear God say, quick as a flash: "I haven't moved."

Do you remember the Broadway play, made into a movie – "Fiddler on the Roof"? One of my favorite and the most engaging characters in this play is Tevye. Before he sings his famous song, "If I were a Rich Man," he complains to God: "Dear God" he says, "you made many, many poor people. I realize, of course, it's no shame to be poor, but it's no great honor either. So what would have been so terrible if I had a small fortune?" Then Tevye sings, "If I were a Rich Man." The lyric begins with Tevye's reminder to God that if he were a rich man, he wouldn't have to work hard. In fact, all day long he'd just "deedle deedle dum, bidi bidi bum." Then in the middle of the song, Tevye sings, "I'd build a big tall house with rooms by the dozen, right in the middle of the town, a fine tin roof with real wooden floors below. There would be one long staircase just going up and one even longer coming down, and one more leading nowhere just for show."

MDP, how wonderful it would be to have that "small fortune." How secure life would be! How fulfilling to possess things "just for show!" Could this possibly be the power of evil speaking? And then, Jesus comes into our lives and tells us that even with "one more staircase," we might be going nowhere. We might be very active in our church; we might be very pious, but we might be relying too heavily on the wrong things for our fulfillment. Sometimes the words of Jesus, "No man can serve two masters," rustles my heart.

I grew up in and around Philadelphia, and I remember that, when Lent began, there was always a vendor with a short pole in front of the Church, upon which dozens of pretzels hung. I never understood the meaning of this until later in life. I found out the pretzels were first baked as a Lenten food going back at least to the fifth century. Monks are credited with twisting dough into the now familiar pretzel shape to represent arms crossed over the chest, which was the posture for prayer back then. Pretzels would appear on Ash Wednesday and disappear on Good Friday. The shape and ingredients of the pretzel were reminders of the Lenten season. They were the food of the poor because these early Christians ate no dairy products during Lent; you see, the pretzel consisted only of flour, salt and water – it could not be simpler. And the coarse salt sprinkled on the pretzel reminded the Christian that salt, so necessary to all forms of life, is what Christ had called them to be for the world – you remember when He told His Disciples to be "the salt of the earth."

MDP, it is my prayer that we embrace the spirit of the pretzel this Lent: that these 40 days, before the great Feast of Easter, be a time of prayer, a time to "reconnect" with God; that the simplicity of the pretzel will remind us to live lives of simplicity, lives centered on the values of God taught to us by Jesus; that the salt of the pretzel remind us that we are called by Christ to become for our families, for our friends, for our world, the "salt" of compassion, of generosity, of love, of forgiveness; that the cross arms formed by the pretzel be a sign of the cross Jesus calls us to take up as we journey with Him to the joy of Easter.

SECOND SUNDAY OF LENT
A – MATTHEW 17:1-9

In this Gospel of the Transfiguration, I find Peter to be such an interesting character. Peter didn't want to leave the mountaintop; after all, he had been an eyewitness to the glory of God. It seems he didn't want to get back into the "rat race." He wanted to build three shelters. But, no, Jesus led him and the other Disciples down from the mountain back into the valley of everyday life. And what did they find? They found people in need. If you read just a little further from this point in the Gospel, the first person they encountered was a father pleading for his son: "Lord have mercy on my son for he is sick, he is an epileptic, and he suffers terribly."

This was driven home to me when I visited the Vatican museum in Rome. I saw the famous painting of the transfiguration by Raphael, the great Italian artist. Raphael died at the age of 37, and as he lay in state, his painting of the transfiguration was placed at the head of his coffin. The striking thing about the painting is that the top half depicts Christ and the three Apostles in their phenomenal mountaintop experience of intense glory. But the bottom half of the painting depicts the epileptic boy and his father in the agony of their need.

In other words, we are being told that as followers of Christ, we must be agents of transfiguration. Wherever we are, wherever God calls us, we must always be willing to walk with Jesus down from the mountaintop into the valley of human need.

When my aircraft carrier was in Mombasa, in Africa, I took the opportunity to leave the ship for a while and visit some of the local missionary priests. One of the priests told me this story. He said, "It was a bright Sunday morning, a most fitting day to preach on the Gospel of the Transfiguration. In the sermon I told the members of the Church to reflect the glory of God's love in everything they did, just as Jesus did in His life. After the sermon, the offering plate was passed. A young native woman who had recently been baptized, had no money to give. So, when the plate came to her, she quietly rose from her seat, placed the plate on the floor and stood on it, and as she carried out that symbolic act of total commitment, a total gift of self, I saw in her face a brilliant, dazzling reflection of God's love."

MDP, if we belong to Christ in anyway, we must be agents of transfiguration. We must walk down the mountaintop with Jesus and work with Him so that injustice will be transfigured into justice, that heartache and hurt will be transfigured into compassion and caring, that sadness will be transfigured into laughter and joy, that despair, loneliness, worry, fear will be transfigured by our love for God and for one another. Yes, that's it: to walk down the mountaintop with our blessed Lord, into the valley of human need.

B (1) – Mark 9:2-10

In the event recounted in today's Gospel, Peter, James and John see in Jesus the very life and love of God that dwelled within Him. This Gospel of the Transfiguration tells us that the same love and life of God dwells within each of us and calls us to transfigure our lives and then to "transfigure" our world into God's image.

"Seeing is the great paradox in the Bible; those with two good eyes are blind, and those who are blind see. The spiritual writers often speak of a 'third eye', a seeing with the soul. In other words, what I believe they are saying is that what we see governs our behavior.

Allow me to give you an example: I remember reading the author Steve Covey who told of an experience he had on a New York subway one Sunday morning. He says that people were sitting quietly. Some were reading newspapers, some were dozing, others were simply contemplating with their eyes closed. It was a rather peaceful, calm scene. At one stop a man and his children entered the car. The children were soon yelling back and forth, throwing things, even grabbing peoples' newspapers. It was all very disturbing, and yet the father just sat next to Steve and did nothing. It was not difficult to feel irritated, he said. He could not believe the man could be so insensitive as to let his children run wild and do nothing about it. It was easy to see that everyone else in the car was annoyed as well. So finally, with what he thought was admirable restraint and patience, he said to the man, "Sir, your children are really disturbing a lot of people. I wonder if you could not control them a little bit more?"

The man lifted his eyes as if coming into consciousness for the first time and said, "Oh, you're right. I guess I should do something about it. We just came from the hospital where their mother died about an hour ago. I don't know what to think and I guess they don't know how to handle it." Steve said, "Can you imagine what I felt at that moment? Suddenly I saw things differently. Because I saw differently, I felt differently, I behaved differently. My irritation vanished. I didn't have to worry about controlling my attitude or my behavior. My heart was filled with this man's pain. Feelings of compassion and sympathy flowed freely." He said to the man, "Your wife just died. Oh, I'm sorry! Can you tell me about it? What can I do to help?"

MDP, nothing changed in that subway car. All was the same: the same people, the same irritation, the same kids. What 'did' change was a way of seeing it all and, with the seeing, a change of behavior. It was Steve's moment of transfiguration.

The point is that we have to see differently; we have to recognize such moments in our lives, and seeing all of this we must transfigure despair into hope, sadness into joy, anguish into healing.

"Jesus was Transfigured before them and His clothes became dazzling white."

B (2)– Mark 9:2-10

A doctor friend of mine tells this story of a wonderful Christian mother and her five year old son who was in the hospital, dying of a painful cancer.

One morning, before the mother arrived at the hospital, a nurse heard the little boy saying, "I hear the bells. I hear the bells still ringing."

Over and over that morning, the nurses and the staff heard him say this. When the mother arrived, she asked one of the nurses how her son was doing. The nurse replied, "Oh, he's hallucinating today. It's probably the medication. He keeps saying he hears bells." Whereupon, that beautiful mother's face came alive with understanding. She looked at the nurse and said, "No, he is not hallucinating. And he's not out of his head because of the medicine. I told him weeks ago that when the pains in his chest got bad and it was getting hard to breathe, it meant he was going to leave us. It meant he was going to go to heaven. And when the pain got really bad, I told him to look up in the corner of the room toward heaven and listen for the bells of heaven, because they will be ringing for him." With that, she went into her little son's room, swooped him out of his bed and rocked him in her arms, until the sounds of the ringing bells were only echoes, and he was gone."

The doctor finished his story by saying, "That great mother, in her act of mothering, left the hospital a different place as the result of her inspiring presence."

C – LUKE 9:28 – 36

Someone told me once that the two greatest days in our life are the day we were born and the day we discover the reason why. Why were we born?

I loved reading, and still do, the author C. S. Lewis and, in his own style, he gives a perspective on an answer: he says, in effect, imagine yourself as a living house. God comes to rebuild that house. At first, perhaps you can understand what He is doing. He is getting the drains right and is stopping the leaks in the roof and so on: you knew that those jobs needed doing and so you are not surprised. But then He starts knocking the house about in a way that really hurts and it does not seem to make sense. What on earth is He up to? The explanation is that He is building quite a different house from the one you thought of – throwing a new wing here, putting on an extra floor there, running new stairs, making yards. You thought you were going to be made into a decent little cottage, but He is building a mansion – and He intends to come and live in it Himself.

Today we read in this beautiful Gospel, "Jesus took with Him Peter and John and James, and went up the mountain to pray." And "as He prayed, the aspect of His face was changed and His clothing became brilliant as lightening."

I need to place this Gospel for you. Just a few days before this Transfiguration event, Jesus had told His followers that He "must suffer many things, be rejected and killed and on the third day be raised." And at this crucial point in their lives, the Apostles desperately needed a mountaintop experience, a once and for all vision of what their lives were all about: why Jesus was born and why they were born.

And as the Transfigured Christ returned to normal, they heard a voice coming out of the clouds saying, "This is my Son, the Chosen One, listen to Him!" You see, Jesus' reason for being born, was to be the Saviour of all mankind.

MDP, like the Disciples we need to be reinforced, for the difficulties that lie ahead. We need to envision where the marvelous plan of God is unfolding in our life. We need to be dazzled by the awesome presence of God in our lives and also in our death.

For years when I prepared a homily on this Gospel, I would see a note I scribbled in the margin: "Reread Mary's letter"

I want to share that letter that I have been holding on to from a wonderful mother to her four year old daughter whom she lost:

My dear little girl: It is six months since you've gone. All day I've seen you out of the corner of my eye, running as hard as you could through the lawn while I cut the grass. And I saw you helping Michael whenever he cried. You would put your arm around him, kiss the hurt, and lead him to me. He misses you as lot. Can you possibly know how much we miss you? Do you ever think of us? Or are you so changed, so complete, so full of love and beauty that we are forgotten? Are you still a little girl or did you become a woman – mature, wise, perfect? It is beyond me, too much speculation makes my head reel. Who can comprehend heaven? At times it's all I can do to believe in it.

Your last birthday party in January – your remember how your friends couldn't come because of illness? And you said quietly, "Next year, Mommy, lots of people will come." I wonder, are there birthdays in heaven? Ah, little one, your mother is weak and weeping. I miss you a thousand times a day. Yet there are times, not often, but times when I sense joy, not in spite of but because you are in heaven. These are glimpses into eternity, however fleeting, that give meaning even to what otherwise seems senseless.

You have everything when you have Christ. He is yours, Elizabeth, and you will never know a single lack, or shed a tear, or feel terror, or disappointment, or pain. You have found your home (Jesus called them mansions) and it is yours forever. You are far beyond me; you've missed so much that is bad, and gained all that is good. I cannot wish you back. What more can I say?

I believe in Jesus just as the Disciples did on that holy mountain: He is with you and with me; that all things do work together for good to those that love and believe in the Lord. Part of me is with you; I feel empty, but someday I'll be full and complete. Until then, I walk by faith in the Transfigured Lord. Lovingly, Mommy.

MDP, we who believe in Jesus, someday we'll be full and complete, more whole, more together than ever before. What a vision of Transfiguration.

THIRD SUNDAY OF LENT
A – JOHN 4:5-42

I had some longtime navy friends visit me from San Diego. They told me about their granddaughter who sees beautifully today because of a cornea transplant. When they were telling me the story, I noticed that their joy was a little tempered by the realization that the cornea belonged to another nine-year-old little girl who was killed in a car accident. They said that the little girl's family finds some peace in knowing that a part of their daughter will live on – and the family of my friends, recipient have also been transformed by what they have received. The deceased child's generosity and selflessness live on; and the girl's family who received the cornea have dedicated their time to work for children who are in need of organs. A moment of grace.

The Samaritan woman is truly a victim. Her religious background and her nationality made her a non-person in the eyes of the Jews. Her life style made her a pariah among her own. But notice – Jesus does not reject her. He actually shows her there is something more to life. He calls from her a sense of faith and joy which enable her to confront her life. We see her putting Jesus at the center of her life. She eventually senses that having Jesus at the center of her life makes her whole life better!

There's a story about a father who wanted to read a magazine but was being bothered by his little girl. She wanted to know what the United States looked like. Finally, he tore a sheet out of his new magazine on which was printed the map of the country. Tearing it into small pieces, he gave it to her and said, "Go into the other room and see if you can put this together. This will show you our whole country today." After a few minutes she returned and handed him the map, correctly fitted and taped together. The father was surprised and asked how she had finished so quickly. "Oh," she said, "On the other side of the paper is a picture of Jesus. When I got all of Jesus back where He belonged, then our country just came together."

Yes, that's it, isn't it. That's the story of the Samaritan woman. That's the moment of grace. When we allow Jesus where He belongs, our whole life just falls into place. Like that Samaritan woman and like the child in the story, each of us has experienced a moment of grace, of generosity, of kindness. Moments that changed our perspective and our approach to life.

All of us who have encountered Jesus and placed Him at the center of our lives, know that our lives are better. All of us are called on this third Sunday of Lent to proclaim to the world what an encounter with Jesus can do; how an encounter with Him will make all things fall into place.

The Gospel put it this way: "Many of the Samaritans in that town began to believe in Him because of the word of the woman who testified, "He told me everything I have done."

B – JOHN 2:13-25

Some of the older comedians knew that they could get a laugh by dipping into their storehouse of husband and wife jokes. They liked to joke about lover's quarrels; for example, they would say, "My wife and I had a fight last night." "How did it go?" "She came crawling to me on her hands and knees." "What did she say?" "Come out from under that bed, you coward!" A lover's quarrel, it is said, 'is like a storm at sea: all the fury is on the surface, but underneath, there is a deep current of love.'

I remember reading that Robert Frost had engraved on his tombstone, "I had a lover's quarrel with God." I feel the same is true with us. We have an ongoing lover's quarrel with God and with the world because of the evil, the suffering, we see all around us. We can't turn on the TV without hearing and seeing the savagery going on in the Middle East; the kidnappings, the beheadings, the torture and killings of Christians by terrorist groups, the senseless murders that we hear and read about daily in our newspapers; sickness and sorrow; anxiety and insecurity; loneliness and emptiness; death! And we ask, why? Why did God make such an imperfect world?

I have never forgotten an interview that I was privy to concerning a symphony orchestra conductor from Eastern Europe. The maestro had just been released from prison where he had spent years in isolation because of his political views. After asking several questions on political matters, the reporter turned to music. He asked the maestro, "What in your opinion is the most beautiful piece of music every written?" The maestro thought about it for awhile and did not answer. The reporter pressed on, "While you were in isolation, what did you want to hear most?" "What music would have come to mind as the most beautiful?" The maestro said with tears in his eyes, "The most beautiful music is the sound of another voice."

But today the voices that we hear are voices of violence, political corruptions, nuclear fears and unconcern for moral consequences of our actions, environmental exploitation, voices that deny that this world is God's world and that we who inhabit this world are God's children.

Yes, the most beautiful music in the world today is the sound of our Christian voices that reflect how we live our lives with moral and spiritual values. The most beautiful music in our world today is the sound of our voices raised in imitation of the voice of Jesus Christ.

In today's Gospel Jesus raises His voice in a "lover's quarrel" with His world. He raises His voice to protest against the exploitation of the poor people – peasants, farmers, fishermen, shepherds who came on pilgrimage to the Holy City to the temple to fulfill their obligations. They were being cheated, overcharged by the temple officials. Jesus sees the situation and yells, "Stop turning My Father's house into a market place!" Scripture scholars say that this was the beginning of the plot by the Sadducees to get rid of Him.

MDP, our Christian love demands that we show compassion toward those who are hurting. There are times when we are called upon, as Christians in this world, to cry out 'stop!' Stop that which is causing human exploitation. Believe me, this requires a lot of courage. What the world needs is an ongoing "lover's quarrel" in which we raise our voices for a revival of spiritual values and for a quality of life that affirms the inherent dignity of God's world and God's children.

There is a story about a stockbroker who lived a life filled with confused and materialistic priorities. One day this stockbroker finds a magic lamp, rubs it, and poof a genie appears. The genie offers him one wish – whatever he would like. After considering this opportunity carefully, he finally makes his one request. He asked the genie for a copy of the newspaper dated one year from today.

Well, the genie thinks that it is a strange request, and asks why he would want such a newspaper. He says, 'Because if I can see what the market is trading one year from now, I'll be able to invest in the high growth stocks now and really clean up." So, the genie grants the stockbroker's request.

Poof, he is reading a copy of the newspaper that will be published one year from the day. The stockbroker quickly goes to the financial pages, and makes notes of the stocks that are doing well. But, as he is scanning the stock listings, he drops part of the paper. As it lands on the floor, the section flips open to the obituary page, and there to his horror, the stockbroker sees his picture.

C – Luke 13:1-9

On this third Sunday of Lent, and with the 'Parable of the Fig Tree,' Jesus seems to be assuring us that while repentance is a matter of spiritual life and death, nevertheless the Lord God is so patient with us. He doesn't call us to repentance, saying, "You can only make this mistake once;" or "you can only do this twice." Rather, He continuously calls us to reform, to change, to do better, to try harder. Better still, He helps us to meet the conditions required for a return to Him. Like the attentive vinedresser in the Gospel, He is always providing us with the nourishment we need for spiritual growth.

A middle aged man was trying to impress a new woman friend with his life story. He said to her: "I was raised by lower middle class parents who wanted me to excel at any cost. And because of their ambition for me, I have tried hard all my life to be number one in several areas. But, he goes on to say, I have made it to the top in none. And now I have arrived at middle age (here he paused in the hope that the woman might notice that he looked younger than his years), and I am forced to admit that in the overall scheme of things I haven't been a success. I can speak six languages, but only three fluently. Therefore, I have failed as a linguist. I play eight musical instruments, but only three of them well. Therefore, I have failed as a musician. And I am just a fair to mediocre writer."

Then, he looked at her expectantly, hoping to score points for his modesty. But the woman was not about to be manipulated. She was too smart for him. She replied: "I was raised by parents who thought I over-achieved when I sucked my thumb. As a result, I speak only one language. I can't even play chopsticks on the piano. And I'm far from being even a mediocre writer. But none of that bothers me a bit because I like myself."

MDP, many of us know from our own life experience, and many of us may have yet to learn, that unless our lives are bearing fruit, in the sense of this Gospel, there is no way we can like ourselves!

Jesus said, "The tree is known by its fruit." And again He said, "There are those who have received the seed in rich soil. They hear the Word and accept it and yield a harvest, 30 and 60 and 100 times." And again He said, "You did not choose Me. I chose you to go out and bear fruit, fruit that will last." But wherever in our lives we find jealousy and blind ambition, small mindedness, pettiness, we find disharmony, we find depression, and a lack of peace in our hearts. You see, the wisdom that comes from the Gospel is a wisdom that makes for peace; it is a kind and considerate wisdom; it is a wisdom full of compassion and it shows itself by doing good. A peacemaker, for example, when he or she works for peace, sows the seeds which will bear fruit.

There's a story from Saudi Arabia, about two friends: Nahib and Mussa. These two friends were traveling on a gloomy road near the mountains of Iran. At some point Mussa lost his footing and fell into awhirling, foaming river; Nahib, without hesitation, leaped in and saved him from drowning. The friend who almost drowned in the rapids, Mussa, called his skilled slaves and ordered them to carve these words on a nearby black boulder: "Wanderer! In this place Nahib heroically saved the life of his friend, Mussa."

And so it happened that after this had been done, the two friends continued on their journey , and after many months went by, they came again to that very spot where the one had saved the other's life. They sat for a while and talked, and then suddenly on some very trivial matter, they began to quarrel. Finally, in a fit of anger, Mussa, the one who had almost drowned, was struck in the face by his friend, Nahib, who only last year saved his life from the whirling river. Mussa, the one who was struck, got up and, picking up his stick, wrote these words in the white sand near the black boulder: "Wanderer, in this place Nahib, in a trivial argument, broke the heart of his friend." When one of Mussa's men inquired why he would record his friend's heroism in stone, but his cruelty in the sand, the wounded friend replied, "I shall cherish the memory of Nahib's brave assistance in my heart forever. But the grave injury he just gave me, I hope will fade from my memory even before the words fade from the sand."

MDP, show me a kind person, a considerate person, a compassionate person, a peacemaking person, a person who does not falsely judge, a person who is not small minded and petty, a person without any trace of hypocrisy, a person who will cherish another's good deeds and forgive and forget the hurts they inflict, and I will show you a Gospel person – a person who understands this Gospel of the fig tree.

This Gospel is Jesus' great assurance that our God is a God of mercy and compassion whose capacity to love and forgive knows no limit or condition, just like the story of Mussa and Nahib.

Despite the times when we crumple up parts of our lives, despite the tears and scars that at times dishearten us, God continues to see our worth and keeps calling us to really like ourselves.

Father Thomas Merton wrote these beautiful thoughts: We think our life is important to ourselves alone, and do not know that our life is more important to the living God than it is to our own selves. We think our happiness is for ourselves alone, and do not realize that it is God's happiness. We think our sorrows are for ourselves alone, and do not believe they are much more than that: they are God's sorrows. There is nothing we can steal from God at all, because before we can think of stealing it, it has already been given."

FOURTH SUNDAY OF LENT
A – JOHN 9:1-41

"NEITHER HE NOR HIS PARENTS SINNED; IT IS SO THAT THE
WORKS OF GOD MIGHT BE MADE VISIBLE THROUGH HIM!"

Kent Nerburn, in his book, "Make Me an Instrument of Your Peace," writes about his experience driving a cab for a living. He remembers one night in particular when he received a call at 2:30 in the morning to go to a small brick fourplex. Thinking he was going to pick up some late night partiers or someone who had just had a fight with his or her spouse, he was surprised when a small woman in her eighties answered the door. She wore a print dress and an old fashioned pillbox hat. By her side was a small nylon suitcase. The apartment was empty, except for a few pieces of furniture covered with sheets and a cardboard box filled with photos and glassware. The driver, Kent, picked up her bag and helped her to the cab. She gave him the address and then asked, "Could you drive through downtown?" "It's not the shortest way," he answered. "Oh, I don't mind," she said. "I'm in no hurry. I'm on my way to a hospice. I don't have any family left. The doctors say I don't have very long to live."

Kent reached over and shut off the meter. "What route would you like me to go?" For the next two hours, they drove through the city. She pointed out the building where she worked as an elevator operator, the house where she and her late husband lived as newlyweds, the furniture store that was once a ballroom where she had gone dancing as a girl. Sometimes she'd ask Kent to slow down in front of a particular building or corner; there she would just sit starting into the darkness, saying nothing. As the dawn broke over the horizon, she said, "I'm tired. Let's go now."

They drove to the small house that served as the hospice. Two attendants came and helped her out of the cab and took her bag.

She asked the driver how much she owed for the fare. "Nothing," he said. "But you have to make a living," she insisted. "There are other passengers," he replied. Almost without thinking, he bent over and gave her a hug. She held him tightly. "You gave an old woman a little moment of joy," she said. "Thank you." Then in the dim morning light, he watched as she walked into the hospice.

MDP, Kent Nerburn ends his story by saying, "We are so conditioned to think that our lives revolve around great moments. But great moments often catch us unaware. When that woman hugged me and said that I brought her a moment of joy, it was possible to believe that I had been placed on earth for the sole purpose of providing her with that last ride. I do not think that I have done anything in my life more important."

In today's Gospel when asked whose "sin" is responsible for the young man's blindness, Jesus replies that the man's blindness might become a manifestation of "the words of God."

The most ordinary aspects of our lives – our day to day struggles to make a living and to make sense out of those things that happen to us, can be moments when the "works of God" are made visible through us.

I have a friend who studied the art of pottery on Longboat Key Art studio for 15 years. Once she invited me to the studio, which was offering free lessons, to try my hand at it. I only did it once, and realized very quickly that it requires great patience, that it requires a certain spirit of love, for example, in creating a bowl. The potter spends many hours creating a beautiful bowl. The bowl she creates is special and she would not sell it at any price. She is making the bowl for her beloved husband. When the bowl is made, she takes it home, presents it to her beloved, and everyday fills the bowl with something precious: fruits, vegetables, lovely flowers. Her beloved cherishes the bowl. He looks at it often; he sees that its color and beautiful shape are the gift of the potter's skill. Even when it is empty, the bowl is a symbol of the repository of their love.

MDP, our lives are just like that, they are empty bowls created by the potter, God. God fills our bowls with whatever we need to live, to grow, to discover, to love, to become the beautiful persons He wants us to be. Jesus says, "God so loved the world that He gave us His Son." He challenges the idea that God is a tyrant, that He is a punishing God. No, He tells Nicodemus that God creates us out of a love He seeks to share with us and wants us to share with one another. He tells Nicodemus and us that God answers all those nagging questions, that He transforms our darkest nights into the morning light of hope, that He Transfigures our good Fridays into Easter joy. He assures us that the first time God ever saw us, it was a love affair at first sight.

B - John 3:14-21

I so enjoyed the comic strip Peanuts through the years. I felt the world was a little less happy, a place with the death of Charles Schultz and the end of his comic strip. Schultz was a happy moralist who brightened our world for nearly half a century with the hapless Charlie Brown, tart tongued Lucy, wise Linus and the rest of the Peanuts crew. These characters in the comic strip taught us about the more important and lasting treasure of life – joy, hope, decency, gentleness, loyalty, perseverance and the dignity of the human spirit.

In his last comic strip before he died, Schultz wrote, "Charlie Brown, Snoopy, Linus, Lucy, how can I ever forget them? There is a Peanuts comic strip in which Linus very candidly admits to his good pal Charlie Brown, "I don't like to face problems head on. I think the best way to solve problems is to avoid them. In fact, this is a distinct philosophy of mine: no problem is so big or complicated that it can't be run away from!

As Charlie Brown, Lucy, Linus, Snoopy and company reflect the gentle spirit of their creator, Shultz, we have been "drawn" to reflect in our lives the Christ of light, the Christ of peace, the Christ of joy, the Christ to whom we can run at any time when we need to face the problems of our lives.

I love the musical "Man of la Mancha". It tells the story of renewal, of freedom, of hope, of joy, of a determination to go on and not be discouraged. The ridiculed Don Quixote lives with the illusion of being a knight of old, battling windmills that he imagines are dragons. Near the end of the musical, Don Quixote is dying and at his side is Aldonza, a worthless woman of the streets whom he has idealized by calling her Dulcinea – "sweet one" – much to the howling laughter of the townspeople. But Don Quixote loves her in a way unlike anything she has ever experienced. When Quixote takes his last breath, Aldonza begins to sing "To Dream the Impossible Dream." As the last echo of the song dies away, someone shouts to her "Aldonza!" But she pulls herself up proudly and responds, "My name is Dulcinea." The crazy knight's love had transformed her.

And here we are – crazy knights of Christ – who believe that God loves us so much that He sent His only Son for us, and so, we can be lifted up, not discouraged, and we can be transformed by that love.

MDP, this beautiful Gospel allows us to believe that the world is animated by a passionately loving God who wants us to make changes in our life, to take risks, to be winners, to be free. And like Aldonza/Dulcinea who was transformed by the love of Don Quixote, we are transformed by the love of the God who gave us His only Son, so that everyone of us who believes in Him might not perish but be transformed to eternal life.

C – LUKE 15:1-3

This Gospel of the prodigal son always brings back a cute memory for me. On one of the bases to which I was assigned, I was visiting young students in a religious education class. The teacher was discussing the parable of the prodigal son. Hoping that the students would focus in on the older brother and his feelings when the father threw a party celebrating the return of the younger brother, I asked these young students, "Who was sorry to see the prodigal son come home?" One little boy raised his hand and said, "the fatted calf!"

MDP, the father in today's Gospel story could have sent one of his servants out with a message for his son: "Don't come home and all is forgiven." He could have gone to his study to think things out and decide on a course of action. He could have ignored his son's presence, given him the cold shoulder. He could have taken his son aside and given him a real tongue-lashing and meted out some severe punishment.

But, no; the father does none of these things. Instead, he receives his son warmly and lovingly. The father forgives with great compassion. The Gospel says, he runs to greet his son, embraces him, kisses him, gives him the best robe, puts a ring on his finger and organizes a party. "My son is alive again. He was lost and is found!"

As followers of Jesus Christ, we must live our lives in terms of His Gospel. Jesus reveals to us in this Gospel what we are to do about the matter of forgiveness. You might remember in St. Matthew's Gospel, the Apostle Peter asks Jesus, "Lord, how often must I forgive my brother if he wrongs me? As often as seven times?" Jesus answers quickly, "not seven, I tell you, but seventy times seven." This is Jesus' way of saying that no limit whatever is placed on our need to live a life of forgiveness.

Jogging ... Roman market ... early in the morning ... butcher-type-person description ... little nun... spit in her hand "That was for me; now give me something for my children."

What a lesson for me! The little nun understood the Gospel of Jesus. She knew that God tells us that in order to become the uniquely beautiful, fulfilled persons He wants us to be, we must learn to forgive unconditionally! We must learn to forgive the one person in our lives who has hurt or wronged us – not seven times, not 70 times, but times without limits.

If our relationship with our good Lord is the single most important thing in our lives, then our relationships with other people will affect our relationship with the Lord God.

MDP, when our relationships with others are enriching and loving, the power and the love of God moves in and through us. But when our relationships with others are destructive, the power of God is blocked and we become lonely and depressed and estranged.

There are so many aspects we can focus on in the parable of the prodigal son. For most of us, it is easy to identify with the older son. After all, most of us are faithful, decent living, hard-working, loving people. But, like the older son, some of us may have become estranged from the Father by living a joyless, loveless life. A life in which "forgiveness" is a strange and foreign word. And yet, the mind-boggling reality that we are given in today's Gospel is that the Father never ceases to pour out His lavish gifts of love and mercy and forgiveness on us – no matter what we have done, no matter where we are in our lives right now! Forgiveness is a gracious circle of mercy. We cannot truly feel God's forgiveness unless we forgive. And our willingness to forgive flows from the fact that God has already forgiven us.

During my last tour in the Navy, I had the opportunity to visit England on a number of occasions. On one occasion I took some time to sightsee. I visited the famous Coventry Cathedral. During the German air war against Britain in 1940 this beautiful Cathedral was leveled. The people of Coventry scoured the ruins of the Cathedral and from two charred beams of wood, they raised up a cross. On the cross they inscribed the words, "Father forgive" – just two words not three. I thought it was significant that they omitted the word "them." They could have said, "Forgive those who perpetrated this horrible crime." But, no! Only Father forgive!

I thought, 'how poignant!' The charred cross tells us something of the way we are as human beings. We all have the capacity of inflicting hurt and pain on others; sometimes we are absorbed totally with ourselves that we are oblivious to the anguish, the loneliness, the despair that others face.

The Coventry Cathedral has been rebuilt, but when the visitor enters the main doors, he or she must walk through the bombed out ruins of the original building, and the visitor must pass the place where the High Altar once stood; and there stands the charred Cross inscribed with the prayer for every generation to see, Father forgive!

MDP, like the older son in the Gospel, the work of forgiveness means putting aside our own hurts and resentments for the ultimate goal of being reunited with those from whom we are separated; the work of forgiveness calls for balance, for healing, rather than vengeance and punishment. This was the path that the father in the Gospel walked between his two sons. This is the path we must walk.

What a powerful Gospel we have been given on this fourth Sunday of Lent. I hope when we begin to think about it, we will remember the Conventry Cross: to forgive without vengeance; to work to bring healing to those who have hurt us; to restore hope and dignity to those who have suffered at our hand. Father forgive!

FIFTH SUNDAY OF LENT
A (1)– JOHN 11:1-45

A couple was preparing for a garage sale at their home. Among the items they put up for sale was an old mirror they had received many years before as a wedding present. Because of its ugly blue colored metal frame, they never found a place in their house where it would look good. During the sale, a man looking over the items saw the mirror and called his wife over. "Look at this beautiful mirror! It still has the plastic on it!" He peeled the ugly blue plastic protective covering away and, to the shock of the sellers, revealed a beautiful gold-finished frame.

MDP, in our own lives, there is so much beauty and joy that are never realized, that are "wrapped" in layers of negativism or discouragement, or joylessness. The Gospel today reminds us that we are called to the work of resurrection, to remove the "plastic" that covers the goodness that we all have in our souls, to free the "Lazaruses" in our lives that force us to live lives of boredom, discouragement, depression, and loneliness. In other words, MDP, each one of us is on the same journey to heaven. And every day brings each one of us closer to that goal. If we treat one another with the care and compassion that honors the fragileness of life, we can bring into one another's life the awesome reality of Christ.

Life is too precious to waste on regrets; life is too short to squander on anger and resentments and grudges and hard-feelings. The promise of this Lenten Gospel is that death is not the end, but it is the beginning! The Christ who raises Lazarus from the grave is calling us out of our own personal graves to walk together – hand in hand – in the light and the promise of His resurrection.

A (2)– John 11:1-45

Not far from here there is a monastery where the Monks were being torn apart by petty squabbles. They asked the Abbot, known for his wisdom, for help. The Abbot told the Monks that "in their dealings with one another, they should say to themselves that 'I am dying and this person is dying too, attempting all the while to experience the truth of those words.' He continued, "If each of you agrees to treat one another according to this practice, bitterness will die out and harmony will be restored among you."

MDP, each of us is on the same journey to heaven; everyday brings each one of us closer to death. But if we treat one another with the care and compassion that honors the fragileness of life, we will bring into one another's life the reality of all that Christ promises. Life is too precious for us to allow anyone to take our joy from us. Life is too precious to waste on regrets, and 'if only's' - if only I would have said I'm sorry; if only I would have told him or her how much I loved them. Life is too precious to squander on anger and resentments, grudges, hard feelings. The promise of this Gospel today is that death is not an end, but it is a beginning. The Christ who raised Lazarus from his grave calls us out of what ever graves we have dug for ourselves and asks us to walk in the light and promise of His resurrection.

B (1)– John 12:20-33

This Gospel for the fifth Sunday of Lent is both powerful and beautiful. We hear Jesus say, "the grain of wheat falling to the ground" and "whoever serves Me must follow Me, and where I am there also will My servant be." "Whoever loves his life loses it."

We can see the growing hostility against Jesus and His impending death. The Body of Jesus was to go into the ground like a planted seed. So too must the follower of Christ bury self.

Jesus is saying that only when we learn to love is love returned;

only by reaching out beyond ourselves do we learn and grow; only by giving to others do we receive. Only by dying do we rise to a new life. Jesus is saying that in taking on the hard work of loving as God loves, we experience transformation and realize the harvest of the grain of wheat. He is saying, in our willingness to 'die' to our fears, to put aside our own needs and wants, to struggle through all the dark moments in our lives, we discover a love that can only be of God.

Please permit me to share a story with you that might bring this Gospel home. There is a man named Sundar who is still alive, born in India, a member of the Sikh religion. He became a convert to Christianity and decided to stay in India to be a missionary and bear witness to Jesus. Late one afternoon, Sundar was traveling on foot high in the Himalaya mountains with a Buddhist Monk. It was bitter cold and the night was coming on. The Buddhist Monk warned that they were in danger of freezing to death if they did not reach the monastery before darkness fell.

Well, it happened that as they crossed over a narrow path above a steep cliff, they heard a cry for help. Deep down in the ravine a man had fallen, and he lay wounded. His leg was broken and he couldn't walk. So the Buddhist Monk warned Sundar, "Do not stop. God has brought this man to his fate. He must work it out by himself. That is our tradition. Let us hurry on before we perish." But Sundar replied, "It is my tradition now that God has brought me here to help my brother. I cannot abandon him." So the Monk set off through the snow, which had started to fall heavily. But Sundar climbed down to where the wounded man was.

Since the man had a broken leg, Sundar took a blanket from his knapsack and made a sling out of it. He got the man into it and hoisted him on his back and began the painful and arduous climb back up to the path. After a long time, drenched with perspiration, he finally got back to the path, struggling to make his way through the falling snow. It was dark now and he had all he could do to stay on the path. But he persevered and although faint from fatigue and overheated from exertion, he finally saw the lights of the monastery.

Then he nearly stumbled and fell, not from weakness. He stumbled over an object lying in the path. He bent down on one knee and brushed the snow from the object and saw that it was the body of the Buddhist Monk who had frozen to death within sight of the monastery. And there, kneeling on one knee in the snow, he said aloud to himself the very Gospel we heard today.

"The one who would save his life will lose it and the one who loses his life for My sake will find it." He understood what Jesus meant and was glad that he decided to "lose his life" for another. Years later, Sundar's own disciples asked him this question, "Master, what is life's most difficult task?" He answered, "No one is really human, really alive, really a disciple of Christ unless that person at some time in life makes the decision to lose his or her life and so to live, to become the grain of wheat in Gospel's figure of speech, to prefer God to self.

MDP, it's the fifth Sunday of Lent and it's decision time. Today we are being challenged to give an answer to life's fundamental question, not the famous question that Shakespeare's Hamlet asks, "To be or not to be," but the question that Jesus asks, "To love or not to love."

There is a story about the great composer, Johann Sebastian Bach that might need to be verified by the combined expertise of a music historian and a musicologist. In any case, the story begins with Bach stopping by his favorite tavern early one afternoon. While he was there, he heard a secular drinking song with a title that translates into English, "One foot in the grave." After hearing the song, Bach went home, had his dinner, and helped Mrs. Bach put their eighteen children to bed. (That's right, they had eighteen children.) Then, having put the children to bed, he went over to the church. We are now at the point of the story that I do not understand.

It seems that, for some reason, there was a local ordinance prohibiting Johann Sebastian Bach and his wife from being in church together after dark. (You figure that one out!) So there was Bach, by himself after dark, in church. Whereupon he sat down at the organ and worked for several hours. And during that working session, he transformed the secular drinking song, "One foot in the grave," into a cantata in praise of Jesus Christ – a cantata so beautiful and so full of power and life that it has been sung for centuries. And it continues to be sung in churches all over the world.

The symbolism there for us is very powerful. It is saying that all those life situations which make you feel like you've got one foot in the grave are the very places where you should be most open to the transforming, resurrection power of almighty God. It is saying that it is possible for you to transform those "one foot in the grave" episodes in your life into something that becomes like a cantata – a song of praise to God in the Lord Jesus Christ.

B (2) – JOHN 12:20-33

I want to tell you about the time when I had a pre-school religious program when I was Chaplain on a Marine Corps base in Orange County, California. It was a Saturday, and I was not in my Navy uniform, but I was wearing my Roman collar – just like this. I passed a group of little ones on their way to class. One little lad of about three or four stopped and looked at me in my collar and asked, "Why do you dress funny?" I told him that I was a priest and that this was the uniform priests wear. Then he pointed to my little plastic collar insert and asked, "Does it hurt? Do you have a boo-boo?" I realized that to him the collar insert looked just like a bandaid. So I laughed and took it out to show him. On the back of the collar are raised letters giving the name of the manufacturer. The little guy felt the letters. And I asked him, "Do you know what those words say?" "Yes I do," said this little guy who was not old enough to read. Looking at the letters intently he said, "It says, 'kills ticks and fleas up to six months'"!

All of like to hear stories about "winners," about the competitive spirit. I want to tell you about a Mrs. Vandermeer who decided to have her portrait painted. She told the artist, "paint me with diamond earrings, a diamond necklace, an emerald bracelet, and a ruby pendant." "But," the artist protested, "you're not wearing any of those things." "I know," said Mrs. Vandemeer. "It's in case I should die before my husband. I'm sure he'd remarry right away, and I want her to go nuts looking for the jewelry."

No doubt about it, the competitive spirit is alive and well. We love a winner. But Jesus had an interesting take on this; we hear Him say "Whoever loves His life loses it, and whoever hates His life in this world will preserve it for eternal life."

Being a true winner has nothing to do with the size of our house or our car or our investment portfolios, etc. Jesus tells us over and over again in the Gospels, that being a winner depends on our day in and day out willingness to renounce ourselves, to take up our cross and follow Him. Jesus says in today's Gospel, "Anyone who loves his life loses it. If a man serves Me, he must follow Me. If anyone follows Me, My Father will honor him." Strange isn't it, to hear Jesus identifying a real winner in these terms.

There's a story about a pastor of a big city church who sat down to prepare his next Sunday's sermon. But he kept up coming up dry and so he decided to go out for a walk. He brought a pen and pad along in case he got some sermon ideas along the way. As he strolled down one of the city's busiest avenues, he saw a big sign in front of a small café. It read. "Had a rough week? Tired, exhausted, bored? All beer, wine and cocktails one dollar between six and eight p.m. Come, and leave with a new perspective on life."

This gave the pastor an idea for his coming sermon. And he began to furiously copy down the words he saw on the sign. Seeing this, the café manager came out and asked, "What are you doing? Are you stealing my advertising?" To which the pastor replied, "Believe it or not, I'm writing a sermon." And so he did. That Sunday he preached a sermon in which he asked the congregation: "Had a rough week, tired, exhausted, bored? Hear the Word of the Lord, and leave with a new perspective on life."

That is precisely what Jesus is telling us today. He wants us to leave with a new perspective on life. He wants us to leave with understanding of what being a "winner" really means.

At the age of 93, Pablo Casals, perhaps the greatest cellist of all time, was practicing his instrument five to six hours a day. When someone asked Pablo, "At your age, why do you still practice the cello every day?" Pablo replied, "Because I think I'm making progress."

C – JOHN 8:1-11

There is a story about a man who had been living with a terrible burden of guilt for many years. He had done something reprehensible which no one else knew about, and he was convinced that he was beyond all hope of forgiveness. As the story goes, he finally met a woman who was renowned for her holiness; she was a mystic. She claimed to have visions in which Christ appeared and spoke to her. The man wanted to test her claim, so he said to her, "You say that you are able to speak directly with Christ in visions. I have a secret which no one else on earth knows. The next time you are in conversation with Christ, please ask Him what sin I committed years ago that destroyed my peace of soul." The holy lady said that she would gladly ask Christ the question.

Well, several days later the two met as agreed. Immediately the man asked, did you visit with Christ in a vision?" "Yes," the lady replied. "And did you ask Him what terrible sin I had committed years ago," the man asked. "Yes, I did," said the lady. "Tell me quickly, what did Christ say?" "He said, 'I don't remember!'"

In today's Gospel, we hear Jesus say to the woman caught in adultery, "Go, and don't sin anymore!"

MDP, all of our tomorrows belong to God. But within the limits of our understanding, all of us can capture glimpses of His love for us; we can all see and feel at times the eternal. These glimpses come in many ways. Sometimes they are offered to us in the magnificent sunsets of our gulf bay area; sometimes they are offered in the birth of a child; sometimes they are offered to us in the simplicity of an earnest prayer in which we quietly listen for the voice of God.

In a strange way I saw this in an ad that a manufacturer of auto parts ran promoting the sale of its shock absorbers. The ad featured a huge football player who weighed at least 300 pounds. This huge man always seemed to be doing something completely out of character – like changing a baby's diaper, or knitting a piece of lace. Underneath this picture appeared a slogan which referred both to the person and the shock absorbers: "Tough, but oh, so gentle."

I thought, 'this is the Christ of today's Gospel – compassionate, forgiving, gentle, yet He is tough on the religious hypocrites of His day.'

MDP, the clearest glimpse of heaven is offered to us through the wonder of unconditional love. Our Blessed Lord says, "Blessed are the merciful," and again, "Be merciful, even as your Father is merciful." We see in the Gospel how the hypocritical religious leaders, "hard-hearted people" caught a woman in adultery and were going to use her to entrap Jesus. Under the religious law they had the right to punish the woman by stoning her to death. If Jesus should oppose the execution, they would accuse Him of dishonoring the law. If He would approve the stoning, He would contradict His own teaching on love and mercy and forgiveness. But Jesus surprises them: "Let him who is without sin among you be the first to throw a stone at her." And then He turns to her and says those beautifully compassionate words, "Woman, where are they? Has no one condemned you...Neither do I condemn you. Go, and do not sin any more."

In a Peanuts cartoon, Charlie Brown says to Linus: "Perhaps you can give me an answer, Linus. What would you do if you felt that no one liked you?" Linus replies, "I'd try to look at myself objectively, and see what I could do to improve. That's my answer, Charlie Brown." To which Charlie replies, "I hate that answer!"

MDP, "Be merciful, even as your Father is merciful."

HOLY WEEK

PASSION (PALM) SUNDAY
PHILLIPIANS 2:6-11

A young boy who lived near the sea loved boats. He would spend hours watching the great ships sail into and out of the harbor. One day he decided to build a small schooner like the great ships that traveled all over the world from his home port. He worked very hard and carefully to get every detail just right. After weeks and weeks of work, the replica was finished – it was a work of art.

The day came to put his boat into the water. He went down to the wharf and gently set the sails. The boy looked on proudly as his schooner sailed straight and tall. Suddenly the wind shifted; before the boy could do anything, the boat was taken out to sea. Every day the boy walked the beach, hoping his boat might have washed upon the shore.

Sometime later, the boy was walking through the town market place. There, in a store window, was his boat. He excitedly ran into the store and told the proprietor that the boat was his. After hearing the boy's story, the proprietor would only say that the boat would cost five dollars. The boy pleaded but the proprietor was unmoved. So the boy immediately went out and did any odd job he could to earn the money. Once he had earned the five dollars, he returned to the store and bought back his boat.

The boat became a cherished toy to the boy, who took special care of it and later would pass the boat on to his son who would later pass it on to his son, telling him of the loving care that went into making the boat and the hard work that went into reclaiming it.

This week we remember a similar story of love and redemption. In the life, death and resurrection of His Son, God reclaims the people He created to be His own, a people lost in the winds of sin. The God of love is not content to forget us but constantly seeks us out and calls us back. Jesus is the perfect manifestation of that love, offering Himself up in death for our sakes so that, for us, He might rise victorious over death.

HOLY THURSDAY

I grew up in an Italian neighborhood in Philadelphia. We lived in a row house. My father worked hard as well as my mother. We did not have very many treasures in our house, but I remember my mother, God rest her, had a pretty vase with roses on the outside; she treasured it and placed it on a mantle in our home. I must have been about six years old and somehow, as I remember it, I wanted to touch the roses to see if they went all the way around the vase. Well, I reached for it in a clumsy sort of way, and it fell to the floor and shattered. I remember how scared I was, that I was in big trouble, and so I began to cry. My mother was in the kitchen and she heard the commotion. She came running into the parlor and saw what I had done. I thought it was the end for me. But my mother gave me a gift. I remember her saying, "Thank God, I thought you were hurt!" And then she held me in her arms and I stopped crying. She made it very clear to me that I was her treasure.

And even though more than sixty years have passed, I still carry this memory in my heart. I wanted to tell you this story because it says something about Holy Thursday, Good Friday, Holy Saturday: that we are God's treasures. He has given us the gift of His precious Son, Jesus.

About 100 years ago Italians emigrated from the southern part of Italy to Philadelphia. They were hard workers. My grandparents were among these immigrants. One of the people I remember was one of these hardworking men who opened an ice making plant in my town. As the years went on, his grandson and I became boyhood friends. I have never forgotten a story from that time.

Before he died, my friend's grandfather had given him a gold pocket watch. My friend treasured that watch. But one day, while he was playing in the ice plant, he lost the watch in all the ice and sawdust. He searched and searched frantically. Then he suddenly realized what he had to do. He stopped running around crazily and became very still. In the silence, he heard the watch ticking.

I tell you this story because it says something about Holy Thursday, Good Friday, Holy Saturday. God has given us today and, throughout Holy Week, a priceless gift in Jesus.

How easy it is for us at times to lose sight of this treasure, to lose our joy in running busily around in life. But we are given a night like this, Holy Thursday, to pause and listen to the beautiful words and to stand in awe at the actions of Jesus.

Tonight, as we pause to listen and relive the beautiful actions of Jesus, we see Him betrayed, His Apostles sleep through His terrible agony in the garden. But, at His last supper, with the man who will betray Him, there is a moment which is among the most beautiful in the life of Jesus. This is the moment when He takes bread and wine into His hands, and He transforms them into His Own Body and Blood. He ordains His Apostles to say Mass, and commands that for all time we will be nourished with His Own Body and Blood.

MDP, we who are nourished by His Body and Blood are expected to represent the Lord at every supper we eat. This is revolutionary in the history of religion! What we must understand about tonight's celebration is not merely that every Mass is the last supper but that every supper is in some sense the Mass – not in its theological meaning, but rather in that the love we celebrate at Mass ought to be carried over into every aspect of our lives, particularly with our families and friends. If we eat the Lord's Supper and are not committed to making our family suppers at least in some way a reflection of the love Jesus showed at His Last Supper, then we fail to understand what Holy Thursday, Holy Week, is all about.

We are God's treasures and He tells us where charity and love are, there He is. The Eucharist is the Bread of Life because it is the Bread of Love. This is a time to pause, be silent and listen to the words and actions of Jesus.

GOOD FRIDAY

You can't turn on the news without hearing something about Russia! However, I had a bit of a surprise. I turned on the Catholic TV channel, and a priest was explaining the celebration of Easter in the Russian tradition, and in a specific way he talked about the meaning of the Russian cross. He spoke about how the Russian cross is shaped differently.

He said, for example, in addition to the usual upright and one crosspiece, there are two smaller crosspieces. One is positioned slightly above the central one and the other down toward the foot of the upright. The small one above represents the sign hung over the head of our Blessed Lord, bearing the inscription, "Jesus of Nazareth, King of the Jews." It is there that everyone would get the message: "Here hangs the King!" The little crosspiece below depicts the wooden block placed under the feet of our Blessed Lord to give Him support and to prevent Him from dying so quickly. This crosspiece is set on the upright at a slant to indicate how Jesus must have pushed down hard with one foot when the pain became severe.

The Russian cross emphasizes that Jesus must have pushed down hard with one foot when the pain became severe. The Russian cross emphasizes that Jesus suffers still, that He suffers wherever anyone suffers in this world; the Russian cross tells us that Jesus is still Victor and still Victim.

What an enormous Good Friday reality! God's total presence in the world is seen not only in the beautiful signs of creation's precise order and dazzling beauty, but also in the shambles of human sorrow, pain and suffering.

I have an interest in reading the author, Elie Wiesel, a Jew. In one of his writings, Wiesel gives a moving reflection of the Good Friday reality of God's presence in a Nazi concentration camp. He says, "One day when we came back from work we saw three gallows rearing in the assembly place. The SS troops were all around us, machine guns trained. Three victims in chains – and one of them, a little boy, a sad eyed angel. The SS troops seemed more preoccupied, more disturbed than usual. To hang a young boy in front of thousands of spectators was no light matter. The head of the camp read the verdict. All eyes were on the child. He was pale, almost calm, biting his lips. The gallows threw its shadow over him. The three victims mounted together on the chairs. The three necks were placed at the same moment in the nooses.

"Long live liberty!" cried the two adults. But the child was silent. "Where is God? Where is He?" someone behind me asked. At a sign from the head of the camp, the three chairs tipped over. I heard a voice within me answer: "Where is He? Here He is – He is hanging on these gallows."

We sing today the old spiritual "Were You there when they crucified my Lord? Were you there? Oh sometimes my heart begins to tremble, were you there when they crucified my Lord?"

This hymn makes me see the scene at calvary taking place under the same stars that I will look at tonight. It makes me wonder if I would have the courage to stand by the Master's side, not when the crowds were shouting, "Hosanna!" but when the mob was crying, "crucify Him!"

The question asked in this hymn should haunt all of us today. Not "were you there?" but are you there? Are you prepared to recognize both Victor and Victim in the sign of the cross? Look again, and see hanging on it some person in your life you now consider undeserving of your love.

Recall Isaiah's classic word picture of the Suffering Servant: "Without beauty, without majesty we saw Him – no looks to attract our eyes; a thing despised and rejected by men."

Again, the question comes to pierce our soul today: "Were you there when they crucified my Lord?" Are you there now?

HOLY SATURDAY — EASTER VIGIL
A – Matthew 28:1-10

Whenever we realize that there is love even in the midst of our worries, our fears, our hurting, and putting up with people we don't like. It is right there where we find Easter! Easter is God's promise that real love will never disappoint, will never be wasted, will never destroy nor be destroyed!

Mary Magdalene and the other Mary are at the tomb. In the darkness of Easter morning, as the Gospel said, they "see the tomb." Who knows what they expected to see – certainly they did not expect a miracle. In all probability they had spent the Sabbath by themselves, grieving the loss of the One they loved. But their unique love brought them to the garden on that Sunday morning.

We can only sense what they must have been going through. We have all lost someone we loved and cared about. And when they were gone, their absence created an emptiness in our life that we struggled to deal with. But at the tomb the words of the angel – "Do not be afraid .. He has been raised" – filled the emptiness of the two Mary's with hope, and transformed their bitterness with an awesome excitement. The words of the angel set them on a new and unexpected road as witnesses of God's greatest miracle. Jesus prepared them for this as He continually prepares us to be witness of His resurrection.

My little town outside of Philadelphia has a long history going back to the late 1600's in Colonial America. William Penn built his house on the outskirts of my town. We have only two Catholic Churches in the town, and about seven or eight Protestant churches. Some of these churches are really old. During my visit, I passed by one of these old churches where workmen were doing some stone-work. I saw one of the men chiseling a triangular piece of stone. I asked him, "What are you going to do with that?" The man said to me, "Do you see that little opening away up there near the spire?" "Well," he said, "I am shaping this down here, so it will fit in up there!" I became very silent when he said this because it seemed that in those simple words, God was giving me an insight into Easter.

Mary Magdalene and the Apostles had to go through the despair, through the challenges, through the bitterness, through fear of the Jews, through doubts; through death of the One they loved. They had to be chiseled so that they would "fit in up there." That is, they had to have a chiseled faith which made them believe that Easter is God's promise that the empty tomb, the tombs each of us have in our lives, will be filled with the brilliant light that only Christ can give.

Easter will not only change us who love, but it will recreate us. The loss of someone we love is devastating; the pain of a betrayed love is not quickly healed. But in "chiseling us so that we fit in up there," God raised His Son from the tomb and promised that love will ultimately triumph, that broken hearts will be healed and made stronger, and that He will guide us along the stony paths we stumble on. And when we "look up to fit in up there," we will hear the angel say, "Do not be afraid! I know you seek Jesus the crucified. He is not here, for He has been raised just as He said. Come and see the place where He lay. Then go quickly and tell His Disciples 'He has been raised up from the dead, and is going before you to Galilee, to Europe, to America, to Africa, to Asia – to Palmetto!

B - Mark 16:1-7

I want to welcome and congratulate our candidates, who will enter the Church through baptism, those who will make a profession of faith and be confirmed in the faith. Your journey in faith has been long and interesting and filled with God's blessings. The Church so wisely welcomes you into its faith community within the splendor of the Easter vigil liturgy.

This evening is the most challenging evening of the whole

Christian year. the Resurrection of Jesus is the most important reality in our lives, and we have great joy over this reality. Our lives
should be so filled with hope and joy that those who meet us could
tell that we believe in Easter, that we are truly Easter people, that we
carry the banner of Jesus Christ, without even being told that we are
Christians.

What a beautiful message this is for you, my dear candidates for
baptism and confirmation, for those making their first communion,
for godparents and parents. You are about to put off the old person,
as St. Paul said, and put on a fresh and new person. When Father
pours the water of baptism on you, when he confirms you in the faith
and gives you your first holy communion, this is actually the beginning of a new life. Your faith will now and forever join you to the
death and resurrection of Jesus. From today you will be one with
Jesus in experiencing His saving death and resurrection. You belong
here this evening!

Now all of you are part of the community of the Church, and
I am really happy to address you and all of our people as "My dear
people."

You – for all time – will be members of the risen Lord. We began
this vigil in darkness – a symbol of aloneness and emptiness. We
could barely see one another. But the whole meaning of salvation
is summed up in the idea that God is a persistent and loving Father.
He is always lighting candles in the darkness so that all of us can see
where He is, and where are brother and sisters are.

MDP, we began this evening by striking a match to light a new
fire. God is always striking matches for us to see where He is and
where our brothers and sisters are. Tonight God lights what seems to
be just a little fire – a light gradually filtering through the cracks of
a stone tomb – but quickly that little fire shatters that tomb and the
darkness is ablaze with the glory of the Risen Christ. And so we shout,
"He is risen!"

C – Luke 24:1-12

I would like to share this story with you. There was a distinguished southern gentleman, who was the only white person buried in a Georgia cemetery reserved exclusively for blacks. He had lost his mother when he was just a baby. His father, who never married again, hired a black woman named Mandy to help raise his son. She was a very Christian lady and she took her task seriously. Seldom had a motherless boy received such warmhearted attention. One of his earliest memories was of Mandy bending tenderly over him in his upstairs bedroom each day and softly singing, "Wake up – God's mornin' has come."

As the years passed this devoted woman continued to serve as his surrogate mother. The young man went away to college, but when he would come home on holidays and in the summer, she would still climb the stairs and call him in the same loving way: "Wake up, God's mornin' has come."

One day after he had become a prominent senator, the sad message came: "Mandy is dead. Can you attend her funeral?" As he stood by her grave in the cemetery, he turned to his friends and said, "If I die before Jesus comes, I want to be buried here beside Mandy. I like to think that on Resurrection Day she'll speak to me again and say, 'Wake up, my boy, God's morning has come'.

MDP, wake up, God's morning has come. Happy Easter! Alleluia, alleluia!

EASTER SUNDAY

A – JOHN 20:1-9

Shortly before His death, the legendary film producer, Cecil B. Demille, wrote this beautiful meditation: "One day as I was lying in a canoe, a big black beetle came out of the water and climbed up into the canoe. I watched it idly for some time. Under the heat of the sun, the beetle proceeded to die. Then a strange thing happened. His glistening black shell cracked all the way down his back. Out of it came a shapeless mass, quickly transformed into a beautiful, brilliantly colored life. As I watched in fascination, there gradually unfolded iridescent wings from which the sunlight flashed a thousand colors. The wings spread wide, as if in worship of the sun. The blue-green body took shape before my very eyes; metamorphosis had occurred – the transformation of a hideous beetle into a gorgeous dragonfly, which started dipping and soaring over the water. But the body it had left behind still clung to my canoe.

I had witnessed what seemed to me a miracle. Out of the mud had come a beautiful new life. And the thought came to me, that if the creator works such wonders with the lowliest of creatures, what may not be in store for the human spirit?

Today's Gospel episode begins on the morning of the first Easter Sunday. Mary Magdalene comes to Jesus' tomb. What is she looking for?

Then one of the Disciples hurries to the tomb. What is he looking for?

He is followed by the Apostle Peter. What is Peter looking for?

More than two thousand Easter Sunday later, we are gathered here in Jesus' name, and what are we looking for? This is our

Easter Sunday question.

MDP, by our own nature we are a desperate people. Each day of our lives we see new incidents of death and destruction and violence and anxiety and war and corruption, so much suffering. We are confronted with this every day on our TV's and newspapers very directly. Each day of our lives, with varying degrees of intensity we ask the question, "Why?" In our heart of hearts we are always searching, desperately searching for the answer to the question, "Why?" and we cry out in desperation, "What are we looking for?"

MDP, that's why we are here this Easter Sunday morning: to discover what we are looking for. Mary Magdalene, Peter, and the other Disciple were desperately looking for the Lord. We too are looking for the Lord Jesus. But the Easter question is: 'Are we willing to find Him buried inside our brothers and sisters everywhere? They, like us, are searching for the Lord, and they need us to discover Jesus in them – so that they may discover Jesus in us.

Easter brings us the Good News of Christ's resurrection; but, it also brings us a mandate: to care about our earth, to care about the human problems most people ignore. To speak up for the downtrodden who are powerless to speak for themselves; to call for forgiveness when others call for revenge; to share our resources without asking, "What's in it for me?" To be loyal to the commandments of God when others have shoved them down the drain.

MDP, what are we looking for? We are looking for love – all of us – for God is love and through Him we are fulfilled in love.

The pyramids of Egypt are famous because they contain the mummified bodies of ancient Egyptian rulers.

Westminster Abbey in London is renowned because in it rests the bodies of many English notables.

Arlington Cemetery in Washington D.C. is revered because it is the final resting place of so many American heroes.

But the tomb of Jesus is empty. There is no epitaph on Jesus' tomb that begins with the words, "Here lies…" There is no epitaph inscribed in gold or cut in stone. Rather, the epitaph of Jesus is spoken from the mouth of an angel: "He is not here…He is risen."

The deep root of our joy is that Easter is not only something that happened then, but something that happens now. This hit me more clearly this year than ever before. Very recently I was in New York and visited Ground Zero. Standing on that observation deck and looking into that pit, that tomb, if you will, in the middle of the financial capital of the world, was a somber and unsettling sight. And along with others, I could not help wondering, where was God? Why did God abandon them and us?

And then I thought of Easter's empty tomb. If God would send an angel to Ground Zero, as He sent an angel to the Easter tomb, I am sure the angel would say to me and all of us gathered on that observation dick, "I know you are looking for God here. But God is not buried in this rubble. God is alive in the dedicated work of the police and firefighters, the rescue workers and medical teams." The angel would say, "Christ and those crucified here have been raised up.

Christ and the crucified are alive in the selflessness of the office worker who carried a disabled stranger down sixty-eight flights to safety. Christ is alive in the compassion of the priest who was killed while giving the last rights to a dying firefighter. Christ is alive in the selflessness of the airline crew and passengers who sacrificed their own lives in order to subdue the terrorists before countless others would have been killed on the ground." And then the angel would say, as he said to Mary Magdalene, "Go and tell others. Christ is risen from this place and goes ahead of you. You will see Him. You will see Him.

MDP, for most of us here and now, our 'ground zeros', places where we see Him, places where we find Easter, occur in the ordinary things that happen to us in our daily lives.

I need to share this personal story with you. I was stationed at a Marine Corps Base not far from Los Angeles. Often, I would go to the Cathedral in Los Angeles for various ceremonies. The Cathedral was in a very poor part of the city.

One Spring day as I left the Cathedral, I saw a familiar face – an elderly woman sitting under a small archway selling corsages, and small flowers spread out on an open newspaper. Everybody called her the "flower lady." She was always smiling, her wrinkled old face so alive with some inner joy. I started down the stairs, and on an impulse, I turned and picked out a flower. As I held it in my hand, I said to the woman, "You look happy this morning." She replied, "Why not? Everything is good."

She was dressed so shabbily and she seemed so very old, that her reply surprised me. "You've been sitting here every Sunday for many years," I said to her, "and you're always smiling; you wear your troubles well." She replied, "You can't reach my age and not have troubles, only it's like Jesus and Good Friday." She paused for a moment, then added, "You see, when Jesus was crucified on Good Friday that was the worst day for the world. And when I get troubles I remember that. And then I think of what happened three days later. Easter, and our Lord, rising. So when I get troubles, I learn to wait three days. And somehow, everything gets all right again." And she smiled "Good-bye."

And to this Easter Sunday her words still follow me whenever I think I have troubles. The tomb is empty! Easter tells us "to wait three days," that life is worth living, that Christ is alive; He is alive in us. He is risen, He is risen, alleluia!

B – JOHN 20:1-9

For two thousand Easter Sundays we have been looking into the empty tomb with Mary Magdalene and the Apostles and asking, "What are we looking for?" This is the Easter question! By our very nature we are a breathless people; we are always seeking an answer to vital questions. Every day in our newspapers and on T.V. we see and hear about incidents of death and destruction, about pirates in the Indian Ocean, about roadside bombs; now we see the caskets of our brave military men and women being so smartly saluted at an Air Force Base as they are carried from the plane. We see suffering, the greed of corporations, the failure of banks, foreclosures. And each day with various intensities, we ask, "Why?" and "What are we looking for?"

On this Feast of Easter, we have the answer. We are looking for Jesus, but are we willing to find Him buried in the heartaches of our world, in our personal fears and anxieties, in the lives of others, who themselves are searching. The world needs us to discover Jesus so that the world and others might discover Jesus in us.

Easter is the Good News of Christ's resurrection, and it challenges us to understand the empty tomb, to know that Jesus is not there: no, that He is with us as we care for our earth, as we try to solve the human problems that we would like to ignore; He is with us as we strengthen our efforts to respect life from conception to death. He is with us as we speak up for the downtrodden, for those powerless to speak for themselves, to call for forgiveness when others are calling for revenge, to be loyal to the commandments of God when our world is saying that God has become meaningless, or as Newsweek Magazine reported that Christianity is irrelevant and on the wane.

What are we looking for? We are looking for love – every one of us – for God is love and through Him we are fulfilled in love.

About three weeks ago, I was talking to a lady who lost her husband. She described her personal disappointment at receiving many cards of sympathy from close friends that kept referring to the loss of her husband. She said to me very bluntly and with a beautiful faith, "My husband is not lost now, and he was not lost when he died. Yes, he may be gone, but I know exactly where to find him. Don't tell me that he's lost."

This good lady knew exactly what she was looking for. She understood the reality of Easter. In the mystery of the empty tomb, she knew that death is not an ending, but a beginning.

"What are we looking for?" The empty tomb consoles us and elates us and challenges us to embrace the faith of this woman, challenges us to live the life of the Gospel. May the Risen Christ be the light in which we always find the answer to the question, "What are we looking for," and in His light we will find the answer that because He rose, He opened heaven for you and me.

C – John 20:1-9

For centuries the world has marked the resurrection of the Lord Jesus with eggs. But the Easter meaning of the egg is found in the struggle of the chick to free itself from its confines, so as to take flight into a much bigger world beyond it. But for this to happen, the egg has to go to pieces. New life always demands the shattering of the old. The real Easter egg is cracked opened, yielding new life that takes flight. This is what the Easter Gospel proclaims to us.

We see Mary and the two Disciples at the tomb. What are they looking for? More than two thousand Easter Sundays later, we are gathered at the tomb in the name of Jesus, and as we look in, we too ask, "What are we looking for? We are looking for the Lord Jesus. But there is more to the question: "Are we willing to find Him buried inside our brothers and sisters everywhere? They, like us, are searching for the Lord; they need us to discover Jesus in them, so that they may discover Jesus in us.

Once a week, I used to take a class in Spanish in Sarasota. My teacher was from Chile. Her heart practically stopped when she heard about the earthquake in Chile. Her mother and brother with his family were vacationing in the very town which was the epicenter of the quake. As she told the class, she tried frantically to make cell phone contact with them, but nothing; not even a ring.

Her hours became days. She was conscious only of the cell phone that did not ring. The television remained on, but she did not want to look at the pictures lest her hopes would be undermined. Finally, the cell phone beeped. The text message read: "We are okay; will call later!" She told all of us in class how those words were the most beautiful words she ever read. She said how empty her life would have been without her family; she realized how unconditionally she loved them; how silly the arguments seemed that occasionally passed between them; how she could not wait to hug them.

After listening to her story, I thought her story had the meaning of

Easter in it. In her life and in the life of the disciples, in our Christian lives, it is daybreak, daybreak after a long, long night of waiting, of hoping. Love transformed the teacher's Good Friday and it transforms our Good Friday's. To know that her family was alive was her Easter morning, a morning that changed her life forever; a morning that will change our lives forever!

MDP, the egg has to go to pieces for new life to begin. Easter is more than one historical moment. Easter is an attitude, a perspective. Easter is a light to guide us along the path of stones we stumble on. It is Easter whenever we realize love in the midst of our fears and worries. It is Easter whenever love pulls us out of our tombs of hopelessness and anxieties. Easter takes place in our midst in such small, simple hidden moments. It is Easter whenever love illuminates our winter hearts and exhausted spirits to believe truly that we are loved by God in the love we have for one another.

SECOND SUNDAY OF EASTER
A, B, C – JOHN 20:19-31

The Gospel began with Jesus saying to the Disciples, "Peace be with you..." and then He breathed on them and said to them, "Receive the Holy Spirit..." When we encounter Christ, part of the change that this encounter brings is His gift of peace. We know that He gives His new church the gift of His 'peace', a peace that is so much more than the absences of conflict. The peace that our encounter brings transforms us, recreates us, and renews us. It is a peace both of gratitude and humility, a peace that values the hopes, dreams and needs of another over our own.

In 1974, the Navy sent me as Chaplain to a Marine Corps Air Wing in Iwakuni, Japan. Iwakuni was about a twenty-minute train ride to Hiroshima, where we dropped the first atomic bomb. Almost weekly I would hop the train to Hiroshima and visit Peace Park. I always remember seeing hundreds of Japanese children visiting this somber memorial. The exhibits of the bomb's destruction were always covered with beautiful and colorful origami, that is, paper cranes. They were draped over statues and trees.

One day I was sitting on a bench in the midst of all of this, just kind of staring at the scene and thinking about the results of the atomic explosion. An elderly Japanese lady came and sat next to me. She was probably a grandmother, and she sensed I was an American. She put her wrinkled hands on mine, and in broken English, she said to me, "Peace starts right here. Peace starts with you and me. It starts today.: ...It brought tears to my eyes.

MDP, Like the Disciples, when we encounter Christ in our lives, we know that it falls to us to make a difference in the kind of lives we live. It falls to us to welcome back the lost, to heal the broken-hearted, to respect the dignity of every man, woman and child as a son and daughter of God. With this beautiful Gospel, with Thomas the Apostle, may we embrace our personal encounter with the risen Christ, not only in the Easter season but in every season!

THIRD SUNDAY OF EASTER
A – LUKE 24:13-35

The Gospel of Emmaus is one of my favorites. For the first time, Jesus makes Himself known after his resurrection not at the tomb or in the temple or in Jerusalem. He makes Himself known when He and His two friends break bread together.

This Gospel always strengthens my faith and reminds me that we walk together with family, with our friends, and, in that walk, Christ is always there. My faith tells me that He walks with us. Yes, Christ walks with each of us on our personal roads to Emmaus. I just want to take a minute to tell you about one of these roads.

In my Navy career, because of long deployments and overseas assignments, I was party to a lot of marriage counseling. I tried to use a gentle technique when I would meet with a military couple having problems. I would have them hold hands while they thrashed out the problem. I remember one couple where one spouse returned after a long deployment. Paying bills was the farthest thing from this Marine's mind. He would forget about them and bury them under a clutter of sports magazines and newspapers. His wife was having a hard time with this and other annoying habits. But when she held his hand as we talked about this and the other annoyances, a gentleness started to flow almost against her will. It almost became impossible to yell at someone who was sitting next to you, looking into your eyes, and holding each other's hand.

MDP, in taking one another's hand – whether in a time of peace or a time of stress, we take the hand of Christ who leads us and directs us on whatever Emmaus Roads we find ourselves. As He did with those two Disciples, Jesus travels with us on the easy roads in our lives and on the difficult and winding roads. He is always present in the broken bread of the love and the healing and the help and the joy we give to any fellow traveler along any Emmaus Road.

Christ, the risen Lord, is in the midst of every challenge we have to make things right for others, and for ourselves. Our challenge is to recognize Him, the risen Christ, in our every day living, in just the ordinary things, in the simple things, and in the comfortable things; our challenge is to see Him in life's bright promising mornings and its dark, terrifying nights.

You know that the intention of this Mass is to thank God for my fifty years of priesthood. What a full and blessed priesthood God has given me: to the men and women of the Navy, Marine Corps, I continue to share joys and sorrows of so many and to comfort them with the Gospel of Jesus Christ. I ask for your prayers at this Mass to continue for many more years to break bread with all I meet in my road to Emmaus.

B – LUKE 24:35-48

There's a famous painting in which the artist depicts a young man playing chess with the devil. The devil has just made a decisive move which checkmates the young man's king. Serious chess players who examine the painting immediately feel sympathy for the young man because they understand that the devil's move has finished him. He has come to a blind alley from which there is no exit. Paul Murphy, one of the world's greatest chess players, once studied that painting for a long time. He saw something that no one else had seen. This excited him, and he cried out to the devil's opponent in the painting, "Don't give up! You still have a move! You still have a move!"

In today's remarkable Gospel, the risen Christ appears in the midst of His Disciples, saying "Peace be with you!" The Disciples are terrified, thinking they are seeing a ghost. Jesus says to them, "Why are you so agitated, and why are these doubts in your hearts? In effect, ' I am still with you and you have not only one more move, but because I am with you, you have hundreds and hundreds and hundreds of moves.'

I don't know if any of you have been to Oberamagau, the place of the famous Passion Play held every ten years in Germany. There is a wonderful and true story about Josef Meier, an actor who, for many years, played the part of Jesus in this play. After hundreds of performances, he gave an interview in which he told the secret of the Passion Play's success. Josef Meier said, "There was a period in the early history of the play when it seemed that the performance would never catch on. There was something about the production that just didn't click. Often, he said, I would meet with the other cast members and discuss the advisability of giving up and disbanding. But a miracle occurred to turn the project from failure to phenomenal success.

Josef continued, "One evening when I was playing the part of Jesus, as I had over one hundred times before, I came to the lines where Jesus said, 'Do not be anxious about tomorrow, oh men of little faith.' I had said these words many, many times. But this particular night, I heard myself saying this line, as I had often done; but something happened. For the first time I asked myself, 'Josef Meier, why don't you have the will to believe these words with your heart? Don't just say them, believe them.' And like a flash, it dawned on me that I was playing the part of Christ without actually believing what He believed or living the faith as He had lived it. Something happened to me: belief, trust, conviction came to me. From that moment on, a change took place with everything connected with the Passion Play and its future."

MDP, for Josef Meier that was the turning point; that was the Jesus we saw in today's Gospel. I wonder how often we play the role of Christ, speak His words, and never have the will to believe that they are the words of life? Take, for example, how we repeat words over and over again, week after week, year after year until they lose their meaning: faith … faith … faith … I believe … I believe … I believe … I believe. Are they just words for us stripped of their meaning? When we say the Creed at Mass, or the Lord's Prayer, are we acting out a role or are we willing to believe these words with all of our heart?

A very pious lady had a dream one night in which one of the town's best known scoundrels died and was on his way to heaven. But because of his many bad deeds, the way to heaven wasn't easy for him. He had to climb a ladder so tall that it reached up far above the clouds. As he climbed the ladder, the man was required to make a chalk mark on each rung for each sin he had committed. As the woman's dream ended, she saw the man coming back down the ladder. "What are you doing?" the woman asked. "I'm coming down for more chalk," the man answered.

MDP, we must really, really believe in the peace that the risen Lord gives us. We must really say our act of faith! And then we must act it out in and through our loving service to one another. And when we can be sure of this, we can throw away the chalk!

C – JOHN 21:15-17

Jesus asks Peter, "Do you love Me?" What He is asking is "Do you love Me, not next week, not when you've resolved all your future doubts? No, Peter, do you love Me **now**, in the present moment; and are you ready to follow Me?"

I must tell you a story from World War I. Three American soldiers—a Protestant, a Jew, and a Catholic—fought together and become friends. They made a pact as the danger increased. Should one of them be killed, the others would do all in their power to comfort the family of the one who died. And so it happened, that the Protestant boy died in battle. It happened in a small town in France. The Catholic and the Jewish boy found the parish priest and asked if their friend's body could be buried in the neat little cemetery near the church. "We want his family to know that their son's body was buried with dignity." But when the priest learned that the boy was not Catholic, he sadly declined, saying that church law permitted only Catholics to be buried in this ground which had been blessed. But the priest made a proposal. He said, "We will bury the boy's body just outside the cemetery fence. And I promise you I will care for his grave just as I do the graves within the fence. Well, the soldiers agreed.

When the war ended, the Catholic and Jewish soldiers promised each other that on the third anniversary of their friend's death they would return to France and meet at his graveside – outside the cemetery fence. When the anniversary day arrived, they met as agreed at the burial site. But they were shocked and angered because they could see no sign of the grave. They found the old priest and demanded that he tell them why he had not kept his word. The priest quietly led the two young men through the cemetery gate to an area along the inside of the fence. There, they saw their friend's grave, neatly tended to. "You see," the priest said, "After you boys left this place, I went back to the rectory to study the Church's regulations. I discovered that although they clearly forbade me to allow the burial inside the fence, there was nothing in them which prevented me from moving the fence.

MDP, if someone were to ask us the question, "Name the causes of division and hatred in the world," we would say among other things, "Greed, jealousy, pride, prejudice, bigotry, self-righteousness. These are the names for the fences that we allow to encircle our hearts! These are the fences that divide people from one another, nation from nation! And there is a sign on those fences which reads "Love postponed." That is, for example, "Let there be peace on earth – but not right now." It's a very large sign: "Do you want peace in the world?" And we respond to the sign, "of course, but be patient, it will take time." And again, there is another sign that says, "Respect life from the moment of conception until death." And we respond, "it is not my business; I don't have the courage to take a stand." And there is another sign which reads, "Shouldn't we give more of our time to our spouses and our children?" How often we answer, "Of course, but you know how it is; I am very busy. As soon as I get something cleaned up" And again another sign, "Do you want to give your parents, your brothers and sisters, your children, your friends, a helping hand?" "Of course, but first I have to pay off the car, buy a new computer, take that vacation."

You see, MDP, we live for tomorrow, we guard our pension plan and our bank accounts – for tomorrow. We are always planning for a time when we are "feeling better," or when the pressure is off us." We lose the brilliant opportunity of the present moment.

MDP, we must take down the sign on our fences which reads, "Love postponed." We must hang a new sign which reads, "Courage, peace and love – right now." We must take hold of any fence around our hearts and move it over. And then – we will find the answer to Jesus' question, "Do you love Me?"

FIFTH SUNDAY OF EASTER
A –(1) JOHN 14:1-12

This story might illustrate the message of today's Gospel. On Memorial Day, actor Christopher Reeve was thrown headfirst from his horse in an accident that broke his neck and left him unable to move or breathe. In the five years since that horrible day, Reeve, best known for starring in the title role of the three "Superman" movies, has not only survived but has fought for himself, his family, and for hundreds of thousands of people with spinal cord injuries in the United States and around the world. In his book, "Still Me" and in his many speeches, Reeve talks about an important lesson he has learned since that horrible day on a Virginia horse farm.

Reeve says, "Anything can happen to anybody. In the last movie I did, "Above Suspicion," I played a paraplegic. I went to a rehab center and I worked with the people there so I could simulate being a paraplegic. And every day I would get in my car and drive away and go, "Thank God that's not me."

I remember the smugness of that, as if I were privileged in a way. And seven months later, I was in this condition. The point is, we are all one great big family, and any one of us can get hurt at any moment. We should never walk by somebody who's in a wheelchair and be afraid of them or think of them as a stranger. (and Reeve ends) It could be us – in fact, it is us."

As I recalled this story I could not help thinking of the three young people who died when the pier collapsed in Philadelphia the other night.

MDP, Christopher Reeve has discovered the truth of what Jesus tells His Disciples in today's Gospel: we are connected to one another; we belong to one another; we are branches of the same vine planted by God. In the love of Christ, we are joined to one another in ways we do not completely realize or understand. As Christopher Reeve has learned, as we learn when some tragedy or sadness hits us, we are not strangers but family.

I began by telling you that God's resources extend beyond our comprehension. In the spirit of Easter may we realize that we can't go it alone and may we have the wisdom and love to realize and rejoice on our belonging to each and every person who, like us, is a child of God, the Great Vine grower.

A (2) – JOHN 14:1-12

Dr. Rachel Remen wrote a little book called "My Grandfather's Blessings." Among the stories in the book, there is one about Dr. Louisa, a highly skilled physician who treats patients with Aids. Louisa keeps a picture of her grandmother in her home. Every morning, before leaving for the hospital, she sits quietly before the picture. Her grandmother was an Italian-born woman who held her family close to her heart. Her wisdom was the wisdom of the earth.

Once when Louisa was small, her kitten was killed in an accident. It was her first experience of death and she was devastated. Her Mom and Dad assured her not to be sad, that her kitten was now in heaven with God. But little Louisa found small comfort in that. She prayed, asking God to give her kitten back. But God did not answer. In her sadness, she turned to her Grandmother. "Why?" she asked her Grandmother. Her Grandmother lifted her up and held her close. She did not tell her that her kitten was with God. Instead, she reminded her of the time when Grandpa died. She didn't know why either. She prayed too; but God did not bring Grandpa back.

Louisa turned into the warm comfort of her Grandmother's lap and cried. At one point she looked up only to see her Grandmother crying too. Although her Grandmother could not answer her question, a great loneliness was lifted and Louisa felt able to move on.

"My Grandmother was a lap. A place of refuge," Louisa says today. "I know a great deal about Aids but what I really want to be for my patients is a lap, a place from which they can face what they have to face and not be alone."

MDP, Louisa has a real grasp on Easter faith. She knows that faith in our good Lord, the resurrected Christ, is a joyful embrace of all that is good. You see, our identity as disciples of Christ is centered in the compassion we extend to others – in our willingness to be a "Lap," A place of refuge, a source of peace for others. Our faithfulness in imitating the love of the risen Jesus is not in having the right answers all the time, or in making dogmatic judgments on others, but in our openness of heart and spirit to love selflessly, completely and unconditionally as God has loved us in Christ. We heard the beautiful command in today's Gospel: "As I have loved you, so you also should love one another."

MDP, we come together at the invitation of Christ to accompany one another through each of our life's journeys – all the way to the kingdom of God. We are called by Christ today to support one another, not in a joyless, severe way, but to "be Christ" lovingly, joyfully, to one another. Our identity as followers of Christ is centered in the joy, the optimism, the fun of loving others as God's children and as our brothers and sisters. Our identity as a parish will only be found in the way we have love for one another.

B (1)– JOHN 15:1-8

When I was in Vietnam, I would say this prayer very often: "Dear Lord, I am at the end of all my resources." And, I could swear that I would hear him answer, "Son, you are just at the beginning of mine."

MDP, God's resources extend beyond our comprehension. We are always at the end of our meager human resources; always in need of opening ourselves up to Almighty God. We get so caught up in our daily worries and annoyances that we keep missing the Good News of Jesus, the truly rich life our Lord promises to those who open up their hearts to His presence. But no matter what, God is so patient with us. He never says, "You can only do this once." Or, "You can only do this twice." Rather, He continuously calls us to do better, to try harder; to bear more fruit as we heard in the Gospel.

The syndicated newspaper columnist Sidney J. Harris once told the story of visiting a Quaker friend. Each night the friend would go to a newsstand to buy a paper. And he always had a cheerful greeting for the news dealer. He would say something like, "Nice to see you, you're looking good. How's business?" But the news dealer's response was always curt, even sarcastic. After observing these encounters for several nights, Sidney Harris said to his Quaker friend, "You are always so kind to that fellow. How can you be so friendly toward him when he is so nasty to you?" The Quaker friend replied, "Why should I let him decide how I'm going to act?"

For many of us, that is an important key to understanding today's Gospel, and the challenge we are given to go and bear good fruit, that is, to go and be fruitful human beings. Many of us unconsciously allow others to decide how we are going to act. We justify responding to hostility with hostility, saying, "Of course I'm upset. You'd be upset too if you had this so and so to deal with." But that is only to admit that our life is being controlled by outside forces, rather than the spiritually nourishing power that comes from following the Gospel of Jesus Christ.

MDP, even if our life experience has been fruitless for many years, we can change all that. By the grace of God, we can choose to transfer control of our life from those things out there that distract us, to those things that Jesus calls us to in the Gospel. We can, for example, turn from self-centeredness, to a poverty of spirit; from insensitivity and indifference to understanding and caring; from taking everything we can get, to sharing what we have been given.

Film producer Sol Hurok said of Marion Anderson, one of the world's greatest singers, "She hadn't simply grown great, she had grown great simply.

Once a reporter began an interview with Marion Anderson by recalling some of the great moments in her career. He mentioned the night that Arturo Toscanini told her that she possessed the finest voice of the century. He mentioned the private concert she had given at the

White House before President Roosevelt and the king and queen of England. He mentioned the honor she had received as the person who had done the most good for the people of her hometown, Philadelphia. He mentioned the Easter Sunday in Washington, D.C., when she stood before the Lincoln monument and sang for a crowd of over seventy-five thousand, then he asked her which was the greatest moment of her career. She chose none of those he had mentioned. Instead, she said simply, "The greatest moment of my life was when I went home and told my mother she wouldn't have to take in washing clothes anymore."

MDP, understanding, loving, caring, these are the characteristics of the followers of Jesus who go out and bear much fruit. The living, loving presence of God is with us. We can keep it turned on or we can keep it turned off. It's our choice how. I hope we choose wisely.

B (2) – JOHN 15:1-8

There is a little story about four men who were on a trip through the woods. Suddenly, they came upon a high wall. Intrigued, they built a ladder to see what was on the other side. The first man to reach the top cried out with delight at the vision below and immediately plunged in. The second man did the same; and so did the third. Finally, the fourth man looked down on the inspiring scene: lush, green gardens as far as the eye could see; beautiful trees bearing every sort of delicious fruits. Never before had he seen such a sight. And, like the others, he was tempted to jump right in. But, no, he paused for a moment to think of his family and friends, he decided to resist the temptation. Then he rushed down the ladder and set out to preach the glad tidings of the beautiful garden to others.

The first three men had seen a new land of wonderful promise and decided to keep it to themselves. The fourth rushed to share it.

MDP, the sure way of enriching our insight into the question, "Who is the Lord our God" is to share with others all the little visions of God we have seen in our lives. It comes down to this: God measures the success we have in trying to live a good and decent life by the love we have for others. He identifies our success with our willingness to carry out His ministry of helping others, of caring for others, of sharing our live with others. For you and me, the basis of our living a wholesome Christian life is our connections with the True Vine, Christ Himself. He has assigned all of us a mission: never to break hearts, but to heal hearts! May the remainder of this Easter season help us realize this and help us to be happy in sharing our visions of God, our hearts and our love with one another, all of us who are children of God, the Vine grower.

C – JOHN 13:31-33, 34-35

It seems that the last month or so I have been reminding anyone who would listen, to go see the movie "Chocolat." This movie is a wonderful fable in which a mysterious chocolate maker comes to a stuffy, pious French village. The village is ruled by a 'holier than thou mayor," Count de Reynard. The whole village, as the movie opens, is in the midst of a very austere Lent. The villagers live and practice their Catholic religion mired in a stiff, cold, joyless, intolerant way. Vianne, the star of the movie, comes to the village – during Lent – and opens her chocolate store. Well, she draws the wrath of the pious mayor who condemns her both for her bad business timing and what he considers her lax lifestyle. But Vianne not only reawakens the palates of the villagers with her wonderful chocolate creations, but by her warmth and kindness, she opens their hearts and spirits to realize that long ago they had buried their sense of joy, a joy that comes from a real faith, a joy that comes from compassion, from generosity, from acceptance, and forgiveness.

Well, by Easter Sunday, the town has experienced a true rebirth in mood and attitude. They discover that their real hunger is not for the bread and sweets they have denied themselves during Lent, but for the love and community they denied themselves out of fear and out of a joyless understanding of their Catholic faith. Even the young priest, who feared the mayor, finally feels released and has the courage to deliver his Easter sermon so beautifully on how "human" Jesus was. He says, "Our faith in the risen Christ cannot be based on what we are not or what we do not do." Then, he stammers, "Our faith is what we are and what we do."

And so the villagers of that small French town discover that Easter faith is the joyful embrace of what is good. They discover that if they are to be true followers of the risen Christ, they must dedicate themselves to the beautiful command that our blessed Lord gives us in this Gospel: "As I have loved you, so must your love be for one another."

You see, MDP, we come together at the invitation of Christ to accompany one another through each of our life's journeys to the reign of God. We are called by Christ's command to support one another, not in a joyless, severe way, but to "be Christ" lovingly, joyfully, to one another in our love and compassion. Our identity as followers of Christ is centered in the joy, the optimism, the fun of loving others as God's children and as our brothers and sisters. Our identity is to be found truly in the love we have for one another.

SIXTH SUNDAY OF EASTER
A – John 14:15-21

I love the work of Jewish humorist Shalom Alecichem. He tells the story of Jake who is well known to his relatives and friends as a 'certified worrier.'

Jake is standing with a friend on a crowded bus. A young man asks Jake, "What time is it?" Jake refuses to reply and the young man moves on. Jake's friend asks, "Jake, why were you so discourteous?" and then Jake, the anxious worrier, replies, "If I had given him the time of day, next he would want to know where I am going. Then he would begin to talk about our mutual interests. If we did that, he might invite himself to my house for dinner. If he did, he would meet my lovely daughter. If he met her, they would both fall in love, and I don't want my daughter marrying someone who can't afford a watch."

For so many of us the story of Jake hits close to home. We worry about so many things, about our future, about our health. We let worry rob us of life and joy; sometimes it even robs us of sleep. It steals our energy. And it can cause sickness. When you are watching television today, notice all the advertisements for medicines, their side effects. Millions buy these products every day.

Our Gospel today can put us at ease. Jesus tells us, "Do not be afraid...don't' worry." He told us in Matthew's Gospel, "Do not worry about your life and what you are to eat, or your body and how you are to cloth it. Think of the flowers in the field, they never have to work or spin; yet, I assure you that not even Solomon in all his regalia was robed like one of these." And then Matthew says, If this is how God clothed the flowers in the field, will He not look after you much more? But, somehow, all of us forget this and we build up a wall of fear and doubt, an anxiety between ourselves and God.

In the Gospel today Jesus tells us to believe in God's love and to respond with a simple trust. He says, "Peace I leave you, my peace

I give you, and this is a peace which the world cannot give.: And then He adds, "This is my gift to you; do not let your hearts be troubled: don't worry; don't be afraid."

I need to tell you about a lady in the parish in which I work in Florida. These words of Jesus were her strength. Not long ago I celebrated a funeral Mass in this parish for four-year-old Elizabeth. Her mother could not contain her sorrow; so to express her deep feelings, she wrote a letter to her daughter, Elizabeth, which she shared with me. I called her before I left for Florida, told her that I probably would be celebrating Mass for you, and I asked her if I could share her letter with you.

She wrote: "My dear little girl: It is six months since you've gone. All day I have seen you out of the corner of my eye, running as hard as you could through the yard while I cut the grass. And I saw you helping Michael. Whenever he cried, you would put our arm around him, kiss the hurt, and lead him to me. He misses you a lot, can you possibly know how much we miss you? Do you ever think of us? Or are you so changed, so full of love and beauty that we are forgotten? Are you still a little girl or did you become a woman, mature, wise, perfect? Too much speculation makes my head reel. Who can comprehend heaven? At times it is all I can do to believe in it. I remember your birthday party last January. Some of your friends couldn't come because of illness, and you said so quietly, "Next year, Mommy; next year lots of people will come." I wonder, are there birthdays in heaven? I miss you a thousand times a day, but there are times when I sense peace because I know you are in heaven. You have everything when you have Christ. He is yours, Elizabeth, and you will never know a single worry, or shed a single tear, because He told us "never to be afraid." You have found your home – Jesus called it a mansion! What more can I say? I believe in Jesus. I believe Him when He gave me His peace. I believe in Him when He told me, "Not to worry, and never to be afraid.? Until I see you again, I will walk by faith in the Risen Lord. Lovingly, Mommy."

MDP, if we live with this kind of faith, we are sure to become the beautiful persons God wants us to be. Listen again: Do not let your hearts be troubled. Do not be afraid. My peace I give you.

B (1)– John 15:9-7

The love that Christ demands of us in today's beautiful Gospel is complete, total, and unconditional; a love that finds itself in the heart and spirit. We are to love one another as He loved us! And if we really want to know what that means, just take a look at the crucifix. Now that's how much we are to love one another.

MDP, love is always a choice. We have the power to choose how we will respond to every living thing that crosses our path. We have the power to love or not to love. I am sure that everyone at Mass today can tell a story of how he or she has made that choice. Allow me to tell you a story that brought this Gospel and it's command to love, home to me.

I have a friend named Maryann who once told me her story: she said in effect: "I grew up knowing I was different, and I hated it. I was born with a cleft palate, and when I started school, my classmates made it clear to me how I must look to others: a little girl with a mis-shapen lip, crooked nose, lopsided teeth and garbled speech. When my schoolmates would ask, "What happened to your lip?" I'd tell them I'd fallen and cut it on a piece of glass. Somehow it seemed more accept-able to have suffered an accident than to have been born different. I was convinced that no one outside my family could love me.

There was, however, a teacher in the second grade that we all adored – a Mrs. Leonard by name. She was short, round, happy – a sparkling lady. Annually, we would have a hearing test. I was virtually deaf in one of my ears; but when I had taken the test in the past years, I discovered that if I did not press my hand as tightly upon my ears as I was instructed to do, I could pass the test. Mrs. Leonard gave the test to everyone in the class, and finally it was my turn. I knew from past years that as we stood against the door and covered one ear, the teacher sitting at her desk would whisper something and we would have to repeat it back, things like "the sky is blue" or "do you have new shoes?" I waited there for those words which God must have put into her mouth, seven words which changed my life. Mrs. Leonard said, in her whisper, "I wish you were my little girl."

Not long ago I took a short cruise to the Bahamas. As I walked down the main shopping street, there was a store which sold the most unusual T-shirts. At first look, the colors in the design of the T-shirt were dull; but when a person touched the colors, and they were warmed by that touch, the warmth caused the special dyes to react, and the dull gray was transformed into a flashing rainbow of color.

In light of this Gospel, I thought what other things can be changed by the warmth of our love and our touch. Think of the story of Mrs. Leonard and Maryann; think of the needs of our family, our friends, our parish, even our world! Love is a choice. We are all hungry for the touch of someone who cares – really cares. Authentic love will always cost something. "This is my commandment: Love one another as I have loved you. There is no greater love than this; to lay down one's life for one's friends."

Let me tell you a legend that has grown through the years about Leonardo Da Vinci's Last Supper, the painting which figures prominently in Dan Brown's book and movie. The story is told that Leonardo could not find a man evil enough to be his model for Judas nor good enough to be his model for John. Consequently, in the painting, both figures are somewhat unfinished. After a long search, Leonardo used the most handsome man he could find as his model for John, the beloved Disciple. Years later, as the legend goes, still looking, still trying to finish the painting, he finds a man whose features have been torn and twisted by years of dissipation. He is really an awful looking person. Leonardo brings the man to his studio to be his model for Judas. But when the man realizes what is happening, he cries out in horror, "Years ago, I was your model for John."

It might only be a legend, but he helps us to remember that God's love for us depends neither on how we see ourselves nor how others see us. What is important is how God sees us! Whether we fancy ourselves as the beloved disciple or despise ourselves as the unlovable Judas, we must remember that we were created neither in John's image nor in the image of Judas, nor anyone else's image. We were created as unique reflections of God's image.

"This is my commandment: Love one another." This is a command that we love one another in a special way. We are called upon by Christ every day of our lives to like Him, to love one another as He loved us, to love one another in the heart of the other's humanity, no matter what they are like, no matter what they have done to us, to love them in their tears, their hurts, their joys, their laughter.

B (2) – JOHN 15

This is My commandment: Love one another…" This new commandment is not simply a command that we love one another. It is a command that we love one another in a special way. We are called upon to be like Christ, to love one another as Jesus loved us. And to be like Christ is to minister to others where they are right now, right at the heart of their humanity: when they cry, when they laugh, when they hurt, when they rejoice.

Mother Teresa was kneeling beside a dying man whom she had just recovered from the gutter. Stripped of his rags, he was one appalling wound. What did Mother Teresa do? She fell on her knees beside him. A young man joined her, and then took over. When he had finished, he said, "When I cleanse the wounds of the poor, I am cleansing the wounds of Christ." He had learned this from Mother Teresa, who echoing this Gospel said, "I see Christ in every person I touch. It is as simple as that." Because we are followers of Christ, because we are a Christian people, from our heart of hearts, we love one another…it's as simple as that.

C (1) – JOHN 14:23-29

There are many fascinating stories and legends about the great magician and illusionist Harry Houdini. Houdini had a standing challenge that he could get out of any locked jail within sixty minutes, provided they would let him enter the cell in his regular street clothes and now watch him work.

There is a story about a little town in the British Isles that decided to take Houdini up on his challenge. The town had just completed the building of a state-of-the-art, escape-proof jail, and they invited Houdini to come and try to break out of it. Houdini accepted the challenge. Wearing his regular street clothes, Houdini was taken to the cell. A locksmith turned the lock and closed the massive steel door. Then the townspeople who had gathered left Houdini to work his 'magic.'

Houdini had hidden a long flexible steel rod in his belt which he used to try and trip the lock. But the lock would not trip. He continued to work, but the lock would not give. Thirty minutes went by. He kept his ear close to the lock to hear it trip…but nothing. Forty-five minutes, an hour had passed and, after two hours, perspiring and exhausted, Houdini was ready to admit defeat. The defeated illusionist leaned against the door; and to his amazement, it opened. The townsfolk had never locked the door. It was their trick on the great escape artist. The door was only locked in Houdini's mind.

MDP, we sometimes live our lives behind locked doors—doors locked spiritually and mentally. Disappointment, fear, mistrust, and cynicism imprison us from living life and from believing the words of Jesus in this Gospel.

The night before He died, Jesus left His followers the gift of His peace. Christ's peace, Father Thomas Merton was accustomed to say, is more than a 'spiritual tranquilizer.' The peace of Christ is the hope in the things of God, the assurance that God loves us beyond our wildest dreams, that He is present in every moment of our lives. Jesus says in the Gospel, "Peace I leave with you; My peace I give to you."

MDP, this Christ-given peace is a perspective that shapes all of our actions, behavior, beliefs, values. May such a mindset of 'not being afraid,' of peace, dwell forever in our hearts and spirits in this Easter Season and in every season of our lives.

I don't know if any of you are fans of the comic strip "Stone Soup;" it's about the trials and tribulations of a modern family as seen through the eyes of two sisters, Val and Joan, and their families. In a cartoon that appeared a few months ago, thirteen-year-old Holly decides to go to California for her spring break. Holly, a drama queen of the first order, has been invited by her 'cool' aunt Margie to come to California for a week. Holly thinks she is going for a week of sun, surfing, and shopping—but when she arrives, she finds that she will be persuaded to work on a "Habitat for Humanity" project.

At first, Holly is furious that she has to spend her week off from school working at a construction site to build a house for some family of 'losers.' But during the week, she meets the family who will move into the house, including their thirteen-year-old daughter, Gini. Holly is genuinely moved by the family's plight; and she realizes that she could not have had a better, more fulfilling spring break. Holly and Aunt Margie spend her last day in California at the beach. Holly's experience has had a profound effect on her. "Aunt Margie thanks for inviting me to visit." "I hope you had fun," Aunt Margie says. "I did! I didn't think I would but helping to build a house for charity...I never thought I could do something so, so important." Holly looks at her red, scarred, and chapped hands. "Who knew blisters could feel so good."

MDP, Holly discovers that the joy that can only be experienced by giving to others, the fulfillment that comes from emptying ourselves of our own wants and putting aside our own needs to realize the wants and needs of others. Like Holly, may we discover the Christ-like 'blisters' suffered in the pursuit of bringing the love of God into our homes, into our hearts. Do not let your hearts be troubled.

C (2)– JOHN 14:23-29

At times, the Gospel of Jesus Christ is very demanding; at times, it asks more of us than we believe we are capable of; at times, the Gospel of Jesus Christ requires us to put aside our own needs and hurts in order to show the world the love of God.

We come to Mass every Sunday, for example, and we say the prayers of the Mass by rote. We say the "Gloria" and we pray out loud,

"...and peace to God's people on Earth..." Yes, we are praying for peace in the Middle East, in the regions of Africa and Asia. We pray for peace in our towns, in our politics, and, yes, in our church.

But where does this desire for peace begin? MDP, it begins at our dinner tables. It is at our dinner table where the peace of the risen Christ reigns. Mealtime in our homes can be an oasis of calm, an island of tranquility. Even in the midst of work schedules and school conflicts, our family table should be a place where fear, stress and anger are put aside and all are welcomed and appreciated. I wonder how many of us take the time to start our meals with a prayer, and so feel a sense of peace? I find it amazing how something as simple as a lighted candle on the table or a vase of flowers can bestow a sense of peace.

That's the idea of what Jesus' peace is all about. Peace – among nations, between husband and wife, within a family is work! Christ's gift of peace is not a warm fluffy blanket, but an attitude we take toward ourselves and others and a perspective by which we live our lives. Peace becomes a reality only through our gratitude and our generosity. Peace is not only prayed for but is a prayer in and of itself. The peace we pray for in the Gloria at Mass, the peace promised by the angels, is hard work. And it begins at our dining room table.

SEVENTH SUNDAY OF EASTER
A – JOHN 17:1-11

C omedian Red Skelton was once asked to speak at a college on the subject of religion. During the question and answer session, a student asked him, "Why am I unable to find God?" Skelton replied, "You can't find God for the same reason a thief can't find a policeman: You're not looking for Him." Then he suggested to the student each morning he should place the word 'good' on a blackboard and then go out and do something for someone in need, expecting and getting nothing in return. "Nothing is zero," he told the student, and, "When you go home, erase a zero from your word 'good' and you will find God."

MDP, there are people that we all know who are hurting in one way or another. The call of today's Gospel is to remind them and to remind ourselves that there is nothing in our lives which is beyond the scope of God's loving concern, nothing which prevents us from changing the word "good" to "God". No heartbreak, no disaster, is the last word for those of us who are trying to find God, trying to live our lives in the presence of God, and in the spirit of God's command that we love one another. Our search for God and our fulfillment as human beings depend literally and absolutely on whether or not we make the connection between a loving God and a loving devotion to one another. Fidelity to God and fidelity to our neighbor are inseparable!

Some of the events happening around our world today, make me believe that we have failed to make this connection, and we will continue to suffer the disastrous and inevitable consequence of the destruction of the human spirit. But should we ever learn to make the connection between God and one another, we will enjoy the inevitable consequence of enriching the human spirit.

MDP, whether on this very day we are in pain or free from pain, whether we have money or don't have it, whether we are living our lives alone or sharing them with another – wherever we are today, - God is present to us and He is loving us right here! As we try to find God and open our lives to Him, we will find that we are living more fully. This is what it means to be holy, to be a completely spiritual person, a whole person.

Let me tell you, in light of today's Gospel, about a friend of mine. Her name is Amelia. Late morning is Amelia's favorite time of the day. The hospice volunteers have already helped her get washed and dressed. After preparing her breakfast, they go quietly about whatever household tasks that need to be done. This gives Amelia some quiet time in her sun room. Amelia is at peace. She is grateful for the days, though now numbered, that she has left. In this quiet time every morning, she fingers her rosary, but the photographs of her family that cover the table near her rocking chair are her real prayer beads. She picks each one up gently. She prays that her son will do well in his new job. That her daughter continues to conquer the challenges of her medical career, that her grandson will choose the right college and grow into a value-centered adult. That her granddaughter will be born whole and healthy. My friend Amelia prays, "Hold them all, oh Lord, in Your hand. Bless them as You have blessed my husband and me these many years."

In today's Gospel we hear Jesus say that eternal life is to know the only true God, and then He prays for the Church He is about to leave behind. The same anxieties and hopes that Amelia voices in her prayers for those she loves and is about to leave behind, Jesus voices in His prayer for those He loves and leaves behind. In this beautiful Gospel from St. John's account of the Last Supper, we see and hear Jesus commending every disciple of every time and place – yes, you and me – to His Father.

As we look for God in our lives, and as Amelia gathers her family in prayer, we must gather one another, always and everywhere, into prayer before the God for whom we all search and to whom we all belong, the One who gives us all things in Christ.

B – JOHN 17:16-19

Over the arches of the triple doorway of the Cathedral in Milan, there are three inscriptions. One is a beautifully carved wreath of roses, and beneath it the words, "All that pleases is but for a moment." Another is a sculptured cross with these words below: "All that troubles is but for a moment." And over the central doorway these words are inscribed, "That only is important which is eternal."

When we begin to trust in God's promise of eternal fulfillment, we've already begun to experience the eternal life Jesus spoke of.

Muriel was a vivacious and fun-loving college co-ed, engaged to be married. God, it seemed, had given her everything. Then, at age nineteen, she began having some physical distress which eventually was diagnosed as multiple sclerosis. Since then, Muriel's life has radically changed. Once, she could with grace and beauty skate with near perfect balance. Today, she can't even shoo a fly from her ear. Her lovely voice has gone. She goes to church in a wheelchair.

But when others come to her door to give Muriel comfort, they go away knowing that it is they who have been comforted by Muriel. The weaker she gets, the more power God seems to give her to project an aura of peace and serenity and other-centeredness. There are those who see her present existence as hell. But others know she already is in heaven – already experiencing the words of the Gospel, eternal life with God now.

There always are people we know who are hurting very badly. We need to remind them and ourselves, that there is no event in our lives which is beyond the scope of God's loving concern. No disaster, no heartbreak has the last word for those who live in the presence of God's love and in the spirit of God's will that we love one another. Our fulfillment as human beings depends literally and absolutely on whether or not we make the connection between loving God and a loving devotion to brother and sister. Fidelity to God and fidelity to neighbor and inseparable. If we fail to make the connection, the inevitable disastrous consequence is the destruction of the human spirit. If we make the connection, the inevitable happy consequence is the enrichment of the human spirit.

Whether today you are in pain or free from pain, whether you are rich or poor, whether you are alone or with other persons, whatever your present situation, God is present to you and He is loving you in whatever situation you find yourself now. As you respond to Him, as you open your life to Him and enter more deeply into union with Him, you will find that you can live more fully now. This is what it means to be a complete person, a whole person.

This is of crucial importance for us to understand because many of us are living in the past. We're not here at all; we're somewhere back in time. For many others, the tendency is to dream about the way things will be. For some of us Christians, the problem is getting so caught up in the next life that we forget to live fully, to the hilt in the present life. "So caught up in heaven that we're no earthly good," is the way Monks used to say it.

Holy Scripture reminds us, of course, that the past and the future, both, are important to us. It is extremely important for us to be aware of our religious heritage and our roots as a people. The Christian life is full of hope and expectation. But what is most important is to be able to live deeply and fully in God's present moment; to be able to experience here and now, the awe and the wonder and the joy of the miracle of our present life.

A middle-aged woman named Harriet was trying to decide what to do with the rest of her life. To help her decide, she took a job in a hospital Chaplain's office.

One day, when the Chaplain was not at the hospital, a distraught, tired looking man came into the office and said, "I'm not sure what I'm looking for but my father seems to need to talk to someone before he can die. We're not church people, but I decided to come here anyway. Something is holding my dad back. He can't seem to let go. Your name tag says 'Chaplain,' so would you please come and see what you can do?"

Harriet began to panic. She was not a Chaplain. Her name tag really said "Chaplain's Secretary". She as not even a social worker. But this man needed help. So she followed him into a darkened room where a pale, emaciated old man lay on the bed. She touched his shoulder gently. He acknowledged her presence with a flutter of his eyelids. She asked if he wanted to pray with her. Again, a flutter of the eyelids. In her anxious state, the only prayer she could think of was the one she taught to her children when they were little ones: "Now I lay me down to sleep, I pray the Lord my soul to keep." Again, she touched the man's shoulder to put him at ease, but still something was wrong. Then Harriet remembered her final gesture in those long ago experiences of putting her kids to bed. "I can do that." She said to herself. "Mothers do that." And she gave the dying man a gentle kiss, and left the room.

Later, the son sought her out. "Thank you," he said. "I don't know what you did, but right after you left the room, he peacefully drifted away." Without thinking, Harriet replied, "Oh, I gave him permission to cross the street."

Eternal life is this to know the only true God. With these words, Jesus gives us permission to cross the street and enter into the life of God, and to do it now!

A REMINDER

Many travelers on religious pilgrimage to the Middle East have heard the true story of Father Demetrius, a priest of the Orthodox, Eastern Rite Church. Father Demetrius was a good and strong Christian man. Like so many others in the Orthodox Church, he was a man for whom the prayer of Jesus was very important. He was a man who had been graced with a special talent for teaching other people to enrich their spiritual lives. He was a man who cared very deeply about other people. He was a man who was very loved by the people he ministered to in the city.

One day, a tragic riot occurred causing extensive property damage. One family lost all its possessions: the family dwelling, the family business, the furniture, the clothing—everything was destroyed.

Friends and relatives provided assistance, of course, including Father Demetrius. He volunteered to help the youngest daughter in the family who appeared to be especially in need. Father Demetrius lived very frugally, but he did have some money. The girl needed shoes, stockings, a dress and a coat, and Father Demetrius bought these things for her. Then, with his remaining money, he bought her a ring.

When the people in the community heard about this, some began to talk about him behind his back: "How foolish it was of him to buy her a ring. He is a good man, a loving person, but he is so naïve to buy a ring in a situation like this." Demetrius happened to overhear some of them talking. He said, very quietly, "I wanted to give her things that would remind her not only of her poverty but also that would help her to know that she is loved."

C – JOHN 13:31-33, 34-35

A little boy was behaving perfectly at the baptism of his baby sister. But when the pastor started to sprinkle water on the baby's bald head, her little brother cried out, "Behind her ears too!"

In a shopping mall, a married couple stopped at a wishing well standing in the center of the arcade. The wife playfully tossed in a coin. The husband looked wistfully into the fountain, then threw in his coin. "What did you wish for?" the wife asked. The husband replied, "I just wished that I could afford whatever it was you wished for."

A few days ago, I was talking to one of my sailors who had just returned from some duty in Bosnia. He was one of these hard-drinking types who didn't wear his heart on his sleeve, yet who I knew came from a good Christian family. He asked me, "Chaplain, can you tell me how it is that sometimes when my nerves are all a-jitter, I suddenly feet calm and ready for anything? I thought for a moment and said, "Might it not be that at such times your mother is praying for you?"

Mothers, remember always to pray for your children. The Gospel the Church gives us this Sunday is so wonderful. It is the beautiful prayer of Jesus that we might know that the power of God's love is always working to transform any darkness we have in our lives to light, and turmoil we have in our lives to peace, and any alienation we have in our lives to affection.

In a "peanuts" cartoon recently, Charlie Brown says to Lucy, "My dad said that someday I might be able to run for President!" "Really, Charlie Brown?" Lucy answers. "He certainly must think highly of you!" "I don't know! Charlie Brown replies, "he also said that he didn't think he'd vote for me."

MDP, more than anything else in life, we need to know and believe that God would vote for us. No matter what we have done in our lives, we need to know and believe that God is with us and that He loves us."

Once when I was flying from Southern Spain to Germany with a stop over in Madrid. At the Madrid airport, during a lay over, I found myself in a group of Americans who had just experienced a bad flight; their mood wasn't good. Their take off had been delayed; they had to wait for their luggage, they were tired; tension was in everybody's face. There was anxiety about the delay from the States causing them problems with making their connections. But in the midst of all of this there was an elderly lady in a wheel chair who was being pushed to one of the gates. And suddenly in a voice that seemed to boom through the terminal, she cried out, "good work, God!"

Nearly everybody within hearing distance turned toward the lady and saw that she was looking out of the massive windows that lined the airport walkway. Our eyes followed her gaze as we saw a majestic sunset lighting up the sky. The atmosphere among the group of tired and complaining travelers seemed immediately transformed by the lady's observation: 'good work, God!"

MDP, we can say, "I know there is a God." We can say "I know God". We can even say with the lady, 'good work, God!" But if we are serious about living good Christian lives, we must identify heart and soul with this Gospel of unity and reconciliation. Without exception we must live with one another in a way that says, "you are my brother, you are my sister, you are my mother in Christ. God created each one of us in His image and saw that that image was very good. "Good work,

God!" If we are really serious about wanting to live good lives, holy lives, we must relate to one another in a way that says, "I want to bring out the best in you!"

On his 30th wedding anniversary, the actor Robert Mitchum was asked why his marriage had endured so long when those of so many of acting friends had failed. Mitchum answered, "Mutual forgiveness. My wife and I have always believed that the other will do better tomorrow."

And that's the way it is with God and us. We know that because of the forgiveness of God, no matter what, we can do better today than we did yesterday. We know that God is always working in our lives to bring out the best in us. We know that with humble thankfulness for so many of His gifts, we can have on our lips the words, "good work, God! Good work!"

FEAST OF THE ASCENSION
A – Matthew 28:16-20

I read an article in "The New York Times" which struck me. I clipped it out and saved it, thinking that somehow there was a homily in the story. Well, as I read and prepared for the Mass of the Ascension today, the words of Jesus, "…I am with you always, until the end of the time," hit me hard. And I thought of the story I read in the "New York Times."

The story was about a sensitive lady named Brooke who had been married for only a year when her life suddenly became a nightmare. The FBI burst into her house at six o'clock A.M. and arrested Brooke and her husband on charges of fraud and conspiracy. Brooke would soon learn that her husband had used her identity to embezzle tens of thousands of dollars from his workplace. Brooke had no idea. In an instant, she lost her home and her marriage.

The federal charges were held against her for ninety days. So Brooke went home to her mom and dad's. For ninety nights, she slept on their couch—and for those ninety nights, Brooke's mom slept on the love seat across from the couch. Brooke did not ask her mom to sleep there, her mom just did. Brooke's mom quietly shared every sleepless night, every meal that went uneaten, every moment of anger, grief and despair, with her daughter. Her mom would often whisper during those long nights, "Are you okay?' Brooke would whisper back, "Are you okay?" Brooke says, "It was our code." She continued, "To know that someone loved me so much, and was willing to feel my pain so intensely…made me feel encased in a bubble of protection."

Later, when the charges against her were dropped and she began to rebuild her life, Brooke shared the whole ugly story with her doctor. Her doctor asked her, "How have you survived this?" Brooke said, "While the charges were held against me, I slept on the couch in my parent's house. I spent ninety nights on that couch." She paused and said, "And my mom? She slept for ninety nights on the love seat." The doctor blinked, unable to hold back her tears. "What a mom," she said softly, "what a mom."

MDP, The Ascension of the Lord is not the marking of a departure but the realization that "God is with us," as Matthew begins his Gospel, and ends it with the promise of the Risen Lord, "I am with you always even to the end of time." Christ is the very center of our church. We meet Him in the scriptures, in our sacraments, in every moment, in every time we are generous, caring…compassionate to another. Christ's constant presence in our midst is realized in every tear we shed and in every sleepless night we share. On this Feast of the Ascension, we recognize His presence in the love and support of moms like Brooke's—and then we become that presence for others in the long, terrifying nights we share with those who need us.

B – MARK 16:15-20

A couple of days ago I was visiting some friends, all of whom had children. We were discussing the negative environment that our kids find themselves in today: drugs, violence, sexual exploitations; a general sense of hopelessness. My friends were wondering aloud how they could bring any light into their children's world. They asked how they could be a positive influence that would help their children not only to survive, but also to possibly change the world around them.

One of the parents, a science teacher in a local high school, remarked, "I think we can make a difference in our children's lives if we would become 'lamplighters'. "What was she talking about?" said the look on everybody's face. The teacher explained, "Around the turn of the century, a lamplighter went around the streets lighting the streetlamps. He carried a long pole that had a small candle on top with which he would reach up to light the kerosene-fed lamps. But from a distance, you could not see the lamplighter very well. The light from the small candle was not very bright in the surrounding darkness of night. However," she continued, "you could follow the progress of the lamplighter as he went along the street. The presence of his candle was barely visible until it joined the flame of the street lamp being newly lit. A radiant glow erased a portion of the night's darkness, and looking back down the street, you could see that the light from the glowing street lamps made the entire street bright as day."

There was a pensive silence, and everyone then agreed that they should be lamplighters for their children, that they should be role models. They agreed that they share from their own flame in order to light each child's individual lamp of wisdom; they agreed that by their love they would provide the fuel necessary to nourish and sustain the flame. They agreed that in doing this they will have helped their children to become bright enough so that they could conquer the darkness and hopelessness of the pressures that surround them.

MDP, I believe this is exactly what today's Gospel on the Feast of the Ascension is all about. The Risen Christ is asking Peter, and James, and John—and all of us—to become lamplighters for His Gospel. In every kindness we do, in every word of encouragement we give, in every moment we take to listen to one another, to make one another happy, to smile, to cheer another on, in every good work we do—be it ever so small and hidden—we are signs of Christ's Light. We are proclaiming that He lives. This is the call of discipleship—to look at one another, to look at our children, at our families and friends, and light the light of hope and joy. The Gospel put it this way: "They went forth and preached the Gospel everywhere." They went forth and were true lamplighters for Christ.

C – Luke 24:46-53

Our television news reports as well as our newspapers are filled with the war both in Iraq and Afghanistan that we tend to miss one of the world's greatest tragedies happening under our noses: the genocide in the Sudan. Since the recent conflict erupted in February 2003, seventy thousand Sudanese have died and almost two million have been driven from their homes.

I wanted to mention this on the Feast of the Ascension because, as I was preparing some thoughts on this Feast for you and me, I happened to see an NBC "Dateline" special report. It was about one of the few American journalists who had the courage to cover the Sudanese war with any depth. The name of this journalist is Ann Curry from the morning "Today" show on NBC. Ann Curry made three trips to Sudan in the past. She traveled to Darfur, one of the most dangerous places on earth to report on the genocide there. She put herself at considerable risk, but she said on the "Dateline" show, "I am more afraid of not having done enough to help others than I am of dying." She actually confronted the president of Sudan—on the air—and asked why he tacitly approved of the genocide. She showed the horror and suffering endured by the Sudanese people; she and her crew spent nights in refugee camps and broken-down hotels to cover a story for the world to know. Ann Curry said she wanted to bear witness to such massive human suffering, and to know that she is the kind of person who would take a risk in doing so.

MDP, the witness of Ann Curry is the same challenge that our Blessed Lord poses to us as He takes leave of His young Church on the Mount of the Ascension. He entrusts His work to you and me, even when it means taking risks, even if when it means doubting. Jesus, the Christ, entrusts to us the work of witnessing His Gospel of compassion, of justice, of love. And He wants us to question ourselves as to whether we are up for it! Do we dare take the risk of witnessing His Gospel in the Jerusalems, the Darfurs; the Palmettos of our daily lives? If we bear the name "Christian," then every one of us takes on the role of being Christ to these places in our world. So...the Feast of the Ascension is as much about Jesus as it is about us. We must embrace the challenging words of the Gospel, and in a quiet, simple, powerful way, we must witness this Gospel of love to our world, to our family, to our dear friends, to the stranger, and make no mistake about it, Jesus assures us in the Gospel, "Behold, I am sending the promise of My Father upon you."

PENTECOST
A – JOHN 20:19-23

On the evening of the first Easter, the Disciples were holed up in a locked room. They were frightened of the Jewish authorities, paralyzed by grief, and utterly perplexed by Mary Magdalene's wild tale that their crucified Friend had somehow come back to life. No one in that room was prepared for what happened next in all the history of the world, there has never been a more dramatic entrance than when Jesus suddenly appeared in the midst of the Disciples and said, "Peace be with you." And, from that moment on, those first Disciples of Christ and all who were to follow would proclaim it from the housetops, "He is risen!" Not, "He represents that He is risen," not, "He is reported to be risen," not, "It is claimed that He is risen," not, "We allege that He is risen," but; "He is risen!"

Moreover, Jesus did not come empty-handed to His frightened Disciples. The Risen Lord came bearing gifts.

First of all, He brought them the gift of His living and eternal presence. The Disciples thought they had seen the last of their beloved Jesus when He was laid in the tomb—but even death cannot separate Christ from those who love Him.

Who or what can separate us from the loving presence of Christ at our side? Will false friends or conniving enemies come between us? Will depression, or financial set-back, or grief? Will troubles at work or troubles at home or troubles within? Will sickness or danger or anxiety? If even death could not keep Christ from our side, then what is there in all the world that can separate us from the constant companionship of our Lord and Savior?

The second gift Jesus brought to His Disciples was the gift of peace. Did this mean a trouble-free existence? Far from it! According to tradition, most of the Disciples in that room would eventually die for the sake of their Lord. They would carry His message to the ends of the known world, they would suffer the hazards of travel, the animosity of strangers, and they would be killed in terrible ways.

Jesus does not promise us ease or comfort in His service, but He still gives us His peace. The Peace of Christ allows us to face the world on its own terms, knowing that our destiny is in the hands of the One who has overcome the world. Even when everything around us is falling apart, we have a refuge within. The world cannot give this kind of peace, nor can the world take it away.

A traveler told of visiting an Arab village and seeing a boy playing the flute. The flute seemed unusual in design, and the traveler asked if he could see it. To his surprise, he discovered that the flute was made from a gun barrel. The boy had found the barrel on a battlefield, filed it down, drilled holes in it, and transformed a weapon of death into an instrument of live music. The Peace of Christ will not necessarily exempt us from life's battlefields, but in Christ, we find ways to surmount those battles. In Christ, we discover possibilities for transformation and renewal even in the midst of strife. In Christ, the storms that rage around us cannot drown out the voice of peace within.

On the Plains of Waterloo, the scene of Napoleon's defeat is a great statue of a lion, made from melted weapons. The lion's mouth is open in a ferocious snarl as the frightful beast surveys the plains. A traveler reported seeing a bird's nest in the bronze lion's mouth. A mother bird was perched on the nest feeding her fledglings, oblivious to the lion's threatening teeth above and below. So it is with those who know the Peace of Christ. We may nest without fear in the very mouth of the 'lions' of this world, entrusting ourselves to the shielding wings of the Peace of Christ.

B– JOHN 15:26-27; 16:22

The wonderful Spirit of God is in our lives. It is the Spirit of God that brings two people together as spouses; it is the Spirit of God that forges strong, lasting and wonderful friendships; it is the Spirit of God that transforms us—all different—into a community of faith.

Yes, even in the most troubling times of our lives, God gives us His spirit, His joy, His power, and through us, He gives the world hope. This Gospel of Pentecost tells us that you and I are supposed to go out and make a difference in this world. Pope John Paul II reminds us so often that we are the hands of the heart of Christ! The small group of early Christians we heard about in today's reading set the world on fire in a manner far out of proportion to their numbers because of the hope and joy they spread wherever they went.

MDP, when we lose our hope and joy, we lose the power to turn the world upside down. The early Disciples found their hope and joy in the Spirit of God breathed into them by the Risen Lord. And so it must be with us: The drive that we need to be holy people, a royal priesthood, a spiritual nuclear power in our world comes from only one source—the Risen Christ! On this Feast of Pentecost, may the Risen Christ breathe into us once again His Holy Spirit.

Because you are you

Moms and dads: If you want your children to grow up to love God, to experience God and the Holy Spirit; if you want your children to love you and believe in you; if you want your children to love themselves and believe in themselves; first, you must communicate these feelings to them as your own. In the words of one loving Father:

When you tuck them into bed, be sure to tell them that you love them just for being themselves. Say to them, "I'm really the luckiest father (mother) in the world to have such marvelous children. I love you not because of your report card, or your talent, or because you're going to do a good job—but simply because you are you."

If this sounds much too simple, I still would like to think that it gets far better results than do demands for obedience based on fear and intimidation. And, the kids will go to sleep with a terrific feeling that, "Gosh, I really am loved for just being me." And that will be a healing touch for children...an experience of the presence of the Holy Spirit of God, of Pentecost, in their lives.

It seems that what our children need now is under-exposure to the tribes involved in commercial exploitation and violence, and over-exposure to the community of love. In order to learn more about who they are our children are watching us. They are searching for role models. If they can plainly see that God's Holy Spirit of love is in us, they'll get a good picture of who they are and what they ought to aspire to.

C – John 20:19-23

The Gospel brings us to the evening of the first Easter Sunday. Three years earlier Jesus called His first Disciples saying, "Come after me and I will make you fishers of men." For three years, the Disciples had followed Him, traveled with Him, prayed with Him; talked with Him. Then came the cross and the resurrection, and how He appears to them in this Gospel saying, "Peace be with you... as the Father has sent Me, so I send you." He breathed on them and said, "Receive the Holy Spirit." Jesus gave His Disciples the strength, joy, and courage to take the magnificent power of His Word to the ends of the earth. And before long, if you remember, the Disciples are being referred to in "Acts" as the men who have turned the world upside down.

MDP, this beautiful Feast of Pentecost reminds us vividly that we are the new disciples of Jesus. And, no matter how ugly things seem in the world, no matter how disheartening things may be in our own lives, we are not to waver, but are to have confidence and the joy, knowing that we are backed up by the power of the Spirit to make things right! The message of the Pentecost is a message of power because God is God and there is nothing that anyone can do to ultimately defeat God!

Some time ago, we all heard or read about the story of Ashley Smith. Ashley was returning home to her Atlanta apartment after a quick run to the store. As she got out of her car, she felt a gun in her side. Brian Nichols, the fugitive who had killed the presiding judge, court reporter and a deputy at an Atlanta courthouse, forced Ashley into her apartment and held her bound in her bathroom. It was the beginning of an extraordinary ordeal for the young widow, mother of a five-year-old daughter. But, displaying courage and levelheadedness, Ashley acted as her faith in

Jesus Christ and the power of His Spirit taught her. Over the next several hours, she spoke to him as one hurting soul to another. She spoke gently but firmly to Nichols. As they talked about Jesus, about the Bible, about family, pancakes and the massive manhunt going on outside; Ashley the hostage became Ashley the confidant. The longer they talked, the more the fear dissipated. As the story goes, Nichols soon untied Ashley. He said at one point, "I feel like I'm already dead," but Ashley urged him to consider the fact that he was still alive, a miracle. After Brian Nichols gave himself up peacefully, Ashley said that she tried not to judge him but to let him take from her a sense of hope. She said that she had several opportunities to pick up the gun, "But," she said, "I did not want him or anybody else dead." She said, "I wanted his mother to be able to look at me and say, "Thank you for making my son understand that nobody else needed to die, not even him.'"

MDP, Ashley Smith, believer and disciple of Jesus, had the Pentecost strength of courage and compassion; she had the Pentecost Spirit that helped her rise to the possibility of forgiveness. The same Pentecost Spirit that invigorated the first Disciples of Jesus, breathed into her hope and strength and peace in a most desperate and dark situation. In her own way, like those first Disciples, she turned a world of fear and darkness upside down.

MDP, you and I, like Ashley, can always be caught up in the power of Pentecost, and so we can find our hope and joy in the Spirit of God, breathed into us by the Risen Lord. The drive that we need to be courageous, holy, joyful, comes only from one source: The Risen Christ! On this Feast of Pentecost, may He once again breathe into us the Holy Spirit, and may He empower us as He empowered those first Disciples and the disciple, Ashley Smith, to go and turn the world upside down!

TEN MILES

MDP, it is the Spirit of God that enabled the Disciples and enables us to do things that we cannot do on our own.

I served as Chaplain to the Third Marine Division in Vietnam. Let me tell you a story which happened there. One of the platoons in my battalion was on night patrol. Suddenly shots rang out in the darkness. As the Marines were trained, they all dove for cover. When the lieutenant gave the all-clear order, everyone was okay—except one Marine. The sniper had seriously wounded him. Instinctively all the Marines in the platoon worked to stop the bleeding. Then they paired up, taking turns carrying him to an aid station—some ten miles away. Some of those young Marines probably never thought that they would be in such a terrifying situation, and they probably never imagined that they could save their buddy. But, somehow, they did! The love for a brother beat being scared to death!

MDP, this is what Pentecost is all about. There is the Spirit of God that surrounds those of us who believe. It is that mysterious, unseen, often unexpected power that gives us the strength to achieve things we never thought we could do.

READING GLASSES

I spent a lot of time in the Pacific, and once in a while, I was called upon to celebrate Mass in one of the small islands. I believe it was the Island of Panope—very Catholic—when one Sunday I said Mass there. The people there really have trouble with eye impairment because of their diet and the exposure to the intense glare of the sun. On this particular Sunday, a lady named Marguerite was in charge of the readings. Her husband got up to do the first reading. I saw him reach over to Marguerite to borrow her glasses. When he finished, his brother, who was to do the second reading, reached over and borrowed the glasses his brother used. When he finished the reading, he returned the glasses to Marguerite for the remainder of the Mass. When I think about this scene, I think that a pair of glasses, shared among the community, speaks to me of Pentecost more powerfully than the readings of that day. The sharing of those lenses by a family, by a community, spoke to me of the presence of the Spirit, Pentecost, helping us to recognize what is good, what is right, what is true, what is ethical in our personal journey to God.

Our Gospel today began by telling us that the Disciples of Jesus had locked themselves behind closed doors. They had shut themselves away in fear. Sometimes we too, new disciples of Jesus, shut out the treasures of the Spirit of God—love, faith, forgiveness. We are afraid of loving too much. We are afraid of being thought of as a 'religious fanatic,' we are afraid of being taken advantage of for our kindness. We are afraid of sharing our glasses.

MDP, it is the Spirit of God which gives life and direction to our journeys as a parish, as a people of God. It is the Spirit of God, which 'breathes' the life of God into us; it is the Spirit of God which opens the doors of our lives, and enlivens us with a hope and strength to go out and renew the face of the earth.

THE SOLEMNITY OF THE MOST HOLY TRINITY SUNDAY
A – JOHN 3:16-18

On the night of their anniversary, he was determined to show her how much he loved her. He took her to a very elegant restaurant for an intimate, candlelight dinner. After dinner as she sipped champagne, he began to recite romantic verse, telling her he would climb the highest mountains, swim the deepest oceans, cross the burning deserts for her, how he would slay dragons and monsters to protect her, how he longed to sit under her window and sing for her beautiful love songs in the moonlight.

She listened to him go on for some time about his immense love for her. The poetry, however, came to an abrupt halt when she asked him, "Ok, but would you wash the dishes for me?"

Such is the love of our God—a love not just celebrated in song and story but revealed in human history. Today's Feast of the Trinity invites us to rediscover the presence of God in our lives.

The one-time atheist communist spy and later American editor and author Whittaker Chambers wrote in his 1952 autobiography "Witness" that his deeply troubled life began to turn when he discovered God in the birth of his baby daughter.

"I was sitting in our apartment on St. Paul Street in Baltimore... my daughter was in her high chair. I was watching her eat. She was the most miraculous thing that had ever happened in my life. I liked to watch her even when she smeared cereal on her face or dropped it meditatively on the floor. My eye came to rest on the delicate convolutions of her ear—those intricate, perfect ears. The thought passed through my mind: No, those ears were not created by any chance coming together of atoms in nature (the Communist view). They could only have been created by some immense design. The thought was involuntary and unwanted. I crowded it out of my mind. But I never wholly forgot it or the occasion. I had to crowd it out of my mind. If I had completed it, I should have had to say: Design presupposes God. I did not know that, at that moment, the finger of God was already laid upon my forehead."

Since the dawn of creation, God has never abandoned nor forgotten His people. God is motivated by a love that we cannot begin to fathom. Despite our ignorance of God, our displacement of God with safer, more comforting and less mysterious concepts, our outright rejection of God, God continues to call us back. Always making the first move in being reconciled with us: God readily forgives Israel and renews the covenant with them (today's first reading, from the Book of Exodus); God is the ultimate source of loving community (even for the deeply divided Corinthian Church, today's second reading); God recreates us by touching human history in Christ (John's Gospel.) Today's Celebration is an invitation for us to share in the work of God's love—the work of forgiveness and reconciliation, of creating communion and community among all of God's people.

The next gift Christ gave to the Disciples was the gift of His earthly mission: "As the Father sent Me so I am sending you." As Christ was sent to bring good news to the oppressed, we are sent on the same mission. If we are to fulfill the mission Christ has given us, then our hands must be His hand, reaching out to the weary and the broken. Our feet must be His feet, carrying us to wherever our ministry of service is needed. Our ears must be His ears, ready to listen to the heart-broken confession, eager to hear the painful story. Our voices must be His voice, promising hope, proclaiming good news, and sharing forgiveness. It is not enough for a person to simply live; a person must have something to live for. And Christ has given us that by sharing His work with us.

There is one last gift mentioned in this Resurrection Story in today's Gospel lesson. In a sense, this gift encompasses all the others. Jesus breathed on the Disciples and gifted them with the Holy Spirit of God.

There is a word in Hebrew that means both 'breath' and 'spirit.'

This is true also in Greek. In Biblical thought, the Spirit is the Breath of God filling us with life. Even our English word 'inspire' means both to inhale and to fill with spiritual energy. In that locked room, Jesus inspired His followers. Just as God breathed life and spirit into Adam, Christ breathed His Life and Spirit into His Disciples.

Many years ago, there was a pastor who accomplished wonderful work among the parish people, but he suffered from severe attacks of asthma. Sometimes he had to be carried to the pulpit and supported on either side while he preached. When he prayed the Lord's Prayer, he added a personal twist, "Our Father who are in Heaven, Hallowed be Your name. Give us this day our daily breath."

The Holy Spirit is our daily Breath from God, the life-giving inspiration that fills us with something bigger than ourselves. The Spirit helps us catch our second wind in this hectic world. The Spirit gives us fresh air when we feel we're going down for the third time. The Spirit pumps us up when life has sucked us empty. The Spirit revives and renews us when our own energy and strength have run out.

All these gifts Jesus brought to the overjoyed Disciples. And what Jesus gave to His followers twenty centuries ago, He still gives to you and me today.

The famous Abbe Pierre, whose work for the homeless and hurting is well-known; one day was called in to help a homeless family who had been forced to live in the fields in a crude tent shelter. Two of their children already had died and a third was seriously ill. Abbe Pierre recalls the experience:

"It was then that I realized some terrible things. I realized that so long as people were supposed to be apostles; as long as a priest like me was incapable of saying to that poor woman, 'Come on, get your things, pick up your child and come along with me and your husband and sleep in my room, I'll take your place in the tent and tomorrow we'll find some way of solving this," until then, well, fundamentally I was simply an imposter."

Christ has given us wonderful gifts. And the measure of how well we use them is how generously we share them.

B (1)– Matthew 28:16-20

"Go, therefore, make disciples of all nations." An incredible challenge that Jesus gives us in today's Gospel.

There is a story of a man who asked the question, "What is the devil?" Before anyone could reply, the man gave his own answer... "The devil," he said, "is not a huge monster with horns and a long tail and a wicket glitter in his eye. No, the devil is 'inertia'—doing nothing, always living a life, taking the path of least resistance."

When Jesus gives us the command in today's Gospel to turn our lives upside down, by following His example of love, and we respond with inactivity and take a path of least resistance, we are giving the devil full play. "Go now, and make disciples of all nations." Go now and share the good news of a loving God.

MDP, if we follow the path of least resistance as a church, as God's holy people, if we fail to bring love into the world, we are failing to bring God into this world of ours which seems to be unconcerned about God, even saying He is absent or He is dead.

The French philosopher, Gabriel Marcel, says that there is one great suffering on this earth and that is to be alone. Man, made in the image and likeness of God, is made for love, for community. Today psychiatrists are saying loneliness is one of the greatest of all human fears. And we are challenged not to be alone, challenged to discipleship—that is, not to sit back and do nothing. God revealed Himself through Christ. Christ returned to the Father. It is up to us—to you and me—to reveal God. When a person looks at us, that person must see love, and so sees God...

I grew up in a town that wasn't so far from Valley Forge. One of the nuns I had in grammar school took advantage of this and, on occasion, took us, her students, to visit these close-by historical sights. I remember a story she told about George Washington. It seems that during the terrible winter at Valley Forge, a government official arrived on the scene to obtain a firsthand report of the actual field situation from George Washington, himself. After Washington had dutifully received him, the government man immediately began complimenting him on his ability to hold the army together under such terribly trying circumstances. "General Washington, you are a great leader, a great man, an inspiration to all of us," the man said. Whereupon, General Washington, standing in the midst of his suffering troops, broke in impatiently saying, "Never mind all that. Just tell me where you stand in relation to the cause I represent?"

The Feast of the Holy Trinity, today, helps me to take that story to heart. We arrive at Church every Saturday evening (or Sunday morning), feeling good, praising the Lord in word, and song, and Eucharist. But if we are really listening, we can hear Him say to each one of us, "Don't take the path of least resistance; tell Me where you stand in relation to the cause I represent; Go make disciples of all nations."

B (2) – Mark 14:12-16

Today's Feast of the Holy Trinity celebrates the many ways God makes His presence known in our world, in the manifestation of His love in our lives. I thought about this when I visited a friend last week. She is the mother of five and spends hours cooking Sunday dinner for her extended family. Her greatest joy is to see her sons and daughters and their spouses and her grandchildren gathered at the family table. While she is not the feast, it is her love that brings such a joyful experience of family into being.

MDP, when it comes to a description of God, even the greatest theologian is left babbling, for human language can never capture God's essence. Such joy to her family helps us grasp the idea that is the heart of Father, Son, and Holy Spirit. It is love who created our world and fashioned it with care; it is love who passionately desired to become one of us and for a little while pitched His tent among us; it is love who could never leave us but remains with us to inhabit every moment of our existence. Love is Father, Son, and Holy Spirit.

C – John 16:12-15

"The Spirit of Truth will guide you into all truth."

W hen I thought about a homily for Trinity Sunday, and living our lives in the Spirit of Truth, I thought about how we need to fill our hearts with a total, innocent, honest, non-manipulative, humble, child-like trust in God.

Several years ago, I saw a science fiction movie called "Close Encounters of the Third Kind." The movie is about a group of the greatest scientists on earth preparing to meet with aliens from an advanced civilization. In the final scene of the movie, when the meeting takes place, the scientists discover that the highly evolved aliens are very child-like. For me the message of the film seemed to be that if the human race is ever to genuinely advance and become truly wise and close to God and close to complete truth, it will have to—somehow— become more child-like!

In an issue of "The New York Times Magazine", I read an article by Dana Tierney entitled, "Coveting Luke's Faith." For Dana and her husband, God was not a part of their lives; He played no role whatsoever in their lives. Like so many young people brought up in strict religious homes, they had enough and simply abandoned the faith of their mothers' and dads'; their aunts' and uncles'; and their grandparents'. They brought up their six-year-old son, Luke, in this atmosphere.

Well, Dana's husband was sent to Iraq for several months. While Dana was numb with anxiety, Luke was surprisingly calm. He missed his daddy, but he wasn't scared. One night Dana and Luke were watching television. A story came on about a soldier on leave from the war to celebrate his wedding. The soldier began to talk about how dangerous it was in Iraq, and how very much afraid he was to go back. Dana reached to switch the TV to another channel, but, no, Luke wanted to watch it. Out of the corner of her eye, Dana saw little Luke bow his head for a split second. She asked, "Sweetheart, what are you doing?" But

Luke wouldn't tell her. A few minutes later, he did it again. Dana said, "You don't have to tell me, but if you want to, I am listening." Finally, Luke confessed, "I was saying a prayer for Daddy." Surprised and almost embarrassed because prayer was never mentioned in their home, Dana said, "That's wonderful, Luke; it's wonderful that you would pray for Daddy in our home." She asked Luke when he first began to believe in God. "I don't know," he said, "but I always knew he was there."

And, in her article in the "New York Times Magazine", Dana writes,

"It was as if that mustard seed of faith had found its way into our son and now he was revealing that he could move mountains. I was envious of him. Luke wasn't rattled because he believed that God would bring his father home safely. I was the only one stranded. For Luke, all things are possible. His prayers can stretch to infinity and beyond, but I am limited to one. O, Lord, help my unbelief..."

MDP, Luke possesses the openness of heart and spirit that enables him to realize God's presence in his life and in the lives of those dearest to him; Luke is able to sense the Spirit of God loving him and protecting him and his mom and dad and family. This is faith at its most basic, at its most enduring. Today, we celebrate the Feast of the most Holy Trinity. With child-like trust, we celebrate God as we behold him in the simple things of every day: God the Father—the giver of our lives; God the Son—Jesus, the human face of the Father; God the Holy Spirit—the love that binds us to one another and back to God.

May we possess the faith of young Luke to be able to find God in the joys and the sorrows, the victories and the hurts, the loves; that are part of all of our lives.

THE SOLEMNITY OF THE MOST HOLY BODY AND BLOOD OF CHRIST

A (1)– JOHN 6:51-59

I come from an Italian family, a great family where many of my values were shaped, many of my beliefs were learned and are still held dear; I am sure you have had the same experience. But when I look back, I realize that my values and beliefs were shaped at the dinner table. I can still hear my father and mother discussing the politics of the town, the demands of the Italian pastor we had, what the President of the United States was up to.

I am sure you can relate to this in some way. This is how we learned out story—the journeys of our parents and grandparents from small villages, for example, in Italy, Ireland; traveling across the seas, to this dinner table. At the dinner table, we first learned how to share with our brothers and sisters. At the dinner table, we came to realize how hard our parents worked to provide what was necessary for our growth and development. At the dinner table, we found affirmation, support, and a beautiful, unconditional love. Whatever traumas, pains, and griefs we were experiencing, the table, the dinner table, was the one place where we always belonged; it was always a place of safety, forgiveness, and welcome; it was the one place we could be family to one another.

MDP, Christ calls us to His Eucharistic table, offering us peace, affirmation, support and love. We come to the Eucharistic table to celebrate our identity as His disciples, to seek the sustaining grace to live the demands of such discipleship. Today, at the table of the Eucharist, we celebrate God's lasting gift to His family, the Church. He gives us the Bread and Wine—His Own Body Blessed and Broken for us. But there is a string attached: like the sharing at the dinner table in our families, we must share the Eucharist with others. If we partake of the Eucharist then we must be willing to become the Eucharist for others—to make the love of Christ real. St. Augustine put it this way, "we must become what we receive."

A (2) – JOHN 6:51-59

We are very happy and relieved when we hear the Biblical assertion that we have been created in the "image of God." It goes down easier than so many other passages like, "Love your enemies," or "sell everything and give it to the poor." But this Biblical phrase—image of God—is very much misunderstood. Many of us, when we think about being made in God's image, create a picture in our mind's eye of having been made somehow to look like God—little copies of God, little models of God. Whatever else the Biblical writers are trying to tell us they are not trying to tell us that we are little gods or that we are copies of God. God is God; God is the creator.

We are finite beings, dependent on God for every breath we draw, for every moment of life. MDP, we are not made to be little images of God; we are made to image God, to reflect in our lives the love of God. The Biblical writers are telling us more about the position of our lives than about the shape of our lives. It is not how we are formed, not what we look like or who we look like. It is, rather, whether we have positioned ourselves before God in such a way as to reflect Him. Only when we have acknowledged that God is God, that we are dependent upon Him, are we in a position to begin to reflect His life to others. This is how we become holy persons.

Today we celebrate the Feast of the Body and Blood of Christ. There is a magnificent line in today's Gospel: "...just as the living Father sent Me and I have life because of the Father, so also the one who feeds on Me will have life because of Me..." In other words, God is God and we are dependent upon Him, and because we feed on His Body and Blood together, we can reflect His life and love to others in this world of ours.

I saw a movie called "Millions." I could not stop thinking about this movie as I was preparing my thoughts for you on this Feast of the Body and Blood of Christ, and the call we have to reflect Christ Jesus to the world. This movie, "Millions," is the story of a lonesome seven-year-old boy named Damian. Damian is trying to cope with the recent death of his mother, a new home, a new school. Helping him deal with it all are his friends—the Holy Saints of the Church whose lives he has memorized the way most kids memorize the stats of their favorite baseball players. Damian has long conversations with his favorite saints: St. Nicholas of Myra (the real Santa Claus), St. Francis and St. Clare of Assisi, and St. Peter—even the martyrs of Uganda show up to help him rebuild the hideaway he has built for himself out of the old cardboard boxes.

One day Damian is bopped on the head by a satchel of money— hundreds of thousands of dollars that have fallen from a passing train. Serious believer that he is; little Damian figures that the money is from God so it should be used for doing good. Damian wants to give it to the poor and needy—and seizes upon some unusual way of locating them. His Christ-like and saintly approach doesn't sit well with his nine-year-old brother, Anthony, a budding, coldhearted capitalist, who wants to parlay the money into a real estate empire.

The terrific joy of this movie is watching Damian give the money away to anyone he perceives as poor and in need. You can't help but be taken up in his delight as he takes a group of homeless people to lunch at Pizza Hut and later watches the water flow from a well he had paid to have dug in an African village.

But when the money begins to destroy his family and those around him, Damian does not hesitate to do what he has to do: he destroys the money by putting a match to it! His dead mother appears to him and Damian soon learns from her—here I could not hold back my tears—that one of the tests of sainthood is the performance of a miracle. In his selfless and simple faith, Damian performed miracles and is well on the road of joining Francis and Clare and Peter and Nicholas and his friends from Uganda.

MDP, Damian reflects the Christ who gave Himself to us in bread and asks us to become, in our love, bread for others. May all of us, as we celebrate today's Feast, possess the depth and integrity of the faith of little Damian, and realize Jesus' vision of becoming His flesh and blood for the life of the world.

B – MARK 14:12-16, 22-26

A few weeks ago, I received a phone call from the wife of a Navy friend with whom I served. She was struggling with the loss of her husband. Her husband, an electrician, accidentally brushed up against a hot wire and was electrocuted. This sudden tragedy put this good lady into a state of hopelessness. She talked and cried, talked and cried. But then she said something that touched my heart. She said that on her way to Church the previous Sunday, she said to her priest that had the Mass, "I don't know how I am going to make it without my husband. I'm thirty-six years old and have three children to raise and I was so very much dependent on my wonderful husband." Then she paused and said, "I know one thing. I have a choice to make. I can either stay bitter or I can get better."

That good woman made a personal faith-decision to get better, and on that Sunday morning at Church, she found God's healing touch. Whenever we come to Church—and most of the time we are not aware of it—but there are people in the pews who are experiencing the harsh side of life—the loss of a spouse, the loss of a parent, the loss of a child. Or, there are others among us struggling with serious illness, struggling to find their way through a relationship gone wrong; or struggling with a financial crisis, or struggling through the trials of the aging process. We come to Church today—the Feast of the Body and Blood of Christ—because we believe that the healing touch of God, can, in some beautiful way, smooth out the rough times in our lives.

In the marvelous Gospel, we have for today's Feast, we see Jesus Blessing, Breaking Bread, and giving this gift of Himself to His disciples. The Gospel tells us that God is with us, ready to transform our bitterness into 'betterness', our despair into hope, our sorrow into joy

Jesus is the Bread that gives life to us, feeds us, nourishes us, sustains us; gives us the power and strength to live as Christians. So we are here on this Feast of the Body and Blood of Christ to feed on the Bread of Life; we are here today not just for ourselves. We are here to nourish others. What a joy it is to come to Church knowing that the Bread of Life will renew and refresh us—spiritually, emotionally, physically—and help us to change "bitter into better;" to continue our ministry of love to the world.

C– Luke 9:11-17

A husband had a worried look on his face when he sat down to have a heart-to-heart talk with his wife. After a few false starts, he said to her..."Sweetheart, just suppose I were to tell you that I had made some bad investments, and had lost money gambling and everything we had was gone; the house gone, the cars gone, the insurance gone, the bank accounts gone, the stocks and bonds gone—everything gone! Now, if I were to tell you all that, would you still love me?" The wife thought about it for a moment; then answered, "Honey, I would always love you, but I sure would miss you!"

MDP, Jesus doesn't promise us a rose garden for our life's journey. Neither does He promise us houses and cars; and gambling money and stocks and bonds. But rather, He promises us life, 'abundant life'. And He will never withdraw His promise. He loves us that much and He always will!

In today's beautiful Gospel, Jesus welcomes the crowds that are following Him and Luke tells us that He "talked to them about the Kingdom of God, and He cured those who were in need of healing." There are many of us, so many in our families and friends who need healing in mind or spirit. The very process of living in today's world is very stressful. And we are so often caught up in a process of spiritual and emotional and even physical disintegration that needs to be reversed or we can be overwhelmed by it.

In her book, "Two-Part Invention: The Story of a Marriage," Madeleine L'Engle tells the story of her forty-five year marriage to Hugh

Franklin. She writes of her bedside vigil as Hugh lay dying of cancer:

"I am who I am because of our years together, freed by his acceptance and love for me…Our love has been anything but perfect and anything but static. Inevitably, there have been times when one of us outrun the other and has to wait patiently for the other to catch up. There have been times when we have misunderstood each other, demanded too much from the other, been insensitive to the other's needs. I do not believe there is any marriage where this does not happen.

The growth of love is not a straight line, but a series of hills and valleys. I suspect that in every good marriage there are times when love seems to be over. Sometimes these desert lines are simply the only way to the next oasis, which is far more lush and beautiful after the desert crossing that it could possibly have been without it."

And Madeline L'Engle writes that she will always cherish the words of the poet Conrad Aiken that her husband spoke to her when he proposed: "Music I heard with you was more than music! And bread I broke with you was more than Bread."

The Jesus of the Gospels challenges us to feel the healing presence of God within us. Madeleine L'Engle felt it in her marriage. The Jesus of this Gospel challenges us to feel ourselves enabled and strengthened to be instruments of healing in the lives of others. The Jesus of the Gospel tells us today that this is our calling as His followers; this is our calling—to be ministers of His Gospel.

MDP, discipleship begins with realizing our own need to hear the "Good News" in our lives and then accept Christ's call to live the Gospel and bring it into the lives of others. It would be a great day if we were to make a serious decision to share our hope in the healing power of the Good Lord to everyone we know. Through the lives we live, in the works we perform, to let it be known that there is a new world coming; to let it be known that everyone counts for something uniquely important in God's eyes; to let it be known that because God loves each of us, we are worthy of each other's love. And so we can say, as Madeleine L'Engle's husband said to her: "The bread I broke with you was more than bread."

SECOND SUNDAY IN ORDINARY TIME
A – JOHN 1:29-34

I would like to ask you a question. If Jesus should come again to earth in human form, would the world recognize Him? Would the Christian world recognize Him? Would you, would I recognize Him? John the Baptist, in today's Gospel, says that when Jesus first walked into His life, He did not recognize Him. He did not realize that Jesus was the promised Messiah.

If we are unable to recognize Christ when He walks into our life, it may be because our expectations are misguided; it may be because we are not able to "switch off" our busyness to recognize Him.

A few weeks ago we celebrated the Christmas story and we were reminded that it was not man's idea that the Son of God should be born in a stable. The first thing we learned from Jesus' birth is that the Lord will not always be found where we expect to find Him. We tend to look for Him in everything that is nice, that is clean, that is warm. We expect Him to be in our churches and in our Bibles, in the beautiful hymns we sing. If these are the only places we search for the Lord, then we are not looking in the stables that confront us in our everyday lives.

The Lord says, "You will see me most clearly in the faces of those brothers and sisters whose need for your concern is hardest to satisfy. You will see me most clearly in the faces of those brothers and sisters whom you find hardest to love."

I read a story in the Boston Globe which brought this Gospel home to me. In a downtown Boston shelter, the large television set is always on. Shutting it off is like tampering with another country's flag. Lesser acts have led to war. But one humid night, a staff member turned the television off. The shelter's wilting guests – even those who paid no attention to the perpetually flickering images – were stunned. Two women stood at the front of the room, under the dark television screen. Each unsnapped a case, lifted out a stringed instrument, and started to tune it. Then they began to play: first a pair of madrigals, a Mozart duet, and then a Bulgarian folk tune. The musicians didn't know anything about the lives of their audience. They didn't know who was listening with one ear while hearing voices with the other. They didn't know who was freshly out of prison and who was heading back in, who was momentarily sober and who was never sober.

News of the concerts spread and the audiences grew. The musicians – professionals who play in the city's renowned symphony – were not surprised. One Wednesday a month the television set at the shelter is turned off and the concert begins. Over the months, little windows have opened. The music manages to bridge the unscalable heights separating people. For a couple of hours – the forgotten, the lost, the desperate, the addicted, and those who struggle to help them – are all the same.

MDP, John the Baptizer urges us to "switch off" the busyness of our lives and realize that Jesus, the Lamb of God, is in our midst. The Spirit of God, like the timeless music of Mozart, brings us together in spite of our differences. Every one of us has been called, as the Baptizer was called, to point to Christ who lives and walks with us whenever we begin to doubt, whenever we hurt in some way, whenever we are fearful and worried about something. John declared his witness, and we must declare our witness in our unfailing compassion for others, in our uncompromising moral and ethical convictions, in our everyday sense of joy.

The Unwrapped Gift

It was about Brandon and Kathy Gunn who received a gift at their wedding from Kathy's Aunt Alice. It was a white box on which she attached a note which read: "Do not open until your first argument."

So Brandon and Kathy placed the unwrapped gift on the top shelf of their kitchen pantry and just left it there. Sure enough, there were moments of tension and disagreement, but Brandon and Kathy refused to open the gift. In spite of hard words and slammed doors, the couple saw opening the box as a sign of failure – they believed that their love for one another could handle whatever life threw at them. The little white box became a challenge.

As the story goes, the couple, now the parents of two children, celebrated their ninth anniversary. That's when they decided to open Aunt Alice's box – not because they needed to but because they were convinced they would never have to.

What they found in Aunt Alice's box was remarkably unremarkable: there was money for flowers; money for pizza; money for a bottle of wine – nothing that could really end a fight at all. But that's when it hit them, that the real gift wasn't anything in the box. The real gift, the priceless gift had been staring at them all those years. By not turning to the box, Brandon and Kathy were forced to learn tolerance, compromise, patience that was the real gift! And they possessed it all along.

How beautiful to think of Christ, making it possible for us to see: to penetrate the darkness, to begin to put things into place; to begin to see what life is all about, to be there to help us with our destructive worries. More than that, the power that comes from Christ gives us the strength to cope, the strength to live, the strength to live creatively, the strength to love unconditionally.

The whole world needs the light of Christ that is in us. The world out there with all its problems, needs to be illumined by the light of Christ that shines within us. To understand this and to be able to take it seriously, we must first open up the window of our hearts so that we can see what the beloved Disciple John saw when he cried out, "Look! There is the Lamb of God who takes away the sin of the world. The real light which gives light to every man."

B - John 1:35-42

I read this story in "Theater Arts Magazine". It seems that one of the magazine's subscribers dialed "information" for the magazine's phone number. "Sorry," said the operator, "but there is no listing for anyone named 'Theodore Arts.'" The subscriber insisted, "It's not a person, it's a publication. I want 'Theater Arts.'" The operator's voice became testy. "I tell you, we have no listing for 'Theodore Arts'" At this point, the frustrated subscriber shouted into the phone, "The word is Theater, T-H-E-A-T-E-R," to which the operator replied, That's not the way to spell Theodore."

MDP, Jesus, the Christ, is the Messiah. Actually, those two names for Jesus, although spelled differently, have exactly the same meaning. Both are titles – Messiah, from the Hebrew, Christ, from the Greek. And we who call ourselves Christians acknowledge Jesus as Christ and Messiah.

Just a few weeks ago, we celebrated how beautifully God makes His presence known to us. But now, as the Sundays the Church calls, 'Ordinary time' pass by, we must be open to the discovery of His presence in our lives, in every new and in every unexpected way. So the question that the Gospel prompts today is, "Have we really found the Messiah, the Lord, the Christ?"

Jesus says, you will find Me most clearly in the faces of your spouses, in the faces of all your children, your brothers and sisters, your cherished friends; you will find Me in those who make the hardest demands on your love.

An impetuous young man spied a beautiful young woman walking through the park. He began to follow her. After a time, the young woman turned and confronted him: Why are you following me?" she asked. "Because you are so beautiful," he answered. "I am madly in love with you and wish you to be mine." To which the young woman replied, "But why don't you take a look behind you to see my younger sister. She is far more beautiful than I." The young man quickly turned around but saw no one. "You're putting me on," he said. To which she replied, "You have lied to me; if you were so madly in love with me, then why did you turn around?"

We heard Andrew say in the Gospel, "We have found the Messiah." I wonder if we really believe this, or do we turn our heads around in the direction of every passing distraction, of everything that pulls us away from the values we really must hold as Christians.

MDP, "To find the Messiah," means that we must know ourselves. We must never stop asking the question, "Who am I?" We must see what is before us. The challenge of being a disciple of Christ is to discern and to respond to that question, "Who am I,?" in the light of the Gospel of Jesus.

A few weeks ago, I saw the movie "Ray with Jamie Foxx," who won the Oscar for his role in portraying Ray Charles in this movie. Before the filming began, Jamie Foxx met with the legendary musician, hoping to receive the blessing of the man whose character he would play. Ray Charles invited the actor to sit down and play some blues. Foxx sang and played on one piano while Charles led the jam session on another. Without warning, Ray Charles strayed into the works of another jazz singer, Thelonious Monk. Jamie didn't expect such a challenge, and – trying to keep up, he hit some wrong notes. Ray Charles abruptly stopped playing to ask, "Why would you do that?" Jamie Foxx didn't know what to say. "Look," Charles said, "The notes are right underneath your fingers. All you have to do is to take the time to hit the right notes." Foxx came away from his jamming with Ray Charles understanding what made him the great musician he was.

The Gospel today invites us to look, to see what is before us, to take the time to live in the presence of God who is in our midst. Regardless of what we do, whether we are grandparents, whether we are retired, whether we are teachers, or artists, or sportsmen, regardless of where we live, God is present in every moment of our lives. Whether we are musicians or stock investors, or parents or students or sages, Jesus the Messiah calls us to see the ways of God before us and to take the time to "hit" the "right" notes of love, and justice, and compassion, and forgiveness, and in the joy of knowing and believing that the life He has given us is worth living.

We do love God, we want to place our identity in Him; we want to be the ideal Christian disciple, but for some of us there are certain areas where we hold back. We may be unwilling to risk our sense of security; or we may be involved in totally destructive relationships; or we might be unwilling to give up a dependence on a chemical, a drug, a food. It may be even a religious hypocrisy. It may be a lot of other things too; but, whatever it is, as long as we are holding back, our response is incomplete and we remain what I like to call "an almost Christian."

There's an anonymous poem that I think of often. It goes like this:

"The Gospels of Matthew, Mark, Luke and John are read by more than a few,

But the one that is most read and commented on is the Gospel according to you.

You are writing a Gospel, a chapter each day by the things that you do and the words that you say. People read what you write, whether faithless or true..

Say, tell me, what is the Gospel according to you?

Do others read His truth and His love in your life?

Or has yours been too full of malice and strife?

Does your life speak of evil, or does it ring true?

Say, tell me, what is the Gospel according to you?"

C (1)- JOHN 2:1-12

In His "first sign" in this beautiful Gospel of St. John, Jesus transforms simple water into the finest and choicest wine. It is a fitting sign of what Jesus has been sent by God to do: to transform our world from darkness into God's banquet table of hope and joy.

I loved reading the columns of the late Erma Bombeck, the humorist. I remember one of her columns in which she tells the story of her being in church one Sunday. Erma was looking at a small child in the pew in front of her. This beautiful, little child was turning around and smiling at everyone. The child wasn't humming or kicking the pew, or making any kind of noise or rummaging through his mother's handbag. No – he was just smiling at everyone. Finally, Erma says, (and I quote) "His mother jerked him about and in a stage whisper that could be heard throughout the church, said, 'Stop that grinning! You're in church!' With that she gave him a slap and as the tears rolled down his cheeks added, 'That's better,' and she returned to her prayers. Erma said, "I was suddenly angry. It occurred to me that the entire world was in tears today. I wanted to grab this little child with the tear-stained face and tell him about my God, the happy God, the smiling God, the God who changes water to wine, the God who had a sense of humor to have created the likes of us." Here was a woman sitting next to the only light left in our civilization, the only hope, our only miracle. If he couldn't smile in church, where was there left to go?"

MDP, in this beautiful Gospel of the Wedding Feast at Cana, Jesus works His first sign by creating wine. He was at a party where there was fun, and joy; where there was dancing and happiness. St. John tells us that Cana is a symbol of God's Kingdom. He tells us that as followers of Jesus we are to be people of joy, that there's no room for doom and gloom in our lives.

The Wedding Feast symbolizes a new age, an age where wine bubbles in our cups, an age where God chose to intervene in our history. When we hear the story of Cana, we need no further sign. Our conviction and happiness is based on the firm belief that God broke into the personal history, the personal lives of each one of us, that God threw a wedding party, that the darkness, the worries, that we sometimes find ourselves in are but a passing state.

MDP, when God causes miracles, He doesn't want us to just believe in miracles, signs, wonders, He wants us to believe in Him and to cause others to believe in Him. For me, and now I hope for you, this is precisely the encouragement we are to take from this beautiful Gospel.

C (2) - JOHN 2:1-12

A little while ago I read a fascinating article about a woman redecorating her family's home. Things went well until her husband overruled the interior decorator and hung a 16 by 20 inch picture of Jesus in the most prominent place in the house. The woman tried to get her husband to reconsider, but he absolutely refused. Then, during a discussion with him, she recalled these words of Jesus: "Everyone who acknowledges Me before others, I will acknowledge before my Heavenly Father."

That settled it; her husband won! Now she says she's glad her husband won, because she thinks that picture of Jesus has had a remarkable effect on her family, and on visitors. For example, one day a stranger kept glancing at the picture. Finally, he turned to the woman and said, "You know, the Jesus in that picture of yours doesn't look at you, He looks right through you!" And one night a friend sitting across from the picture said, "I always feel so peaceful in your home."

The picture's most striking impact, however, is in conversations, says the woman. It inevitably draws them to a higher level. The woman ended her article by saying she knows people will smile at her remarks and even ridicule them, but she doesn't care. "This much I know," she says, "when you invite Jesus into your home, you're never the same again."

The young couple in today's Gospel would agree with that woman. They invited Jesus into their home, and He worked His first miracle there. And they were never the same again!

A little known fact about Jesus is how often He worked miracles in people's homes. For example, when Peter first invited Jesus to his home, the first thing Jesus did was to cure Peter's mother-in-law. When Jairus, the synagogue official, invited Jesus to his home, the first thing Jesus did was to restore life to Jairus' daughter who had just died. Neither Peter's family nor Jairus' family was ever the same again!

Then, there was a leading Pharisee. He invited Jesus to dinner one day, and one of the first things Jesus did was to cure a sick man at his house. And can we forget Zacchaeus, the tax collector of Jericho? He welcomed Jesus into his house one day. The two talked for a while, and Zacchaeus ended up giving half his belongings to the poor and paying back from those he cheated, four times what he took. And finally, there's the episode at Emmaus on Easter night. Two men invited Jesus to supper, although at the time they did not know it was Jesus. Jesus ended up celebrating with them the very first Eucharist after the Last Supper, and they were never the same again!

MDP, I wonder if some of us have ever invited Jesus into our homes in a practical way? If an interior decorator, for example, checked over our home, would he or she see any evidence that we are followers of Jesus? Or would the decorator merely say, "I see that your kids are big followers of Bruce Springsteen or Michael Jackson." Or suppose your daughter brought home a friend from college: would that friend say to her on their return to college: "Your family is really Christian. I can never remember praying at meals in our home, but we prayed before meals in your home. There was something else. I can't remember hearing your family put anyone down." That college friend would never be the same again, because she had met Jesus in your home!

MDP, this is one of the messages of today's beautiful Gospel. It is a message we all need to hear. It is a message we all need to take to heart. It is a message that could change our family life together. In the words of my friend who wrote the article: "This much I know. When you invite Jesus into your home, you will never be the same again!"

THIRD SUNDAY IN ORDINARY TIME
A −(1) MATTHEW 4:12-23

Father Robert McCahill is the only Catholic in the predominately Muslim town of Kishorganj in Bangladesh. He lives alone in a small hut in the village. The law of the Islamic country forbids him from any form of proselytizing, including saying Mass and preaching publicly. But in his quiet life among them, this Maryknoll priest has taught his Muslim neighbors a great deal about Christ, and about practical Christianity. He has lived this beautiful Gospel of today.

By the first light of each day, people begin to gather at his door seeking his help. He provides them with medicine for the sick and help in getting the seriously ill to a hospital. He offers food and what help he can to the poor. He is a familiar figure in the village, going to homes of those too sick to come to him. Father McCahill is a regular at a small restaurant in the town. The owners are used to him inviting beggars and the poor to join him at his table. What they can't figure out is why the priest serves them and pours their tea for them as if he were their hired servant. Father McCahill simply tells them what St. James wrote in his epistle: "In the eyes of God, perfect and practical religion is helping those in need." That makes sense to his Muslim friends who have learned the same lessons from the Koran. On Ash Wednesday, people ask him about the black smudge on his forehead. He uses it to tell them about Lent and Easter. His Muslim friends understand because each year they celebrate a month of prayer and fasting called "Ramadan." As he walks through the streets of Kishorganj, Father McCahill is greeted with Bhai Bob, Brother Bob.

My dear people, in the ordinary events of every day we are presented with the opportunities to uncover the extraordinary love of God. Those of us who truly hear Christ's call to be His disciples (in this Gospel), and embrace the real spirit of such a calling such as Peter, James, John and Father McCahill, we are able to celebrate God's presence in their lives and help others realize that same love in their lives. With this beautiful Gospel Jesus is calling us now. He wants us to become real true, practical "fishermen". He wants to put us in circulation as His ambassadors of love.

A (2)- MATTHEW 4:12-23

The Apostles left their nets behind and walked down the beach after Jesus to begin the work of preparing for the Kingdom. That work continues even now, and all who are followers of Christ in any way must be fishers of men. But we "trap" others not by laying snares for them, not by tricking them, not by pressuring them; we catch them by the strength of our faith, the generosity of our love, and the confidence of our hope and joy. It might be easy to turn men into Christians by force; but it is extremely difficult to charm them by our faith and our love. Yet, this is how Jesus worked. We are to be fishers of men not because of the persuasiveness of our arguments but by the witness, the kind of persons we are, and the sort of lives that we live.

If our nets are empty today, the reason may be that there are so many holes in the nets – in other words, so many weaknesses in our faith, that those to whom we are trying to preach can see right through us.

B - MARK 1:14-20

In today's Gospel, Christ's first words to Peter and Andrew have a curious explosiveness. They struck Peter and Andrew with such power that they immediately dropped their nets to go with Him. "Come with Me; I will make you fishers of men."

Jesus noticed Peter and Andrew with their nets and in the act of fishing; He sees a relationship between what they are doing now and what they might do. Peter and Andrew have fished all of their lives; fishing is their living and their competence. Any attempt to persuade them to abandon a livelihood, to scrap a career on the spot in order to pick up another, had to have a special flavor. Jesus observed what Peter and Andrew were doing; they fished in one way now, and they might fish in another way in time to come. In this sense, He turned their present into their future.

Former Speaker of the House, Thomas "Tip" O'Neill recalled one of the most important lessons he learned early in his career: in 1935, just before election day in O'Neill's first campaign, a neighbor told him, "Tom, I'm going to vote for you tomorrow even though you didn't ask me to." A shocked O'Neill replied, "Why, Mrs. O'Brien, I've lived across from you for 18 years. I cut your grass in the summer. I shoveled your walk in the winter. I didn't think I had to ask for your vote." Mrs. O'Brien replied, "Tom, let me tell you something: people like to be asked."

Like Peter, Andrew, James and John, we are asked by Jesus to take on the work of discipleship; we are asked to leave our "fishing nets" – our own needs and wants – to follow the example of love and servanthood given to us by Jesus; we are asked to rebuild our lives, our families, our cities, our world, in justice and peace, to proclaim in whatever circumstances we find ourselves, the love God has for us.

I read a simple but beautiful thought in an issue of "Spirituality and Health." It was written by Mary Ann Rollano. She writes about how a mom learns about the power of a mother's kiss. Mary Ann says: My youngest daughter always had me kissing her boo-boos. I did it because, as every mother knows, it makes it feel better. What I never understood was the thought process behind the action. One day my daughter asked me to kiss her boo-boo when I was so pressed for time; so I hurriedly obliged. She cried, telling me it wasn't any good because my kiss didn't have any love in it. I realized that kissing boo-boos was really about loving the pain away. This simple truth, along with the value of mindfulness my daughter taught me, has encouraged me to slow down to become more aware and present in the moment. Slowing down is a conscious decision to live life at a gentler pace and to make the most of the time I have.

When my own mother passed away, I did not forget the love she gave me; it will live on in my heart forever. She gave me life, but beyond that, she gave me love. With that errant kiss, I realized it was my responsibility as a mother to watch over my child's spiritual growth. By simply showing my child kindness through listening, I believe I have satisfied my child's earliest spiritual needs. By being genuine – that is personally connected and physically present – I have satisfied my child's developing spirit.

MDP, as God is present to us in the person of Jesus, we are called to be present to one another in our love and care. To be the "fishers" that Christ calls us to become is to "cast the net" of God's love that we have experienced in the waters of our own time and place, to reach out and grasp the hand of those who struggle and stumble, to "love" away the hurt and pain and fear of all those we love, to walk with Jesus to become "fishers" of the life and love of God.

C - Luke 1:1-4;

We saw in today's beautiful Gospel that Jesus began His public ministry with the words from Isaiah the prophet: The Spirit of the Lord is upon Me, because He has anointed me to bring glad tiding to the poor, to proclaim liberty to captives and recovery of sight to the blind, to let the oppressed go free, to proclaim the Lord's favor." In Christ, Isaiah's words are fulfilled, and we who follow Christ must be willing to bring His vision to the world.

I must tell you a very personal story about two friends of mine, Nina and Vinney. My friend, Vinney, was a widower; his wife had suffered a long and painful death from cancer. He met Nina, and they came to love each other and each other's children dearly. Less than a year into their courtship, Nina discovered a lump in her breast. She had gone to the doctor alone, and was alone when she received the devastating news: the lump in her breast was malignant. Almost her first thought was of Vinney and his children. They had been profoundly wounded by cancer only a few years before. They were still healing from it. How could she bring this terrible thing into their lives again?

She called Vinney immediately and without telling him why,

simply broke off their relationship. For several weeks she refused his phone calls and returned his letters. But Vinney would not give up and begged her to see him. Finally, Nina relented and arranged to meet him to say good-bye. When they met, she could see the deep strain and hurt on his face. Vinney gently asked Maria why she had broken up with him. Finally, on the verge of tears, she told Vinney the truth: that she had found a lump in her breast, that it was malignant, that she had undergone surgery a few weeks before and would begin chemotherapy the following week. She said to Vinney, "You and the children have lived through this once already, and I won't put you through it again." Vinney looked at her, his jaw dropping. "You have cancer?" he asked. Nina nodded, the tears beginning to run down her cheeks. "Oh, Nina," he said, and began to laugh with relief. "We can do cancer. We know how to do cancer. I thought that you didn't love me." Oh, but she did. And they got through it together – happily married.

MDP, today's Gospel of compassion is "fulfilled" every time we try to imitate Jesus. Whether we can "do cancer" or whether we know how to comfort and console another, whether we can help in soup kitchens or meals on wheels, or in our own parish, we can make Isaiah's vision a reality in our own particular Nazareths. As followers of Christ we must "bring glad tidings" and we must proclaim the Lord's favor to the poor, to our family and friends, to this world of ours. Whatever gifts and graces we possess, we can work wonderful things when we do them in the name and spirit of the Lord.

FOURTH SUNDAY IN ORDINARY TIME
A – Matthew 5:2-12

In the 1950's Dr. Tom Dooley captured the imagination of the world. After graduating from medical school, Dooley enlisted in the Navy as a doctor. The big day of his life came one hot July afternoon off the coast of Vietnam. That's when his ship rescued 1000 refugees who were drifting helplessly in an open boat. Many of the refugees were diseased and sick. Since Dr. Dooley was the only doctor on the ship, he had to tackle, single-handedly, the job of giving medical aid to these people. It was backbreaking, but he discovered what a little medicine could do for sick people like this. He said, "Hours later, I stopped a moment, to straighten my shoulders and made another discovery – I was happy treating these people, happier than I had ever been before." Dooley's experience that hot July afternoon changed his life forever. When he got out of the Navy, he returned to the jungles of Asia and set up a small hospital to serve the poor and the sick.

In reading the life of Tom Dooley one finds out quickly that one of his favorite Bible passages was the one I just read – the Beatitudes or Sermon on the Mount. Tom said that his work among the poor gave him a new insight into the meaning of the Beatitudes. Take, for example, he says, the Beatitude, "Blest too are the sorrowing," which we sometimes translate, "happy are those who mourn." Applying this beatitude to himself, Dooley said: "To mourn is to be more aware of the sorrow in the world than of the pleasure. If you are extra sensitive to sorrow," he said, "then you must do something, no matter how small, to make it lighter – you can't help but be happy. That's just the way it is."

Let's take another Beatitude: "Blest are those who are poor in spirit." The "poor in spirit" are people like those Dr. Dooley ministered to in the jungles of Asia. They are people whose helpless situation in life forces them to place all their trust in God. They are the "humble people of the land" that Zephaniah talks about in the first reading.

They are the weak and the despised that Paul talks about in the second reading. The 'poor in spirit' are the people who are detached from worldly things and totally attached to heavenly things. They are the people who regard material things as nothing and the good Lord as everything. They are found not only among society's rejected people but also among it's most successful people.

There's a story I like about Pope John XXIII. One of John's first acts as Pope was to visit a large prison in Rome. He told the inmates, "You couldn't come to me, so I came to you." He also told them that the last time he went to a prison was to visit his cousin. The next day the Vatican newspaper omitted the Pope's reference to his cousin. The paper was afraid some of the readers would be shocked to learn that a Papal relative was in jail. Pope John illustrates the fact that many of the world's truly great people rarely see themselves as great.

There's a Malayan Proverb which compares great people to rice stalks in a rice field. It goes like this: "The more grain a rice stalk has, the lower it bends down to the ground. The fewer grains it has, the higher it lifts itself into the air."

To be rejected is a devastating experience. A friend turns against us, a favorite teacher is unfair to us, we work up enough nerve to ask for a date and get a flat no. We try to have a party and no one can come, we make an overture toward friendship and are ignored; we offer a gift and it is scarcely noticed. We work hard on a good dinner and no one seems to enjoy it – great or small, experiences of rejection hurt, and they particularly hurt when they come from those we love. They hurt even more when the basic reason for the rejection is envy, when our loved ones turn against us because we do well. Envy would kill if it could; it would kill the goodness in us, the excellence; and if the matter is serious enough, it can actually destroy physical life.

So the Gospel today tells us to take a hard look at ourselves, to ask to what extent we qualify to be called "Blest" by the good Lord. Am I a person whom Jesus would give the name merciful? Am I a person whom Jesus would give the name peacemaker? Am I a person to whom Jesus would give the name poor in spirit?

MDP, may we live lives centered in the compassion, mercy, justice and peace of God, so that we may be worthy to be counted among the "Blest" in the reign of God.

B – Mark 1:21-28

In the story "The Fugitive" by the famous Indian writer Tagore, a father returns home from the funeral rites of his wife. His boy of seven is standing at the window with eyes wide open and a golden chain hanging from his neck. The boy is full of thoughts, too difficult for his age. His father takes him in his arms and the boy asks him "Where is Mother?" The father answers, "In heaven," pointing toward the sky. The boy raises his eyes to the sky and stares in silence. His young mind sends out into the night the question, "Where is heaven"? No answer comes and the stars seem like burning tears in the darkness.

"Where is heaven"? Where is this place? What is it like? If we study the Gospels, we find that our Blessed Lord always talked about God. He talked about God as being the One and only real necessity. He talked to the rich young man about disposing of all his possessions because they were getting in the way of his knowing and loving God. He said that knowing and loving God is like a treasure hidden in the field, so valuable, that a person would sell everything he or she had in order to possess it. He said that the people who are really happy are those who are "poor in spirit" because they know they need God.

He tells His Disciples again and again what eternal life is: to know and to love God!

So, where is heaven? Where is hell? How should we, as followers of Christ, think about these questions?

It reminds me of the time when I was driving through a small town near a base where I was stationed. I took notice of a sign in front of the Unitarian Church announcing the subject of next Sunday's sermon. It read, "There is no hell!" and just across the street, in front of the little Baptist Church, there was another sign which read: "The hell there isn't."

I suppose it's natural to think of heaven and hell in terms of a geographical location; we really don't have the language to deal with this. So we sing about putting on our shoes and "walking all over God's heaven." Or we sing, "I want to be in that number when the saints go marching in." What are we marching into?

There's another story about a group of American tourists who were visiting Mount Vesuvius, the volcano in Naples, Italy. It happened that the volcano was in one of its active periods. One woman was completely awed by the hot smoke and steam coming from the crater, and cried out, "It is just like hell!" Well, there happened to be a British person standing nearby who turned to his friend and said, "My goodness, these American tourists; they've been everywhere!"

You see, MDP, there is a symbolic notion that heaven and hell are geographical locations. But Jesus never speaks in these terms. What He talks about is God, His Father. What He says is that we must think of heaven and hell in our relationship to God. The important thing in our lives is trying to know God, trying to live every day to be present to God, trying each day to enter into a loving relationship with God. So, heaven is being with God; and hell is being away from God, and worst of all, knowing that we are separated from Him.

In the Gospel today Jesus is confronted by a man possessed by a demon. The demon had taken over his life. He was living a kind of hell, a life separated from God.

This Gospel always reminds me of an incident that took place a few years ago in Ann Arbor, Michigan. A black, 19 year old teenager named Keshia Thomas was one of three hundred people who had assembled in downtown Ann Arbor to protest a rally by 17 members of the Ku Klux Klan. The anti-Klan protestors spotted a white male spectator wearing confederate flags on his vest and t-shirt. Keshia wanted to yell at him "What did I ever do to you?" But, before she knew it, one of her members hit the man with a sign and a swarm of angry demonstrators began beating him. Appalled, Keshia threw herself over the fallen man, shielding him from the kicks and punches. Thanks to Keshia, police were able to step in and disperse the crowd and rescue the unidentified man who suffered only a bloody nose. It was later learned that the man was not a member of the Klan. "You don't beat a man because he doesn't believe the same things you do," Keshia said. "He is still somebody's child." A photograph of Keshia protecting the man who only moments earlier had been a target of her protest became the enduring image of that day in Ann Arbor. A nineteen year old student changed a lot of minds and hearts that day – including more than one member of the Ku Klux Klan.

Keshia Thomas cast out the demons of racism and violence. There are demons all around us.

The Gospel forces us to ask ourselves if there is a demon in our lives forcing us to separate from God. Could the demon be, for example, a destructive relationship that has made us push God aside and is tearing us to pieces? Or could the demon be a lust for power, for material possessions? Or could the demon be the demon of unforgiveness toward someone who desperately needs our healing words? If so, the Gospel tells us to identify the demon, face up to it, confront it in the name of Jesus of Nazareth. "What do you want of me, Jesus of Nazareth"? The demon shrieks in the Gospel. Jesus answers, "I want to give you peace; wholeness of life. I want you to know yourself for who you are and what you ought to be doing with your life. I want you to understand that the way to heaven is heaven when you are living your life every day in the presence of almighty God.

There is a story about Thomas Jefferson when he founded the University of Virginia in the years after his presidency. Jefferson established a code of discipline for the students which was very lax. He trusted them; he trusted that the students would take their studies seriously. But Jefferson's trust was betrayed when one day a group of rowdy, drunken students rioted. Professors who tried to restore order were attacked with bricks and sticks.

The following day the defiant students were called before the University's Board of visitors, chaired by Jefferson. Here sits Thomas Jefferson who once held the honor of being a Governor of Virginia, the architect of America's Independence, Secretary of State, and President.

He looked at the students and began saying, "This is one of the most painful events of my life." But he could say no more. Overcome by emotion, Jefferson broke down and could not continue. Another member of the board had to take over the meeting. No amount of censure or reprimand could have had such an extraordinary effect. Each of the students came forward, admitted his guilt and accepted his punishment. One of the students said afterward, "It was not Mr. Jefferson's words, but his tears."

C – Luke 4:21-30

Sometimes I think God has taken a calculated risk with man! By working through us rather than revealing Himself directly, like some lightening bolt, God really becomes vulnerable. You see, He leaves Himself open so that His Word could be rejected.

This is what happened when God made Himself vulnerable in Jesus, and Jesus was nailed to the cross by the people He came to serve and to save. And this is what the Psalmist was saying today when he wrote, "I will sing of your salvation."

There is a marvelous Jewish story about a remote Polish village that had not been visited by a clock maker for many years. After a while, the clocks in the village got out of whack and were all telling different times. Most of the villagers gave up on even winding their useless clocks. Finally, a wandering clock maker did show up. The villagers ran to him with their clocks to have them set and repaired. But the clocks had rusted and corroded from long years of disuse – except for one clock, whose owner had wound it each day. Even though he knew it was not telling the right time, he remained hopeful that a clock maker would one day come to the village.

MDP, the man and woman of faith, the faithful Christian, is often like that one man. Through prayer, through the daily practice of our faith, we can keep our spiritual works wound up even though we sometimes are not sure of the specific direction God intends for our life. But God is always active in our lives no matter how far we might think He is from us! In every decision we make, we must be alert to signs of God's direction for our lives. We must never let ourselves be deceived by routine, by boredom, by the "everyday ordinaries" of our lives. God can and does break through routine! He breaks through what we might consider trivial! He's there in all the interruptions of our lives! He's there in every step we take.

On one of the Marine bases on which I was stationed in California, I had invited a professor to speak on the occasion of a national holiday. Well, I sent my clerk, a young Marine named Ralph, to meet the professor at the airport. Ralph was an unusual man, and the professor soon realized it. As they headed toward the baggage claim area, Ralph kept disappearing: once to help an older woman with her suitcase; once to lift kids so that they could see Santa Claus; and again to give someone directions. Each time Ralph came back smiling. "Where did you learn to live like that?" the professor asked. Ralph told the professor about his tour in Vietnam. His job was to clear the mine fields, and he saw many of his fellow marines meet untimely ends, one after another, before his eyes. Ralph said, "I learned to live between the steps." "I never knew whether the next one would be my last, so I had to get everything I could out of that moment between picking up my foot and putting it down again. Every step felt like a whole new world."

In today's beautiful Gospel we read that 'Jesus began speaking in the synagogue.' "Today this Scripture passage is fulfilled in your hearing." All who were present spoke favorably of Him. They marveled at the appealing discourse which came from His lips. And so it is with us. So it is in our daily lives, in our routines, in our interruptions. Each step of the day can be a moment of grace, of an encounter with the Jesus who spoke in the synagogue; we can make the minutes of our days, the stories of our lives with family and friends, be moments of rebirth, of transformation, of healing. May we remain ever alert and attentive to His voice in the steps in our lives. And when we recognize His voice, even if we hear it today, like my clerk, Ralph, let us know that every step can be a whole new world!

FIFTH SUNDAY IN ORDINARY TIME
A - MATTHEW 5:13-16

The Gospels of Jesus Christ are so beautiful, and I am sure that you, like myself, have some favorites, some that strike at the heart. This is one of those for me. I cannot tell you how many times in my life, in my priesthood, when I have met and been inspired by so many good people, that I tell them, "you are the salt of the earth; you are really a light in this world."

You know them, ordinary people, just like you and just like me. That is what this Gospel is all about: Jesus challenges us ordinary people to do extraordinary things. When He calls us to be "salt" and "light" He is pleading with us to live the Gospel we have just heard and to profess it and to believe it. He is telling us that we must be committed to work for justice in our world, for the protection of life from the moment of conception to the grave, to pray for peace and holiness in our homes, with our husbands and wives, with our children, our friends; He is telling us we must profess our faith in the God who is Father of all, and unless this profession, this commitment affects every one of our relationships, then our lives mean as much to the world and to one another as salt that has gone flat or as useful as a light hidden under a bushel basket.

In 1993 I was the command Chaplain for the Marine Corps base in El Toro, California. One quiet afternoon, the phone rang in my office, and it was a priest Chaplain who worked for me at the helicopter base not far from El Toro. He was crying. I said, "Ed, what's wrong?" He told me that the police had just found the bloodied body of his sister, murdered in her apartment up in the Los Angeles area. I listened to the details of the senseless murder. Father Ed said to me, "I know I must follow the Lord's model and teach mercy and forgiveness, but I am having a hard time with it." To make a long story short, I attended his sister's funeral in Los Angeles. Father Ed preached the homily, and in effect, he said this: "It is not just the man who killed my sister who is on trial. We are all on trial. So much of what each of us does fosters violence in our families, in our societies. When we attempt to solve family problems through temper, ugly and harsh words … when we view television programs or movies where violence is glorified, when we use or condone the use of alcohol or drugs, we support and fuel the climate of violence." I often recall his words, and they came back to me as I took today's Gospel to heart.

MDP, we are at Mass today to ask for the grace to be "salt" for our families, our sons and daughters, our grandchildren, our friends, to make God's presence and grace realities in wherever we find ourselves during this week. It's a challenge to be "light for a world" that has many dark corners. It's a real challenge to light a world that is trying to find its way to almighty God and to His Son Jesus Christ.

B – MATTHEW 5:13-16

I want to tell you a little story that has stayed with me for years. I was the command Chaplain for a U.S. Marine Air Wing in California. One day we received the news that one of our Marines was killed in a Marine Corps operation. I remember how we all gathered on a Friday morning to have the funeral Mass. The lovely and faithful wife of this Marine was there with her four children. She was a model of grace throughout the Mass and the ceremonies that followed. As she was leaving the church, I hugged her and offered to do whatever I could to help her. She said to me, "Thank you, Father, but we will see you Sunday for Mass." And, foolishly, I said, "You have enough on your hands right now, don't be too concerned about Mass; I know it's a very hard time for you." She said, "I know it's hard. It's already hard, but you see, this is my church, and my church is going to see that my children and I are okay."

The church reminds us today that we are God's very own people, and because we are God's people we can be people of joy. We know in our hearts that God gives Himself to us in the dark moments; but, He also gives Himself in moments of joy. It is summed up in those beautiful words of the Gospel: "Do not let your hearts be troubled; do not be afraid. Have faith in God and in Me!"

One of the worst moments in World War II came when the Nazis occupied Warsaw and proceeded to slaughter the Jews. There was a young Jewish girl who managed to escape and hide herself in a cave outside the city. She died there all alone. But before she died, she scratched on the wall of the cave these words:

I believe in the sun, even when it is not shining.

I believe in love, even when feeling it not.

I believe in God, even when He is silent.

MDP, Jesus put it this way: "Do not be afraid; do not let your hearts be troubled. Have faith in God and faith in Me." God is God! As the old spiritual song says, "He has His eye on the sparrow, and so, He has His eye on me."

I hope and pray that His resurrection becomes the meaning and purpose of our lives, and helps us with all the 'whys' of our lives as we make our journey to the kingdom of His Father.

A (1)– MARK 1:29-39

Earlier in today's Gospel lesson, Jesus and the Apostles James and John go to the house of Simon Peter and his brother Andrew. There they learned that Simon Peter's mother-in-law had gone to bed with a fever. Jesus "went to see her." Mark tells us, "He took her by the hand and helped her up. And the fever left her."

There is an amusing little story about a woman who went to church one Sunday morning and listened to the very same Gospel that I just read to you. The woman was listening to her priest preach a sermon about Simon Peter's mother-in-law who was ill with a fever. For the woman, not only was the Gospel an obscure text, but also the priest gave a boring sermon on the Gospel. The woman lasted through the experience, but left the church feeling somewhat unfulfilled. So, she decided to go to church again that day, out in the country where she had grown up.

When she arrived, she discovered to her dismay that the same priest from her parish had been invited to be the guest preacher, and again he chose to preach the same sermon about Peter's mother-in-law being ill with a fever.

Believing that there was still time to redeem the day, the woman decided to go to the hospital chapel. As you may have guessed, the same priest was there doing hospital duty, and he preached the same sermon on Peter's mother-in-law and her fever. The next morning, the woman was on a bus riding downtown and, believe it or not, the same priest boarded the bus and sat down beside her. An ambulance raced by with sirens roaring. In order to make conversation, the priest said, "Well, I wonder who it is?" The woman replied, "Surely it must be Peter's mother-in-law. She was sick all day yesterday!"

There is another scene in today's Gospel that is so significant. Mark says, that Jesus slipped away to pray. His Disciples went looking for Him, and when they found Him, said something that has echoed through the centuries: "Everyone is searching for You."

MDP, everyone is still searching for Him! At the deepest level of our being we long to fulfill our potential, and at times we imagine that we can do this by honoring one passing whim or another, one limping value system or another. But I must tell you that only when we are 'right' with God, when we stand on our own two feet and live our lives in the presence of God, will we experience happiness.

I need to tell you about a woman who was recently diagnosed with cancer. Despite being well off financially, she always had a feeling of emptiness. Seeking to fulfill that void, she amassed more and more things – books, and magazines, and antiques, and closets full of clothes, and more and more people made demands on her life. But the more she accumulated, the less time she had to enjoy them or appreciate them, and even worse, to know what she really had. Her motto had become, "Have everything, experience nothing."

This all began to change with a bathrobe, one of the few things she took to the hospital for her cancer surgery. Every morning she would put it on and took comfort in how soft it was; she enjoyed its beautiful color, its warmth, the way it moved around her when she walked. She later told her doctor, "One morning as I was putting my bathrobe on, I had an overwhelming sense of gratitude. I know it sounds funny, but I felt so lucky just to have it. But the odd part is that it wasn't new. I had owned it and worn it now and then for quite a few years. Possibly because it was one of the five bathrobes in my closet, I had never really noticed it before."

When she completed her chemotherapy, she had a huge garage sale and sold more than half the things that cluttered her home. Her friends thought she had gone "chemo-crazy," but getting rid of so many possessions brought a new joy and appreciation to her life. Until her illness, she had no idea of what was in her closets; she didn't even know half the people whose telephone numbers were in her address book. But the few things she has she now enjoys; she has fewer but much deeper friendships. Having and experiencing, she discovered are very different.

MDP, again St. Mark tells us that Jesus sought out a "deserted," and out of the way place to pray. We all need that deserted place in which we can reconnect with God and the things of the heart, things that really matter. That "deserted" place may be a set time for prayer every day, a walk in the neighborhood, a quiet corner of the house or apartment or condo – or even a bathrobe – whatever keeps us aware of God's presence in our life and renews within us a sense of gratitude for the blessings we receive by living our lives in His presence.

B (2)- MARK 1:29-39

I remember telling you this during my Christmas homily that one of the deepest secrets of the spiritual life is this: when God gives us light unless we share it, it fades out, dissipates, and darkness returns. This explains some of the problem areas in the lives of so many of us. Sometimes when the darkness in our lives is at its worst, God gives us light in a wonderfully healing way. But how we lose it again; how often that grace, that light God gives us fades and is gone! And the darkness returns! Not because God isn't there but because we have turned it in on ourselves; we have let God's grace stagnate and die. If our lives seem to be in a rut, if things seem to be getting us down, if we don't seem to be growing spiritually, if our development, as a uniquely beautiful person seems to have ceased, it's not that God isn't there, it's that we like Job in the first reading are living our very own lives like the wind.

In the Tennessee Williams play, "Streetcar named Desire," Blanche is a person whose world is falling apart. She is looking for some solid ground to stand on, some center for her life. She desperately needs to be loved. Unfortunately, she is one of those people who talks all the time in a way that denies them the very thing they want most, which is for people to love them. That is Blanche's ongoing problem as her life keeps falling apart until, in the play, she meets a man named Mitch. He too has a problem. He is much overweight and, as he explains to her, he perspires profusely. Mitch is a very lonely person and very much in need of love too. They get to the point where Blanche is able to share with him one of the tragic moments in her life. She tells him about it and about its terrible consequences and when she is finished, Mitch takes her in his arms and says, "You need somebody and I need somebody too. Could it be you and me, Blanche?" Blanche stares at him in disbelief and then, with a soft cry, she gives herself to his embrace. Sobbing in joy and in continuing disbelief, she says this beautiful line just before the curtain goes down: "Sometimes there's God – so quickly!"

This is exactly what most of us have experienced. When we need it most, when our worries, fears and anxieties are most frightening, there's God – so quickly! This happened to Blanche in the play and it happens to many of us.

Maybe the reason why we don't grow spiritually, that we don't feel fulfilled is that we have not opened ourselves outward to share our love, to communicate it to others.

Since Vatican II, the Church has been going through some turmoil and rebellion in some sectors. Countless numbers of people have turned off the church. I am beginning to think that some of us in the church have really built walls around ourselves and have not shared ourselves and our faith with the world.

For example, this incident I am about to relate which makes me shake my head in disbelief, truly took place recently in one of our downtown Christian churches. Apparently, this church had purchased some new cushions for the sanctuary and held a ritual called the "blessing of the cushions!" This is how it went: "The Lord be with you. And also with you. Dear God we bless and dedicate these exquisitely beautiful, three inch thick reversible cushions that have been made with heave duty damask of Italian renaissance design, with welted seams and self covered buttons, which have been provided by the wise plans and effort of the St. Luke's Ladies Guild and the gracious contributions of a visitor. May the Blessing of God the Father, the Son and the Holy Ghost descend upon these cushions."

Horrible as the example is for me I think it helps indicate something of the image that a great many people have of the church. Here is a church blessing cushions while, less than a block away, there are people because of the earthquake with no beds, no cushions, no place to lay their heads. There are people three miles from this church sharing drug needles, scared with aids. Around the corner from this church, are young women planning their abortions.

Today's Gospel lesson tells us that Jesus entered the house of the Apostle Peter and cured his mother-in-law who was sick with a fever. Later in the day, the Disciples "brought to Him all who were sick or possessed with demons. And the whole city was gathered about the door. And He healed many who were sick.

There's a smart story about a parish church that was having a homecoming service to which ex-members who had moved away were invited. Now one ex-member who attended was a man who had become a multi-millionaire. He, along with others, were giving a little testimony on their faith experience. The rich man spoke of the time when, as a little altar boy in that church, he had earned his first dollar – a silver dollar at that.

He said, "I had decided to keep it forever. But a visiting missionary came to the church and preached about the urgent need for funds in his mission work. Consequently, when the offering basket was passed a great struggle took place inside of me. As a result, I put my treasured silver dollar in the basket. I am convinced that the reason God has blessed me so richly is that when I was a boy I gave God everything I possessed."

The congregation was spellbound by the rich man's testimony until a little old lady in the front pew rose and said to that multi-millionaire, "Brother, I dare you to do it again."

Only when we are 'right' with God will we experience happiness.

An elderly priest known for his preaching and good works in many parts of our county, was one day traveling by plane. Seated next to him was a famous and fabulously rich lady who was very often in the news. The priest who recognized her, engaged her in conversation.

"What is it like to go into a store knowing you can buy anything?" he asked. She replied, "Oh, you get used to it." But being sharp herself, she turned his question around. She asked, "What is it like to go into a store and know you can't buy anything?" The priest answered, "Oh, you get used to it." Then he said, "I wish I could trade places with you for just one day!" And it was the lady's turn. She told him what it would be like if they traded places: Lots off money; yes, but two bitter divorces that left her angry and hurt; never ever knowing who was your real friend; never knowing if people were there because they really cared about you as a person or because they were attracted to your money.

Then, the priest talked about his life. He told her what it was like to travel the country talking about Jesus Christ. He told her what it was like to work in the ghettos with young people, helping them get to college, helping them to get moving with their lives. He told her what it was like to pray with the people he loved. He told her what it was like to have the loyalty and support of the members of his parish congregation. And when he finished the rich lady said, "I would give everything I have for a life like yours."

And then there was silence. They were both thinking about the same thing: she had the money; he had a life that was right with God. I am sure it was clear to both who was truly rich.

C – Luke 5:1-5

One of the finest tours I had in my Navy career was being the command Chaplain for the Marine Corps Recruit Depot, San Diego, where in three years I was pastorally responsible for 50,000 young men graduating as Marines.

From the first moments the young recruits arrived at the base, they encountered the legendary drill instructors. In booming voices these drill instructors would say to the recruits, "You will get to know me better than you know your mother!" How true! The young recruits experienced the drill sergeants through most of their senses: they heard them, they saw them, they thought about them, they responded to them. The drill sergeants were the most significant part of their lives.

MDP, after Simon Peter, James and John encountered Jesus on the lake, they would see Him, think about Him, respond to Him. From that moment on the lake, they would never be the same again. And just like those young recruits, it all began when Peter listened to Jesus: "Put out into deep water and lower your nets for a catch." They did it, and how generously the good Lord rewarded them: those fishermen gave up all – their nets, their boats, their very lives – to be with Jesus. Three simple fishermen – three recruits – were caught in Christ's net. He was now the Lord of their lives. "Follow Me," He said; they listened and today we call them Saints.

During the reign of Oliver Cromwell, the British government began to run low on silver coins. Cromwell reportedly sent some of his treasury people to see if they could find any silver in the great cathedrals. After visiting a major cathedral, the investigators reported to Cromwell, "The only silver we could find is in the statues of the saints standing in the corners." To which Cromwell replied, "Good, we'll melt down the saints and put them into circulation!" Even though he didn't intend it, Cromwell proposed some good theology, that is not to cram silver coated saints into the corners of elegant churches; no, the first priority of the everyday Christian is to be a real, live, good, saintly human being in circulation.

The first priority of the everyday Christian, whether he or she is a mom or dad or grandparent, teacher, musician, computer expert, doctor, lawyer, engineer, or priest is to be "catchers of people for God." The first priority of the everyday Christian is to melt down the hearts of others with the fire of God's love and to proclaim the Good News of our Lord Jesus Christ.

Once, on the Oprah Winfrey show, I heard the American poet, Maya Angelou, talk about her rediscovery of God. She said, "In my twenties in San Francisco, I became an acting agnostic. It wasn't that I stopped believing in God; it just seemed that God wasn't around the neighborhoods that I frequented." One day," she continued, "my voice teacher asked me to read a passage from a book, a section which ended with these words: 'God loves me.' I opened the book, and sarcastically read, 'God loves me.' No, he said, read it again." Maya said, "After the seventh repetition, I began to sense that there might be truth in the statement, that there was a possibility that God really did love me, yes me, Maya Angelou. I suddenly began to cry at the wonder of it all. I knew that if God loved me, then I could do wonderful things, that I could do great things, achieve anything. For what could stand against me and God?" She ended by saying, "That knowledge humbles me, melts my bones, closes my ears and makes my teeth rock loosely in their gums."

MDP, in today's beautiful Gospel, Jesus invites us to feel what Maya Angelou felt; He wants us to inspire others, to encourage them, to enable them to become the beautiful persons He has created them – and all of us – to be. In the simple, ordinary events that we live every day, we are presented with hundreds of opportunities to "catch" others by the fire of our love, to melt their bones and rock their teeth, and put them in circulation as ambassadors of Jesus Christ.

SIXTH SUNDAY IN ORDINARY TIME
A – Matthew 5:17-37

When I taught a "creative writing" class I sometimes gave my students writing assignments which involved various aspects of their everyday living. Once, as the course was drawing to a close, I gave them a final assignment which put them in a state of shock. "Write your own obituary," I said. Later, one of the students said, for him, "the weirdest part of carrying out the assignment was choosing a date of death." Another said, "summarizing, in a few short paragraphs, who I was and what I did before I died was a growth experience." Still another said, "It brought home to me, as never before, the one thing we all share in common: at the moment of birth we begin our journey toward death."

Many years ago, a Eugene O'Neil play called "Lazarus Laughed" was produced on the Broadway stage. The play was based on the New Testament episode in which a friend of Jesus named Lazarus dies and his body is placed in the burial tomb. Three days later, Jesus raises Lazarus from the dead. In the death experience, Lazarus learned to appreciate the greatness of life, and he sees things in a whole new perspective. He is able to look upon the affairs of mankind with a cosmic insight. And it is all so funny that he laughs. He cannot contain himself from laughter over the way people worry and struggle and relate to one another. "Why are your eyes always watching one another with suspicion?" he asks.

The play reminds us that we all are destined to share in Lazarus' experience of death and seeing the affairs of mankind in a whole new perspective. Like Lazarus, perhaps, we shall ask: "Why are you always watching one another with suspicion? Why are you bearing grudges against one another?"

At a family reunion, the discussion turned to the subject of "living each day as though it were your last." When it was grandmother's turn to speak, she said, "I think it's a fine idea to live each day as though it were your last. But I've always tried to live by one that is slightly different. It is this: 'Treat all people you meet each day as though it were their last.'

In today's Gospel lesson, taken from the "Sermon on the Mount," Jesus says:

If you are bringing your offering to the altar and there remember that your brother has something against you, leave your offering there before the altar, go and be reconciled with your brother first, and then come back and present your offering. (Matthew 5:23-24)

The actor Michael Landon was driving home one Friday afternoon on a Los Angeles freeway. It was hot, and the traffic was horrendous, horns were blaring, tempers were flaring, and people were hurling insults at one another from open car windows. Landon asked himself why there is so much anger everywhere? Why do people hate one another so much? Why is so much energy wasted on rage? His mind went back to his own childhood and the anger that often raged between his Catholic mother and his Jewish father. Suddenly a thought flashed across his mind, why couldn't there be a television series dedicated to the idea that kindness, not anger, is the real answer to life's problems? At that moment, he conceived the idea for the television show "Highway to Heaven." The point of each episode of "Highway to Heaven" is the same point our Blessed Lord is making in today's Gospel: Show kindness to one another even to the point of "turning the other cheek."

My dear people, I have often tried in my homilies to tell you that the church is all wrapped up in the message that God so loved the world that He gave His only begotten Son. In other words, God gave us His Son to show us how much He loves us! And it's the Son who is saying to us in the Gospel: "If you are offering your gift at the altar, and there remember your brother or sister has something against you, leave your gift before the altar and go be reconciled to your brother or sister."

We cannot come to have any kind of a life in and with Christ with unforgiving hearts; we will never grow spiritually! Often, I have come to feel that a long-term unforgiving heart is the consequence of wanting to be in control of someone else's life. It's usually a case of wanting that 'someone else' to be just like us, without respect or regard for the other's individuality. It is hard at times to actually believe that certain people around us – people whom we can't stand because they are so full of faults – are capable of becoming better persons – without putting us in charge of the project. We just can't forgive them for that!

Here we are now at the altar with that Gospel ringing in our ears and our Blessed Lord is saying, "First be reconciled to your brother or sister or parent or child or friend or colleague or enemy, and then come and offer your gift."

You remember that old Indian saying which goes, "If you want to understand someone else, you must walk a mile in his or her moccasins." To be the kind of person Christ wants us to be we must empathize: put ourselves in another's place, feel another's pain, sense another's need. We need to listen to the other person. We need to understand; to call forth the best from the other person; to forgive and to accept forgiveness.

Let me return to Michael Landon for just a minute: one of the shows in the "Highway to Heaven" series dealt with child cancer victims. Landon and his staff got the idea to have real life victims play the parts. One victim was a boy named Josh Wood. His case was especially tragic because he had already lost a leg to cancer. But what bothered little Josh even more was the fact that he had a speech defect that caused him to stammer badly. People avoided talking to him because of his stutter, the more he stammered. Landon surprised everybody by asking Josh to audition for one of the parts, saying to the boy: "The important thing about acting is to be a good actor; if you stammer, that's okay. You're just a good actor who stammers." To everyone's amazement, when the boy read for the part, his stammer disappeared completely. Two years later Josh's cancer was in remission, and his stammer has never come back. Josh Wood's an example of the tremendous power that is contained in a little assurance and a little affirmation of what it means to call for the best from another person.

My dear mothers and dads, if I may speak to you just a bit personally: If you find yourselves in conflict with your children and, there will inevitably be some conflict during the adolescent and teenage years, I think it would be good to remember that you are just a little better equipped to empathize and try to understand than your child is. As parents most of you have been there, you have traveled the same road. You have experienced the same growing pains, for this reason the responsibility for empathy and understanding rests gently on your shoulders. Fathers and mothers would do well to remember what it was like for them during those sometimes bewildering, sometimes frightening early years of their lives. And parents who are unwilling to do that find themselves responding to their children's mistakes and misadventures as personal affronts. "How could you do this to me, I'll never forgive you for this." On the other hand, I would think that parents who are able to say, "I remember, that was me twenty years ago," are more likely to succeed in passing on the message of today's Gospel.

Empathize, put yourselves in the other's place; feel the other's pain; sense need; listen to one another; understand, call forth the best and forgive – and then come to the altar and bring your gift.

B – Mark 1:40-45

The leper says to Jesus in today's Gospel, "...you can make me clean..." Jesus put His hand on the leper and says, "I do will it." At that moment Jesus had effected a radical change in the man's life. He could begin to live again as a full human being.

MDP, the request of that leper is a challenge to all of us who follow Jesus. When we really follow Jesus, our lives are changed, almost inevitably. The Gospel is filled with examples of those who have accepted the challenge to follow Jesus: Peter and Andrew, James and John, Mary and Martha, the woman at the well, the woman caught in adultery, the blind, the lepers. When our Blessed Lord touched them, they started to come alive to God.

Nicodemus put it this way, "it's like being born again." So when we spend even a little time with Jesus, we are born into a whole new life! We are changed in the way we care for one another, in the way we love one another, in the way we share our gifts with one another. We find ourselves caring, for example, about what is going on in our world; caring about those among our friends who are shattered by some trauma; we care about those in this world who are devastated by injustice.

There is a scene in John Drinkwater's play, "Abraham Lincoln", where this exchange takes place between President Lincoln and a Northern woman, an anti-confederate zealot. Lincoln tells her about the latest victory by Northern forces – the Confederate Army lost 2700 men, while Union Forces lost 800. The woman is ecstatic. "How splendid, Mr. President!" Lincoln is stunned at her reaction. "But, Madam, 3500 human lives lost." "Oh, you must not talk like that, Mr. President. There were only 800 that mattered." Lincoln's shoulders drop as he says slowly and emotionally: "Madam, the world is larger than your heart."

MDP, the Christ who healed the leper comes to us to perform much greater miracles. For whatever reasons we are here today, there is a need in all of us to be touched by Christ in a way that will give us healing power and a renewed life. And so in experiencing this, we get in touch with one of life's most interesting paradoxes: that the more we are able to move out of ourselves and see the sacredness and dignity of those in our world, in our lives that we demean as "lepers," the more intensely we will experience the presence of God within ourselves.

One clever officer with whom I served in the Navy had this plaque on his desk: "When in charge, ponder; when in trouble, delegate; when in doubt, mumble!" The humor of all that is turned against us when we reflect on how often we respond to the 'leper at our door,' how we respond to our husband and wife, to our brother or sister, to a friend in need. How many times are we guilty of 'pondering', of endless discussions and idle reflections? How many times do we 'delegate' our consciences and not stand strong to defend our ethical values? How many times when we merely mumble pious words, on questions that require honest, firm, conscientious answers?

We have just celebrated Valentine's Day. I heard about a lovesick Romeo who wrote this letter to Susan, his love: "Dearest Susan, I would swim the mighty ocean for one glance from your lovely eyes. I would walk through a wall of fire for one touch of your soft hand. I would cross the widest river, climb the highest mountain for a single word from your warm lips." And he signed it, "As ever, your faithful, Arnold. P.S. I'll come to see you next Sunday if it doesn't rain!"

We, the people who are drawn close to the Christ who healed the leper, must resist the temptation of placing a "PS" on our love for one another. "PS – we are pondering your misfortune. PS – we are delegating our responsibility to heal your sadness, to alleviate your worries. PS – we mumble, PS …PS…PS"

MDP, we can never forget or overlook the 'lepers' at our door, whoever they may be. They will be the very agents of our salvation.

C – Luke 6:17, 20-26

I was moving things around in my house yesterday, and came across a box which contained all the medals that I wore on my uniform during my Navy career. The interesting thing was that in preparation for this Mass, I had just finished reading this beautiful Gospel on the Beatitudes. Looking at my medals, I remembered a cartoon in the New Yorker about two generals, with all their gold braid and complete with more than a dozen medals on their uniforms and carrying briefcases filled with military intelligence data, .are marching down the corridors of power at the Pentagon. One general says to the other: "I had a dream last night which really shook me up. I dreamed that the meek inherited the earth."

MDP, what Jesus is telling us in today's Gospel is that our fulfillment as beautiful persons created by God, depends necessarily upon our willingness to acknowledge that, if we are living our lives apart from God, we are nothing, and that we are truly blest and happy and fulfilled, when we are meek enough in spirit to stand before God, and look up to Him, and say to Him, 'This is me; this is the way I am; I really want to live my life in Your presence, but I need Your help.'

And the worst thing we can do for ourselves is to think that we can live our lives apart from God. It takes a powerful pride to do this, something akin to conceit and arrogance.

There is a story about how in the very depths of winter, a bird of prey was scouring the frozen landscape for food. On a large ice flow in the river, the bird saw the remains of a deer left behind by hunters. The bird swooped down and began to feast. The bird was so consumed by what he was consuming, that he ignored the sound of thundering water that was becoming increasingly louder by the minutes. In a second the ice flow was about to go crashing over the rivers falls. The bird immediately flapped its wings to escape, but its claws had become frozen into the icy remains of the deer. He was trapped, powerless to escape.

MDP, like that bird, sometimes we become so consumed in our

worries, our fears, our busyness, that we just forget to live our lives in the presence of God; we become so consumed by amassing the things that mark success that we lose our souls in the process. We are so absorbed in pursuing 'la dolce vita,' the good things of life, that we devalue and miss the real riches of the love of family, of husband for wife and wife for husband; we lose and miss the real meaning of friendship, the special sense of joy we experience in giving of ourselves to others; and we lose the peace and serenity that can be ours when we center our lives on the things of God.

In the Gospel today, Jesus spares no words in challenging us to embrace a new attitude and vision as to what separates us from God. Jesus puts it this way: "How Blest are the meek, for they shall inherit the land." And further He says, "Some who are last will be first and some who are first will be last." And again, "How happy, how Blessed, how fulfilled are the poor in spirit, for the Kingdom of Heaven is theirs."

SEVENTH SUNDAY IN ORDINARY TIME
A - MATTHEW 5:38-48

Some years ago *Newsweek* magazine carried a moving story. What first got you interested in the story was the photograph that accompanied it. It showed three boys, ages seven to eleven, kneeling in the front pew of a church. Below the photograph were the words, "This Was Left Behind."

The story went on to say that the eldest boy, Jerry, always turned on the radio immediately after he woke up in the morning. He liked to listen to the news while he dressed for school.

This particular morning the news was bad. Someone had placed a bomb on United Airlines Flight 629. It exploded over Colorado in mid-air, killing 44 persons.

Jerry finished dressing and started down the stairs. As he did, he saw his grandmother and the parish priest standing at the foot of the stairs.

Jerry took one look at them and said, "My mother and father were on that plane, weren't they?" Jerry was right.

Later that day the children of St. Gabriel's, where Jerry and his brother attended school, asked their pastor for a prayer service for their three classmates. The pastor asked Jerry if this would be all right. Jerry said it would. Then he added, "Could you also pray for the man who killed my mother and father?"

That story illustrates Jesus' commandment in today's Gospel, when He says:

"You have heard that it was said, 'you shall love your neighbor and hate your enemy.' But I say to you, love your enemies, and pray for those who persecute you."

I think it's interesting that the hero in that story is a child. Somehow children seem to understand the difficult teachings of Jesus so much better than adults do.

Perhaps that's why Jesus said, "Unless you turn and become like children, you will not enter the kingdom of heaven." Matthew 18:3

Some of you know how difficult it is to forgive others. The words of forgiveness can get stuck in our throats. It is easy to keep an argument alive! I know of moms and dads, children, aunts and uncles, friends, who, for a time, we would prefer not to be with; colleagues with whom we work who have done us wrong. It's strange but the "getting even," the argument that we engage in, is not usually with sworn enemies, but with those who we claim to love.

It seems that human intimacy, brings together different personalities, and so almost always involves tension and friction and conflict. With the closest of friends, with the most passionate of lovers there is friction at times; indeed, the stronger the feelings the more powerful the potential for argument, for friction, for conflict. Intimacy is so wonderful and so necessary, but intimacy demands that lovers, friends learn how to forgive. Sometimes I feel that if we could get inside the heart of the person we are in conflict with, that we are arguing with, if we could walk around their heart, we would find enough pain and sorrow there to disarm us of the hard feelings we have toward that person. We would see that person, in all of his or her humanity! We would see him or her as a father, a mother, a son. Daughter, aunt or uncle, a loved friend – all of them, who have their own song to sing, their own special love to give, message to speak. Yes, we will see them as God saw them when He created them!

Let me share with you a story I experienced not long ago. I was at the Tampa airport preparing for a flight to Philadelphia. I was in the line to check bags. At the head of the line, a man with several suitcases was arguing loudly with the airline clerk who had just told him that there would be an extra charge because his luggage was over the weight limit. The angry man did his best to embarrass and belittle the young clerk. All this was taking place with a long line of passengers listening. When the woman whom I was standing right next to, reached the head of the line, she said to the young clerk, "I'm so sorry that the man was rude to you. You really didn't do anything wrong. And it was good that you did not answer him. Yes, you did not do anything wrong; you were a perfect gentleman." To which the clerk replied, "Thank you, ma'am. I am a perfect gentleman." And then he smiled with a twinkle in his eye, he said to the lady, "That man is going to Philadelphia, and he doesn't know it yet, but his bags are going to Albuquerque!"

This is what our good Lord has in mind in today's Gospel. We who strive to follow Him must make up our minds whether we are strong enough and gentle enough to make these sacred words live in our hearts and lives: "You have heard it said that you shall love your neighbor and hate your enemy. But I say to you, love your enemies and pray for those who persecute you, that you may be children of your Heavenly Father."

B – Mark 2:1-12

In February 2001, the USS Greenville, a Navy submarine stationed in Hawaii, was on maneuvers in the Sea of Japan. During a test, the nuclear-powered submarine accidentally rammed a Japanese fisheries – school training boat. Five teachers and four students were killed. An investigation of the accident led to a letter of reprimand for the Captain of the submarine, Scott Waddle, and forced his retirement from the Navy.

The victims' families received letters of apologies from the highest levels of our government, as well as written apologies from Scott Waddle himself. But Scott Waddle knew he had to do more. Two weeks before Christmas, now civilian Waddle traveled to Japan to meet with the families of the victims and survivors. It was a difficult trip. Some of the families refused to meet him. The school did not want him to come to the campus, but relented, allowing Waddle to place a wreath at the school's memorial to the nine who died. Family and friends of Scott Waddle tried to discourage the trip, but the disgraced commander had made a promise to seek forgiveness in person.

He said, "I wanted to make sure that they knew my plea for forgiveness was sincere. I wanted them to understand, as a human being, that there was compassion from me." And he continued, "As a parent, there isn't a day that goes by that I don't look at my daughter, and my wife, and I feel that we know there's an emptiness that the families who lost loved ones, experience.

Jesus asks in today's Gospel: 'what is easier, to forgive one's sins or cure an illness.'

Some of us would answer, 'Curing the illness. Forgiveness requires too much from us: to forgive demands letting go of our own hurt and anger. Far easier to take a pill, stay in bed, set the broken limb, surgically repair the damaged organ, than to put our own pride, reputation, self- interest on the line.

MDP, when we strip away the fancy words about what it means to be a follower of Jesus Christ, it all comes down to whether we are loving, caring, forgiving persons. No amount of ornamentation, or superficial displays of piety can cover that up.

You remember in the Gospels that Jesus sets no limits on forgiveness. He tells us we must keep forgiving again and again. There really is no possibility of a Christian forgiving too often. Sometimes we say, "I'll forgive him or her for what he or she did to me because my religion says I must. But I'll never forget it." And the resentment keeps churning up inside. There is no real forgiveness here.

The Hebrew Talmud says that a person who harbors a resentment is like one who, having cut one hand while handling a knife, avenges himself by cutting the other hand. Many people are ill not because of what they are eating, but what is eating them inside. The medical and social sciences have long been telling us that harboring grudges and resentments literally help to make people sick. Forgiveness on the other hand can do more to make them well than pills and medicine.

All of us have known someone who is a "half-a-minder," that is someone who is always saying, "I have half-a-mind to do this or that." Actually, we are all half-a-minders, in many areas of our lives. But in the area of forgiveness, Jesus is telling us that half-way measures simply will not do.

In the art of forgiveness, we have to go all out. We have got to forgive unconditionally, with all our minds and all our hearts. We have got to forgive and forget the other's transgression until it has no meaning. How often? Don't even ask, because it is never enough.

On the way out of church one Sunday morning, an uptight parishioner said to the priest who was greeting her, "There is so much resentment between groups in this city that the very air is filled with it." To which the priest replied, "No, if you were to take a sampling of this air to a laboratory for analysis, you wouldn't find a trace of resentment in the air. Resentment is in the minds and the hearts of people who breathe the air."

Forgiveness is a way of living. It means letting go of past resentments and bitterness and moving on. Of course, it is not always easy, but it is worth every difficulty. And there is nothing mushy or softhearted about loving and forgiving.

Doctor Jonas Salk puts it this way: "The end result of forgiving is to release the power in the nucleus of the individual – a power much greater in its positive effects than atomic power in its negative."

If we can be courageous one more time than we are fearful. Trusting one more time than we are anxious, cooperative one more time than we are competitive, forgiving one more time than we are vindictive, loving one more time than hateful, we will have moved closer to the next big breakthrough in our human growth, and closer to the next big breakthrough toward our human potential.

We heard in the Gospel, after hearing Jesus' words of forgiveness, the scribes in the area thought to themselves, "How can this man talk like that?"

There are times for all of us when forgiveness doesn't come easy. And when we hear Jesus saying we must forgive unconditionally and without limit, we are tempted to ask, along with the scribes, "How can that Man talk like that?"

MDP, at every Mass we pray "Forgive us our trespasses as we forgive those who trespass against us." How can we not talk like that?

"Forgive us our trespasses as we forgive those who trespass against us," It's as simple as that!

C – Luke 6:27-28

There's a story about a woman in a fast food restaurant, who was about to eat. She bowed her head and said, "Thank you, Lord, for these vittles." A teenager at the next table overheard her and asked, "What are vittles?" The woman answered, "These are the blessings that God gives me – my food to eat." The teenager replied, "But don't you know you're going to get food to eat whether or not you thank God for it?" "Perhaps so," said the woman, "But everything tastes better when I'm thankful."

MDP, if our life seems to be in a rut, if things keep getting us down, if we don't seem to be growing spiritually, if we are wondering why life just isn't good, it is not that God needs changing. It's us who needs changing. And as followers of Jesus Christ, we have been given this powerful Gospel to help us live a fulfilling, rewarding, good life. It is really a Gospel of love, a challenge for us to become holy, which we must share.

In 1982 I had a tour in a Naval hospital in Oakland, California. I will always remember a bright, cheerful nurse and a story about her life as a nurse, when she was attending a patient named Tom. Tom was desperately ill and my nurse friend did all she could to make him comfortable. But Tom was downright surly and rude. His only response to the nurse's cheerful charm was a string of profanities and blasphemies. My nurse friend was broken-hearted because she knew the man was dying that there was little she could do but pray for him. When she had the opportunity, she tried to speak to him gently and tactfully about God's goodness and mercy. But Tom would turn on her fiercely and, one time, with a curse on his lips, he used his last ounce of strength to slap her across the cheek. Immediately, the scene in the ward turned chaotic as some of the other patients rose from their beds to defend her. But the nurse calmed the situation and told the patients to back off. She noticed that Tom, though still conscious, was gasping for breath. He couldn't last long. So she drew close to him and prayed hard. After a bit, she stopped and whispered his name and said, "Tom, God loves you." She was smiling at him, and to her surprise, Tom smiled back, his feeble lips forming just three words, "Sorry… please pray."

Tom seemed to rally enough just to join in whispering the "Our Father." When they came to the words, "Deliver us from evil," Tom's eyes sank back and he breathed his last. Tears flowed from my nurse friend's eyes, but there was a gladness in her heart, as she whispered this final prayer: "Thank you, Lord, for that blow on the cheek."

I recently read in an inspirational book these thoughts:

To Whom it May Concern:

- If you find me stumbling and falling, I may be trying something new – I just may be learning.

- If you find me sad, I may have realized that I have been making the same mistakes again and again – I may just be exploring.

- If you find me frightened, I may be facing a new situation, unique in my experience – I just may be reaching out.

- If you find my crying, I may have failed – I just may be lonely.

- If you find me quiet, I may be planning – I just may be trying again.

- These are life signs of my nature. You see, I am chronically human.

We are so, so human! We are creatures of God and totally dependent on God not only for our life, but also for the way we live our life!

I remember last year when I was watching an interview on Dateline with Mel Gibson and his movie "The Passion of the Christ". He said very poignantly to Diane Sawyer, that Jesus came into this world to do the Father's will; that in the film, Mel tried to show how, unconditionally, Jesus staked His life on the power of the Father's love for us.

A young Romeo falls in love, and he goes to his girlfriend's father to ask his blessing. The father asks him, "What do you do?" The young boy answers, "I go to church every Sunday; I'm very religious." "But my daughter will have to be supported," says the father. "Don't worry," says our Romeo, "God will take care of that."

"But she'll want a family," says the father. "Oh, I love children. God will take care of that," says the young lad.

"She needs a house to live in." Again the same answer from the young Romeo: "God will take care of that."

Later on, the father's wife asks him, "Well, what do you think of our daughter's lover?"

The father says, "He seems very nice. But he things I'm God."

MDP, how foolish we are to imagine, even for a single day, that we can go our own way, do our own thing, live as we please and ignore the challenge of today's Gospel. That we can expect to enrich our lives in the process. Yes, how foolish we are to think that we are God!

The Gospel is so powerful! The only way to make our life good, holy and balanced is to share the gift of God's challenge to forgive, to do what is right and to love one another.

EIGHTH SUNDAY IN ORDINARY TIME
A (1)– MATTHEW 6:24-34

One of my favorite musicals is "Fiddler on the Roof." I am sure I have seen it more than a dozen times. The Jewish humorist who wrote it, one of my favorites, Shalom Aleichem, loved to portray the "Worrier." There's a line in "Fiddler", said by Tevye, who is always needling God: Tevye says: "Sometimes I think when things get too quiet up there, you say to yourself, 'Let's see what kind of mischief can I play on my friend, Tevye, today'.

Shalom Aleichem tells in the wonderful accents of a Jewish storyteller, another story about a true, certified worrier. This worrier, an old man, is standing with a friend on a crowded bus. A young man asks him, "What time is it?" The old man refuses to reply, and the young man moves on. The old man's friend says to him, "Why were you so discourteous?" The old man replies, "If I had given him the time of day, next he would want to know where I was going. Then we might talk about our interests. If we did that, he might invite himself to my house for dinner. If he did, he would meet my lovely daughter. If he met her, they would both fall in love. And I don't want my daughter marrying someone who can't afford a watch!"

We all worry about something or another, and some of the worries we carry around with us can rob our days, can steal joy out of our life. Worries drain our energy and our vitality. Some doctors even say that worrying contributes to many forms of sickness.

And then today we hear this beautiful Gospel. Our blessed Lord tells us about a better way, He says very gently, "Don't worry; don't be anxious; Look at the lilies of the field…"

But still we worry, we build a wall between ourselves and these words of the Lord. This wall, I believe, has two components: one is the anxiety we feel about our final moments. In other words, when life just seems to be bearing down on us in a heavy way, we worry about it; and then we worry about death. The second component is our anxiety about our daily life: what are we going to eat, shall we eat at home or shall we go out, what are we going to wear, what shall we do today, should we pay cash for this or should we put it on credit.

Just maybe we might allow ourselves to hear – in the quiet of our hearts – the powerful words of the Gospel, Jesus saying that worry will rob us of life, drain our energy unless we respond to God's love with unconditional trust. As finite beings we will never be able, realistically, to rid ourselves completely of all anxiety. But we know that the good Lord really cares for us; He enables us to cast off the destructive kind of anxiety that robs us of joy and prevents life from being worth living.

I heard a story once about a man who worried so much, that he was on the verge of a nervous breakdown. Life was becoming more and more unreal for him. He began to imagine that he was other than human. He decided to see a psychiatrist. The psychiatrist asked him, "What's your problem?" The man said, "Actually, I have two problems. My first problem is that I think I am a soda drink vending machine. I can dispense six different kinds of soda for 50 cents each: orange, grape, lemon, lime, cherry, and cola." The doctor thought about the man's claim for a while. Then he decided on a course of action. He put two quarters in the man's mouth and said: "I'll have an orange soda, please." Whereupon, the man answered, "That's my second problem. I'm out of order."

MDP, in just a few days we will begin the season of Lent. One of the things we might do during this Lenten season, is to tear down the walls of destructive worry so that on Easter we will experience new life. Once in a while, take a walk at night and just look up at the trillions of stars in the heavens and be impressed that the God who made each one of them cares for each one of us as if He had nothing else to care for.

A (2)– Matthew 6:24-34

I remember a story that I heard long ago and have carried around with me for years; actually, in some way this story, as simple as it is to tell, has helped me bring this Gospel close to my heart, and I hope it will do the same for you.

Once upon a time, there was a king who held a grand ball at the palace to celebrate the anniversary of his coronation. Everyone in the kingdom was invited to attend. The king asked that all in attendance be dressed in formal attire. A poor apprentice carpenter, named Peter, wanted to attend, but he did not own any appropriate clothes for such an event. As he passed by the palace gate the afternoon of the ball, he stopped to look at the preparations being made, imagining what the evening would be like. Her heard someone say, "Why the long face, son?" Peter turned to the questioner. Again the questioner asked, "Why the long face? You should be getting ready for my party."

Peter couldn't believe it. It was the king himself, talking to Peter, a common carpenter. "I'm sorry, your majesty, I would very much like to attend the party, but I do not have the proper clothes to attend such a royal event." "

"Why that's no problem at all," the king said. The king then summoned the prince and instructed his son to find suitable attire for Peter. The prince escorted the young carpenter to a royal dressing room where he picked out a beautiful set of clothes. "I think you will be very pleased with these," said the prince. "They are made of the finest material and will not wear out quickly like your other clothes."

"Thank you kindly, sir," said Peter as he reached to gather up his old clothes piled on the floor.

"Leave those," the prince said. "They're of no use to you now."

"But what if something happens to my new garments?"

"Then you can come to me again and I will give you something else to wear."

Peter thought for a moment, "No sir, I may need these someday."

"As you wish, my friend, "Come! The ball is beginning. Go and enjoy every minute of it."

Peter carried his old clothes with him all during the ball. Refusing to part with his bundle, Peter stayed on the edges of the great ball-room. He was not able to dance or participate in the evening's festivities. When the servants came around with platters of food and drink, Peter could only sample a few delicacies because he had only one free hand, his other hand refusing to let go of his bundle of rags.

At the end of the evening, all the people of the kingdom left the palace filled with joy and awe at having spent such a grand evening at the king's ball. Except for Peter, who had spent most of the time clutching his ragged bundle of old clothes.

B – MARK 2:18-22

"No man pours new wine into old wineskins," Jesus says in today's Gospel. In other words, the pressure of fermenting new wine would break a shriveled, old, dried out wineskin. Jesus is using this figure to make the point that the old, rigid laws of Judaism are unsuitable to receive His new teachings. Jesus comes and expands our capacity for good. Living under His new law of love, we have the absolute capacity to break through the boundaries imposed by the old law of vengeance.

There's the story about the night a cheerful truck driver pulled up to a road side diner for some food. As he was eating, three wild looking motorcyclists roared up to the diner's entrance. The atmosphere became tense as they stalked in, wearing dirty leather jackets and swastika tattoos. Immediately, they selected the truck driver as the target of their meanness. One poured salt and pepper on the truck driver's head. Another took the truck driver's apple pie, placed it on the floor and squished it under a dirty boot. The third upset the trucker's coffee, causing it to spill in his lap.

Well, the truck driver did not say a word. He merely rose, walked slowly to the cashier, calmly paid his check and made his way to the door. One of the bikers said, "That dude sure ain't much of a fighter." The waiter behind the counter was peering out into the night and then replied, "He doesn't seem to be much of a driver either. He just ran his truck over three motorcycles."

That is called "instant vengeance," and the revenge couldn't be sweeter. If we stop to think about it for a minute, we see the enormous amounts of time and effort that some people invest in 'getting even', in playing the tit-for-tat game; saying, if you cross me, I will cross you; and an eye for an eye, a tooth for a tooth!

But Jesus came and said a flat "no" to vengeance. He commanded us, His followers, to forgive our enemies and to suffer wrong rather than repay it. He said we should repay evil with good.

I heard recently that a professor in a local university gave his students an opportunity to evaluate his course at the end of the semester. One student said, "I like the course but I feel very strongly that the professor put too much of the responsibility for learning on the students."

When it comes to our blessed Lord's law of love, we are like that student. We like what Jesus says, but we act as though He has put too much responsibility on us in learning how to live His law of love. It is easier to cry 'tit-for-tat' or 'I'll get even with you," than it is to pray for our enemies. It is more palatable to taste sweet revenge than to return evil with good. It is much easier to rely on the laws of men that it is to believe and to hope and live the spirit of Christ.

MDP, in Jesus we are given the opportunity to explore the inexhaustible depths of another human being; and in doing so we learn more about who God is and who we are. The reality of another human being is inexhaustible. Each one of us is a mystery to the other; a mystery of joy and sorrow, of hope and fear, of strange hurts, and strange ecstasies. And, we are a mystery to ourselves. It is, in the words of St. Paul, only in God's kingdom that "We shall know ourselves even as we are known."

We cannot be the new wineskins into which Jesus pours His new wine of love unless we see the inexhaustible goodness of each other.

Rigid, old, wineskins who don't know the law of Jesus' love, continue to pile human disaster upon human disaster. Nothing is learned. Kids leave home because they hate their parents; parents can't wait until the kids clear out. We build new jails and then we need two more. One nation develops the capacity to destroy the entire world in a single blow. Another discovers how to do it two times over. The rigid, old wineskins are bursting at any suggestion of a new and better way.

There was once a rigid, old wineskin who sought advice from a marriage counselor (another rigid, old wineskin, as it turned out). She said to him, "I hate my husband. He is making my life miserable. I want a divorce and, more than that, I want to make things as tough as possible for him. What do you advise?"

The counselor replied, "Begin by showering him with compliments, indulge him in every way. Help him in everything. Then, when he realizes how much he needs you and wants you, start divorce proceedings. That will really fracture him."

Six months later, the counselor met the woman and asked, "Are you following my advice?" "I am," she answered. "When are you going to file your divorce papers?" he asked.

"Are you out of your mind," the woman replied indignantly. "We're divinely happy! I love him with all my heart!"

MDP, that's what happens when an old wineskin embraces the spirit of Christ. Love can make all things soft and pliable and new again. Let me remind you, revenge is always sour. Love is so sweet.

C – Luke 6:39-45

I would like to tell you the story of a family – and just maybe it might have a familiar ring: the family are friends of mine, and the father had a problem with one of his daughters, a little girl who was very quiet, very shy, unable to express herself outwardly. The father was an outgoing person and most of the other children took after him. So he could not figure why this one daughter was so different.

On one occasion he gave this quiet little daughter a present. It was an elegant, small glass elephant on a gold chain, to put around her neck. He put it down on the table in front of her and said: "I've brought you this present."

Well, the littler girl was overwhelmed! Her mouth dropped open and she stared at this beautiful gift. It shone more beautifully than any star of Bethlehem because it symbolized her father's love for her. She sat there for several minutes, staring at the little glass elephant, but she was unable to speak, to say anything. Then she got up and went into the other room to try to tell her mother what had happened. When she came back, she was thunderstruck because she saw her beautiful little elephant dangling from her sister's neck.

The father said, in a kind of offhanded and insensitive way, "Well, you didn't say anything, you didn't want it, so I gave it to your sister."

That father wasn't listening! He wasn't listening to the joy of her silence. He hadn't listened enough to this child to know who she was and how she expressed herself. And years later this child was in therapy, trying, with her doctor, to trace back to the tragic feeling she had that no one was listening down through the years! So even in our families, we don't know one another because we are not listening!

Those of us who have really identified with Jesus, the Christ, have been taught a very special kind of love, which among other things, is a listening love. It's not the kind of love that says, "How can I use you for me, and how can I use you to give me pleasure and how can I use you to exalt me?" No, it is the love that asks, "How can I give of myself in order that you can be happy, that you can be fulfilled?"

The New Testament calls this kind of love agape love: the love that is for the other, the love that affirms the life of the other, the love that rejoices in the difference in the other. It is a listening love.

We all talk too much – talk, talk, talk. Even when we are not talking, we are not listening. We at times are trying to think of what we're going to say when the other person slows up enough for us to break in. What a contrast to our Blessed Lord, who in all of history, had more right to speak with authority than anyone else.

Yet how often we find Him just listening! He listened to Nicodemus. He knew what this proud member of the establishment's problem was from the beginning, but He listened. He heard him out. He listened to Peter, patiently, even when Peter was making a fool of himself. He listened to the woman at the well.

"The measure you measure with will be measured back to you," we heard in today's Gospel. MDP, if we want to be heard, we had better start listening. Listening, after all, is the way to get to know another person. It presents a quality of knowing in which we discover the other's uniqueness – their strengths and weaknesses, their joys and sorrow. When we know something of the other, we can give of ourselves in order to affirm his or her unique personhood. But unless we listen, we will never get to know. This is the tragedy of so many long-term relationships which remain untouched by love because people just don't get to know one another truly.

When I was up North for the past holidays, I went to the classic Philadelphia diner. Seated not far from me was a grandmother, mother, and a little boy: three generations. The waitress came to the table to take the order. She took the grandmother's order, then the mother's and then she turned to the little boy and said, "What would you like?" The mother immediately said, "Oh, I'll order for him." In many cases this is necessary and typical. But the waitress, without being overly rude, ignored the mother and said again to the little boy, "what would you like?" Glancing over at his mother to see how she was reacting to all of this, the boy said, "A hamburger." "How would you like your hamburger – with pickles and the works?" asked the waitress. And with his mouth dropping open in amazement now, he said, "The works!" The waitress went over to the short order window, and hollered the grandmother's order, the mother's order, then in a very loud voice she said, "and a hamburger with the works!" The little boy turned to his mother in utter astonishment and said, "Mommy, she thinks I'm real.!"

This is what happens when we listen to other persons. They

suddenly become real. They realize that someone cares enough to recognize their unique worth as human beings.

MDP, in this beautiful Gospel, Jesus, our Blessed Lord, tells us to be compassionate, not to judge, not to condemn, to pardon – even to love our enemies. But none of this is possible if we are not good listeners. Husbands, wives, grandparents, children, friends – listen, listen and listen again! Listen and then love.

NINTH SUNDAY IN ORDINARY TIME
A – MATTHEW 7:21-27

I am sure some of you have heard of Rabbi Harold Kushner. Years ago he wrote the book "Why Bad Things Happen to Good People." He has a follow up book called "Overcoming Life's Disappointments." In this book Rabbi Kushner tells the story about a prominent Rabbi who ran into a member of his congregation on the street one day and said to him, "I haven't seen you in the Synagogue the past few weeks. Is everything okay?" The man answered, "Everything is fine, but I've been worshipping at a small Synagogue on the other side of town."

"I'm really surprised to hear that, the Rabbi responded. "I know the Rabbi of that congregation. He's a nice enough fellow, but he's not the scholar I am. He's not the preacher I am. He's not the leader I am. What can you possibly get from leaving my synagogue to worship at his?"

The man replied, "That's all very true, Rabbi, but he has other qualities; for example, he can read minds, and he's teaching us how to read minds. I'll show you. Think of something. Concentrate on it. I'll read your mind and tell you what you were thinking of."

The Rabbi concentrated for a few moments; then, the former member of his congregation ventured, "You're thinking of the verse from Psalm 16: "I have set the Lord before me at all times."

The Rabbi laughed, "You couldn't be more wrong. I wasn't thinking about that at all."

The former member said, "I know you weren't. That's why I don't worship at your Synagogue anymore."

MDP, faith is not lived in buildings bearing God's name; it is not lived in boasting about degrees in theology. Faith is grounded in the heart; it is grounded in the way we show love to one another, in how generous and gracious we are to one another, in our willingness to forgive those who have hurt us. It is not grounded in putting oneself first, but it is in "setting the Lord before us at all times!"

There's a story about a hungry boy traveling with his father through a dense forest. Suddenly the boy spots a patch of ripe berries and begins to pick them and eat them. When the hour grows dangerously late, the boy can't bring himself to leave the patch. What could the father do? He loves the boy in spite of his childish behavior. The father says: "I will start out; you may stay a few minutes longer. But to make sure we don't get separated, keep calling, 'Father! Father!' and I will answer you. But as soon as my voice begins to fade, come running to me."

This is what Jesus meant when He said we must build our house, build our faith, on solid rock! The Gospel today challenges us to "set the Lord before us at all time," to call out 'Father, Father,' when we feel we are separating ourselves from Him, to bridge the divide between what we say and believe and what we do.

To build our house on solid rock is to "set the Lord before us at all times." Call out 'Father, Father' when we feel ourselves separating from Him.

B – MARK 2:23-3:6

In "Tis," his sequel to "Angela's Ashes," author Frank McCourt writes about coming to America after the war. He was 18 years old and he was struggling to establish his life as a teacher. One of his first jobs was teaching English and Social Studies at a vocational high school on Staten Island. His students are loud and rude; they pelted each other with chalk, erasers and sandwiches; they ridicule and abuse their teachers; they have little or no interest in learning. Then, one day, while his students are taking a test, McCourt explores the old closets at the back of his classroom. They are stuffed with old newspapers, books and hundreds of uncorrected student compositions going back to 1942.

He starts reading through some of the compositions: he reads about how the boys back then yearned to fight, to avenge the deaths of brothers, friends, neighbors killed by the Japanese and Germans.

The girls write how they will wait for their boyfriends to return, get married and make a new life for themselves "in New Jersey."

Then McCourt begins reading them to the class. He gets their attention; they sit up as they hear familiar names. "Hey, that was my father. He was wounded in Africa." Another student said, "That was my Uncle Sal; he was killed in Guam." Dozens of Staten Island and Brooklyn families are named in these papers, papers which are so brittle that they crumble at the mere touch. But he got the students' interest. They want to save the papers so they begin to copy them. For the rest of the term they decipher and write. Tears flow as students read about their mothers and fathers, aunts and uncles.

"This is my father when he was 15." "This is my aunt and she died having a baby." So, in a stack of crumbling, forgotten student compositions, a class of Staten Island students discover the richness of their past and the possibilities for their own future.

MDP, In these old compositions, Frank McCourt's students come to realize the love and values of their families that now exist within themselves and in their own young lives.

In today's Gospel we hear Jesus, like Frank McCourt, talking to the Pharisees, trying to teach them, trying to give them new insights into the Sabbath Law, trying to tell them that it is love, and not the letter of the law, that motivated Him to heal people's ailments and to forgive their sins; it is love, not the letter of the law, that will lead Jesus to calvary and to the cross. You see, Jesus looks beyond the letter of the law, beyond these old dusty compositions. He trims away the externals and goes to the spirit of the law.

For example, in His Sermon on the Mount, He said, "You have heard the commandment, 'You shall not commit murder'. What I say to you is: Everyone who grows angry with his brother shall be liable to judgment.: Then again He says, "Thou shall not kill." He means this as not just a simple command against murder, but He means it to be a call to divest ourselves of all traces of hatred and lack of compassion. Christ teaches us with this Gospel the lesson that the law in itself is not the answer. He describes His mission as one of bringing the law to fulfillment, changing those human attitudes which make law necessary in the first place.

Since the dawn of human curiosity, man has gazed into the night sky and wondered whether there is life somewhere out there, hoping, or perhaps fearing that we are not alone in the universe. Even as we attend this Mass, there are powerful transmitters sending messages out into the vast unknown. Scientists are hoping somebody out there will hear the messages, and respond. But don't hold your breath! They don't expect a quick answer. But they are listening. Tiny bits of static from deep space are being examined in the hope of discovering a "message" from out there.

As exciting as this might be, just think about this, how lucky we are: we have the privilege of listening to the Word of the Lord Himself; the Creator of the universe speaks to us. Not a word from little green men in outer space, but from the Lord Himself!

Hear the Word of the Lord in this Gospel: The Sabbath is made for man, not man for the Sabbath." As James McCourt tried to do with his students, our Blessed Lord calls us, instructs us, to see the love which lives within each of us, calling us beyond our own needs, and wants and interests. A love that calls us beyond the mere letter of the law, is transforming.

So our challenge as Catholics, as followers of Christ, the challenge of this Gospel is to allow the Spirit of Christ, His call to love, to change our lives. To change our world by transforming despair into hope, sadness into joy, worry into freedom, anger into forgiveness, to radiate to all who see us, the Face of Christ.

C – Luke 7:1-10

It's in times like these that I really cherish my Catholic faith.

This is what St. Paul is telling the Corinthians this morning, and this is what I want to share with you. Our faith is the very foundation of our spiritual life. It's faith which gives meaning to our present existence. It's faith which is our passport to heaven.

Without faith 'right' and 'wrong' are empty words. Morality is a matter of convenience. Without faith sickness, like that of my father's, is nothing but a puzzle, and self-sacrifice is stupid.

Sometimes I think we who have been Catholics since birth tend to underestimate our faith. We take it for granted. We may even grow careless and expose it to dangers. All of us have a fear of the unknown. We don't know when sickness will strike; we don't know what will happen within the next hour. So, it comes down to faith. Let us spare no effort in coming closer to Christ, in letting our religion shine through all of our actions.

TENTH SUNDAY IN ORDINARY TIME
A – Matthew 9:9-13

M DP, we heard in the Gospel that Jesus was at dinner and a number of tax collectors and sinners came to sit with Him. Some of the Pharisees asked the Disciples, in effect, "Why does our Master eat with gangsters and prostitutes?" and we heard the searing response of Jesus, "It is not the healthy who need the doctor, but the sick… I did not come to call the virtuous, but sinners, and I desire mercy, not sacrifice."

Once, during my Navy career, Chaplains were required to attend Alcoholic Anonymous meetings on the base, simply to get a feel of what was going on in the mind and hearts of alcoholics. One evening I was about to leave one of the meetings, which was held at my chapel. As I was walking out of the building, I noticed a young sailor crouched over the hood of his old car. I took a minute to introduce myself. The man looked at me, saw the cross on my uniform, let out a deep breath, and told me how long he had intended to "get back to the church."

I invited him to come to services at the chapel any time. His face became flushed and he launched into the story of his life. He told the familiar story of a string of regrets and losses which usually accompany a life of addiction. I listened, let him talk, and when he was finished, I said a prayer with him, and wished him a "good night."

As I was walking to my car, he called out to me, "Father, did you really mean what you said?" "Did you really mean I could come to this church?"

On my drive home, I realized that this young sailor told me his life story as a response to my invitation. I thought it was his polite way of saying he could not accept my invitation, that he wasn't "clean enough" to be included in my congregation or any congregation.

The words of Jesus in today's Gospel came to me, "I have come to call sinners… and I desire mercy, not sacrifice," came back to me as I read the Gospel today. I remembered that young sailor.

MDP, if the work of Jesus is to be done in this world, it will only be done through Christians like you and me. There is no walking away from it! The work of Jesus must become our work, because in our world we are the only hands, and feet and heart that Jesus has. We are called to be His hands and heart and feet, so that we can extend His love and peace and compassion and forgiveness and support to those who have done nothing to deserve them. This is the cutting edge of the Gospel of Jesus! Let's face it: before almighty God every one of us is a sinner.

Everything we have on this earth is a gift from a God whose profound and limitless love compels us to become the beautiful persons He intended us to be. We must leave church this morning thinking about what the words of the Gospel really mean, that is, God seeks no greater gift from us than for us to extend His mercy and kindness and forgiveness to others, to all who come through the doors of this church, to all whom our life will touch today!

B – MARK 3:20-35

To dream the impossible dream! Sometimes when I read these beautiful Gospel stories, I think it is easy to conclude that to be a follower of Jesus Christ is simply to pursue the impossible dream.

Lewis Carroll's masterpiece, Alice in Wonderland, "Through the Looking Glass," includes this following exchange between Alice and the Queen:

"I can't believe that!" says Alice.

"Can't you?" the Queen replies in a tone dripping with pity. "Try again, draw a deep breath, and shut your eyes."

Alice laughs. "There's no use trying," she says. "One can't believe impossible things."

"I dare say you haven't had much practice," says the Queen. "When I was your age, I always did it for half an hour a day. Why, sometimes I've believed as many as six impossible things before breakfast."

MDP, before breakfast, before lunch, before dinner, morning, noon, night our Blessed Lord is calling you and me, His followers, to pursue the vision of Jesus Christ. But in reality, those of us who try to follow His vision wonder at times if we are pursuing an impossible dream. In any case, we discover real soon that following the vision of Jesus can be a risky business – as we can see in today's Gospel.

The Gospel tells us that it is still early in Jesus' public ministry and the things He is saying and doing are beginning to rankle the religious establishment. You see, they see Him as a non-conformist, a threat to their authority. They say He does things by the power of Beelzebub. His own relatives think He has gone out of His mind and, as the Gospel says, "They set out to take charge of Him."

I often thought it would be fun to make a list of the risks that Jesus asks us to take, for example, in our relationships with others. And then after making the list, show it to somebody who knows us very well, a spouse, a close friend, a relative. Tell them that we are going to live in this manner; for example, tell them we are going to strictly follow the instructions Jesus gives us for achieving greatness: He says, "Anyone who wants to be first among you must be servant to all." You know, our spouse, our friend or relative might just think we have gone out of our mind.

Some of the popular "self-help" books seem to be saying that we need to become hard-nosed "realists." They tell us to set aside our dreams and abandon our visions in order to come to terms with the "real world," but it so happens that their "real world" mentality has led us into a lot of social injustice and such fierce competitiveness.

The Biblical truth is this: "Where there is no vision the people perish." But we as a Christian people have such a great vision, a mystical vision that can inform and shape our interaction with the world. And because we can look at the world with the eyes of Jesus Christ, we can stand firm in the Lord, in the words of St. Paul. We can stand firm against the proposition that "everything will be all right if only we think everything is all right."

We stand firm in the Lord against the proposition that the highest goal in life is to look out for number one.

A wise doctor once said, "I have been practicing medicine for 30 years, and I have prescribed many things. But in the long run, I have learned that for most of the ills of the human creature, the best medicine is a patient understanding of another's problems."

When someone asked him, "What if that doesn't work?" He replied, "Double the dose!"

Again St. Paul prescribes, "Put on love!" And if that doesn't work, "double the dose!" And even if it seems to others that we have gone out of our minds, the peace of Christ will reign in our hearts!

Three men set out on a journey. Each carried two sacks around his neck – one in front and one in back. The first man was asked what was in his sacks. "In this one on my back," he said, "I carry all the kind deeds of my friends. In that way they are out of sight and out of mind and I don't have to do anything about them. They're soon forgotten. This sack in front carries all the unkind things people do to me. I pause in my journey every day to take them out and air them, lest I forget them. It slows me down, but nobody gets away with anything."

The second man was asked what was in his sacks. "In this one on my back, I keep all my bad deeds. I keep them behind me, out of my view. This sack in front carries all my good deeds. I constantly keep them before me. I pause in my journey every day to take them out and air them, lest I forget them. It slows me down, but I take great pleasure in them."

The third man was asked what was in his sacks. "I carry my friends' kind deeds in this front sack," he said. "It looks full, but it is not heavy. Far from slowing me down, it is like the sails of a ship. It helps me move ahead. The sack on my back has a hole in the bottom. That's where I put all the evil I hear and receive from others. It just falls out and is lost, so I have no burden to slow me down.

MDP, guess who has the vision of Jesus Christ, and guess who finished first!

C – LUKE 7:11-17

Compassion is the beautiful virtue of today's Gospel. If you take apart the word, it literally means "to suffer with." Compassion is the ability to put oneself in the place of someone and readily take on – with them – their suffering, their despair, their brokenness, and to transform their pain and struggle into hope and healing.

I must tell you a story that accompanied me throughout my career in the Navy. In 1979 the Navy selected me to go to post-graduate school at the University of Berkeley in California. The Jesuit School of Theology there was offering courses in counseling. Every time the story of the widow of Nain comes around, I think of an incident that one of the Jesuit priest/professors described. He told the story of a woman who was eaten up with guilt over the terrible treatment of a loved one. That person had died, and the lady could not find peace or forgiveness. She felt rejected by God.

She met several times with the priest counselor, but she could not break out of her depression. Finally, the priest/professor said he tried a new approach. He took a chair and placed it facing the lady, and said to her, "Pretend God is sitting in this chair." He said, "I want you to tell God whatever you want God to know about how you feel, about what you have done. Whatever you want to tell God, just let it out. I'm just going to sit back and listen. But I want you to talk to God, and not me. Reluctantly, she began to pour it all out – her guilt, her shame, her embarrassment. Finally, after a long time, she seemed to be finished.

The priest then asked her to move to the chair where God has been sitting. A little puzzled, she took the chair. He said to her, "Now, I want God to respond to this woman and to all she has just said. What would God say if God was sitting where you sit now?" The lady sat there for just a minute and then said, "Can I move back to the other chair for just a minute?" The priest nodded and she moved. She talked again for about a minute, and then moved back into "God's chair." She looked for a long time at the chair in which she had been sitting, pouring out her hurts to God. Then, very lovingly she spoke, "I want to tell this woman that I know how she feels, and I know that she means everything she said, and I forgive her right now. But it will probably take her a long, long time to realize that she is forgiven." Without a word, she moved from God's chair back to her own. Tears streamed down her face, and over and over again she said the same thing, "Thank you, thank you; I am overwhelmed!" Her encounter with God was a new beginning for her!

MDP, this is what the Gospel is all about. The compassion manifested in Jesus' embrace of the grieving widow and mother. God's compassion is constant in our lives no matter what we have done. The very heart of the Gospel of Jesus Christ is that we have been created by a God out of a love, and sometimes we have a hard time understanding this. God forms us in His love, and He continues to love us in spite of our brokenness, the feelings we have at times that we are beyond His forgiveness.

ELEVENTH SUNDAY IN ORDINARY TIME
A – Matthew 9:36 – 10:8

Jesus talks straight and direct in this Gospel. He does not promise a life of ease; He says there's a lot of work to be done. "The harvest is rich and the laborers are few."

In many languages the words 'hope' and 'wait' express the same idea. To hope for something is to wait for it, to adjust one's life to its coming. This thought prompts me to tell you a little story. I call it "The Waiting Woman" story.

The "Waiting Woman" was a very depressed young woman who clung to the hope that religion – Christianity – might restore a sense of meaning and purpose to her life. She could never quite bring herself into a church building. Every Sunday she could be seen waiting outside the church door, sitting on the steps, looking at the faces of people who filed into the church and later emerged from it. She eventually wrote down her reason for not going in. She wrote, "I looked at their faces and I saw their faces preoccupied with anxiety without even a smile – faces very much like my own. If only I could have found one face which reflected a new light, a sense of joy, as a result of the religious event that they had just experienced, I surely would have rushed into the church and flung myself before the altar. But no, not one, not a clue that a seed had grown, that a ray of light had burst, that a bright note had sounded."

What the "Waiting Lady" saw, perhaps, might sound to some of us like our own response to the invitation of Jesus to proclaim His Gospel. We immediately begin to think of rules and structures, that is, what we can and cannot do. And yet, what Jesus is saying is that all He asks of us is to love one another. This was His message to those first Disciples whose names we heard in today's Gospel. He summoned them and instructed them to go out and "proclaim that the kingdom of heaven is at hand." Jesus had unraveled the mystery of God's Kingdom for those first Disciples, that the Kingdom of God is a Kingdom of love, that in love they were to "cure the sick, raise the dead, cleanse the lepers, cast out devils."

MDP, in that same loving spirit, we, His new disciples, embark on the same ministry of service, to do God's work on earth, to serve one another in the name of Jesus, to proclaim justice in a world of inequity, to open eyes that are blind to the needs of others, to enlarge the hearts of those who manifest a greater concern for power and wealth, than for a ministry of service.

Over one hundred years ago Robert Ingersoll wrote these words: Happiness is the only good. The place to be happy is here; the time to be happy is now; the way to be happy is to make others so.

B – MARK 4:26-34

I would like to tell you about a Jewish friend of mine named Leon. I met Leon early on in my Navy career. He told me that he had grown up in Poland during the Second World War. Leon and his family were Jews. He was just a child and he saw his parents and other relatives and friends killed or hauled off to the concentration camps by the Nazis. Little Leon fled to a nearby farm and hid there. He was so young and could not fend for himself.

One day he revealed himself to the farmer. The farmer and his wife happened to be very sensitive people. Very good Catholics, and they hid Leon for years. They fed him and clothed him and took care of him even though, had they been caught doing so, they would have been instantly executed. After the war Leon grew up and moved to the USA. He went to school, was a brilliant student, and became a Rabbi. To this day, Leon, as an older man now, tells the story of his childhood and the people who saved him. He humbly shares with his Jewish friends his great appreciation for the Catholic Church, because those Catholics of long ago were so good and gracious to him. What happened to him long ago operates every day in his life as an ongoing outreach to other religious communities.

MDP, I tell you this story because, as I told you, we all are mustard seeds possessing within us the ability to do great things for others and for God Himself. Think about it: forty years ago a seed was planted in a little Jewish boy who is now a famous Rabbi in New York.

We all have the opportunity, the courage, to do the big things; and every day we have the opportunity to do the small ones that show our values and the values of Jesus, values small as a seed, but a seed that will bear fruit, thirty, forty, fifty years from now. This Gospel makes me ask, 'who planted a mustard seed in me?' And to ask, 'who planted a mustard seed in you?' Who made you and me what we are; who helped put values and meaning and grace into our lives? He or she must have been so good because here we all are expressing our faith in God at Mass.

This Gospel gently allows me to ask you and me, who is planting a mustard seed maybe very quietly and gently in helping others to be caring, sensitive, open-hearted people? Only we, in our hearts, know the answer to this, and if we fail, the mustard seed will not grow and will never bear fruit.

C – Luke 7:36-8:3

Do you remember when Jesus taught us His prayer? He placed in this prayer a petition for forgiveness. It was the one petition, "Forgive us our sins as we forgive those who sin against us," that He emphasized the most. In fact, it was the only petition he commented on specifically, saying that if you forgive others, then you will experience God's forgiveness.

In today's Gospel we saw a woman of the streets standing behind Jesus, weeping, and wetting His feet with her tears.

MDP, the person who loves much is a forgiving person. The person who forgives much is a forgiven person! We cannot experience God's forgiveness unless we are willing to forgive.

TWELFTH SUNDAY IN ORDINARY TIME
A – MATTHEW 10:26-33

Today's Gospel is so beautiful and so encouraging. Listen again: "Even all the hairs on your head are counted. So do not be afraid; you are worth more than many sparrows."

I have a friend who just went through cancer surgery. After the surgery she began chemotherapy treatments. Every morning, she would comb her hair – and every morning she would pull out another clump of her long hair from the brush. This side effect was hitting her harder and harder. One morning, she felt the top of her head and for the first time, she could count the strands. But she felt strangely at peace. She held each strand – just as God, in His providence, could count them from the moment God breathed His life into her. She became aware of God's presence in the love of her family and friends who were supporting and encouraging her. She said to me in effect, "I felt comfort knowing that God knew how many strands were in my brush, on my pillow, in my hat and in my hand. With or without my hair, God knew me and what my future held. I am still afraid – of the cancer, of the chemo, the upcoming brain scan – but I know that God would be with me through it all."

MDP, in this Gospel, Christ reveals a God who loves us and cares for us, who has counted every hair on our heads. We are all called to be vehicles of God's love for those who need His presence in their lives.

Mother Theresa of Calcutta was a vehicle of God's love for so many years, ministering to the dying poor on the streets of Calcutta. One time she said, "For them and for me the greatest development of a human life is to die at peace with God. I remember once after we had picked up one man from the street, he said, "I have lived like an animal in the street, but I am going to die like an angel, loved and cared for. And he did. He died like an angel."

My friend who has cancer, the lowly street person, the most brilliant doctor, are all the concern of a loving God. They and we have our origins in God and we know we are going back to God. So, He says in the Gospel, 'Courage, my friend, do not be afraid.'

God is alive. We might get confused once in a while, we might make mistakes from time to time, but we are never alone, never lost. Never!

A – MATTHEW 10:26-33

In today's Gospel lesson Jesus and His friends are riding the crest of a rising wave of popularity. The crowds had turned into multitudes. Whole towns had come into the wilderness to hear Jesus preach and to see Him perform miracles of healing. Jesus is the "Man of the hour." Had there been a first-century Hebrew edition of *Time* Magazine, Jesus would have been a shoo-in for "Man of the Year." Everything is coming up roses! Then Jesus takes the twelve Apostles aside for some quiet, adult conversation. Maybe they expected a strategy session or a state of the kingdom address. Instead, Jesus says to them, "There is no need to be afraid."

Jesus knows what the future will bring. Soon He will send the Disciples out to continue His work, and the twelve will feel like sheep among starving wolves. In many places, the message of Jesus will be greeted with scorn and mockery. Doors will be slammed in their faces; city gates will be locked. Christian preachers will be flogged in the streets.

Hearing these things, the Disciples must have been utterly demoralized. They had a hundred things to be afraid of, thousands of dangers to fear, yet Jesus looked them in the eye and said, "Don't be afraid!" Why not? Because the enemies of the Gospel cannot bury Jesus – not for long – nor can they bury His message. So the Disciples preached and even though no one would listen, they preached anyway.

Contrary to all reasonable expectations, the truth about Jesus began to spread. There were converts among the Jews! Greeks became followers! Even Romans were baptized in the name of Jesus! More and more people believed in Christ, in spite of all the reasons not to believe. The truth spread because the truth could not be stopped. The world would kill Peter and Paul, the children of darkness could martyr Polycarp and Justin. The rebellious powers would nail the truth to a cross, but they couldn't keep it there.

The Good News of Jesus Christ will not be held back – not by threats, not by cover-ups, not by bullets, not by hangmen's nooses. The message of Jesus will triumph – the message that enemies must love each other, that wealth is a snare, that you cannot end bloodshed, by shedding blood. No matter how the world resists, the truth in the life and teachings of Jesus ultimately will penetrate.

"Don't be afraid." Jesus said. God will take care of you who belong to Christ. In order to assure His Disciples of God's loving care, Jesus reminded them of the sparrows which were sold in the market as an inexpensive source of meat for the poor. Sparrows were so plentiful, and so easily netted, that they sold two for a penny. If you bought four sparrows, the vendor would throw in a fifth bird for free. A single sparrow had almost no value, and yet the eye of God is fixed even upon this insignificant bird. "Not one sparrow falls to the ground without your Father knowing it," Jesus said to the Disciples.

So, the Disciples preached to whomever would listen. With boldness and power they told the truth to the rulers of their day. They faced danger and persecution fearlessly because they knew that the God who watches over the landing of a sparrow was most certainly watching over them. They lived in the unshakable conviction that God loved them down to the last hair on their heads.

B – MARK 4:35-41

We heard Jesus say to His frightened Disciples in the Gospel, "Why are you so frightened? How is it that you have no faith?"

This reminds me of the story about a great storm which was roaring as a train traveled across country. All the passengers were terrified as lightening flashed and thunder rocked the sky. But there was one little boy who seemed totally oblivious to the raging storm and the panic going on around him. He just continued playing with his toys as if nothing was wrong. One of the passengers asked, "Little boy, aren't you afraid to travel alone in such a storm?" The little boy lifted up his head and said, "No, sir, I'm not afraid at all. My father is the engineer of this train."

It has been said that "When fear knocks at the door, and we send faith to answer, nobody is there." Through the eyes of faith, we see things in the light of how they are when we place them in God's hands. Through those kinds of eyes, we will always be able to see beyond panic and fear.

MDP, on a daily basis, when we encounter 'storms' in our lives, God moves in beside us and whispers, "Do not be afraid. I am with you. I will never abandon you."

I heard recently about a politician who went to see the local Bishop for counsel. The Bishop advised the politician that the next time it rained, he should go outside and lift his face to heaven. "It will bring a revelation to you," the Bishop assured the politician.

A few weeks later a very upset politician ran into the Bishop. "I followed your advice but no revelation came. All I got was dripping wet. I felt like a fool." The Bishop replied simply, "Not a bad revelation for a first try."

MDP, the words Jesus addressed to the storm in today's Gospel, He is always addressing to us: "Peace! Be still!" It goes without saying that all of us encounter some adversities, some sadness, maybe even a tragedy in our lives which can either help us grow in our understanding of what life is all about or consume us with a sense of despair and loneliness. But within each of us is the presence of the "awakened" Jesus telling us, "Peace, be still." Telling us to make time for peace, for stillness, for quiet in our lives in order to hear the whispers of the Spirit, to re-set our compass as we navigate our small boats through life's storms, to check our bearings to make sure that we are really becoming the beautiful persons the good Lord wants us to become.

C (1)– Luke 9:18-24

"Who do you say that I am?" This question in today's Gospel has haunted me for years.

MDP, wherever we are at this very moment on our life's journey, I believe that the light of Christ is shining at the center of our being. This helps us to answer the question, "Who do you say that I am?" This light of Christ at the center of our being allows us to drop our defenses, relinquish our excuses, so that we can allow the light of Christ to shine through us and to penetrate our lives.

A fifteen-year-old boy and his father were driving past a local airport in a small Ohio town. Suddenly a low flying plane spun out of control and nose-dived into the runway. The boy yelled, "Dad, stop the car!" Minutes later the fifteen-year-old boy was pulling the pilot out of the plane. The pilot was a twenty-year-old student flier, who had been practicing takeoffs and landings. The young student pilot died in the fifteen-year-old boy's arms.

When the boy got home, he threw his arms around his mother and cried, "Mom, he was my friend; he was only twenty years old." Well, that night the boy was still too shocked to eat dinner. He went to his room, closed the door, and lay on his bed. He had been working in a drugstore to save every penny for flying lessons. His goal was to get his pilot's license when he turned sixteen.

The boy's parents wondered what effect the tragedy would have on their son. Would he stop taking lessons, or would he continue? They agreed that the decision would have to be his.

Two days later the boy's mother entered the boy's room. On his dresser she saw an open notebook. It was one he had kept from childhood. Across the top of the page was written, in big letters, "The character of Jesus." Beneath was listed a series of qualities: "Jesus was sinless; He was humble: He championed the poor; He was unselfish; He was close to God."

The mother saw that in her son's hour of decision he was turning to Jesus for guidance. Then she turned to her son and said, "What have you decided about flying?"

The boy looked into his mother's eyes and said, "Mom, I hope you and Dad will understand, but with God's help, I must continue to fly."

That boy was Neil Armstrong. And on July 20, 1969, he became the first human being to walk on the moon.

Few of us who watched that historic event on television knew that one of the reasons Neil Armstrong was walking on the moon was our Blessed Lord.

"We didn't know that it was from Jesus that Neil drew strength and guidance to make a crucial teenage decision that was now responsible for his walking on the moon."

I like that story because it answers Jesus' question in today's Gospel – "Who do you say that I am?" In a way that we are not used to hearing it answered.

Young Neil Armstrong didn't answer the question by saying to Jesus, "You are the Son of God," or "You are the Messiah," or "You are the Second Person of the Trinity." He answered it much more simply. He said: "You are a sinless Person. You are a selfless Person. You are a Person who cares. You are a Person who is close to God."

In other words, Neil Armstrong didn't give a theological answer to the question "Who do you say that I am?" He gave a personal answer. He looked into his own heart and described how Jesus touched his heart.

Each one of us must do the same thing. We must answer Jesus' question – "Who do you way that I am?" And once we ask that question, we must ask another: What are we going to do about it?

Reminds me of a story: I debated whether to tell you this story told to me by a Bradenton police officer. A woman in this area stopped behind another car at a traffic light. The light turned green, but the driver in the car ahead of her is on his cell phone, and he doesn't notice the light change. The woman, who is running late, begins to pound on her steering wheel and begins to scream at the man to move. The man doesn't move, still talking on the phone. Well, the woman is now going ballistic; she's ranting and raving at the man. The light turns yellow. Now the woman blasts her horn; she screams a litany of obscenities and she makes an awful gesture with her hand.

The man finally looks up, sees the yellow light, and accelerates through the intersection as the light turns red. The woman, now stuck at the intersection, is beside herself. Still ranting, she hears a tap on her window. As she looks up, she sees a very serious looking police officer, hand on his gun, telling her to turn off her engine, keep her hands in sight, and exit the car. She's speechless, but does exactly what he says. When she gets out of the car, he tells her to place her hands on the roof and then locks her wrists in handcuffs. She is hustled into his patrol car, taken to the station where she is fingerprinted, photographed, searched, booked and placed in a holding cell. She is too frightened to ask any questions.

A couple of hours later, a sergeant comes to the cell and opens the door. He escorts the woman back to the booking desk where the arresting officer is waiting with her personal effects. The officer says to her, "I'm very sorry for the mistake, ma'am. But, you see, I pulled up behind your car while you were blowing your horn, cursing, and making obscene gestures at the guy in front of you. Then I noticed the two bumper stickers on the car: "We worship at St. Joseph's" and "What would Jesus do?" I saw the Christian fish emblem on the trunk of the car. So, naturally, I assumed you had stolen the car."

MDP, Jesus confronts us with the same question he poses to His Disciples: "Who do you say I am?" Everything we say, every gesture, everything we do is our response to that question. Every decision and choice we make proclaims exactly who we believe this Jesus is. Every moment of our lives declares our faith. In the words of Neil Armstrong, in Jesus, the sinless Man, the Selfless Man, the Man who cares, the Man who is close to God.

C (2)– LUKE 9:18-24

In today's Gospel Jesus asks the question: "Who do you say that I am?" I want to tell you a story of how a military Chaplain, a priest, Father Emil Kapaun, answered that question.

Sixty years ago, a group of American soldiers walked out of a North Korean prison camp, carrying a large wooden crucifix they had made from firewood and bits of wire. The cross was a tribute to a fellow prisoner who had touched their souls and saved their lives – Father Emil Kapaun.

After the Communist invasion of South Korea in 1950, Chaplain/ Father Kapaun was among the first American troops to hit the beaches and pushed their way north through hard mountains and bitter cold. When 20,000 Chinese troops swept down on the outnumbered American forces at Unsan, Father Kapaun raced across no man's land, dodging bullets and explosions to drag the wounded to safety. Father Kapaun and a dozen other Americans were taken prisoner. As they were being led away on the tiger death march to the North Korean prison camp at Pyoktong, the priest saw another American lying in a ditch, unable to walk, his ankle shattered in a grenade blast. A Chinese soldier was about to execute the American – but Father Kapaun pushed the Chinese soldier aside. As the stunned soldier watched, Father Kapaun picked up the wounded soldier and carried him for miles. When other prisoners stumbled, he helped them up as well. When they wanted to quit, knowing that stragglers would be shot – Father Kapaun begged them to keep walking. During that brutally cold winter, Father Kapaun took care of the sick, gave away his own clothes to freezing prisoners, fashioned pots to boil water to battle dysentery, and prayed with the men in their huts. He was known as "the good thief" for his ability to steal food and trade anything he had for meager supplies. He celebrated Mass with a small missal and some bread he and the prisoners kept hidden. But Father Kapaun did not survive.

Crippled by a blood clot in his leg and weakened by dysentery and pneumonia, Father Kapaun died on May 23, 1951. He was 35 years old. Two years later the camp was liberated.

President Obama awarded Father Kapaun the medal of honor, our nation's highest military honor. He is the fifth Catholic Priest in our Military history to be so honored. His men always referred to him as their "shepherd in combat boots." And now because certain miracles have been attributed to his intercession, he has been presented to the Pope in the first inquiries for canonization.

Jesus asks, "Who do you say that I am?" We see how Father Kapaun answered.

MDP, everything we say and do is our response to that question; every decision and choice we make proclaims exactly who we believe this Jesus is; every moment of our lives declares our faith in this Jesus. As Father Kapaun understood, to lay claim to the title of disciple of Jesus Christ we must in every time, in every place be willing to risk our safety and security for the Gospel of justice and peace, never looking back but always looking forward to the possibilities of making the reign of God a reality in our lives, in our time and wherever we find ourselves.

NATIVITY OF SAINT JOHN THE BAPTIST
— JUNE 24 DAY
A LUKE 1:57-66, 80

From the very beginning of His public ministry Jesus proclaimed this theme: "Reform your lives!" His call to transform our lives and to follow Him are inseparable. He is telling us, in effect, "I understand how human you are. I know each one of you is anything but perfect. And yet I want you to know that to follow Me – to be My Disciple – you must be devoted to the task of bettering yourselves."

To follow our Blessed Lord is to work at ongoing change in our lives necessarily. To follow Jesus is to work at letting go of everything we have crowded in at the center of our lives that is not God-centered. You see, MDP, this is not a once in a lifetime transformation Jesus is calling for. It is an ongoing, continuing change, a process of development and growth that stretches out over our entire life.

A priest friend of mine had in his parish his nephew who was the most egotistical, the most self-centered, the most selfish, young person imaginable. One Sunday, my priest friend decided to preach a sermon aimed directly at his nephew. From the pulpit he looked directly at his nephew who was seated in a front pew, and he denounced egotism, self-centeredness and selfishness in the strongest terms. "Surely," the priest said to himself, "this will motivate my nephew to change his selfish ways!"

Later, as my priest friend was greeting members of the parish as they were leaving church, his nephew shook his hand and said enthusiastically, "Great sermon, Uncle! You sure gave it to them today!"

When we hear the call of our Blessed Lord to change our way of living, we are inclined to identify with the priest's nephew. But Jesus is not talking about "them." His words are intended for me and for you!

In today's Gospel, we see the name John given to the eight-day old baby. We see his father cured of a speech impediment. We see the neighbors filled with awe, and we hear Luke tell us that "the child grew up and his spirit matured." So John the Baptist, great desert preacher, needed to prepare himself for the task. And so it is for all the New Testament figures who wanted to follow Christ.

Take the prime example of Peter, the great Saint, Peter was constantly blowing hot and cold, making mistakes, dropping the ball, not getting things right. Three times Peter denied Christ. St. Peter, a good man but far from perfect. But that is not the whole story, because God never gave up on Peter and his willingness to change.

There is an ancient fable about a water-bearer in India: the water-bearer had two large pots hung on each end of a pole which he carried on the back of his neck and shoulders. Each day he took a long walk from his master's house to a running stream. There he filled the pots with water and walked back to his master's house. One of the pots had a crack in it and always arrived only half full. The other pot was perfect and always arrived with a full portion. This went on daily for more than two years. Of course, the flawless pot was proud of its perfect record. But the poor cracked pot grew more and more ashamed of its sorry record of accomplishing only half of what it was made to do. Sensing this, the water-bearer said to the cracked pot, as he filled it with water: As we return to the master's house, I want you to notice the beautiful flowers along the path. Notice also there are flowers only on your side of the path. That's because I have always known about your flaw and I put it to good advantage by planting flower seeds on your side of the path. And every day, as we walked back from the stream, you watered them. And for a long time now I have been able to pick those beautiful flowers to decorate my mother's table."

MDP, each of us has his or her own unique flaws. We are all cracked pots – crackpots – in this sense. But, along the way, despite our flaws and imperfections, each of us has the God-given potential to do something beautiful for our Lord Jesus Christ, and for one another. This is the very process of growing up spiritually and entering fully into the life of God.

So, like John the Baptist, "grow up," Jesus says. There never is a point at which our potential for spiritual growing up stops. There is never an age at which we can say there is no need for change in our lives. In all honesty we simply have to see the need for reform in all of us crackpots.

B – Luke 1:57-66

We celebrate the Feast of the Birth of John the Baptizer. No one, except for the Mother of God, no one had a higher function in unfolding the story of salvation. John challenges us Christians to live our dependence on God in Christ Jesus.

There is a recently published book titled "Beautiful Souls: Saying No, Breaking Ranks, and Heeding the Voice of Conscience in Dark Times" by reporter Eyal Press. Press's book is a collection of stories of unexceptional, ordinary people who took great risks for others, at great sacrifice. He tells the story of Paul Gruniger who was a police officer. Paul guarded the border in a Swiss town near the Austrian border. He was a quiet, church-going man; he served with the Swiss army in World War I. He married and had a family. His job as police officer involved completing reports and arranging security for visiting officials.

One morning in 1939 he went to work and found his office blocked by a uniformed officer who said, "Sir, you no longer have the right to enter these premises." His credentials were taken from him; he was stripped of his uniform. An investigation had discovered that Gruniger was secretly altering the documents of Jews fleeing Austria for safety in Switzerland. When the Nazis came to power in Austria, Austrian Jews headed to the Swiss border. To avoid confrontation with the Nazis, Swiss police were directed to deny the Jews entry, but Officer Gruniger would make minor alterations in their passports to allow them to enter safely. He paid the price for this. He was dismissed from his position.

The Nazis circulated false rumors that Gruniger had demanded money and sexual favors from those he helped. Paul was shunned by his neighbors. He could only peddle raincoats, and animal feed until he died, and he died broke and disgraced. He died in 1972. He was buried with his wife near St. Gallen in Austria. Seventy years after the war, a plaque was placed on his grave. It read: "Paul Gruniger saved hundreds of refugees in 1938-1939." At his funeral a Rabbi read from the Talmud: "He who saves a single life, saves the entire world."

MDP, Paul Gruniger is just one of the prophets of our time who are not afraid to proclaim the reign of God as they challenge what they see as immoral and evil and disgusting and horrible in our world. Today the Church celebrates the Birth of John the Baptizer, the last great Prophet who bridges the Old Testament and the New Testament.

John gave his life, as the 4th Gospel says, to "testify to the light," who is Christ. He paid the price for his testimony! May we possess the courage of Paul Gruniger and John the Baptizer to be prophets of the "Light of Christ when darkness threatens to snuff out that light in our lives, in our parish, in our town, in our world.

THIRTEENTH SUNDAY IN ORDINARY TIME
A – Matthew 10:37

A good number of years ago, I sat glued to the TV watching Archie Bunker and his bickering family pick on each other. Even as I watch the reruns from time to time, somehow, I still notice the deep love, the awkward tenderness and strong concern felt by each member of that family. The sitcom, "All in the Family", did not portray a model, ideal, artificial family; but a living, breathing, real one. For me it depicted average, every day, and ordinary people, often annoyed with one another, often angry with one another. But still, there was a strong bond of love between them. There was a readiness to forgive that often resulted in sincere, sometimes clumsy efforts to bring out the best qualities in each other. I remember when the day came for Gloria (the daughter) and "Meathead" (her husband) to leave the Bunker nest. I, as well as many in the audience, felt a tangible sadness as if we were losing a close friend.

MDP, separation can be tough. But, isn't that the way it is in life? No family lasts forever, no matter how loving, how fulfilling, how tender the warm family circle, all families break up, eventually. Children grow up, and go off to chase their own personal rainbows. And, eventually, inevitably, family members are separated by death. When we are living in the warm and comforting glow of a happy family life, it is so difficult for some of us to acknowledge that God comes first in our lives, that He is our closest, and our most constant love.

There is one line from an ancient Psalm that has always haunted me: "Unless the Lord builds the house, they labor in vain that build it." We may accept the concept in principle, but it is tough to put into practice. Sometimes our family circle is so happy and complete to us that we forget that it is God who must come first. We heard it in the Gospel today: "Whoever loves father or mother, son or daughter, more than me is not worthy of me." If God does not come first in our lives, we are in deep trouble. All that will be left when it is said and done, will be an aching void, a terrible loneliness, a desperate fear that nobody cares about us.

One of the most touching songs in the musical "Les Miserables" is the song "Empty Chairs and Empty Tables." Its theme: 'All the old, familiar faces are gone!' But when God is first in our lives, we know passionately that we are never alone. We are never without love; we are never abandoned by God. And, you know, MDP, when we put our love for God first in our lives, our ability to love others increases. We are secure in God's love and this, paradoxically, frees us to love others with a respect for their integrity, and in a way that will enhance their lives.

There's a scene in an old Noel Coward play, called "Cavalcade." This particular scene takes place on the deck of an Atlantic Ocean liner. It is about 7:00 PM, Sunday, April 14, 1912. Standing on the deck at the ship's rail are Edith and Edward—on their honeymoon trip. The conversation between them reveals that they are very much in love and so very happy. Edith says to Edward, "This is the best sort of happiness. But what happens when you begin to get tired of me?" Edward says, "I never shall. Anyhow, look at Father and Mother; they're perfectly happy and devoted, and they have always been," Edith says. "They had a better chance at the beginning. Things weren't changing so swiftly; life wasn't so restless." Then Edward asked, "How long do you give us?" Edith says, "I don't know, and Edward, I don't care. This is our moment—complete and heavenly. I'm not afraid of anything. This is our own forever."

Edward takes Edith in his arms and kisses her. Edith then takes up her coat which has been hanging over the ship's rail, and they walk away. The coat has been covering a life jacket. On it, in big black letters appear the words, "S.S. Titanic." The stage lights fade into complete darkness, but the letters remain glowing as the orchestra plays very softly and tragically, "Nearer My God to Thee."

MDP, from the moment of our birth to the moment of our death; that is our song: "Nearer My God to Thee." It doesn't matter what age we are now the seconds are ticking away, relentlessly one-by-one; we must take today's Gospel to heart and believe that God not only wants us to realize that our lives are moving toward Him, but He also wants us to experience His loving presence here and now. "He who will not take up his cross and come after me is not worthy of Me," He says in the Gospel. What He is saying is, "Love one another as I have loved you." He is telling us to harmonize our love for one another as proclaimed in the Gospel; He is asking us to allow our love for God to draw us closer to one another; and to let our love for one another draw us closer to God. With the Gospel, he is challenging us not to forget that by placing God first in our lives, we are living life to the fullest, singing our theme song, "Nearer My God to Thee!"

A BACKPACK

Not long ago I remember seeing an NBC news report about two young hikers, Brandon Day and Gina Allen who took an afternoon off from a sales conference they were attending near Palm Springs, California. They decided to hike through the snowy San Jacinto Mountains. They ventured off from the main trail and soon found themselves completely lost. They spent the next three days alone in the wilderness, hungry, cold, with very little hope of rescue. They needed a miracle to survive—and they got one...from a dead man.

After spending a cold night on the mountain, the young couple came upon an abandoned campsite. There they found a discarded backpack—and inside the backpack, they found a book of matches. They started a fire that saved their lives. In the backpack, they also found a sweater for Gina and a pair of warm socks for Brandon. Rescue teams saw the smoke and went to the dehydrated and scared Gina and Brandon to bring them down from the mountain.

The backpack also contained a diary belonging to John Donovan, a sixty-year-old hiker from Virginia. Donovan, an experienced hiker, wrote that he was caught in icy weather in a place where he wasn't going to be found and where nobody would know to look for him. Amazingly, the diary entry was dated exactly a year to the day that Brandon and Gina found it. John Donovan was never found! Brandon and Gina will always be grateful for the man whose tragic end gave them a new beginning.

FEAST OF SAINT PETER AND SAINT PAUL
—JUNE 29
MATTHEW 16:13-19

Jesus Christ taught us the meaning of love not just with words, but with our life. This is the call of Christ to all of us, and He began with Peter and Paul.

One was a poor fisherman, a man with little or no education. For three years, he followed Jesus, the Rabbi, from Nazareth, even though he did not always grasp what Jesus said and did. Once, this fisherman suggested that Jesus, the Rabbi, not speak so openly about the suffering he would endure because people would not understand and would be needlessly upset. Jesus responded angrily, sending him away. The night before Jesus died; the fisherman was too embarrassed to allow Jesus to wash his feet. And just as Jesus had foretold, the fisherman, who at first took out a sword to defend Jesus from the guards who came to arrest him, and a few hours later, he denied even knowing him. Jesus gave him the name, Peter.

The other was a learned Rabbi himself, a skilled craftsman who was an expert maker of tents. He was a passionate writer and preacher, and a loyal defender of Judaism. He was a man of stature in the community, respected by both his own people and the Roman occupiers of his nation. He was ruled by his convictions and so he led the first persecutions against the new sect of radicals and troublemakers who threatened the Jewish faith—the so-called "Christians." His name was Paul.

It was upon the fisherman-Peter, the Rock, that the Rabbi Jesus established his new Church. And it was upon Paul, the Apostle to the Gentiles whom the Lord called to proclaim the Gospel to the farthest ends of the earth.

A fisherman and a scholar; a poor simple worker who scraped together whatever living he could from the fish he could catch, and a man of letters and position, one who was quiet, simple, rough around the edges and often overwhelmed by the events swirling around him. The other: a man of great intelligence and passion, a masterful writer, preacher, a visionary. Both were called by God to the role of Apostle—messengers of the Gospel.

I want to tell you briefly of a modern-day messenger of the Gospel of Jesus…

Father Frans Lugt, a Dutch Jesuit, worked in Syria since 1966. He was loved by both Christians and Muslims in the old city of Homs. Two weeks before Easter, just days before his seventy-sixth birthday, a lone assailant dragged him into the street, beat him and shot him twice.

For years, every Syrian who came to his door for help was welcomed. He would say, "I didn't come to Syria to help just Christians. I don't see Muslims or Christians; I see only human beings who hunger to lead a good life." Father Frans brought Muslims and Christians together to talk and study the art, culture and history of their homeland.

As hunger took hold of the city, a Muslim charity would give Father Frans nine pounds of flour every week, which he turned into bread and gave a loaf to the neediest people in the town. A few days before his murder, Father Frans wrote to friends, "We are preparing for Easter, reflecting on the crossing from death to resurrection. We feel like we are in the valley of the shadows, but we can see that flight far away, leading us to life again. We hope that Syria experiences resurrection soon…" Father Frans, an apostle of Jesus Christ, changed the lives of thousands of people. He taught the meaning of love not just with words, but with life. This is the call of Jesus Christ.

MDP, the lives of Saint Peter and Saint Paul and Father Frans, show how God uses us, you and me, persons of every kind of background, intellect and talent to be apostles—people sent forth to proclaim, to reveal, to teach the story of God. On this Feast of these great Apostles, the Church asks us to recommit ourselves to use whatever talents and abilities we have to proclaim the Gospel we love and have embraced.

FOURTEENTH SUNDAY IN ORDINARY TIME
A – MATTHEW 11:25-30

Seven hundred years before Jesus' birth, a Greek slave named Aesop compiled a collection of stories. Today we know them as "Aesop's Fables." One of the fables deals with a dispute between the sun and the wind. The dispute was over which of the two was the stronger…

One day an opportunity arose to settle the dispute. A person dressed in a coat was walking down a deserted country road. The sun said to the wind, "Whoever makes that person remove the coat faster will be the winner." The wind not only agreed but decided to go first. He blew and blew, but the more he blew, the tighter the person held on to the coat. Finally, exhausted, the wind gave up. Then the sun took over. It merely shone in all its glory. Within minutes, the person took off the coat. Aesop said that the moral of the story is this: You can achieve more by gentleness than by violence.

Today gentleness is not as highly regarded as it once was. There was a time when the best compliment you could pay someone was to call him or her a gentle person—a gentleman…but today violence is more popular than gentleness; and television (and the movies have given it a widespread audience.) I believe three years ago an older brother killed his younger brother by duplicating some of the kicks seen on wrestling shows.

Sometimes our own families reflect the violence of our age. We shout at one another, we slam things around the house, we throw things, we yell at one another and sometimes we even strike one another… And Jesus comes along in this Gospel and says, "Learn from me because I am gentle and humble of heart." A beautiful example of the gentleness of Jesus was the way He handled the woman caught in adultery. He didn't shout or rave and rant, He simply bent over and wrote in the sand with His finger. His action stood out like a clap of thunder in the silence of a summer's night.

Or do you remember the father in the story of the prodigal son. The father didn't shout at his wayward son. He didn't call him names or hassle him; no, he hugged him!

There's an old Navy story about Henry "Butch" O'Hare. Butch was the Navy's number-one ace (six pilot year) in World War II, and the first Naval Aviator to win the Congressional Medal of Honor. Chicago's International Airport is named for him. What Butch O'Hare became was because of a gentle conversion in his father's life. Butch's father, Edward J O'Hare, was a quick, tough-talking lawyer for the gangster Al Capone. They used to call him "Artful Eddy". He had money; he had power. He was ruthless! But one day he woke up, saw the effect his violent lifestyle was having on his family, especially his son, and had a change of heart. He squealed on Al Capone! Before long the violent mob that he belonged to, silenced artful Eddie with two shotgun blasts. Because of his turn away from violence to gentleness—because he paid with his life for his son to make good—his son subsequently was accepted into Annapolis and became that Ace of World War II.

Today's Gospel contains an important invitation for all of us. It invites us to learn from our Good Lord because He is gentle and humble in spirit. What does this mean as we leave Church and try to live another week of our Christian lives? It means we must try to respond to our family, to our friends, to other people as the sun did in Aesop's Fable of the wind and the sun with genuine warmth. It means we must respond with gentleness and understanding to those who wronged us as Jesus did in the case of the woman caught in adultery or the father with his prodigal son. It means, like Artful Eddie, we must pray for a conversion of heart and place the interests of our children, our family above our own. Listen again to those haunting words of the Gospel: "Learn from Me because I am gentle and humble of heart."

B – Mark 6:1-6

A father took his two daughters shopping for a new bicycle for five-year old Jenna. Jenna picked out a shiny 'Starlett' with a banana seat and training wheels. Andrea, three years old, decided she wanted one as well. Dad explained to Andrea that she was not big enough for a two-wheeler, that she was still having trouble with her tricycle. Andrea was not convinced. She still wanted a 'big girl' bike, like her sister. Her father tried to make her understand that a big bike would bring her more pain than pleasure, more scrapes than thrills. Pouting, Andrea turned away and said nothing. Dad promised that when she was older, she would get a 'big girl' bike. Andrea just stared at him. Finally, Dad sighed and said, "Look Honey, Daddy knows best, okay?" Andrea then screamed loud enough for everyone in the store to hear: "Then I want a new daddy!"

Three-year-old Andrea's response is not much different than our own response to the realities we do not want to face, a wisdom we refuse to embrace, a truth that clashes with the way we live our lives.

MDP, we are crippled in our search for wisdom by a society which describes 'success' as the ability to acquire knowledge for personal gain. We have reached the point of progress where our capacity to gather, store and interpret data is almost limitless. This knowledge-gathering explosion has brought us some good things, to be sure. However, we need to be reminded that it has brought us problems and complications that we have never faced before. As a society, and as individuals we are acquiring knowledge at breakneck speed without slowing down, ever, to reflect on how to handle it, what to do with it, how to use it to uplift the human spirit. Living our lives wisely means developing a lifestyle which in itself is an act of faith in God's promise of ultimate, total fulfillment when the tourist season of our life is over. If we want to discover the meaning of life, Scripture tells us that we must be in touch with God. We must love the Lord with our heart and soul and mind. We find wisdom, then, only to the extent that we are in touch with God on this level.

There is a story about an American tourist visiting a nineteenth century Polish rabbi who was looked upon by his people as an extremely wise and saintly person. On his arrival at the rabbi's residence, the tourist was astonished to discover that it consisted of only one simple room. The walls were lined with books. A table and chair were the only furnishings. "Rabbi," the tourist asked, "where is your furniture?" to which the rabbi replied, "Where is yours?" "Where is mine?" said the puzzled tourist. "I'm only a visitor here, just passing through." "So am I," answered the rabbi, "so am I."

In today's Gospel lesson, Jesus begins teaching in the synagogue, and most of His listeners are astonished to hear His words of wisdom. "How did He get this wisdom? Isn't He the carpenter's Son?" They refused to take Him seriously.

MDP, because of our deep personal faith in God, we are empowered to take the teachings of Jesus Christ seriously. We are empowered to live wisely, to take each day of our earthly journey a preparation for a new life in the Lord Jesus Christ. Because of our deep, personal faith in Jesus Christ, we are empowered to make each day of our earthly journey a time for loving one another as Jesus has loved us.

A Spelling Bee

Let me tell you about an inspiring movie called "Akeelah and the Bee". Akeelah Anderson is a bright and gifted eleven-year-old—and doesn't want anyone to know it. She hides her brilliance in slang talk and posing; she skips a lot of classes because the curriculum doesn't challenge her. It's the only way to survive at her South Central Los Angeles school, where being labeled a 'brainiac' is dangerous. You'd better keep your smarts to yourself or be mercilessly ridiculed by other students whose own self-esteem has been eaten away by defeatism; and who are mired in an inferiority complex that extends beyond the walls of their school to their entire neighborhood and community.

Akeelah has a real talent for spelling. Beating time with her hand against her thigh, she triumphantly cranks out the letters of the most obscure words. A college English professor takes an interest in her and teaches her not only to spell, but how to succeed. Tasting victory at her school spelling bee, Akeelah puts aside her "cool" detachment to learning and finally admits that she wants to win. Her success and hard work transforms not only her school but her whole South Central neighborhood. Family, friends and teachers become her coaches, even the local 'Gangstas', even the mailman. Akeelah wins the national spelling bee. Her daring to use her talent and intelligence to succeed challenges them to pursue wisdom, the wisdom of their own dreams.

I thought this movie was very much in line with today's Gospel when the people of Jesus' hometown reject him when his prophetic words call them to move beyond their own safe, insulated world. Akeelah dares to challenge the pessimism, the mindlessness, the lack of reflection and wisdom of her environment. And Jesus calls us—no, He dares us, to change our perspective, to slow down, to see if we have really placed Him and His teaching at the center of our lives and so empower ourselves to make each day of our earthly journey a chance to let the masterpiece of Christ shine through us. He wants to help prepare us for a new and dynamic life in Him, Jesus Christ.

KIND ECHOES

When I was stationed in Italy, I would often go to an area in the Abruzzi where the slopes were high; and the valleys deep. Once while there, I was caught up in the words of a tour guide who was trying to explain the wonder of the echoes that resound in certain areas. But instead of giving the tourists a technical explanation of how echoes are caused by reflected sounds, the guide offered them a bit of his own wisdom. He said, "When you speak kind words, you will be answered by kind echoes." Our Blessed Lord has come to show us His wisdom and the possibilities of living a life of love to the fullest in our homes and in our hearts…and to know that our kind words will be answered by kind echoes!

C (1) – Luke 10: 7-12

So many people—among us and all around us—seem to find little cause for rejoicing in the lives they are living. So many people today are discovering that the quest for happiness, apart from living their lives in the presence of God, inevitably leads to boredom and frustration and depression, and the disintegration of marriages and families. So many people are discovering that money after all, isn't really, what life is all about; that fame after all, isn't really what life is all about; that power after all, isn't really what life is all about. And yet, Jesus tells us over and over again in the Gospel that God is what life is all about; that accepting God's love and entering into a lifelong love affair with God is what life is all about.

Accepting God's love and living in this love affair with God we become whole, we 'get it all together,' we become the uniquely beautiful human persons God created us to be. And, out of this wholeness comes the strength to love other people in a life-enhancing way—not manipulating them, not trying to dominate them, not trying to take life from them; not trying to use them.

I have a priest friend who works with the homeless. He told me this story. I will try to recount it as he told it to me.

There's a story about a bag lady in New York that the author, Bobbie Probstein, tells and I want to share with you. He says, "This lady used to sleep in the Fifth Street post office. I could smell her before I rounded the entrance to where she slept, standing up, by the public phones. I could smell her through the layers of her dirty clothing and the decay from her nearly toothless mouth. If she was not asleep, she mumbled incoherently.

Now they close the post office at six to keep the homeless out, so she would curl up on the sidewalk, talking to herself, her mouth flapping open as though unhinged, her smells diminished by the soft breeze.

One Thanksgiving we had so much food left over, I packed it up, excused myself from the others and drove over to Fifth Street.

It was a frigid night. Leaves were swirling around the streets and hardly anyone was out, all but a few of the luckless in some warm home or shelter. But I knew I would find her.

She was dressed as she always was, even in summer. The warm wooly layers concealing her old, bent body. Her bony hands clutched the precious shopping cart. She was squatting against a wire fence in front of the playground next to the post office. "Why didn't she choose some place more protected from the wind?" I thought, and assumed she was so crazy she did not have the sense to huddle in a doorway.

I pulled my shiny car to the curb, rolled down the window and said, "Mother…would you…" and I was shocked at the word 'Mother." But she was…is in some way I cannot grasp.

I said, again, "Mother, I've brought you some food. Would you like some turkey and stuffing and apple pie?"

At this the old woman looked at me and said quite clearly and distinctly, her two loose lower teeth wobbling as she spoke, "Oh, thank you very much, but I'm quite full now. Why don't you take it to someone who really needs it?" Her words were clear, her manners gracious. Then I was dismissed; her head sank into her rags again.

MDP, if we try to build relationships apart from God in our own lives, if we try to do something for another apart from having God in our lives, we will end up hurting rather than healing one another. You know how it is: people are always doing things to us and our immediate reaction is either to be hurt and feel rejected or to get mad and fight back in kind. And the alienation sets in: husbands versus wives; parents versus children; nations versus nations. This is a natural reaction. Ask yourself, "If there had been a time this past week when the presence of God in your life had made a difference in the life of another? Will there be a time this coming week when the presence of God in your life convinces someone else that a gracious God is in control and that you can show Him to someone who needs Him?"

A FIREMAN

There's a story about a boy named Bopsy I want to share with you…

It begins with a twenty-six-year-old mother staring down at her son who is dying of terminal leukemia. Although her heart is filled with sadness, she also has a strong feeling of determination. Like any parent, she wants her son to grow up and fulfill all his dreams. She knows that this is no longer possible. The leukemia would see to this. But she still wants her son's dreams to come true.

She takes her son's hand and asks, "Bopsy, did you ever think about what you want to be when you grew up? Did you ever dream and wish about what you would do with your life?"

"Mommy, I always wanted to be a fireman when I grew up."

Mom smiles back and says, "Let's see if we can make your wish come true." Later that day she goes to her local fire department in Phoenix, Arizona, where she meets Fireman Bob, who has a heart as big as Phoenix. She explains her son's final wish and asks if it might be possible to give her six-year-old son a ride around the block on a fire engine.

Fireman Bob says, "Look, we can do better than that. If you'll have your son ready at seven o'clock Wednesday morning, we'll make him an honorary fireman for the whole day. He can come down to the fire station, eat with us, go out on all the fire calls, the whole nine yards. And, if you'll give us his sizes, we'll get a real fire uniform made for him, with a real fire hat—not a toy one—with the emblem of the Phoenix fire department on it, a yellow slicker like we wear and rubber boots. They're really manufactured right here in Phoenix, so we can get them fast."

Three days later Fireman Bob picks up Bopsy, dresses him in his fire uniform and escorts him from his hospital bed to the waiting hook and ladder truck. He helps Bopsy sit up on the back of the truck and lets him steer it back to the fire station. Bopsy is in heaven.

There are three fire calls in Phoenix that day and Bopsy gets to go out on all three calls. He rides in the different fire engines, the paramedics' van and even the fire chief's car. He was also videotaped for the local news program.

MDP, having this dream come true, with all the love and attention that was lavished upon him, so deeply touched Bopsy that he lived three months longer than any doctor thought possible.

One night all of his vital signs begin to drop dramatically and the head nurse, who believes in the hospice concept that no one should die alone, begins to call the family members to the hospital. Then she remembers the day Bopsy spent as a fireman, so she calls the fire chief and asks if it would be possible to send a fireman in uniform to the hospital to be with Bopsy as he prepared to go to God. The chief replies, "We can do better than that. We'll be there in five minutes. Will you please do me a favor? When you hear the sirens screaming and see the lights flashing, will you announce over the PA system that there is not a fire? It's just the fire department coming to see one of its finest members one more time. And will you open the window to his room? Thanks."

About five minutes later a hook and ladder truck arrives at the hospital, extends its ladder up to Bopsy's third floor open window and fourteen firemen and two firewomen climbed up the ladder into Bopsy's room with his mother's permission, they hug him and hold him and tell him how much they loved him.

With his dying breath, Bopsy looks up at the fire chief and says, "Chief, am I really a fireman now?" "Bopsy, you are," the chief said. With those words, Bopsy smiles and closes his eyes for the last time.

MDP, all of us experience sorrow, pain, grief and despair in our lives. As He appoints the seventy-two in today's Gospel, Jesus commissions every disciple of every time and place especially those disciples of Marine Corps Air Show El Toro to go before him to bring 'peace' into the lives of others, to be firemen of compassion, reconciliation and hope to those in need. Such is the 'work' of faith, the 'labor' of discipleship. It is in extending such blessings to others that we are blessed in return.

C (2) – Luke 10: 25-37

Those of us who grew up in neighborhoods—like I did in South Philadelphia—are able to understand this morning's Gospel very easily. The 'neighbor' is someone special to us. We can encounter people from the neighborhood halfway around the world, and even if we didn't know them all that well at home, they still seem like long lost friends: they are one of us, people who share something terribly important with us. A neighbor is a person for whom we feel responsible, and who feels some kind of a responsibility for us. Among neighbors, there are strong links of support, of respect, affection, and trust.

The priest and the Levite in today's Gospel quickly passed by the wounded man because they did not see him as a human being. He was a stranger, and no one had any obligations to strangers. Indeed, it is of the very essence of being a stranger that one can make no claim on others to be treated as full human beings. But when the Samaritan came by, he did not see a stranger; he recognized a neighbor, a fellow human being who had the same claims on him, as did the man who lived next door. For the follower of Christ Jesus, everyone lives next door; everyone grew up just down the street; everyone's mother knows your mother. Yes, for the follower of Christ Jesus, the neighbor is mankind.

I listened and watched a good Samaritan story that most of the TV news stations reported on, a Samaritan story with not so good an ending...

The news report came from Queens, New York. Hugo Alfredo Tale-Yax was a thirty-one-year-old immigrant from Guatemala. Finding work as a day laborer in the current economy had been all but impossible. Hugo had been without a place to live, and most nights he slept in the public park. On a Sunday morning in April, Hugo was walking down a street in Queens when he saw a man and woman having a violent argument. He crossed the street to intervene. The man swung around and stabbed Hugo several times in the stomach. Leaving Hugo in a puddle of blood, the man and woman fled in opposite directions. Hugo lay unconscious on the sidewalk for an hour. A surveillance tape showed dozens of people walking by Hugo and doing nothing to help him. Two people stopped and discussed the situation; one even paused to take a picture. The others turned to look out of curiosity, and then hurried away. Finally, someone bent down to shake Hugo and saw the blood. Police and emergency medical personnel were called—but it was too late. Hugo died. Helping a stranger was the last act of a broken man. We are the world we live in!

MDP, today's Gospel and this sad story of Hugo Tale-Yax, remind us that sometimes we are the victim and sometimes we are the Samaritan. But our blessed Lord makes it clear that we are always the neighbor, we are always the brother and sister who must reach out to help another. The Gospel of the good Samaritan calls us to embrace a vision of faith that sees every man, woman, and child—regardless of whatever labels society has assigned to them—as our 'neighbors.' Yes, 'our neighbor' is every one of us who sees one another with the eyes of Christ as sons and daughters of God, brothers and sisters of the Risen Lord.

Twinkies and Root Beer

I often feel we can learn something of the Gospel of Jesus Christ and the art of successful living from children. There was once a little boy who wanted to meet God. He figured it would be a long journey, so he filled his backpack with Twinkies and a six-pack of root beer. And then he sets off.

When he had gone about three blocks, he met an old woman. She was sitting in the park quietly, just watching the pigeons. The boy sat down next to her on the bench and opened his backpack. He was about to take a drink from his first root beer when he noticed that the old lady looked hungry, so he offered her a Twinkie. She gratefully accepted it and smiled at him. Her smile was so wonderful that the little boy wanted to see it again, so he offered her a root beer. Once again, she smiled. The boy was delighted. They sat there all afternoon eating and smiling, never saying a word.

As it grew late, the boy got up to leave, but before he had gone a few steps, he turned to the old lady and gave her a hug. She gave him the biggest smile ever.

When the boy opened the door to his own house a short time later, his mother was surprised by the look of happiness on his face. "What did you do today?" she asked. "I had lunch with God." But before his mother could respond, he continued, "You know what? She's got the most beautiful smile I've ever seen!"

About the same time, the old woman returned to her home. Her son was stunned by the rare smile on her face. "Mother, what happened that brought such a smile to your face?" "I ate Twinkies in the park with God." Before her son could respond, she continued, "You know, he's much younger than I expected."

MDP, in our love for others, God resides in us; in the kindness and care we are able to extend to others, we realize the presence of God in us. Like the seventy-two in today's Gospel, Jesus appoints every disciple of every time and place to go before Him to bring 'joy' and 'peace' into the lives of others, to be His messengers of compassion and hope in this very, very needy world. This it the work of what it means to be a disciple of Jesus Christ: to bring the peace of God into every home and heart, to make one person happy, with a healing word, a smile and a root beer.

FIFTEENTH SUNDAY IN ORDINARY TIME
A – Matthew 13:1-23

MDP, if we want to be true followers of Jesus Christ, we have got to do something about it; we have got to do something about it clearly through the rest of our lives!

There is a story about a little girl who sat at her grandmother's feet listening to the Creation story from the book of Genesis...

As the grandmother unfolded the story, she noticed that her grandchild was unusually quiet. "Well, what do you think of it, dear?" "Oh, I love it," the child answered, "You never know what God is going to do next." That little girl was making a profound distinction between our preconceived notions of who God is and what He does, and who He really is and what He really does. It is the difference between being a passive listener to God's Word and an actual hearer of God's Word. It is the difference between some vague, general understanding that God has spoken, and the conviction that God is speaking to me—right here and now! And, this is the point of today's Gospel of the sower.

Jesus likens the seed to the Word of God, and the ground in which it is sown to people like you and me to whom the Word is addressed.

There's another story about a preacher who was about ten minutes into his sermon when a voice from the very last pew called out, "Louder! Louder!"

The preacher raised his voice a bit, but again the voice cried out, "Louder! Louder!" This time the preacher bent down to talk as close as possible to the microphone, but the voice from the back pew persisted: "Louder! Louder!" whereupon, there was a man sitting the front pew who spoke up, turned around, and said, "Can't you hear back there?" "No, I can't!" "Then move over, I'm coming back where you are." How often we are the man in the front pew! We miss the point of God's Word; or, even worse, we don't want to hear God's Word. We might be listening, but we are spiritually deaf. The Word of God is exciting, and life changing, and will flower and bear fruit only on good ground, only on soil that is properly conditioned to receive it. Perhaps the little girl in the first story I told gave us a terrific insight: to listen and to expect the unexpected from the good and gracious God because "You never know what God is going to do next!"

The brilliant writer, C.S. Lewis, wrote a thought-provoking book called "The Great Divorce." It is not about a divorce that occurs between a husband and wife. It is about a divorce that occurs between our souls and God. In his book, C.S. Lewis gives us a picture of hell as a big city, with all its big city pressures and problems. The weather is always cold and wet with a heavy rain. The light is always grey and murky. The people in this city of hell become more and more aware of the great divorce that has taken place between their souls and God, and they sink deeper and deeper into their dismal surroundings. But…there is a way out! C.S. Lewis says there is a way out of this terrible condition! God has provided a shuttle-bus service from hell to heaven: Regular bus service. All you need to do is to get on the bus and, by the power of God and His Word; it will carry you into the light. But the most incredible thing about the story is that very few people board the buses, even though they keep coming right on schedule. The people find all kinds of excuses for putting the journey off to some vague future time. Hardly anyone wants to get on the bus right now! Consequently, most of them miss the opportunity to be carried by the power of God from death to life.

MDP, our good and gracious God never ceases to sow His seed; He is always trying to get through to us. We can hear his voice only if we truly listen. We must turn toward him in the spirit of complete openness and complete trust, just as a sunflower turns toward the sun to absorb its creative light.

Mother Theresa of Calcutta was first refused by her Bishop and her religious order to start her work for the poor and dying. Her superiors told her she would never see results and they asked her what resources she had. Her answer was, "Three pennies." "What can you do with three pennies?" they scoffed. "Nothing," Mother Theresa said. "But with three pennies and God, I can do anything."

MDP, only with this kind of an attitude, reverential listening and determined action, can we confront our own deepest and most authentic self. There's a saying which goes like this, "Religion is a way of walking, not a way of talking." MDP, listen to the Lord. The more we listen, the closer we will get to Him; the more we listen to Him; the closer we will get to one another. So, with C.S. Lewis, let us board the bus; with Mother Theresa, "with three pennies and God, we can do anything."

B – Mark 6:7-13

There are so many people who come to church, and maybe even some of us here today, who feel that life is a drag, who feel less enthusiastic about the life they are living as followers of Jesus Christ.

There's a story about the pastor of a large parish who decided to try and whip us some enthusiasm in his lifeless congregation...

So one Sunday morning, as the people came into church, he gave each a helium-filled balloon on a string. The pastor then asked them to let go of their balloons at any point in the worship service during which they felt moved by God.

At one point, a single balloon went up. Toward the end of the sermon, two more went up. A few more rose during the singing of a hymn. But that was it! At the end, the great majority of the worshippers were still clinging to their balloons.

MDP, it is time for us to let go of our balloons. There is work for the Lord to be done. There is a mission to perform. And just as we heard in the Gospel, the Lord Jesus is sending us out for the very same purpose he sent out those first Disciples. But before we go, we need to search ourselves. We must honestly look at ourselves to see if we are lacking in wholeness. Sometimes we long to be changed from what we are to what we know God wants us to be. Oh, yes, in this desire to transform our lives, some of us join classes; read books; order CDs; have group sessions. But there is something that just doesn't connect, something that doesn't seem to last; perhaps, it is because we have not discovered the secret of the Gospel. It was given to us today: repent, change, create a turning point in our lives. Mark told us in the Gospel. After the Apostles listened carefully to Jesus' instruction…they went off preaching the need of change.

If we too were to go off by ourselves to a quiet place where we would be able to take an honest look at ourselves, what would we begin to see? What shape would the changing of our lives take? Change begins with recognition. We must recognize the fact that we really need it. We must recognize the fact that there are areas in our lives that separate us from God. As followers of Jesus we cannot go along with the modern idea which says, "…Nothing is really wrong if it feels good, or if we can get away with it."

 In one of my Navy tours, I had a young clerk, a Yeoman, named Ralph. Ralph had also served in Vietnam. He had an unusually beautiful attitude about his job, about life. I would often see him helping old people into our chapel services, picking up toddlers during military parades so that they could see what was going on. He was always the first to volunteer in anything that would help others. Once we had time to chat about personal experiences, I asked Ralph, "Ralph, where did you learn to live such a joy-filled, enthusiastic life?" He told me that during his tour in Vietnam, before he became a Chaplain's assistant, his job was to clear mine fields; he said he saw so many of his shipmates meet death right before his eyes. Ralph said, "…I learned to live between the steps… I never knew whether the next one would be my last, so I had to get everything I could out of that moment between picking up my foot and putting it down again. Every step felt like a whole new world."

MDP, we need to let go of our balloons, and like the twelve in to-day's Gospel, we must begin an enthusiastic walk with God. Each step, like my friend Ralph's, will be a whole new world. Each time we make the effort to change will be a moment of grace, an encounter with what is holy, a rebirth, a transformation.

A poet once said, "…Years wrinkle the skin, but to give up enthusiasm wrinkles the soul…" Jesus awaits our enthusiastic response to change, to go out and make disciples of all nations, to let go of our balloons, no matter what they are!

GUITARS AND GARDENS

Jesus told us how to live our daily lives... I would like to tell you two short stories that brought the message of Jesus and the walking stick home to me.

Not long ago, I visited a friend in the hospital. As I walked into the room, I heard guitar music. I heard the guitarist playing Bach's "Jesu, Joy of Man's Desiring". I stood there in silence as I watched a young lady moving her fingers over the strings of her guitar with the quiet confidence of years of practice. She next played an Irish song, then a Bob Dylan folk song, and finally, something that she created. She was playing for an audience of one, a seventy-five-year-old lady who was dying of cancer. Music was her walking stick and, like those Apostles in the Gospel, she provided a measure of peace and tranquility for a person who soon would be taking her leave for eternity.

The second story I would like to share with you is one a little closer to my own heart; it's about my own father and his simple way of living the mission entrusted by Jesus Christ. My father was from Italy, and, like many Italians, he had a small garden in our backyard. When he got home from work, he always headed for that small garden; it was like his favorite place on earth. He grew tomatoes, basil, peppers, corn and string beans. He saved some of this produce for my mother, my sister and myself, but he always, always shared the rest with some needy families in our neighborhood. You see, the young lady with the guitar, and my father with his garden—yes, the guitar, the garden, were their "walking sticks" of the Gospel. They used them, in their own small way, in their mission to live the Gospel of Jesus. The lady with the guitar and my father with his garden knew that Christ had sent them forth to be prophets of goodness; apostles of compassion; ministers of kindness.

MDP, as we make our own personal journey in this life, may we realize, may we use our own small and seemingly insignificant walking sticks to heal the broken-hearted, to show kindness, a smile, to lift a helping-hand to those who stumble, just as the good Lord does for us when we stumble.

C – Luke 10:25-37

MDP, today's Gospel contains a phrase we never should go beyond until we are sure we understand its implications... "You must love the Lord your God with all your heart, with all your soul, with all your strength, with all your mind; and your neighbor as yourself..." We have been given so many good things by Almighty God, and we can say, "Thank you, Lord...Thank you, Lord..." and still not have understood the implications of the command to love the Lord our God. You see the command to love God cannot be understood as long as we make the mistake of regarding the command to 'love neighbor' as a separate command. According to the Gospel of Jesus Christ, love of God and love of neighbor are inseparable! We cannot say we love God, in a Christian way, if, at the same time, we have something against our brother or sister. We show the depth of our love for God in the depth of our love for our neighbor. If our concern for our neighbor is shallow, so too is our love for God shallow.

MDP, if we tell people we have faith, we can't expect them to believe us unless we demonstrate our faith through the kind of life we live.

Two farmers were talking to one another. The first farmer says to the second farmer, "If you had two fields wouldn't you be willing to share one of them?" "Of course!"

"If you had two houses, you wouldn't live in both, so you'd be happy to share the other, wouldn't you?" "Of course! Absolutely!"

"If you had two cars, you would be willing to give one to your neighbor who had none, wouldn't you?" "Yes, indeed!"

"Suppose you had two horses. You would give one to your neighbor, wouldn't you?" "No, I couldn't do that." "Why not?" "Because I have two horses."

Now I would like to contrast this story with the story of an inner-city priest who was making his daily rounds in ministering to the poor...

He stopped in front of a small, broken-down house, the home of a poor family in which there were two sons. The younger of the two boys was physically handicapped. As the priest parked his car in front of the house, he was greeted enthusiastically by the older brother. "Wow, your shiny new car really looks great." the boy said. "Where did you get it?" The priest replied, "You know, son, I don't make much money in my work and I couldn't afford to buy a car like this for myself. But, I have a brother in Houston who makes a lot of money in the oil business. He gave me this car." The boy looked up at the priest and said, wistfully, "I wish I could be a brother like that!"

You see, he might have said, "I wish I had a brother like that", but, clearly, that young man was in on the secret of life's true meaning and purpose...caring is everything. There is no other way to make ourselves rich in the sight of God. There is no other way to experience genuine holiness of life!

MDP, on our life's journey, we do not travel alone. We are all companions on this adventure through this life to the life of God. As 'neighbors' to one another, as the Gospel teaches today, we are called to lift one another up, to seek what is good for one another, to put one another first—and allow ourselves to be lifted up and assisted when we stumble and fall.

I was traveling the subway system in Barcelona, Spain, and I saw an incident in which I thought, 'Boy, there is a sermon in this.' It was cold in Barcelona that day, and the train I was on was preparing to leave the station. A young man was running late and managed to leap into the train car just as it was leaving, before the doors closed. As he took a seat on the car, he looked out the window and saw that in his rush, he lost one of his fur-lined leather gloves, and it was laying on the platform. It probably had fallen out of his coat. There was no time to retrieve it; there was no one who could pass it to him through the train's window. So the man did the only thing he could do. He reached into his coat pocket, pulled out the glove he still had, and threw it out the window where it landed on the platform near its mate. At least, I am sure he reasoned, someone would have a pair of warm gloves on a cold day.

The spirit of the good Samaritan lives in such unexpected, unheralded acts of selflessness, in making good on the many opportunities we have in the course of the day we can make the love of God very real in our homes, in our lives, in this world of ours.

SIXTEENTH SUNDAY IN ORDINARY TIME
A – MATTHEW 13:24-43

One of the Old Testament stories most often told to children is the flood story, featuring Noah and Noah's ark. All of you know that history has recorded many great floods that have ravaged the earth down through the ages, not the least of which is the famous Johnstown Flood in my own home state of Pennsylvania.

Well, there is a story of a survivor of the Johnstown Flood who was extremely fond of telling all about it to any and all who would listen… but with each telling of the story, it became more embellished…

The flood waters got deeper and deeper and his struggle for survival became more and more heroic. Finally, the old man died and went to heaven. When he had settled in, Saint Peter stopped by to ask him if everything in heaven came up to his expectations. "Everything is great," the old man said, "but I would like to tell the story of the Johnstown Flood to some of the others up here." Saint Peter obliged. He assembled a large heavenly audience. But as the old man rose to address them, Saint Peter whispered in his ear, "I think I'd better warn you, Noah is in the audience."

MDP, we listen to the Gospel week in and week out and we hear the story of Jesus and His loving service; and in the spirit of a response to the Gospel, we tell our own story. But when we tell our story, we must remember that Jesus is in the audience. He is there to listen to us as we report our failures and successes, and He really wants to comment on what we say. For example, in today's Gospel, the parable of the sower, He instructs us on our place in His kingdom. He describes any follower of His as good seed. He is telling us that we are called to be the yeast, the leaven is our world; He is asking us to be healers, to be reconcilers, to be peacemakers, and especially never to condemn or judge others.

To return to the parable for just a minute: We heard about the famer who sowed good seed into his field. Then, under cover of night, an enemy sowed weeds among the wheat. And when the new wheat sprouted and ripened, the weeds appeared as well. It's hard to believe that someone would go to the trouble of sowing bad seed in another person's field, but among the people who lived in Jesus' time this was a favorite method of revenge. The farmer could have burned off the whole field; but instead, he pursues the only course which would allow him to salvage his original crop; he allows the wheat and the weeds to grow side by side until harvest. Then, every plant will be cut, the wheat will be stored in barns, and the weeds will be burned.

And then Jesus explains, "The Son of man will send His angels, and they will gather out of His kingdom all things that provoke offenses and all who do evil, and throw them into blazing furnaces." It's probably safe to say that most of us depict ourselves as the wheat, the "good guys." We see the angels collecting all those other guys, throwing them into the fire while we sit back and wait to be escorted into heaven! And perhaps, this parable of Jesus is about how we judge other people. It is God's prerogative to judge others. If he is willing to let the wheat and weeds grow side by side, why should we ever presume upon God's decision?

There is a story about a woman who decided to take a break after a long afternoon in a huge shopping mall…

She sat down on a bench, opened her newspaper, and reached down to take a bite of the candy bar she had just purchased. A well-dressed man was sitting next to her and, much to her chagrin; he suddenly reached down, took a piece of the candy bar and popped it into his mouth! The woman was a bit shocked, but she figured, "I'll just ignore it." Then she took another piece of the candy—and he took another piece of candy and popped it into his mouth. Then, he beat her to the punch and took another piece of the candy bar. By this time, the lady was livid, angry. She grabbed the remaining candy, threw it into a trash basket, and stormed off through the mall, muttering to herself, "that awful person, I should have slapped his face." A few minutes later, she spotted the same man standing in front of a bakery in the mall with a donut in his hand. Later she said, "I couldn't resist the temptation. I grabbed that awful man's wrist, took a big bite of the donut, and walked away." Then she confessed, "When I got home, I put my things down, opened my purse—and there was my unwrapped candy bar! All the time she had been eating his candy!

MDP, the constant willingness to pass judgment on others can bruise feelings; kill relationships; and box people into stereotypes. Instead of being constantly judgmental, the follower of Christ who really listened to today's Gospel should strive to be the yeast, the leaven, to bring out the best in one another.

Please allow me to tell you just another story about a Persian king who wanted to discourage his four sons from making rash judgments…

At his command, the oldest son made a winter journey to see a mango tree. When spring came, the next oldest son was sent on the same journey. Summer followed, and the third son was sent on the same journey. Finally, after the youngest son had made his visit to the mango tree in autumn, the king called them together and asked them to describe the tree. The first son said it looked like a burnt stump. The second disagreed, describing it as lovely—large and green. The third son declared its blossoms were as beautiful as roses. The fourth son said that they were all wrong. To him it was a fruit just like a pear. "Well," the king said, "each of you is right." Seeing the puzzled look in the sons' eyes, the king said, "Each of you saw it in a different season; thus all of you are correct in describing what you saw. But the lesson for you," said the king, "is to withhold your judgment until you have seen the tree in all its seasons."

MDP, if we really appreciate today's Gospel, we will see that Jesus assures us that our relationship with God is the single most important thing in our lives. He tells us that we are leaven, that our relationships with other people affect our relationship with God. When our relationships are rich and loving, the power of God moves in and through us. But when our relationship with another person is destructive, the power of God is blocked and we become estranged from Him.

The story of this beautiful Gospel is about judgment and good seed and bad seed, about saints and sinners living side by side in God's world. In the end, God will sort everything out, and His judgments will be just. Meanwhile, in the short life God has given us, we must strive for the best in ourselves, and look for the very best in others—and leave the harvesting to God. After all, it is God alone who sees each and every one of us in all our seasons!

B – Mark 6:30-34

The Gospel today, which shows the compassion of Jesus, reminds me of the time when I walked into a religious education class on one of my Navy base assignments. The teacher was discussing the words of Jesus where he says, "Come to me all you who labor and are burdened, and I will give you rest. Take my yoke upon you..." The teacher asked, "Who can tell me what a yoke is?" A young boy answered: "A yoke is something they put on the necks of animals." Quizzing him a little further, the teacher asked: "And what is the yoke that Jesus puts on us?" The young boy answered: "It is Jesus putting his arms around our necks." What a marvelous insight into this Gospel of compassion.

MDP, how often do we hear the cries, see the anguished looks, feel the hurt that another is going through, and do very little to help? We all know people who push and shove, and compete and lean on their car horns when an elderly pedestrian is slow in his or her driving habits. We know how to say "No!" very quickly when someone approaches us for financial help. We know persons who automatically 'look the other way' when they see someone in distress—in order not to 'get involved.' We all know persons who can quickly change the subject whenever someone tries to share a problem or hurt them. But today's Gospel shows a God who has come to us through Jesus Christ as a "Man for others, a Man of compassion, a Man, as the young CCD student said "who puts His arms around our necks."

For people who had anxiety problems, Jesus had compassion; for the crowds who were hungry, Jesus had compassion; for the sick and sore and disabled, Jesus had compassion. But what we fail to miss at times is that from the moment people came in contact with Jesus, and wanted to identify with Him, He began to prepare them for a ministry of compassion for others. That's the way it is with those of us who follow Jesus. When we come into contact with Him, He feeds us; He nourishes us; He shows us compassion. He gives us His great love, and then He says, "You go and feed others, nourish them, show them compassion, love them."

A cartoon appeared not long ago in the Wall Street Journal in which a pastor is delivering a sermon on church finances. "I want you good people to understand," he says, "that the cost of salvation is going up." MDP, the cost of salvation has always been high! Because we are infinitely precious in the sight of God, we have certain feelings about who we are and how we want to be treated. Then Jesus raises the cost. He says, in effect, "You will treat others with goodness because they too are infinitely precious in God's eyes."

We are also told in the Gospel today that Jesus and His Disciples went to a deserted place to rest awhile. We need our periods of rest and relaxation; our tired bones need to be refreshed, relaxed and renewed. And, whatever else they do for us, our times of 'getting away from it all' are golden opportunities to take stock of our lives, opportunities to ask ourselves, "Am I really being the person God wants me to be? Am I really doing what God wants me to do? Am I really doing all I can to make Christ visible in me? Do I really follow Jesus and try to be a person of compassion for others?"

I want to tell you a story told to me by a nurse friend; this story said something to me of the kind of compassion characteristic of a follower of Jesus…

Once during her evening shift of duty, my nurse friend escorted a tired, anxious young man to the bedside of an elderly man. She whispered to the patient, "Your son is here." She had to repeat the words several times before the patient's eyes opened. He was heavily sedated and he simply saw the figure of the young man standing beside the bed. He reached out his hand, and the young man tightly wrapped his fingers around it, squeezing a message of encouragement. The nurse brought a chair to the bedside and, all through the night, the young man sat, holding the old man's hand, and whispering general words of hope. The dying man said nothing. As dawn approached, the old man died. The young man gently placed on the bed the lifeless hand he had been holding. My nurse friend began to offer words of sympathy to the young man, but he interrupted her. "Who was that man?" he asked. My friend replied, "I thought he was your father." "No," the young man replied, "I never saw him before in my life." "Then why didn't you say something when I took you to him?" the nurse asked. The young man replied, "I sensed that he really needed his son, and that his son just wasn't there. Then I realized he was too sick to tell whether or not I was his son. And, I knew how much he needed me."

MDP, do we hear the cries of those who really need us? The challenge of the Gospel is: Do we really listen; do we personalize them? Maybe we can find an answer if we take the invitation of the Gospel seriously to go, take a vacation, find a deserted spot, locate a quiet place in hearts, find a space for prayer, and re-center our lives in the life of Christ and His Gospel.

C – Luke 10: 38-42

There's a wonderful story about a man who bought a used suit of clothes at the Goodwill Industry Store…

In one of the pockets, he found a fifteen-year-old ticket for a shoe repair job. The store was still doing business at the old neighborhood location. So, as a lark, the man decided to try to redeem the shoes. When he presented the ticket, the proprietor looked at it for a moment and then disappeared into the back room. A few moments later he reappeared, saying very calmly, "They'll be ready next Tuesday."

"Martha, Martha, you are anxious and upset about many things; one thing only is required. Mary has chosen the better part and she shall not be deprived of it." (Luke 10:42)

But the 'Martha' within us is always there to remind us of our responsibilities; the 'Things to Do' list that is never completed, the calendar that is always full, the deadlines that forever hang over us. There simply aren't enough hours in the day to possess 'The Better Part'.

Today's Gospel recounts the 'tiff' between two sisters: Martha, the practical, no-nonsense housekeeper, and Mary, the romantic, the 'free spirit' who is captivated by the charismatic Jesus. For Martha, there is a household to run, beds to be made, meals to be cooked and served; for Mary, nothing else matters because Jesus is in their midst. It is easy to understand the tension that could arise between two such very different women.

But, in our own experience, Martha and Mary can be and often are the same person. There is something of both Martha and Mary within each one of us—and the conflict between the two is just as real. Our 'Martha' side is consumed with the work and necessities of living and surviving; careers to establish, mortgages to meet, food and clothing to pay for, college tuition payments to cover. But our 'Mary' side seeks something better, something more meaningful and purposeful for our lives. The 'Mary' within us longs to spend more time with our children, longs to be able to give more of ourselves to causes we believe in, longs to turn off the world and be at peace with God, ourselves and others.

Like Martha in the Gospel, sometimes we set our priorities wrong; we bury ourselves in our work, our calendars, our agendas to avoid loving and being loved. Jesus, our Good Lord, invites each one of us today to make a place in our lives for the 'better part' of listening to Him, welcoming the joy and love of family and friends where we will find the very presence of God.

AN OLD ENGLISH PRAYER

There is an old English prayer that goes like this:
*Take time to **work** – it is the price of success.*
*Take time to **think** – it is the source of power.*
*Take time to **play** – it is the secret of perpetual youth.*
*Take time to **read** – it is the fountain of wisdom.*
*Take time to **be friendly** – it is the road to happiness.*

*Take time to **dream** – it is hitching your wagon to a star.*
*Take time to **love and be loved** – it is the privilege of the Gods.*
*Take time to **look around** – it is too short a day to be selfish.*
*Take time to **laugh** – it is the music of the soul.*

Most of us would agree that there is a time for all those things. There's a time to work and a time to play and a time to think and a time to dream and a time to laugh, and all the rest. But, having just heard the story of Jesus' visit to Martha and Mary, I think that the author of the old English poem missed the boat. He left out the most important activity of all. Jesus refers to it in today's Gospel as 'the better part'.

SEVENTEENTH SUNDAY IN ORDINARY TIME
A – Matthew 13:44-52

This beautiful Gospel challenges us to believe that "treasure" and a "pearl" exist in every one of us, and that we must work our way through the disappointments of life, through the distractions that life gives us, so as to discover the treasure and the pearl of what it means to place Almighty God at the center of our lives. The Gospel challenges us to know that it is so possible to live and to work and carry out our responsibilities with complete trust in God. So the treasure and the pearl in us is trust.

There are so many superficial ways that we choose so as not to realize the treasure and trust and the pearl of trust within us. Some of those we know use alcohol or other drugs to tranquilize fear and anxieties; some of us use repression, that is, we pretend and refuse to confront our problems. Some of us are workaholics. Others of us use the gift of speech; that is we never stop talking. If we do, we fear that our anxieties will catch up to us, and some of those we know use the quest for money, for things, to buy relief from anxiety. In every case, we have lost sight of the trust we must place in God.

This was brought home (USN Champlain School) to me years ago when I had the opportunity to visit the Gardener Museum in Boston. In one of the rooms in the museum, I suddenly found myself face to face with Rembrandt's large painting of "The Storm of the Sea of Galilee". I remember just staring at the painting for the longest time. I saw the little boat being hit by large waves and I could feel the shudder of the Apostles. I felt the dangerous high winds blowing through the rigging. I sensed the panic of the Disciples. But something else struck me; in the midst of the storm, the danger, and the panic, the Disciples had to awaken Jesus to tell him about it. I thought that Jesus had such complete trust in God, and He had sunk himself completely into that trust, that He was sleeping through the storm. I felt then that God was sending me a message. Actually, the message of today's

Gospel, that I had to learn that kind of trust in my own spiritual life, that I had to listen and learn from Jesus.

MDP, this same Jesus calls us to seek the "treasure of trust", the "pearl of trust" that we all have within us. When it seems that so many things are crashing down on us, we must trust He will never abandon us. In His own powerful words, "We will shine like the sun in the kingdom of our Heavenly Father."

Story of widow with six children

Several years ago, a man died leaving his wife with six children to raise. The widow reflected seriously on her talents and what she would do with the rest of her life. She realized that she loved children, had a way with them. Consequently, she decided to take in several foster children—in addition to her own six. For years, she ran a beautiful, loving, good home for all those children. From time to time, she needed and received help largely from persons in her Church community.

As the years went by and the children were turning out beautifully, a newspaper reporter came to interview her for a feature story. The reporter asked her how in the world she had managed to raise so many children so gracefully. The woman replied with a smile, "Well, it was the partnership." "What partnership?" asked the reporter. Still smiling, the woman answered, "My partnership with God. A few days after my husband died, I looked at my situation and I said to God, 'From now on, Lord, I'll do the work if You'll do the worrying!' and all through the years I've done what needed to be done. I have upheld my end of the bargain." Then her smile broadened, and she said with great joy in her voice, "And He has upheld His!"

Even when it seems as though the total anxieties of the whole world will come crashing down on us; God will never abandon us. Uphold our end of the bargain. God will uphold His. Apply for membership in a partnership of love and, in Jesus' words, we will "shine like the sun in the kingdom of our Heavenly Father."

B – John 6:1-15

We have heard this Gospel so many times—this Gospel of the loaves and fishes. In one way, some people may think it is just another fish story, and in another way, some of us will think about it more deeply.

This is the story that is told in all four Gospels. There are so many ways to look at it. Because of an anniversary we celebrated last week, I thought it might be good to look at the meaning of the Gospel with this anniversary in mind.

More than fifty years ago last week, our eyes were focused on the skies. On July 20, 1969 American astronauts Neil Armstrong and Buzz Aldrin took their historic first steps on the surface of the moon. But something else, which was kept very quiet, took place before the two astronauts climbed out of the lunar module Eagle and set foot on the moon!

Two Sundays before the launch of Apollo 11, Buzz Aldrin participated in a private Holy Communion service at his Presbyterian Church. During the service, a small piece of bread and a small chalice of wine were sealed in plastic packets. The packets were safely stowed in Aldrin's personal preference kit. When the lunar module touched down on the moon, Aldrin took out the communion elements and set them in front of the guidance system computer. He then radioed Houston: "Houston, this is Eagle. This is the lunar module pilot speaking. I would like to request a few moments of silence. I would like to invite each person listening in, whomever or wherever he may be, to contemplate for a moment the events of the last few hours, and, give thanks in their own individual way." Next came the moment of communion. Aldrin writes in his autobiography, "I opened the little plastic packages which contained the bread and wine. I poured the wine into the chalice our church had given me. In the one-sixth gravity of the moon, the wine slowly curled and gracefully came up the side of the cup. It was interesting for me to think the very first liquid poured on the moon, and the very first food eaten there, was Holy Communion." Buzz Aldrin continues, "Just before I partook of Communion, I read the words which I had chosen to indicate our trust that as man probes into space, we are in fact acting in Christ. 'I am the Vine, you are the branches. Whoever remains in me, and I in Him, will bear much fruit for you can do nothing without Me.' I sensed especially strongly my unity with the church everywhere. I gave thanks for the intelligence and spirit that had brought two young pilots to the sea of tranquility."

MDP, bread blessed and broken on the surface of the moon; bread blessed and broken on a Palestinian hillside centuries ago; bread blessed and broken uniting all humankind into a community which transcends time and space. Christ, the Bread of Life, present to us in this sacrament for one another. The Eucharist demands more than just extending our hands when we come to receive communion. The Eucharist demands that we open our hearts and spirit so that we may become what we receive. We should now say this prayer, which we say at every Mass with greater feeling: "May all of us who share in the Body and Blood of Christ be brought together in unity by the Holy Spirit. Lord, I am not worthy to receive You, but only say the word and my soul shall be healed."

C (1) – Luke 11:1-13

The power of prayer! There once was a small Kentucky town that had two churches, and one whiskey distillery. Members of both churches complained that the distillery gave the community a bad image. "Besides," they said, "the owner is an atheist." They tried many times to close the place down, but were unsuccessful. At last, they decided to hold a joint Saturday night prayer meeting. They would petition God to intervene. Saturday night came and all through the prayer meeting, a terrible electrical storm raged. To the delight of the church members, lightning struck the distillery and it burned to the ground. The next morning, the sermons in both churches were on "the power of prayer." Fire insurance adjusters promptly notified the distillery owner they would not pay for his damages. The fire was caused by an "Act of God," they said, and the coverage for "Acts of God" was excluded in the policy. Whereupon, the distillery owner sued all the church members claiming that they had conspired with God to destroy the building. The defendants denied absolutely that they had done anything to cause the fire. The trial judge observed, "I find one thing about this case that is perplexing. We have a situation where the plaintiff—an atheist—is professing his belief in the power of prayer, and the defendants—all church members—are denying the power of prayer!"

We can all identify with that judge's feelings. We talk a lot about prayer, about its importance, about the necessity of prayer, about different kinds of prayer, and some of us do a lot of praying—morning and evening, and sometimes in between. Our trust and hope in prayer as the ultimate problem solver is deep rooted and profound. Yet, sometimes we become a little perplexed about prayer and find ourselves wondering how we should pray. In this beautiful Gospel, Jesus tells us just how we should pray. "Father, hallowed be Your name. Your kingdom come..." This is the prayer that Jesus teaches, a prayer that does not so much as ask God to do what we want but a prayer that asks that we do what God wants of us—and being ready and willing to make God's will a reality in our lives. Any prayer worthy of God's ear seeks the grace to do the work God calls us to do—to be forgiving, to have charity, to be just—and so to become the beautiful people God wants us to be. It enables us to realize God's love in our love for family and friends and their love for us. Prayer is an awareness of God as the source of all that is good. Today, Jesus calls us to be men and women of prayer—to embrace the spirit of God and to be embraced by that spirit that actively celebrates God's presence in all things.

C (2) – Luke 11:1-13

W hen you pray, say: "Father hallowed be Your name. Your kingdom come…"

In today's Gospel, Jesus gives us more than a prayer text—He
teaches us the attitude necessary for authentic prayer. Rabbi Harold
Kushner writes in his book, "The Lord is My Shepherd" that "Gratitude,
the sense that life is a gift, the awareness that life has given us a wonderful bounty…is where religion begins in the human heart."

Jesus calls us today to be men and women of prayer—prayer that
begins and ends with realizing how blessed we have been by God; and
how we must embrace the spirit and attitude of prayer that actively
seeks out and gratefully celebrates God's presence in all things.

I want to tell you a story about a little boy who approached his
slightly older sister with the question, "Susie, can anybody ever really
see God?"

Busy with other things, Susie curtly replies, "No, of course not,
silly. God is so far up in heaven that nobody can see Him." Still wondering, he approaches his mother: "Mom, can anybody ever really see
God?" "No, not really," his mother says gently. "God is spirit and he
dwells in our hearts, but we can never really see Him." This answer
satisfies him for the moment but he still wonders.

A few days later, his beloved old grandfather takes him on a fishing trip. They have a great time together—it has been an ideal day.
As the sun begins to set, the grandfather stops fishing and turns his
full attention to the beauty unfolding before their eyes. On seeing the
peace and contentment on his grandfather's face, the boy thinks for
a moment and asks hesitatingly, "Grandpa, I—I wasn't going to ask
anybody else, but I wonder if you can tell me something I've been
wondering about for a long time…Can anybody ever really see God?"
The old man does not even turn his head. A long moment slips by
before he finally answers, "Son," he responds quietly, "It's getting so I
can't see anything else."

MDP, authentic prayer is not a formula or ritual but an awareness of God's presence in our lives, of God's hand as the one who sustains us and nurtures us of God's love giving breath to every moment of our existence. In the Gospel today, Jesus calls us to be men and women of prayer: to embrace the spirit and attitude of prayer that actively seeks out and gratefully celebrates God's presence in all things.

KNITTING

I remember one of the Chaplains who was with me on a base in California told me that one of his parishioners came to him and told him how she was struggling to pray. She told him that it just wasn't working for her; she said she had all the right words, but she could not sense God's presence. He told her to go to her room each day and, for fifteen minutes, take out her knitting before the face of God. He told her 'not to say a single word of prayer;' he said, 'just knit and try to enjoy the quiet of your room.' He said that the women thought and said to him, "Fifteen minutes to do nothing and not feel guilty!" so she gave it a try.

Slowly she began to enter the silence created by her noiseless knitting. And she began to perceive that this silence was not simply the absence of noise but that 'this silence had substance, that is not the absence of something, but it was the presence of something.' She said, that 'she continued to knit, and at the heart of the silence, there was God—a God of stillness and peace...'

EIGHTEENTH SUNDAY IN ORDINARY TIME
A– MATTHEW 14:13-21

We see a beautiful miracle in today's Gospel, and perhaps it allows us to think a little bit about miracles—miracles that happen every day. Whether in the intimacy of our family life, or in the joy of a friendship, we must realize that God is always working miracles—and at times, we can only stand in awesome silence in front of them. We must believe that the person we are married to, the children we have brought into the world and nurtured, our blood brothers and sisters, nieces, nephews, grandparents, the friends we love—without exception—are honest-to-goodness miracles. If we try to see life in this way, if we honor, respect and revere human life, we have found the secret to holiness, to living a wholesome and balanced life in Christ.

In my Navy career, I had the opportunity to speak to several Vietnam prisoners of war. Almost all of them talk in terms of 'miracles.' I remember once when I was on a long deployment on an aircraft carrier in the Indian Ocean—we had been at sea for two and one half months without ever seeing land. Admiral Jim Stockdale, Vietnam prisoner of war, was flown aboard to give a talk to the ship's company. (You might remember him as the Vice Presidential running mate for Ross Perot.) He told us how the prisoners of war at the infamous "Hanoi Hilton" survived the isolation and torture of the place because of what he called the "Miracle of the Two Codes," that is, the honor code and the 'tap' code. The North Vietnamese never mastered the 'tap' code, a code each prisoner used for communicating with one another between prison walls. The code laid out the alphabet on a simple five-by-five grid. The first taps indicated the line of the grid; the next tap the position of the letter on that line. For example, the letter 'B' would be tap-tap-tap; the letter 'M' would be tap-tap-tap...tap-tap. He said that the Hanoi Hilton "sounded like a den of woodpeckers." The code flowed so fluently that the men told jokes. Every Sunday, in a coded signal, the men stood and recited the Lord's Prayer and the Pledge of Allegiance. You see, the miracle of a few simple taps against the wall, helped a group of POWs establish a respect and reverence for one another.

MDP, before this Sunday is over, take a look at your wife or your husband, your child, your grandchild, your loving friends, and see that a miracle is taking place before your very eyes. And, like Admiral Jim Stockdale and the other prisoners of war, you will sense a fool-proof way of knowing when this is happening; when you never lose heart, no matter what the circumstances. When you look and really understand that all the persons in your lives are supreme masterpieces of God's Creation, you will know how you are empowered by God to touch these lives and live the miracle of the Gospel of Jesus Christ.

B (1) – JOHN 6:24-35

"No one who comes to Me shall ever be hungry: no one who believes in Me shall ever thirst."

If we were in that crowd with Peter, James and John, and heard these words and believed, we would be well on our way to possessing the key to living a life of hope and joy! All of us want to listen to words which tell us of our own worthiness. All of us want to listen to someone who will give us an insight into who we are, what we are doing here, where we are heading. We all look for that flicker of light at the end of the tunnel of pain and anxiety and death…and in this beautiful Gospel, Jesus gives us the key—'known only to saints and children'—He offers Himself as the Bread of Life!

During World War II, thousands of Belgians were imprisoned in internment camps by the German SS Troopers. When I was stationed in Europe, I had the chance to visit a few of these horrible internment camps. At the internment camp at Breendonk, near Antwerp, the conditions were among the worst in the camps of

Western Europe. But even worse were the violence and the cruelty of the SS Troopers in the camp. Thousands were executed, or perished as a result of the harsh conditions.

I listened carefully as the guide took us through the camp. There was a moment in the tour that I will never forget. The guide took those of us on the tour to a small isolated cell in a remote corner of the camp. There in that cell there was a little slit in the stone wall. The only way to reach this corner and the small slit was to crawl under some high benches. The guide then asked for my hand and placed it against a portion of the stone wall. He said, "Run your hand over this. What do you feel?" I felt the carving of a face. The guide confirmed my feeling that the carving was the face of Jesus. He explained that in the midst of all the horrors surrounding them, the imprisoned men and women of Breendonk would come to this cell and place their hands on the face of Jesus. This carving, carved by an unknown prisoner, was their way of remembering that they were not alone, that the words of today's Gospel, "Whoever comes to me will never hunger and whoever believes in me will never thirst," would give them strength to eternal life.

MDP, when storms blow through our lives, the Good Lord is saying in this Gospel, "Don't worry; Listen to me! I will satisfy your hunger; I will quench your thirst for the truth that will make you free." We may worry about the deteriorating health problems of a loved one; we may at this moment, be concerned about an estrangement, a deep hurt within our family. We may not be getting along with a son or daughter or sister or brother or even a parent. We may feel sorry for ourselves because we lack certain material resources that we really think we need; or we may simply be bored with our marriage, or with a career that has become lackluster and humdrum, and then we hear this Gospel, "Listen to me! Don't worry! Hang in there! No one who comes to me shall ever be hungry; no one who believes in me shall ever thirst," and, like the prisoners of Breendonk, when they touched the face of Jesus on the wall, we are strengthened.

Silent Sermon

I ended my Navy career in Spain, and lived about an hour's drive from Sevilla (Seville.) Seville is known for its Cathedral, the third largest in the world. There's a story they tell about an incident in this Cathedral during the Middle Ages. It was announced that a very popular preacher, a monk, was going to preach on the "Love of God" on an appointed Sunday. When the day came, the great Cathedral of Seville was filled to the overflowing. But, instead of going to the pulpit, the monk merely sat in silence in front of the Altar. The sun was setting and its last rays were shining through the magnificent stained glass windows, flooding the Cathedral with color and warmth. Still the preacher sat, in silence. And finally, when the sun had set and the Cathedral was dark, he went to the Altar, lit a candle and carried the candle to the image of Jesus hanging on the cross. In silence, he held up the candle to the wounded hands for several minutes. Then he moved the candle down to the feet; then up to the open side; and finally, after a few minutes, to the crown of thorns. The old monk said nothing; yet, everyone left the cathedral knowing that he or she had heard an unforgettable sermon on the love of God.

MDP, every time we come to Mass and listen to the Gospel; it is like the first Easter Sunday, when we rediscover again the empty tomb and our spirits are transformed. The darkness in our lives become light; our worries become easy; our thirst is quenched, and we hear the Good Lord saying, "Hang in there; Don't worry so much; Listen to Me…I myself am the Bread of Life. No one who comes to Me, whoever eats of this bread will live free of hunger; no one who believes in Me shall ever thirst."

B (2) – John 6:24-35

In this beautiful and powerful Gospel, Jesus says, "Do not work for food that perishes, but for the food that endures for eternal life..." I really enjoy going to the movies, but I am not so big on animated films. I can remember when I was a kid how the animated film "Bambi" touched me. Well, about a month ago, I saw one of the finest animated films ever. (If you have a chance, look for it should it come on television or, if you can rent the DVD.) The name of the film is simply called, "Up", and it begins with one of the most touching and poetic four minutes ever seen in the movies—all told without a word of dialogue.

A quiet, shy kid named Carl meets Ellie, a real spitfire. They both dream of being explorers, of going on great adventures to faraway places. Ellie and Carl grow up, fall in love, marry; transform a ramshackle house into their dream home. They save all their loose change in a glass jug for their dream trip—but real life gets in the way as it usually does: work, home, car repairs, medical bills, but they are happy. And in an instant, they are celebrating their fiftieth wedding anniversary. Soon after, Ellie succumbs to cancer, leaving the grieving Carl lost and alone.

After Ellie is gone, Carl finds the scrapbook Ellie kept since they were children. She called it "My Adventure Book." The first pages are filled with the silly, funny little treasures and memories of childhood. Then there is a page Ellie has labeled "Stuff I'm Going to Do." On these pages, Ellie planned to chronicle her dream trip with Carl. Carl is stung with sadness that he never kept his promise to Ellie to take her on such a trip. But as Carl turns the page, he sees that Ellie has collected pictures of their life together—their wedding, working side by side on their house, the simple joys of going out for ice cream together. Under one of the last pictures taken of the two together, Ellie wrote, "Carl, thanks for the great adventure—Go and have a new one! Love, Ellie..." Carl realizes that he and Ellie had indeed shared a great adventure; they dreamed together, faced and survived crushing disappointments together, grew happily old together. Carl realizes that love and friendship are life's great adventure.

MDP, Carl and Ellie discover that life does not have to be exotic and exhilarating to be lived to the fullest. A life of true joy and meaning is driven not by 'perishable' material things and fleeting experiences, but by the 'nonperishable' things of God. Perhaps the most difficult challenge of our time is to make a place in our hearts and in our homes for the 'bread' that is Christ especially amid the 'fast food' being shoved in our faces from every direction. Jesus told us about the food that doesn't perish. May He give us the wisdom to live lives grounded in that unperishable food.

A man named Harley had a morbid fear of thunder. He went to a prominent psychiatrist who specialized in the treatment of this phobia, which is called 'brontophobia.' The psychiatrist said, "It's silly to be afraid of thunder at your age. Just think of it as a drum roll in the symphony of life." The patient asked, "Will that cure my fear of thunder?" "If it doesn't," the doctor replied, "then do as I do. When you hear thunder, stuff your ears with cotton, crawl under the bed, pull a blanked over your head, and sing, 'Mary had a Little Lamb' at the top of your voice." We are all struggling with something. This is the setting of the Gospel.

Brian Pirko was a straight-A student at the U.S. Naval Academy in Annapolis. He was considered among the best and brightest of his class of midshipmen. But instead of graduating this year from Annapolis and continuing on to fulfill his dream of becoming a Navy aviator, Brian Pirko was scouring the Want Ads looking for a job.

Pirko was dismissed from Annapolis for cheating officially. But Pirko was caught between two Naval codes—the official "Code of Honor" that midshipmen do not 'lie, cheat or steal; and the informal cynical but no less powerful code among all midshipmen: 'don't bilge (turn in) your classmate.' Teamwork in all things, that code maintains, is the only way to survive at Annapolis.

In December 1992, some of Pirko's classmates got hold of a copy of the final exam in electrical engineering. Ever the team player,

Pirko—who was already pulling an A in the course—helped other 'mids' figure out the answer. A group of 'mids' met secretly after the exam. They decided that although they had committed an honor violation, they invoked a loophole under the honor code. It permitted midshipmen suspected of honor violations to 'counsel' one another—and not press charges. So the group 'counseled' one another and pledged to keep the exam heist secret. Pirko, who learned of the meeting later, knew that the counseling option was 'bull' but didn't want to 'bilge' on his classmates.

The incident was soon uncovered and grew into the worst cheating scandal in Naval history. Pirko recognized that the cheating was wrong and admitted his role. He was dismissed from the Academy. In the end, the 'honor system' had protected the liars and cheaters and punished those who came forward.

But in transcripts from his disciplinary hearings, Brian Pirko stood tall—like the officer and gentleman, he wanted to be. He told the President of the Naval review board: "Whatever happens, you know, I feel better from this moment on, just knowing that I've come here and cleared my conscience. I guess that's all I have to say, sir."

["Gouging" the Honor System – U.S. Navy: How the Academy Let Cheaters Go Free," Newsweek, 6-6-94]

There comes a time when we must stop rationalizing what we have done or not done and decide what we really believe, what values are most important to us. There will come a time when the 'perishable food' of power, wealth and prestige fails us, a time when we hunger for the 'food that remains for life eternal"—the food of compassion, justice, integrity, reconciliation and mercy of Christ, the bread of life. In the Eucharist, Christ speaks to us, challenges us, reconciles us; assures us. The Eucharist demands more than the opening of our hands to take and our mouths to consume, it demands that we open our hearts and spirits as well so that we may become what we receive. The "Amen!" we say when we take this bread is our assent to the Holy One who gives us Himself in this sacrament—a gift that is given to us to give to others.

C– Luke 12:13-21

We just heard a powerful, powerful Gospel. Jesus says emphatically that the man who stores up treasure for himself in place of making himself rich in the sight of God is a fool. When I read this Gospel, I am reminded of a story in which an organization offered a bounty of five thousand dollars for any wolf captured alive. It turned old Sam and old Jed into fortune hunters. Day and night, they scoured the mountains and forests looking for their valuable prey. One night, they were exhausted and fell asleep on the ground, dreaming of their potential fortune. Suddenly, Sam awoke to discover that he and Jed were surrounded by at least, fifty angry wolves, with flaming eyes and bared teeth. Sam nudged his companion and said, "Jed, wake up! We're rich!" Sometimes we confuse our wants with our needs. How many times have we said, "I need a new car," or "I need new clothes," or "I need a new house", or "I need" this or that, when those 'needs' were actually wants. The point is that we can legitimately want all those things, but they aren't needs that address any of life's real issues, like, the need to forgive, the need to love. Jesus once said, "Set your hearts on His kingdom first, and all these other things will be given to you.

In the pages of "The New Yorker", humorist Calvin Trillin talks about life in America. He often speaks about his wife, Alice. Alice was a woman of great compassion, grace, and style, a writer, an educator. She died a year ago awaiting a heart transplant…Trillin once wrote, "Alice believed in the power of pure, undiluted love."

Once when Alice was serving as a counselor at a day camp, she befriended a sunny little girl whom she simply called, "L." "L" was a magical child who was severely disabled. "L" had two genetic diseases—one which kept her from growing and one which kept her from digesting food.

Well, Alice and "L" became fast friends. One day, "L" asked Alice to hold her mail during a game of hide and go seek. While the children played, Alice saw at the top of the stack a note from "L's" mom.

Alice could not resist taking a peak at the note. She said, "I simply had to know what this child's parents could have done to make "L" so spectacular, to make her the most optimistic, most enthusiastic, most hopeful human being I have ever encountered." Alice continues, "I snuck a quick look at the note, and my eyes fell on the sentence, "If God had given us all the children in the world to choose from, "L", we would have chosen you." Before "L" got back, Alice passed the note to the counselor sitting next to her, "Quick, read this," Alice whispered. "It's the secret of life."

MDP, this is what Jesus is telling us in the Gospel. The 'Secret of Life' is not to build bigger barns, but to possess a love that manages to trump every problem, heal every hurt; bridge every division. God has not given the precious time we call life to fill our barns with 'more' of the latest, the best, the biggest—things that could be gone in an instant. (I could not help reflecting on this as I watched the news of the bridge collapse in Minneapolis.) The 'Secret of Life' is a selfless and affirming love that is centered in Christ and that seeks to be shared with all those whom we are privileged to share life with. In Christ, God has revealed to us 'the Secret of life." It is up to us to pass it on!

ASSUMPTION OF THE BLESSED VIRGIN MARY – AUGUST 15

(1) – Luke 11:27-28

There was a young boy leafing through a book that his mother had been reading, entitled "Child Psychology, Ages Five through Ten." He turned to a friend and said, "Wow! You should read what a pain-in-the-neck I'm going to be next year… "

I am positive that Mary went through all of the problems that every mother goes through. But Luke, in this beautiful Gospel, gives us a chance to reflect on and to discover the attitude and approach of the loveliest lady of all time: Mary, the mother of Jesus. When the angel told her what would be happening, and with pressure bearing down upon her, she gave that beautiful response, "Let it be…", "Let it be." And that response was the cornerstone of Mary's life—the unconditional acceptance of God's will! And for us—following Mary's example, that is the cornerstone of our lives as mature Christians.

Our Blessed Lady was supremely faithful to the mandate God had given her that she was to be a real mother to a real child. In some of my own reflections on Mary, I have always felt that it is a tremendous tribute to Mary to realize that so much of the parent turns up in the child. There may be some protesting along the way; there may be vast differences in lifestyles between back to back generations, but when one looks beneath the surface, he or she discovers very real similarities between a parent and his or her child. So, when we realize what Jesus came to be, we can see what a marvelous thing Mary did in that day-to-day mother/child relationship.

It doesn't take much Biblical expertise to realize what a time she must have had: the birth, the flight into Egypt, becoming displaced persons, losing her Son in the temple, Cana and the lecture she received; and then the moment of the cross. But remember the cornerstone of her faith: "Let it be!" And that is the key to weathering whatever crisis we have in our lives as followers of Christ. We do what we can; we work and pray with faith; we turn to others for help; we give others the help they need. But in our hearts are the words of Mary, "Let it be!"

All of us turn to God frantically when we are in some kind of crisis. We come to church; we pray more. But perhaps it would be good to keep our eyes on tomorrow, on our lifestyle for Monday, and Tuesday, and Wednesday; at home; in front of your class; behind your computer; at the kitchen table. Maybe we need to whisper, or say in our hearts, "Let it be, let it be."

Our Blessed Lady said in the Gospel, "My soul proclaims the greatness of the Lord, and my spirit exults in God my Savior." That really describes her! Through her unconditional surrender to God, she proclaimed His greatness; and so, she became our model for a healthy, balanced, lovely life as we follow her Son.

There's a wonderful story about the composer Franz Joseph Haydn who, in Vienna, on the twenty-seventh day of March 1808, attended a grand performance of his work, "The Creation." He was seventy six years old and was feeble; he had to be wheeled into the theatre. His presence aroused intense enthusiasm among the audience, which could no longer be suppressed as the chorus and orchestra burst with full power into the passage, "And there was light."

Amid the enthusiasm of the enraptured audience, the aged composer was seen trying to raise himself. Once on his feet, he mustered all his strength, and in reply to the applause of the audience, cried out loudly as he was able, "No, no! Not for me, But," he said, pointing to heaven, "from Him—from Him in heaven above—comes all!"

This is what Mary proclaims in today's beautiful Gospel, she points to the Lord and says, "My soul proclaims the greatness of the Lord and my spirit exults in God my Savior." That's what Mary is all about. She is there to point us to God! Through her unconditional, surrender to God, she proclaimed His Greatness and she became a model of fruitful living for all ages to come. This is her charm! She gives us the secret to living a beautiful Christian life when, pointing to the Lord, she says, "Let it be done according to your will."

MDP, to point our lives in the direction of Almighty God, to love one another as he has loved us, is why we celebrate Mary, our blessed mother on her Feast of the Assumption.

(2) – Luke 1:39-56

When Elizabeth heard Mary's greeting, the infant leaped in her womb, and Elizabeth, filled with the Holy Spirit, cried out in a loud voice and said, "Blessed are you among women, and blessed is the fruit of your womb."

"Blessed are you…"

So Elizabeth greets Mary when the pregnant teenager comes to be with her elderly cousin, who is also with child through the work of God.

Have you ever been greeted like that?

When someone thanks you for waiting with them, giving them space to vent and time to talk—it is Elizabeth speaking to Mary: "Blessed are you…"

When your little one hugs you before going to sleep after another long, busy day—it is Elizabeth's good night prayer for you: "Blessed are you…"

When you continue to do what is right when those around you expect or demand you act otherwise or when you continue to be patient and kind when everyone else has gone off the deep end, the simple nod or sad smile of thanks gives you is Elizabeth's blessing: "Blessed are you…"

Mary of Nazareth, the "first Disciple" of her Son, is a model for all of us of what it means to be a disciple of Jesus. As she gave birth to the Christ Child, we are called to make a home for the Christ of compassion and peace in our lives. As she journeyed with her Son to Jerusalem, we are called to journey with Him; and take up our crosses. As she held the Body of the Crucified, we are called to hold and support and heal one another despite our own brokenness and pain.

And in our own humble attempts at such "blessedness," we, like

Mary, bring her Son's vision of the Kingdom of God a step closer to reality – and our place in it, with her.

On this solemnity of Mary's Assumption into the Kingdom of God, let us give thanks to God who blesses us as he blessed our faithful and loving sister Mary.

NINETEENTH SUNDAY IN ORDINARY TIME
A– Matthew 14:22-23

"When Peter saw how strong the wind was he became
frightened; and, beginning to sink, he cried out,
"Lord, save me!"

On occasion, I tell you—and myself—to pay attention to things
that happen to us every day; at times, we will find Gospel
homilies in these. I read this Gospel, for example, at the beginning
of the week. During the week, I had the opportunity to use the
large pool at the community where several of my friends live. I
witnessed a young dad giving his six-year-old son his first swimming lesson. His dad held the little boy up as he got the rhythm of
the stroke—hands gliding through the water and legs kicking to
propel him forward. The dad waded alongside of him, holding him
up then slowly, almost imperceptibly; the dad lowered his arms
and let his son float. The six-year-old was swimming on his own.

He was doing well—until he looked over and saw that his dad
was no longer holding him up, and so he began to panic and sank
like a rock. The dad pulled his son up out of the water and held
him close until he coughed up the water. You could see that the
little boy was shaken—but he trusted his dad to be there. Now, the
dad said to his son that he had to trust himself to do it.

So the father and son tried it again, when the young swimmer
got a good, even stroke going, his father slowly pulled away—and
this time, the boy continued on his own. He was swimming; and he
knew it and he understood. From now on, the six-year-old would
feel safe and secure in the water.

MDP, this scene was a Gospel homily for me. What happened
to the young swimmer, what happened to Peter in the Gospel, happens to all of us at one time or another: things happen to us that

make us panic! We don't trust ourselves to know what the right thing to do is; and our ability to do it. And then God reaches out and catches us, but we are not ready to risk giving up control and taking God's hand. So the beautiful Gospel today challenges us to know and trust what it means to live as a disciple of Jesus Christ. Jesus, in turn, promises to make His presence known to us, to hold us up and support us as we make our way through some of the rough waters of life.

What would Jesus do

A few years before I retired from the Navy, I was assigned as Chaplain to a Naval hospital. A little incident happened there that often comes back to me. A young sailor was dying of Aids. He had no connection with any church, but as he was getting worse, the nurses called down to the Chaplain's office to ask for help. One of the older Chaplains so afraid of Aids responded, but he would not go into the dying man's room. He stood by the door in the passage-way, and shouted a prayer and a blessing into the room and quickly left. But, a young female Chaplain, who just reported aboard, heard about this from one of the nurses. She rushed to the sailor's room hoping that he was still alive. When she got to his room, she pulled up a chair by the bed. The young sailor was gasping. She lifted his head and cradled him in her arms. She prayed while he died. Later, I asked her why she did this beautiful act of compassion. Her answer has remained with me all these years: "I just imagined if Jesus had been there, He would have done the same!"

B (1) – Matthew 14:22-23

I have come to believe that God teaches us in every human experience; God 'speaks' to us in every act of generosity, in every moment of forgiveness. God touches us when we are compassionate, when we are humble, when we extend these virtues to others.

I read a true story in the March issue of the "Metropolitan Diary" of the "New York Times." A woman was refilling her MetroCard at a crowded subway station. Just as she was about to retrieve her card from the machine, a man came up behind her and grabbed the card and put it in his pocket. She shouted, "You took my card; give it back." But he just looked at her and walked away. A man who had witnessed the theft yelled, "I saw you take her card. Give it back." Both the woman and the man followed the thief; the man even started shoving the man to get back the card. But the thief ignored them both, did not fight back, and just kept walking. The woman yelled for the police. No one else moved.

The woman followed the thief up the subway steps to the street. When he stopped at the red light on the corner, she said, "You took my card. It's in your pocket. Give it back." He put his hand in his pocket and took out the card, and with tears in his eyes, said, "I'm hungry." "If you give me back my card, I'll give you some money," she said. "But you must give me back my card first." He handed her the card. She gave him five dollars. "Thank you," he said, and walked away.

The woman stood there and thought. "What have I just done? Risked my life for a twenty dollar MetroCard, any normal thief would have grabbed the card and run, I'm not sure what to make of the whole thing. My oldest son told me this was a great New York Story. My younger son said, 'Way to go, Mom.' and my husband was horrified and scared for me."

MDP, today's Gospel confronts us with the 'bread' that so many of us eat but which offers us little nourishment or fulfillment. The New York woman realized that what drove her to confront the thief could have had catastrophic results—the experience caused her to rethink her priorities. Today Jesus invites us to eat 'living bread:' the bread of compassion, of generosity, of graciousness, of forgiveness, of solid values, of respect for life, of understanding what another is going through. This kind of 'living bread' not only nourishes us but inspires us to become 'bread' for others, the bread that is not only from Jesus but is Jesus Himself.

B (2)– JOHN 6:41-51

For the second week in a row Jesus tells us in this uplifting Gospel that "He is the living Bread that came down from heaven..." I want to tell you a true story with which I am very familiar.

A six year old boy was born unable to see. His family doctor read about a new medical procedure developed by a young surgeon in Boston that might restore the six-year-old's sight. After tests and a review of his medical history, it was determined that the boy was a candidate for the surgery.

The boy and his parents went to Boston, and the boy brought his teddy bear with him. The bear was showing his 'age'; one eye was missing, stuffing was oozing out of its seams, patches of cloth were worn away. His parents offered to get him a new teddy bear but, no, he wanted his own bear. The boy and his teddy bear were inseparable through the consultations, tests and X-rays, right up until the anesthesia itself. The surgery was a success; after six years of blindness, the boy could see.

On the morning the boy was to return home, after signing the discharge papers, the surgeon gave the boy a big hug and said, "Listen, I own stock in you; I expect to get letters from you regularly. Do you understand?" Then the boy did something totally unexpected. "I want you to have this," he said, and handed the doctor his beloved teddy bear. The surgeon's first impulse was not to take the bear, but he was sensitive enough to understand what the boy was trying to do. You see, the boy wanted to return joy for joy, grace for grace. The wise doctor accepted the teddy bear with a hug and a promise to take good care of his new friend.

For years, the surgeon displayed the teddy bear near his office at the hospital. He placed his card in front of the teddy bear. Under his name, the doctor wrote, "This is the highest fee I have ever received for professional services rendered."

MDP, a teddy bear becomes a sign of God's grace working in our midst. A doctor realized the life he was able to give through skill; and a little boy discovers gratitude for the greatest gift he was given. This is the 'Bread of Life' Jesus is talking about in the Gospel. This is the 'Bread of Life,' which is Jesus the Lord; this is Jesus, who nourishes us with the bread of compassion, of gratitude, selflessness, graciousness which we give to one another. May this Jesus, our Bread, continue to nourish all of us on our own exoduses to the dwelling place of God.

C– Luke 12:32-48

In the last few months, I have been asked to officiate at the funeral Masses for some of our dear parishioners who have gone to God. I thought about the 'time' God has given all of us. As I read and prayed that the Good Lord would give me an insight into this Gospel of today, Jesus says, "…Be like servants who await the master's return from a wedding, ready to open immediately when he comes and knocks…" Jesus, I believe, is offering us this parable to emphasize the preciousness of the gift of time.

There is a story about a fifty-five-year-old CEO of a top corporation in the United States whose job made demands on his time and forced him to travel. He began to realize that he missed too many of his children's birthdays, ballgames, and recitals; he began to realize that he was not home many evenings of the week when his children needed their dad, and when he did find himself at home, he usually closeted himself in his office with his laptop and smart phone.

Then, one day, he came across an interesting statistic; the average person, he read, lives to be about seventy-five years old. Multiply seventy-five by fifty-two, the number of weeks in a year, and the total is three thousand nine hundred. That's three thousand nine hundred Saturdays in the average lifespan. He did some quick math and realized that he had about a thousand Saturdays left until he turned seventy-five. He realized this was a mind-blowing wake-up call! So he went to a toy store and purchased one thousand marbles—one for each Saturday until his seventy-fifth birthday. He kept the marbles in an array of jars that lined the wall of his study. And every Saturday, he removed one marble to remind him to make that day count. So he did. Watching the number of marbles diminish helped him focus on the number of important things in life.

And then, one Saturday, twenty years later, he had one marble left. Rather than feeling sad, he felt gratitude for the wonderful memories of those one thousand Saturdays with his wife, his children, his friends—and saw the unknown number of Saturdays ahead of him as extra gifts from God.

MDP, we tend to carry on our lives as if we are immortal, that we will live forever; that we have 'all the time in the world.' But, we don't! There are a fixed number of 'marbles' in our lifetimes. We don't really think about how fragile and fleeting life is, but if we have truly listened to today's Gospel and embraced its spirit, we will be conscious of the brevity of this life and live our days in humble gratitude for these days and in a joyful anticipation of life to come.

TWENTIETH SUNDAY IN ORDINARY TIME
A - MATTHEW 15:21-26

It was reported in the Star Tribune from St. Paul, Minnesota that an 85-year-old woman, ill, sick, no family, fatally shot her husband, 86 years old and also ill, and then shot herself. This scene of despair and hopelessness touched me because day after day I witness the demands that life makes on us, and how some of us lack the energy and the know-how to replenish and strengthen ourselves. Just going through our daily routines reading startling news in our daily papers and hearing it on television, worrying about our children, trying to help elderly and sick family members, trying to sell a home and move elsewhere, coping with the demands of our professions and jobs, can exhaust us. Before we know it, all of our minutes become crowded and seem to collide with our hours and days. If only we had an evening at home with nothing to do, an evening just to breathe, to just be! But if you are like me, even when we are home, we still think of all those things that we ought to be doing, and we feel guilty because we are not doing them!

When I was stationed in San Francisco, on my way to my carrier, I would often pass a storefront funeral parlor, a kind of dingy place with beige colored curtains covering the windows. In front of the curtains there was sign which read, "Why walk around half dead when we can bury you for ninety-eight dollars." I thought it was a slick piece of advertising because a lot of people these days are ready to take that funeral parlor up on its offer.

But there is a better way to ask the question. The Scriptures tell us again and again: "Why do we walk around half dead when there is a way of replenishing our strength!" The Good News of the Scriptures, of the readings at Mass today, is that God just didn't create us and then let us flounder on our own. The God who created us is always with us, always empowering us, always telling us that life is worth living.

B - JOHN 6:51

In this beautiful Gospel Jesus invites us to embrace the life of His Father. A life that finds joy in a humble service to others, a life that is centered in unconditional, total love, a life that seeks fulfillment not in the wisdom or the selfish values of this world, but in the holiness of the next.

During World War II, the Red Cross made blood available to all who needed it – ally or enemy. The Red Cross would also provide the soldier, who received blood with the name of the donor so that if he wanted, he could write a letter or note of thanks. But a custom developed among the medics in the European theater that if a Nazi officer needed blood, they would find a Jewish donor. "The bad news is: if left to your own strength and resources, you will die. The good news is we have blood that will save your life – from a Jewish donor. All you have to do is accept it."

A few refused the blood, saying they would rather die than accept the blood of a hated Jew. But most wanted to live and gladly accepted the blood from a fellow human being – who happened to be a Jew. To accept life demanded, on their part, a new view and a new attitude toward this group of fellow human beings.

MDP, in the "Bread" that Jesus gives us to eat, we become the Body of Christ with and for one another. We become His "Blood" of the New Covenant, His life of compassion and forgiveness, and unconditional love, and we truly become what we receive: the very image of the risen Christ!

C - LUKE 12:49-53

In the beginning of the week when I first began reflecting on the readings, I thought they were somewhat grim: Jeremiah is tossed into a cistern and is stuck in the mud; Jesus is opposed by sinners and He himself warns that conflict will accompany His Gospel of love.

It reminded me of a "Peanuts" comic strip, where Lucy and Charlie Brown are engaged in an earnest conversation about the meaning of life. Lucy feels that life is simply a matter of one's perspective. She says, "Life is like a deck chair. Some people place it so they can see where they are going; some people place it so they can see where they have been, and some people place it so they can see where they are now." Charlie Brown ponders Lucy's thinking, and then he says, "I can't even get mine unfolded!"

I am sure most of us have had days like this – maybe even weeks or months. We have a hunger deep within us, a hunger for fulfillment, for happiness. Really, you know what it is – it is a hunger to live our lives in the presence of God and His love. This is why today's Gospel comes as such Good News. Jesus, the One who came to ignite fire upon the earth, is our center; He our direction.

A few weeks ago I had dinner with some friends, who have a five year old son named Ben. It was dinner time. Ben comes to the table, looks at the food, and says out loud, "Broccoli again." He wants no part of it! His Dad says, "Ben, you're not leaving the table until you eat your broccoli." "No! I don't like broccoli! I hate broccoli." His Dad says, "Ben, vegetables are important for you to grow. Now eat your broccoli." "No, I hate broccoli. And I hate you for making me eat broccoli!" His Dad says, "I'm sorry you feel that way, pal; but I love you." That seemed to stop Ben in his tracks. But his response is a bit surprising. He says, "Don't say that!" "But it's true, Ben. I love you – no matter what." Ben says, "Stop saying that! Stop saying that you love me." "Sorry, pal. Now listen to me: I love you, like it or not." Ben lost. Love won. He ate the broccoli!

MDP, I thought that this scene at the dinner table reflected the sense of the Gospel. Love does not always make us feel "loved." Care is not always appreciated. Seeking what is best for someone we love can become a point of tension. Jesus' striking words in the Gospel are painfully clear. The Gospel is not easy. It is not comfortable; it is challenging and demanding and it can put us and those we love on opposing sides. But the ultimate hope of the Gospel is the never-wavering love of God.

Even at five years old, Ben realizes that in the face of unconditional love, he is powerless. There are no negotiations here. It is not "I love you if" or "I'll love you when." No, true love does not bargain or measure; real love does not seek the upper hand or controlling interest. Love seeks the best for the beloved; love finds its happiness in another's happiness.

TWENTY-FIRST SUNDAY IN ORDINARY TIME
A – MATTHEW 16:13-20

This is an awesome Gospel: Christ calls each one of us to be the "Rock" of His church; to bring His love and justice and mercy to wherever we are, whatever we are called—one small act of kindness at a time.

When I retired from the Navy, my Bishop sent me to Rome, to the Vatican, for an update course in theology, Church Law, etc. This course is offered to men who have been priests for more than twenty years. The course was about five months. The curriculum called for all of us to spend at least ten days in the Holy Land. Once, we were all at a hotel on the Sea of Galilee, and we had some free time. The village in which we were was famous for its diamond cutters and silversmiths. I found myself in the shop of a silversmith, who made religious jewelry (I thought I would wear the ring I purchased from him today), and watched as he began to work on a new piece of jewelry. He showed me how the silver ore is held in the heat of the refining fire until it is purified. I remember asking him "How do you know when the ore has been in the fire long enough?"

Jesus calls Peter and His followers to become a Church that reflects the image of God Himself. In taking on God's work of love and forgiveness and compassion and justice, the Church reflects the face of God to this world.

MDP, God is always looking at us and He must see His own Image reflected back. The ministry of Peter the "Rock" belongs to every one of us who had taken on the name of Christ and claim to be His Disciples. Christ calls each of us to be the "Rock" of His Church, to mirror the very love and compassion of God not only in our own struggles, but also in our families and friends, our parish, our world. .

B – JOHN 6:60-69

I need to tell you a very beautiful story; and what prompts me to share this story with you are the words of Peter, the haunting words of Peter in Today's Gospel: "Master, to whom shall we go? You have the words of Eternal Life."

A young man from the poorest section of Brooklyn, New York, was attending the ordination of five young men as Deacons for the congregation of Priests and Deacons founded by Mother Teresa. Mother Teresa herself and several sisters from her congregation were there. It was a very hot afternoon and the humidity was a killer. After the rite of ordination, the Bishop returned to the altar to begin the Eucharistic part of the Mass. Suddenly there were shouts and screams coming from the rear of the church. A man about 30 years old was lunging up the main aisle of the church. His face was covered with blood; he waved a bloody T-shirt in the air, begging for help. Mother Teresa got up and led two of her sisters and two ushers in to gently carry the man to the sacristy. Eventually the Mass was able to continue. At the end of the Mass, a young man came up to the bishop and asked if he could talk. He said, "I've got to talk to someone. I helped carry the bloodied man into the sacristy. He had been beaten and his language was horrible. But never in my life had I seen anything like the way he was treated." He continued, "Mother Teresa and her sisters were wonderful. They calmed the man. They washed the blood off of him. They found a clean shirt and they arranged a place for him to stay. It was everything that Jesus Christ had ever taught. It was everything that Jesus ever taught!" The man was crying with emotion and he said to the Bishop, "I'm making a whole pile of money in the stock market. But I need to be part of what I witnessed in the sacristy. The money just isn't doing it. I need something more."

This young man stayed in touch with the Bishop, who later accepted him into the Seminary and four years later ordained him a priest. Within a year after his ordination, he was stricken with leukemia, and after months of suffering, this man, this priest, realized his hope of becoming part of the reality and compassion of Christ. Peter said in the Gospel, "Lord, to whom shall we go?" This young priest knew the answer.

MDP, those of us who are followers of Jesus Christ understand that God is the ultimate source of all that is good. As we live our lives, we might have a lot of questions, a lot of doubts, a lot of fears, but in the end, we know that the words of Jesus will triumph. We know that we constantly rediscover our blessed Lord in our acts of love, and generosity and support and healing we extend to others. Peter's simple question and answer, "Lord to whom shall we go? You have the words of eternal life," will never let us abandon the hope of God's love for us.

C – Luke 13: 22-30

In the first year of life, a baby struggles to take his or her first steps. The child can charge around the room—as long as there is furniture, or railings or Daddy's long legs to hold on to. But the child will never walk until he or she lets go and stands on his or her own.

First graders begin school excited about the great possibilities that await them: the books and stories they will be able to read, the numbers they will be able to use to count things, to measure things, to keep track of things. But first, they have to master the 26 letters of the alphabet and their sounds and the basic tables of numbers.

Later, in high school and college, come the opportunities to learn the skills on which to build successful and satisfying careers – once the future writers, scientists and economists pass the basic '101" courses.

A man meets a woman, they get to know each other, their friendship blossoms into love. But there is no chance of "happily ever after" until one of the two – usually the man – works up the courage to propose marriage.

Life is a series of difficult passages, "narrow gates" through which we have to pass – and there is no easy way to pass through them.

The Gospel today is about service. When Jesus washed the feet of his Apostles, he used His hands. In light of the Gospel someone has suggested four possibilities for using our hands.

- First we can wring them. This is a popular option. There are so many hand-wringers around these days, saying "Isn't it awful? Life is unfair. The world is going to hell."

- Second, we can quietly fold our hands. In other words, be apathetic. Be unconcerned, do nothing. This too is a popular option.

- Third, we can lift our hands in prayer. As we endeavor to center our lives in the presence of God.

- Fourth, we can choose to use our hands as instruments of loving service – use them for good. Use them for welcoming, healing, hugging, sharing, loving.

TWENTY-SECOND SUNDAY IN ORDINARY TIME
A– MATTHEW 16:21-27

"WHOEVER WISHES TO COME AFTER ME MUST TAKE UP HIS CROSS AND FOLLOW ME..."

Sometimes what makes a problem tough is not that we don't know what to do, but that we know all too well what to do. To do nothing is so much easier. But our taking the easy way out can have destructive consequences for us and others. We see Jesus sharply rebuke Peter for trying to diminish or skirt around the cross. And we see Jesus urging us to let go of those things that overwhelm our lives with sadness, confusion, maybe some despair, with misplaced priorities. He urges us to embrace values, the Gospel values of love, justice and forgiveness.

Many years ago a book was making its rounds. I think everybody was reading it – it was Rabbi Kushner's book, "When Bad Things Happen to Good People". A good book and still helpful.

Not long ago I saw a replay on television of an interview Rabbi Kushner had with a member of his congregation. A woman from his synagogue came to see him. He said that she was a single mother, divorced, working to support herself and three young children. She said to the Rabbi Kushner, "Since my husband walked out on us, every month is a struggle to pay our bills. I have to tell my kids we have no money to go to the movies, while he's out living it up with his new wife in another state. Rabbi, how can you tell me to forgive him?"

The Rabbi answered her, "I'm not asking you to forgive him because what he did to you was unacceptable; it was mean and selfish. I am asking you to forgive because he doesn't deserve the power to live in your head and turn you into a bitter and angry woman. I'd like to see him out of your life emotionally as completely as he is out of it physically; but, you keep holding on to him. You're not hurting him by holding on to that resentment; you are hurting yourself."

MDP, if we are serious about the call of Jesus to be His disciple, we will center our lives on values that run counter to what so much of our culture, our world promotes and honors! If we are true to the call of Jesus to be His disciple, we will center our lives on values that run counter to what so much of our culture, our world promotes and honors! If we are true to the call of Jesus to be His disciple, we will take the first and often, very lonely and difficult steps toward reconciliation and peace; we will put aside our own needs and wants for what is best for our family, our children, for our loving friends, for our community. Today Christ invites us to take up the cross, not out of a sense of pessimism, but because we want to transform our lives into moments of joy and to really become the beautiful persons God wants us to be.

B (1) Mark 7:1-8

I saw in various places two houses which stood across from each other on the same neighborhood street. The first house was right out of Better Homes and Gardens. The house was beautifully designed and detailed. The yard had been professionally landscaped, the manicured lawn would be the envy of any gold course. Expensive late-modeled automobiles were parked in the driveway. Silk curtains lined the windows; the rooms were filled with fine furniture and antiques. There were maids keeping everything immaculate from the wine cellar to the master bedroom suite.

The second house I saw was far from being a dump but it would never make a decorator magazine. Bicycles, ball games, plastic wading pools were all over the lawn. The driveway had skateboards, basketball hoops. There was a durable van in the driveway, which had seen better days. The house was decorated in a style that was pretty eclectic: large, stuffed chairs, bunk beds in the boys' rooms, a small desk in the girls' room – that belonged to Mom when she was a girl. Everyone had their chores, but I could see that it was a challenge to keep things neat and clean.

Now in that first house, everything was quiet. I thought the people living there might be like two ships passing in the night. The dining room seemed seldom used. The father was always on business; the mother was consumed with meetings; the sons and daughters had their own schedules, activities, friends. Four separate existences in the first house.

Something always seemed to be going on in the second house. School work, games, videos, music. The menu was pretty simple and everyone had his place around the dinner table. It seemed that cold formality chilled the interior of the first house. Love, compassion, forgiveness and support transformed the second house into a real home!

It was strange but as I read the real estate ads in the newspaper this last month, they all seemed to be offering houses for sale, not homes. I thought a house is a garment easily put off or on, casually bought or sold; but a home, a home is skin. If one merely changes houses, he becomes a little disoriented; but if he changes homes, he bleeds.

MDP, when the frame you live in has taken on the savor of your love, then your house is a home.

In this poignant Gospel today, Jesus challenges us to see beyond externals and facades to 'inside' our souls and hearts and homes to the place where God dwells. You know, MDP, we all possess within ourselves the potential for great good or for monstrous evil. Who we are, what we believe, how we respond to life's challenges begins within our hearts – the place where God dwells. And it is here, in our hearts, that God is often displaced by selfishness, anger, greed, hatred. The Gospel today calls us to open our spirits and consciences to listen to the voice of God speaking to us in our hearts, calling us home, calling us to live in a home where love is born, where compassion reigns, where peace lives.

B (2)– MARK 7:1-8, 14-15, 21-23

Jesus says in the Gospel, "Nothing that enters one from outside can defile that person; but the things that come from within are what defile."

Wow! So powerful; really makes you think! I always say that one of the most difficult challenges in being a follower of Christ, a Christian, is not to let those things "outside" us diminish what we are "inside" ourselves, not to let such things as anger, vengeance, false values, walking away from our moral center line, displace the things of God in our hearts. But to let the presence of God that is within us transform those tendencies, drives and temptations.

New York Times Joe Queenan, the humorist, critic and author, remembers one of the great life lessons he learned – of all places, a bubble gum factory. Queenan writes about working summers on the night maintenance crew at the Fleer Bubble Gum Factory, in of all places, my hometown, Philadelphia. While he was a student at St. Joe's Catholic College, it was tedious and boring, but it was steady. And it gave Queenan a chance to read hundreds of great books during the frequent down times. One afternoon during the summer between his junior and senior years, Queenan was approached by a young assistant manager, a guy Queenan went to high school with. "We've notice the way you handle yourself around the other employees," he began, "and we think you've got real management potential. We were wondering if you might be interested in entering our management trainee program?"

Queenan listened politely to his friend's spiel. But the last thing Queenan wanted was a career in bubble gum management. He thanked the assistant manager for his consideration and said he would definitely think about it. Queenan thought the whole thing was hilarious and told all of his friends, who all thought it was hysterical as well – all except Queenan's Irish, right from Ireland, Father. Mr. Queenan was livid at his son's arrogance. So, Joe writes in the New York Times article, "My Father understood what it meant to be in management, even at some fifth rate bubblegum factory, because, coming from Ireland, he had once clawed his way up to the top of the white collar world as an expediter at an appliance company, but had then been purged and cast back down into the blue collar darkness. He knew precisely what the difference between blue and white collar jobs was. To thumb my nose at an opportunity for a good salary and a pension and a future and a chance to wear a tie on the job was the height of arrogance and stupidity. This was not so much because he would have wanted the job himself. It was because I acted as if the whole thing was a joke. In his Irish accent he said, "If that's all they taught you at that Catholic college, you'll never amount to a whisker on your grandfather's beard.

I believe that, thanks to his Irish father, Joe Queenan came to understand that who we are, what we believe, and how we respond to life's challenges, is defined by the attitudes and values we hold "within, that is 'right here' in the heart".

MDP, the kind of human beings we are begins in the values of the heart, the very place where the awesome God dwells; but, the evil we are capable of, the hurt we can inflict on others, the degrading of the world that God created, the lack of concern for life from beginning to end, also begins "within" when we displace God by ignoring His laws, by our selfishness, greed, anger, a lack of forgiveness and generosity. So may we take this Gospel to heart and listen, really listen, to the voice of God who is always calling within us.

C – Luke 14:1-7

At God's banquet table sometimes we are the guest; in other words, we are welcomed and are served by God in the disguise of our family, friends, and even strangers. And sometimes we are the waiter, enabling others to share in the good things at God's table.

I spent three years on the aircraft carrier, USS Carl Vinson. I was the only Catholic Chaplain who served with two Protestant Chaplains, one a Lutheran and one an American Baptist. Once a week, when we were deployed, the three of us would get together in the evening hours and talk about the Scriptures for the following Sunday. I remember the discussion we had once when we read the words of Jesus in today's Gospel: "When you hold a banquet, invite the poor, the crippled, the lame, the blind; blessed indeed will you be because of their inability to repay you."

The Baptist Chaplain told us about a time he was invited to preach at a large church in the south. The pastor of that church offered him the use of his apartment for the weekend. So my Chaplain friend arrived on Saturday and settled in. He found a note on the refrigerator door. It read, "If you usually eat breakfast, you can go to the church; we have a breakfast for the homeless." Early Sunday morning, my Chaplain friend, before the service at which he was to preach, walked down the street to the church. He realized that he was in a dangerous part of the city, and he stood in line with maybe two hundred people, waiting to be served. He struck up a conversation with those waiting with him. "Well, what put you in this situation?" One man said, "Alcohol. Might as well be honest with you, it's alcohol. But now I'm dry." Another said, "It was a woman. She took it all." Several people shared their stories of illness, financial disaster, unemployment, divorce, broken relationships.

Then someone, who did not know he was a minister, asked him, "What put you here?" Not knowing what to answer he said, "I was invited." Not wanting to create any distance, he sat with them for breakfast, ate what they ate, talked with them, and got to know them a little more before heading to the church.

Later that morning, dressed in his preaching robe, he stood in the pulpit. As he listened to the choir, and looked out at the congregation, he said to himself: "who am I? I'm only a guest, a guest of God, a guest of Christ, a guest of this church."

MDP, today Jesus asks each of us to see one another from the perspective of Gospel humility – a humility that realizes that we are not the center of all things, but part of a much larger world, a humility that is centered in gratitude for all the blessings we have received as a result of God's love for us and not because of anything we have done.

God's banquet table includes places of honor for every one of us. The humility that the Gospel teaches today is the ability to see one another as God sees us and to rejoice in being ministers to one another in all of the joys and the struggles that we all experience.

TWENTY-THIRD SUNDAY IN ORDINARY TIME
A – Matthew 18:15-20

"For when two or three are gathered together in my name, there I am in the midst of them..." Jesus gives us His definition of what it means to be "Church."

I would like to tell you two short stories about how I came to see this definition of Jesus in a personal way.

When my aircraft carrier pulled into the Philippines for some repair, I knew we would be in port for about four weeks. I wanted to get some of the Sailors aboard the ship involved in something wholesome. At first I visited the missionaries in a very poor parish in town, and I was deeply moved by the joy-filled faith of the people there in spite of their overwhelming poverty. When I returned to the ship, I got on the ship's T.V. system and invited some of the sailors to come with me, to bring help to this poor parish.

A group of sailors and myself went to the parish with extra clothes, blankets, hammers, nails, etc. to do whatever was needed. We brought a lot of happiness to the poor people and to the missionaries. It struck me hard that we were being 'church' with a small 'c."

 On another occasion, I was the Chaplain for a Marine Corps base in California. One of the Marines in the parish came up with the idea of what we called, "the list," that is, we gathered the names and telephone numbers of people in the base parish who could be called on day or night. A person, for example, needed a ride to the doctor. Well, we called Susan. A young Marine couple were struggling through a difficult pregnancy. We called Sheila and Pat who would make sure that they had supper and groceries. The car of a family, whose father was deployed, broke down. We called Neil who knew what to do. So, "the list" was more than names and telephone numbers. It was "church" with a small "c."

MDP, in the Gospel today, Jesus speaks of the "church" – not the institutional church with the capital "C," – but the one with the small 'c' that you and I, ordinary human beings who struggle to follow Jesus belong to. That's the meaning of the Gospel today: the ability of all of us who come together as followers of Jesus Christ, to accomplish works – be they ever so small, works inspired by the Gospel, works of compassion, of love, of healing. May this Gospel and the grace of God bring us together, even just two or three of us, in the name of Jesus, enabling us to mirror God's love to our families, to our beloved friends, to our community, to our world.

B – MARK 7:31

The people who witnessed this miracle were filled with awe and wonder...and the Gospel says, "Their admiration was unbounded, He has done all things well." If we are disciples of Jesus Christ, we are called to do all things well; we are called to a ministry of healing. In one of the great Ringling Museum renaissance paintings portraying the Lord and His Disciples, Jesus is reaching out to touch and heal a blind ("deaf") man. The Disciples are leaning over his shoulder watching. The scene reminds me of a senior doctor making hospital rounds with the young interns following along, watching him, trying to learn, saying to one another, "How did he do that?"

As disciples of Jesus Christ, we are expected to learn lessons in the art of healing and to put this learning into practice.

I want to tell you a Vietnam war story. Vietnam, a place I am familiar with. Major Dan Cherry was an American Air Force pilot during the Vietnam war. On an April morning, flying a F-4 phantom, Major Cherry engaged a North Vietnamese MIG-21. The dog fight ended with Cherry shooting down the MIG; the Vietnamese pilot managed to eject from the burning aircraft.

Dan Cherry retired from the Air Force, but he always wondered what had happened to that pilot – who he was, whether he survived, if he had a family. While working on an exhibit of his old plane for Aviation

Heritage Park in Bowling Green, Kentucky, Cherry thought again about the Vietnamese pilot. With the help of American veterans groups, the ministry of defense in Hanoi, and a Vietnam television network, Cherry found the pilot he had shot down. A meeting was arranged between the two old fighter pilots – on live television in Ho Chi Minh City. When the two former adversaries met, Nguyen Hong My grasped his nervous counterpart's hand firmly. "Welcome to my country. I'm glad to see that you are in good health. I hope that we can be friends."

After the program, Hong My invited Dan to his home in Hanoi where he met Hong My's son, daughter in law and grandson, who was celebrating his first birthday. Earlier this year, Hong My returned the visit to Dan and his family in Kentucky. Both men have appeared together around the country on behalf of veteran's groups to tell their story of healing. Their ability to forge a lasting and trusting friendship has helped many veterans – and two nations – to put a long, agonizing war behind them.

MDP, I thought this story was so appropriate to this Gospel of healing; it is the story of EPHPHATHA – which means "Be open." We must, as Christians, have that powerful word, EPHPHATHA on our lips. EPHPHATHA means we must open our eyes, and we must see beyond labels, and stereotypes, beyond hurts and old grudges. EPHPHATHA means we must listen to the hopes and aspirations of those who seek what is good and right and honest in their lives. EPHPHATHA means that we must have the courage to confront wrong in our lives, in our families, in our community, in our culture. EPHPHATHA must become our word of healing; it must become our prayer that we may be 'open' to the presence of God in our own lives and in the lives of those we are privileged to touch.

C–(1) Luke 14:25-33

A small boy sat in church with his mother, listening to a sermon entitled, "What is a Christian?" During the sermon, the preacher made several dramatic pauses and then with a loud voice would boom out the question, "What is a Christian?" And, for emphasis, his fist would bang down on the pulpit. The tension produced by this fiery preaching style built up in the boy until, finally, he whispered excitedly to his mother, "Do you know, Mama? Mama, do you know what a Christian is?" "Yes, my dear," Mama replied, "Now be quiet!" Then, as the preacher was winding up the sermon, he again thundered the question – "What is a Christian?" and he slammed his fist down on the pulpit with tremendous force. This was too much for the little boy. He jumped up and cried out, "Tell him, Mama, tell him!"

What is a Christian? I suppose we could say that a Christian is a person who has been baptized in the faith; a Christian is one who believes in the true God who is the Creator of all things; a Christian is one who believes that because God loves us so much He gave His only Son in order to redeem the world and to bring us to salvation; a Christian is a member of the worshipping community.

The Gospel of Jesus today reminds us that we must have courage if we are to follow Him. Recently a radio station in New York invited people to call in and tell them the first thing they said when they woke up in the morning. The responses, as desired, were usually funny: "Do I smell the coffee burning?" "Honey, did I remember to put out the dog last night."

One morning the station phone rang and the perky DJ said his usual, "Good morning. This is station FM 106. You're on the air. What's the first thing you said when you rolled out of bed this morning?" A voice with a very pronounced Bronx accent said, "Hear, oh Israel, the Lord our God is one; you shall love your God with all your heart, with all your soul, with all your mind, and with all your strength." He was, of course, a devout Jew reciting the Jewish Shema, or holiness prayer. The DJ didn't know how to handle this and, after a moment of embarrassed silence, said, "sorry, wrong number," hung up on him and cut to a commercial.

The Gospel today asks what does it cost us to be a Christian? Has our fidelity to the Gospel ever cost us embarrassment, money, reputation, family harmony? The Gospel message is costly, and it might mean being ridiculed for it, being called "a wrong number."

Just for a minute, let's look back over our last week and ask, was there any time we felt that we had to pay a price, even a small one, for being a Christian? Listen again to our blessed Lord: "Whoever does not bear his own cross and come after Me cannot be My Disciple."

The episode surrounding this Gospel finds Jesus at the height of His popularity. Crowds were turning out to hear Him speak, and for many different reasons. Political revolutionaries saw Him as a potential ally, a spell binder who could excite crowds and enlist them in their cause. To others, Jesus was "in vogue," as it were, the "in group" coming out to His talks and inviting Him to dinner. Only a very few among the crowds had caught even a glimpse of what He was all about. So it was time for Jesus to reemphasize the conditions necessary for His followers. To be my follower, He says, you must "leave your father, mother, wife, brother, sister, even your own self." If you are going to be My disciple, even your most intimate relationships must be placed within this context. Moreover, if you are going to be My disciple there can be no "wrong numbers," No cutting to a commercial. He says, you must put Me first in your lives! And when you have the courage to put Me first, life will take on a new meaning. Life will become exciting and beautiful and worth living.

After I retired from the Navy and came to Florida, I helped out at Sts. Peter and Paul Parish in Bradenton. I got to know a woman in the parish who was a junior executive in a local company. She told me that once, in a meeting, she happened to mention a point from a homily she heard the previous Sunday. "Well", she said to me, "You would have thought that I belched in public. Everyone around me reacted as if I had dropped out from some weird planet and said disdainfully, "You go to the church?"

MDP, May we have the courage to take the Gospel of Jesus to heart and not to dismiss His Gospel as nothing but a collections of pious teachings; may we take on the demanding task of courageously making the Gospel a reality in our lives and our world.

C (2)– Luke 14:27

There is a tendency throughout life to search for the easy way of doing things; we all search for that elusive 'easy street.' In fact, in Honolulu, Hawaii, if you take the Pali Highway northbound, proceed about one-third of the distance to Pali Pass, and, turn right at Park Street, and continue for one block, there it is: "Easy Street." But if you go one more block, you come upon another sign which says "Dead End".

In Today's lesson, and in many other places in the Gospels, Jesus warns us that if we are looking for an easy way to follow Him, we're on a dead end street. If we want to be His follower, Jesus says, we must "Bear your own cross." If we want to be His disciple, Jesus says that we had better first "count the cost," (Luke 14: 27, 28).

Whoever does not bear his own cross cannot be My disciple. For which of you desiring to build a tower, does not first sit down and count the cost, whether he has enough to complete it? (Luke 14:27-28)

If anyone would come after Me, let him deny himself and take up his cross and follow Me. (Matthew 16:24)

When a man and a woman stand at the Altar of God and enter into a marriage covenant with one another, they agree that the union of their life and love will be a permanent, enduring, lasting union. They promise to love "until death us do part." And one of the beautiful things about a good marriage is that love endures, deepens, and grows through the years. It is relatively easy for a man and a woman, during the early romantic, ecstatic days, to say that they love each other and that they will always remain together. But as time goes by, the daily pressures are upon them, they feel the nitty grittiness of married life, and the honeymoon is over. And both parties in the relationship soon discover that if their love for each other is to endure and deepen and grow, they must be willing to pay the high cost of loving.

Now I know this itemized list doesn't answer the question completely, but it does take us to a point in the relationship between Christ and His followers where the honeymoon is over. This is the point at which the Christian must be willing to pay the price if the relationship is to endure and deepen and grow. This is the point at which the Christian must be willing to pay the high cost of obedience to Jesus' command: "Love one another as I have loved you" (John 15:12)

It is almost as if Jesus is saying to us, "Unless you are willing to get serious about being My Disciple, unless you are willing to get serious about following Me, unless you are willing to get serious about becoming the person God created you to be, unless you are willing to get serious about my invitation to new life, you would be better off not to try to follow Me."

There are Gospel episodes in which people come up to Jesus wanting to talk about religion, and about God, and about eternal life. But because they are not really serious, Jesus days "No! Don't bother! All this talk is useless, unless you are ready and willing to make God's presence in your life your number one priority."

If we want to have this new life we must love one another, Jesus commands. And that's fine with us as long as we can carry out this command with certain limits. We are always ready and willing and able to love the lovable. But then comes the heavy duty pressure, the nitty gritty of the Gospel, the command to love the unlovable, and the honeymoon is over. And it is at this point that we must be willing to count the cost and take up your cross and deny yourself.

In a "Peanuts" comic strip, Lucy and Charlie Brown are engaged in earnest conversation about the meaning of life. Lucy feels that it's a matter of one's perspective. She says that "Life is like a deck chair. Some people place it so they can see where they are going. Some people place is so they can see where they have been. And some people place it so they can see where they are now." Charlie ponders Lucy's little discourse, then replies, "I can't even get mine unfolded."

In terms of our life in Christ, we may wish to look back so that we can see where we've been. We may wish to look ahead to try to see where we're going. But to see where we are right now, if we are not ready and willing to pick up our cross and love the unlovable, like Charlie Brown we haven't even unfolded our chair yet.

TWENTY-FOURTH SUNDAY IN ORDINARY TIME
A – MATTHEW 18:21-35

The Bishop of the Diocese asked us to reflect in some way—sharing our thoughts and prayers on this anniversary of 9/11. All of us have been watching the many tributes on television—and they are so touching, so well done.

But I want to share a personal story with you. By now, you all know that I had the most amazing career as a Navy priest—thirty years of service to your sons, grandsons, and daughters, to our nation. One of the blessings of being a Navy Chaplain is that, if one is lucky, he gets to serve with the United States Marines. I was lucky: I began my career with the 3rd Marines in Vietnam and then had another 13 years with them. I loved the Marines.

 The story I want to tell you will demonstrate why Navy Chaplains love to serve with the Marines. A close Chaplain friend of mine, a Navy priest, was assigned to Henderson Hall, right near the Pentagon on 9/11. He told me what happened at a daycare center right near where the terrorist plane impacted the Pentagon. The daycare center supervisor was in panic, looking to evacuate the toddlers as wells as the infants. There was no time to try to bundle them into carriers and strollers. Just then a young Marine came running into the center, and seeing what the director was trying to do, he ran back into the hallway and disappeared. The director thought, "Well, here we are – on our own." Two minutes later, that Marine returned with twenty other Marines in tow. Each of them grabbed a crib with a child, and the rest started to gather up the toddlers. They took the children out of the center and down toward the park near the Potomac and the Pentagon. Once they got about three fourths of a mile outside the building, the Marines stopped in the park, and then they did a "Marine thing" – they formed a circle with the cribs, which were quite sturdy and heavy, like

the covered wagons of the old west. Inside this circle of cribs, they put the toddlers to keep them from wandering off. Outside this circle were 40 Marines, forming a perimeter around children and waiting for instructions. There they remained until the parents could come and get their children.

My Chaplain friend told me, "I don't think any of us saw nor heard of this on any of the news stories of the day. It was a beautiful 9/11 story of our men in uniform. The thought of those Marines and what they did and how fast they reacted; could we expect any less from them? I always remember Ronald Reagan's great compliment for the Marines: "Most of us wonder if our lives made any difference. Marines don't have that problem."

MDP, in today's Gospel our Lord Jesus Christ, demands a new mind set and He wants us to see our brothers and sisters, to see our nation as God's people wanting peace and freedom. May 9/11 help us put God first in our nation, in our hearts; may the good Lord grant eternal peace to those who suffered and died on this day. May God help their children and families. May God bless the United States of America. My God bless our troops. May God bless each and every one of you.

B– Luke 15:1-32

I would like to tell you a story. A little boy, the son of a minister, pulled his father's favorite hymn book from the bookcase. Picking up a pen, the boy began scribbling all over the first page. Just then, his father walked in. The boy looked at his father, and immediately knew he had done something wrong. The father picked up his favorite hymnal, looked at it carefully, then sat down without saying a word. He did not scold his son. He simply took the pen from the little boy's hand and wrote in the book himself, right alongside his son's scribblings. He wrote: "John's word, 1959, age two. How many times have I looked into your beautiful face and your warm eyes looking up at me and thanked God for the one who has now scribbled in my favorite hymnal? You have made this book sacred as have your brothers and sister to my life."

The hymnal has been handed on to the minister's children and grandchildren who scribble in it themselves and write their names in it – and their parents and their own "hymns" of thanks.

MDP, both the little boy's father and the prodigal son's father in today's Gospel possess a vision of compassion and an ability to forgive that truly mirror the compassion and forgiveness of God. Both fathers understand what really matters in life: people really matter, not objects! Kindness really matters; love, which has no limits, really matters. Both fathers forgive their sons even before the boys ask and put aside their own hurts to love them totally and unconditionally. The most precious lesson that we can take home from the Gospel today is that God loves each and every one of us uniquely and individually, just as parents love their own precious children, and that His love for us is eternally forgiving, never limited or qualified. It is this love that Jesus asks us to bring to others, to this good world of ours.

C– JOHN 3:13-17

It's a privilege to be with all of you as we celebrate this great day of the Holy Cross in our parish. May God continue to bless all of us as we strive to make the cross of Jesus Christ the cornerstone of our parish life. This Feast has its roots in the fourth century, and was known as the "Triumph of the Cross."

The story goes like this. Early in the fourth century St. Helena, mother of the Roman emperor Constantine went to Jerusalem in search of the holy places in Christ's life. She had the temple of Aphrodite, which tradition said was built over the Savior's tomb, knocked down. During the excavation, workers found three crosses, and legend has it that the one on which Jesus died was identified when it was placed on and healed a dying woman. So … today we remember St. Helena's pilgrimage and what a surprising reversal it was for those relics of the cross to arrive in Rome, the capitol of the Empire, and Empire that used the cross as a means, not only of killing Christ, but as a means of assuring that not only would He die, but everything He stood for would die as well. The relics were brought into Rome in the kind of triumphant procession that the Romans reserved for the victories of Caesar over his enemies.

I always thought it was so ironic that it was Caesar who bowed low before the relics of the cross, demonstrating that Christ the Lord was the true King, and the Lord of the nations. For all of us the image of the crucified Savior is one that has been before our eyes through our lives, and its meaning is inescapable. God suffered; God died for us, that we might have His life. This is the awesome mystery of our Christian faith.

I want to tell you a story that I hope will make the mystery of the cross more understandable for you as it did for me.

A wealthy man and his son loved to collect rare works of art. They had everything in their collection, from Picasso to Raphael to Van Gogh. They would often sit together and admire the great works of art. When the Vietnam conflict broke out, the son went to war as one of our Marines. He was very courageous and died in battle while rescuing another Marine. The father was notified and he grieved deeply for his only son.

About a month later, just before Christmas, there was a knock at the father's door. A young man stood at the door with a large package in his hands. He said, "Sir, you don't know me, but I am the Marine for whom your son gave his life. He saved many lives that day, and he was carrying me to safety when a bullet struck him in the heart and he died instantly. He often talked about you and your love for art." The young man held out this package. "I know this isn't much. I'm not really a great artist, but I think your son would have wanted you to have this." The father opened the package. It was a portrait of his son, painted by the Marine. He stared in awe at the way the Marine had captured the personality of his son in the painting. The father was so drawn to the eyes that his own eyes welled up with tears. He thanked the young man and offered to pay him for the picture. "Oh, no, sir, I could never repay what your son did for me. It's a gift."

The father hung the portrait over his mantle. Every time visitors came to his home he took them to see the portrait of his son before he showed them any of the other great works he had collected.

The wealthy man died a few months later. There was to be an auction of his paintings. Many influential people gathered, excited over seeing the great paintings and having an opportunity to purchase one for their collections. On the platform sat the painting of the son. The auctioneer pounded his gavel. "We will start the bidding with this picture of the son. Who will bid for this picture?" There was silence. Then a voice in the back of the room shouted, "We want to see the famous paintings. Skip this one." But the auctioneer persisted, "Will somebody bid for this painting? Who will start the bidding? $100, $200?" Another voice angrily shouted, "We didn't come to see that painting. We came to see the Van Gogh's the Rembrandts. Get on with the real bids!"

Finally a voice came from the very back of the room. It was the long time gardener of the man and his son. "I'll give $10 for the painting..." Being a poor man, it was all he could afford... "We have $10, who will bid $20?" "Give it to him for $10," someone shouted; let's see the masters" The crowd was becoming...they didn't want the picture of the son, they wanted the more worthy investments for their collections. The auctioneer pounded the gavel, "Going once, twice, sold for $10!"

A man sitting on the second row shouted, "Now let's get on with the collection!" The auctioneer laid down his gavel. "I'm sorry, the auction is over." "What about the paintings?" "I am sorry. When I was called to conduct this auction, I was told of a secret stipulation in the will. I was not allowed to reveal that stipulation until this time. Only the painting of the son would be auctioned. Whoever bought that painting would inherit the entire estate, including the paintings... the man who took the son gets everything!"

The awesome God gave His Son 2000 years ago to die on the cross. And His message is "The Son, the Son, who will take the Son?"

MDP, who ever takes the Son and His cross gets everything. "For God so loved the world that He gave His only begotten Son, that whoever believes in Him shall have eternal life."

TWENTY-FIFTH SUNDAY IN ORDINARY TIME
A– MATTHEW 20:12-16

I officiated at a wedding in San Francisco last week, and had the chance to spend time with a Navy couple, Bridget and Jack, with whom I was stationed years ago. Bridget told me that her marriage to Jack was failing. She insisted that Jack had become insensitive and insisted that he see a marriage counselor. Jack didn't want to, but finally agreed to go just to get her off his back. I understood that after talking to him for several minutes, the counselor suggested that Jack needed to communicate his feelings with Bridget a little more. Jack said to the counselor, "How can you say that? I communicate my feelings all the time!" Wanting to be fair and objective, the therapist asked Jack, "In what ways do you share your feelings with Bridget?" Jack said, "Well, I tell her all the time that I feel she talks too much, that she spends too much money, that she worries too much, that she nags me too much. Doc, how much more can a guy do?"

MDP, I hope that somewhere in San Francisco, Jack listened to today's Gospel. In this Gospel, our blessed Lord demands a change of perspective in the way we live our lives. If we want to be exalted by God, if we want Him to give us peace of heart in our lives, if we want Him to give us the power to become the uniquely beautiful persons we were created to be, then we must genuinely trust Him. We must abandon the need we feel to manipulate and control and dominate the lives of others. It is difficult for so many of us to see our lives in a new perspective; our very culture points us in the other direction.

Most of the "how to do it" books on the shelves of the major bookstores these days are about how to win by intimidation; how to be first; how to be number one. As a matter of fact, just a few years ago, Robert Ringer wrote a book entitled, "Looking Out for Number One." In it Ringer argues strongly against generosity. He says, for example, that "if you make the other person's happiness your first responsibility, you pervert the laws of nature…" and he continues, "unless someone is poor because you robbed him, no downtrodden, homeless individual is our responsibility!"

But in every line of the New Testament Jesus tells us that if we follow such advice we are perverting the law of God! The troubling thing for me about Ringer's book is that it became a bestseller. Have we slipped so far down the ladder that we are ready and willing to embrace the "looking out for number one" notion that other people are just things? Are we ready and willing to join those in this dizzy world who see the Christian faith, our whole religious outlook, as irrelevant and out of touch? Are we ready and willing to join those who seem to laugh at the teachings of Jesus that the number one priority in people's lives is not to satisfy personal greed but to satisfy their brother's need?

Our beautiful Gospel today begins with the words, "The kingdom of heaven is like …" As the parable unfolds we learn that the kingdom of heaven is so unlike the feeling that people have about labor and reward. When we hear people say "he has it made," they usually mean "he's made lots of money." But in today's Gospel we learn that for residents of the kingdom of heaven, working in the Lord's vineyard is its own reward; that the number one priority is to be of service – not to get, but to give!

The famous psychiatrist Karl Menninger once asked a very wealthy patient, "What are you going to do with all your money?" The patient replied, "Just worry about it, I guess." "In that case, said Doctor Menninger, "do you experience much pleasure out of worrying about your money?" With a heavy sigh, the patient answered, "No, but I feel such terror when I think of giving any of it away." Commenting on his patient's money sickness Doctor Menninger said, "Generous people are rarely mentally ill."

MDP, how cautious and afraid are we to be totally present to our life situations, to tell others how much we love them. We hold back in our relationships; we never get very close; we are always ready to look down and away; we lose opportunity after opportunity to live life to the fullest, to relate, to forgive, to show compassion, to be warm, to understand, to give, to listen to another, and to put the other's interest first.

I saw an old rerun of "All in the Family" recently. Edith and Archie Bunker are attending Edith's high school reunion. Edith encounters an old classmate named "Buck" who has allowed himself to become very obese. Edith and Buck have a delightful conversation about old times and the things they did together; remarkably, Edith doesn't seem to even notice how extremely obese Buck has become. Later Edith and Archie are talking and she says, "Archie, ain't Buck a beautiful person?" Archie replies, "Edith, I'll never figure you out. You and I can look at the same guy, and you see a beautiful person and I see a blimp. And Edith replies simply, "Yeah, Archie, ain't that too bad! Ain't that too bad!"

"The last will be first and the first will be last." MDP, only God is number one!

The Gospel according to Matthew: notice how Matthew, the superb teacher, often ends a parable with a helpful memory line. The parable refers to the chosen people as first, and to the Gentiles as late-comers. This presents a consoling picture of divine generosity which goes beyond the limits of strict justice.

B – MARK 9:30-37

When my aircraft carrier visited the Port of Mombasa in Africa, I had the opportunity to spend an evening with one of the British missionaries. Somehow, we began talking about the very Gospel of today's Mass.

I remember this simple but powerful story he told. He said, "It was a bright Sunday morning, and I had prepared a few thoughts on the words of Jesus, "If anyone wishes to be first, he shall be the last of all and the servant of all." He said, "I told the congregation to reflect the love of God in everything they do, just as Jesus did in His life and ministry. After the sermon, the collection plate was passed. A young native woman, who had recently been baptized, had no money to give. Consequently, when the plate came to her, she quietly rose from her seat, placed the plate on the floor and stood on it. And as she carried out that symbolic act of total commitment, total giving of self, I saw in her face a brilliant, dazzling reflection of the glory of God's love."

MDP, when we look at the early Christians, we realize that their mission to the world was very effective because every man and every woman who gave themselves to Jesus, went out with the understanding that they were totally engaged in His ministry. They experienced the presence of God in their lives as in no other way. In carrying out their ministry of loving service to others, they truly experienced the God of love in their lives. The whole New Testament tells us in so many ways that it's not the ego trip, not the quest for power and control, not the longing to be rich, that moves us towards fulfillment, toward holiness, as persons who have been created in the image of God on this earth. Rather, the Gospel of Jesus tells us that we must be present to others in a way that makes them feel loved, feel wanted, feel worthwhile; this is what will enable us to experience holiness in our lives.

We heard it in the Gospel, "If anyone wishes to rank first, he must remain last, and be the servant of all." True holiness arises out of our ability to love in a way that says, 'I am the servant of all.'

The challenge of this Gospel – "To be the servant of all", always brings to mind an incident when I was with a company in the Third Marine Division and we were ready to go into Vietnam. There was a young captain in charge of several platoons. I remember precisely what he said when he spoke to his troops. He said, "I don't know what awaits us when we jump off this boat, but I'll tell you this. If I have to give my life for any of you, I will do it in a heartbeat."

MDP, There may be some lonely souls out there, in our parish, among our friends, who are hungry for our immediate, genuine, loving, caring presence. It may even be a daughter, a son, a nephew, a husband, wife or parent. Not our job, nor our possessions, not our money, but the persons we find in our lives are our number one priority.

The Gospel today tells us that our Christian faith is not a luxury, but a necessity now, because now is when we need to know who we are and how we ought to be living. To live humanely, to live lovingly in Christ, is to live for others. The words of the Gospel, these magnificent words of Christian wisdom, will remain only "words" unless we translate them into action.

C – Luke 16:1-13

This powerful Gospel says to us very bluntly that it's not the things we possess, the new car, the stock portfolio, the quest for riches, for money; it's not the quest for power and control that moves us toward fulfillment as human persons who have been created to image God on this earth. Rather, it is the act of being present to others in a way that makes them feel loved, feel wanted, feel worthwhile; it is the priorities that we set for our life so that we can experience wholeness, balance, holiness.

No, Jesus says that true success arises out of our ability to love in a way that says "I am the servant of all." What He is saying about the dishonest manager in the Gospel is that we must realize that the only way to a future security is to live a generous life now. Everything we have is a gift: our husbands, our wives, our children, our friends, our time, our health, our money. How thankful we should be and how this thankfulness should lead us to generosity.

I want to tell you a little story about an ultimate generosity that I personally experienced. My first tour in the Navy was in Southeast Asia, Vietnam. I was assigned to the Third Marine Division. I was told the story that a young Marine in one of our companies was wounded. A fellow Marine wanted to go and retrieve his wounded buddy. But the company commander stopped him. He said to the young Marine, "Don't be stupid! He's dead and if you go you'll be dead." But the young Marine persisted, "No, I want to go; I have to go." But the lieutenant said, "Nobody expects this of you."

But the young Marine ignored the lieutenant's orders and crawled up over the rim of the foxhole and out into the open field. He returned hours later dragging his dead buddy. But he himself was badly wounded, and he wasn't going to make it. In frustration and anger the lieutenant yelled, "I told you. I told you. It wasn't worth it." But the dying Marine said, "Oh yes it was. You see, when I found him he wasn't dead yet and when I knelt to pick him up he looked into my eyes and said, "Jim, I knew you would come."

I anointed this Marine as he was dying. Generosity- to put another's needs, hopes and dreams ahead of our own. This is it; this is the message of the Gospel. I often feel that all of us during the week, during the month, that we meet some lonely soul, someone who is hungry for our immediate, genuine, loving, caring presence. It might be a daughter, a son, a husband, wife, a parent, a niece or nephew, a friend. So, it's not going to be our jobs, it's not going to be our possessions, but these persons we know or meet are the number one priority, and if we are giving them anything and everything but ourselves, we are just not making any sense out of the Gospel of Jesus Christ.

MDP, the power we have as followers of Jesus grows with use and withers with disuse. As people who call ourselves Christians, our goal is to become ever more sensitized to the reality of human need, wherever it exists. We're all in the same boat moving toward a common destiny. As honest followers of Jesus Christ we just have to become sensitized to the reality that just as Jesus is God's gift to us, we must make ourselves a true and generous gift to others. Our family needs us, our friends need us, the world needs us because we are all children of God. We must pray with this Gospel in our hearts that our good Lord will make our lives windows for His light to shine through so that we will reflect His love to everybody we meet.

TWENTY-SIXTH SUNDAY IN ORDINARY TIME
A – Matthew 21:28-32

"Tax collectors and prostitutes are entering the Kingdom of God before you..."

I want to tell you a true story told to me by a good friend, the mother of a large family. One day her mother took her six-year-old son Martin to a restaurant. Martin had been learning how to say his prayers in Catechism class, so he asked his mother if he could say grace before they ate. As they bowed their heads, Martin prayed: "God is great. God is good. Thank you for this food. And I would even thank you more if Mom gets us ice cream for dessert. And liberty and justice for all. Amen."

Well, the people at the nearby table laughed – except for a woman who remarked: "That's what's wrong with this country. Kids today don't even know how to pray. Asking God for ice cream. How silly! Little Martin heard the woman, and with tears welling, said to his Mom, "Did I do it wrong? Is God mad at me now?" His Mom hugged him and assured Martin that he had done a good job with the prayer and that God was not mad at him.

Just then an elderly gentleman came up to their table and said to Martin, "Son, that was a beautiful prayer you said." "Really?" asked Martin. "Cross my heart," the man answered. Then, in a loud whisper, just loud enough for the snobbish woman to hear, he added, "Too bad she never asks God for ice cream. Sometimes a little ice cream is good for the soul."

At the end of the meal, Mom ordered ice cream for them. Martin stared at his ice cream for a moment. Then, to his mother's surprise, he picked up his ice cream and carefully brought it over to the critical woman's table and placed it in front of her. Martin politely said, "Here, this is for you. Ice cream is good for the soul, and my soul is good already."

MDP, in today's beautiful Gospel, Jesus upholds the importance of the spirit of sincerity and compassion behind the words we use every day, behind our actions rather than the words and actions themselves. Martin's prayer, though so informal, so simple, is in itself worthy of God in its sincerity and simple joy. Too often we are quick to judge, quick to gauge people according to our own dubious standards. The externals of dress and speech and pedigree fail to take into account the true meaning of a person's worth; we fail to see the love in that person's heart. Jesus Christ calls us to look beyond labels like "tax collector" and "prostitute" and recognize, instead, the goodness, the holiness, that is in every person, who is, like us, a child of God.

B – MARK 9: 38-43, 45, 41-48

There's an old "Peanuts" comic strip that begins with an obviously sad little Lucy sitting next to Snoopy, the dog. Lucy sighs and says, "Sometimes I think no one is going to love me." In each succeeding panel, she goes on with her lament. "Sometimes I think no one is ever going to want to lean over and kiss me. No one loves me. No one even likes me. No one cares about me." Meanwhile, Snoopy is in distress. He has lost his balance. He can't seem to stand up. He is teetering, "look at me,: he says to Lucy. "I'm leaning over. Hurry up and look. I'm falling! Hurry up! Hurry up, I'm falling! Then clunk! Poor Snoopy has fallen flat on his face. Through it all, Lucy has remained oblivious to Snoopy's need. She's been ignoring his plight, just looking straight ahead, all wrapped up in herself, agonizing over her own problems. "No one will ever love me," she says for the last time. And Snoopy, still flat on his face, mutters "You're right, sweetie! You're right!"

Before this week is over, we all will have dozens of opportunities to be sensitive to another's need. Before this week is over, we will have dozens of opportunities to care for someone. Before this week is over, we will have dozens of opportunities to give that "drink of water in

Jesus' Name" as we are missioned to do in today's Gospel.

A Navy Chaplain friend of mine once preached an entire series of sermons on a very brief conversation he had overheard while serving on one of our Navy bases. The base had been struck by a severe storm, with very high winds, and heavy rains coming down in sheets. Two officer's wives were watching the storm through a big picture window in the officer's club. My Chaplain friend was sitting at a table nearby. Suddenly, through a flash of lightening, one of the women saw a young Sailor outside doing guard duty – totally at the mercy of the raging storm. "Oh dear," she said, "Look at that young Sailor out there in the storm." To which the other lady replied, "My dear, it's perfectly all right. He's only a Sailor."

What a terrible thing to say: "He's only!" We hear it all the time. Sometimes, we ourselves are guilty of saying it: "He's only... she's only... he's only that boy down the street, the one with no father... he's only an old drunk ... she's only the secretary." As long as the "he's only ... she's only" attitude prevails in our lives, God's love is not released within us and we wither spiritually.

We need to hear and to accept without reservation Jesus' promise to use in today's Gospel lesson: Any person who gives a drink of water in My name will never go unrewarded. Because we are who we are – because we are all in this boat together - we cannot bear the notion that our lives should go unrewarded. Our human nature is constantly driving us in search of fulfillment, of peace of heart.

Jesus is telling us today precisely where the search for a rewarding, fulfilled life begins and ends. The most rewarding experience in life, Jesus tells us, comes in the giving of that drink of water – especially to those who thirst most for someone who really cares. The act of caring and giving is life's most fulfilling experience in terms of getting to know who we are, why we are and where we are going.

In his famous novel, "The Diary of a Country Priest," Georges Bernanos, creates a moving scene in which the priest encounters a woman who is completely turned in on herself. She has been abandoned by her daughter and betrayed by her husband. Death has claimed her young son. And her heart has hardened. Beseeching her to unlock her hardened heart, the priest says, "Hell is not to love anymore."

MDP, to tuck ourselves away in a little ego-world of our own is hell. To deceive ourselves into believing that our own little world is the world, is hell. To search for any kind of lasting fulfillment outside the context of "giving a drink of water" is hell. But St. Mark in today's Gospel gives us the assurance, the faith, the strength of the true Christian. He says, "When we break out and give of ourselves in Jesus' name, He says, "I assure you, you will not go without reward."

C – LUKE 16:19-31

When my aircraft carrier was in the Philippines for repair, I and several other Catholic Chaplains on base decided to place a courtesy call on Cardinal Jaime Sin, the Archbishop of Manila. He had a great sense of humor. When he greeted us at his front door, his first words were, "Welcome to the house of sin." And then he said, "When I was little, they would call me a 'venial sin.' But after I die, I am sure they will realize that I was a 'mortal sin.'"

This meeting with Cardinal Sin reminded me of something the New Testament writers have to say about each and every one of us: we are all sinners and we are all mortal. And since we are all sinners to one degree or another, we are all subject to the dangers of our life getting out of control. And, as always, now is the time to check the progress of our journey to our ultimate destiny as mortal humans.

As always, now is the time to take stock of anything in our life that is stalling our effort to follow Jesus. And so we have these magnificent parables of Jesus. In today's Gospel, a wealthy man lives a fabulously privileged life; he, as you hear in the reading, routinely ignores a pitiful beggar, Lazarus, lying at his gate. The parable is telling us to take stock of our lives, to see if we are living in a stubborn resistance to the call of Jesus for us to pick up our cross in loving service to others. When we ignore the "Lazarus" at our gate, the risen Christ will have a hard time getting through to us.

In the Gospels Jesus calls us to "come and follow Him." He says, "Follow Me on the road to happiness," but first, as the Gospel today says, we must eliminate the principal cause of frustration and disillusionment that present a road block: our own self-centeredness! MDP, God made us to be happy. God wants us to experience fulfillment. But some of us have the mistaken notion that we can be happy "on our own." Some of us have the mistaken notion that we can substitute our own happiness formula for God's. Some of us have the mistaken notion that we can do it our way. Some of us have the mistaken notion that our happiness is unrelated to the happiness of others.

Permit me to tell you the story of a Maryknoll priest, who, before he served with me in the Navy, was a missionary in the mountains of Bolivia. He told me the story of the time he went to a poor village in the mountains. On his first day there, he gathered up all the bread and blankets and medicine he could and began his visit to his parishioners. At the first hut, a mother was caring for a child sick with a fever. My priest friend watched as she nestled the child in her arms, wiping his face with a wet rag. For hours she held the child, patiently wiping her little boy's brow, whispering a little song as he slept. Father blessed the child and his mother, left some medicine and went on his way. At another house, Father arrived in time for supper. The mother had prepared a weak soup of water and a few vegetables she had begged that day. She happily welcomed my priest friend and offered him a small cup. As he took the soup and joined the other members of the family, he did not see a cup or bowl for the mother. He blessed the family, left some bread and moved on.

As he arrived at the last house, a cold rain began to fall. An elderly couple lived there. The small fire offered little warmth from the damp cold. The old woman was lying on a mat, trying to sleep, shivering, she had pulled the threadbare blanket around her. Her husband had taken off his own tattered coat and tucked it around her, then sat beside her in the dark cold, rubbing her back to help keep her warm. Father blessed the couple, left blankets for them, and returned to his own small house. That night, having given away all of the food, all of the medicine and blankets he had, the priest sat down and looked at his own empty cupboard and realized that he had been the one who was blessed that day.

MDP, in calling us to check the progress of our journey to eternal life, Jesus calls us not only to care for the poor but also to learn from the poor. The Lazaruses in our midst can teach us so much about compassion and generosity; in their poverty, they can show us what the real treasures of life are and how to possess them; in their humility, they reflect the dignity of being made in the very image of God. The rich man of today's Gospel is too self-absorbed and satisfied to grasp the wisdom that the poor have to teach: that the many blessing they – and we – have been given by God, are a responsibility and a means to realize God's dream of a just and merciful community of those who follow the Gospel of Jesus Christ.

TWENTY-SEVENTH SUNDAY IN ORDINARY TIME
A – Matthew 21:33-43

The death of the 'landlord's son' should remind us of the high price that is demanded from us who try to live life proclaiming the Gospel of Jesus Christ. At times living the challenging values of the Gospel can be discouraging, even isolating. Yet each one of us who proclaims to be a disciple of Jesus and a witness to His resurrection is called to embrace values which will yield a beautiful harvest in God's Kingdom.

There's a Native American Indian legend about the Chief of a certain tribe who was on his deathbed. He called his three sons to him. He said, "My sons, my life is at its end. Soon one of you will succeed me as Chief. I want each of you to climb our ancestors' holy mountain and bring back something beautiful. The one whose gift is most precious will become Chief."

Several days later, the three returned from their journey. The first son brought back a flower that was extremely rare and beautiful. The second son brought back a stone of precious gold. But the third son said, "Father, I have brought nothing back. As I stood at the top of the holy mountain, I saw that on the other side was a land of fertile green pastures and crystal waters. I could imagine our people settling there and establishing a better life. I was so taken by what I saw that I had to return here before I could find something to bring back." The old Chief smiled and said to his third son, "You will be our Chief for you have brought us the gift of a vision for a better future."

MDP, God, the owner of the vineyard, calls all of us to follow the Gospel of His Son, to create a better life, that is, a vineyard that will yield a harvest of justice, peace, forgiveness. Christ comes to us with a new vision for the vineyard – a vision of love rather than desire, a vision of peace rather than hostility, a vision of forgiveness rather than revenge. Our challenge is to welcome Christ into this vineyard of our life determined to sow and reap blessings for ourselves and for those whom we love, for our community and world and for the kingdom of God.

B – MARK 10:2-16

"WHOEVER DOES NOT ACCEPT THE KINGDOM OF GOD LIKE A CHILD WILL NOT ENTER IT."

We have all experienced things like words, tastes, etc. that bring back a memory. These words of Jesus about the faith of children did that for me. About twenty-one years ago, I was the Chaplain for the Navy Seabees in California. (The Seabees are a rough and hardy bunch of the Navy's construction persons, carpenters, electricians, bricklayers, engineers, etc. They were a lot of fun.)

I had a perfect base parish with great people. On a Saturday before the first Sunday of Advent, two good friends invited me for dinner, especially to be with them and their five-year-old daughter to participate in the blessing and lighting of the Advent wreath. Well, we were gathered around the table, and Theresa, the Mother, asked her five year old daughter, Tracy, what song we should sing as we light the Advent candle. Little Tracy said, "Rudolph the Red-nosed Reindeer." But Theresa, the Mother said, "Tracy, don't you think we should a sing a Jesus song?" But Tracy was insistent that "Rudolph" was a Jesus song, but could not explain why. As her eyes filled with tears trying to articulate her reasons, Kent, the Father, said quietly to Theresa, "You're making too much of this...anything can be a prayer." So we all sang "Rudolph the Red-nosed Reindeer" – but Theresa had a revelation. She said to us, "Have you ever listened, really listened, to the words of 'Rudolph'? How he was an outcast and was laughed at and excluded? Sounds a lot like the Suffering Servant songs in Isaiah. And how did he come to us? As a light, on Christmas Eve, bringing gifts."

When we had finishing singing, Theresa shared her newfound insight with Tracy. "Tracy, you meant that Jesus suffered too, and that He comes as a light on Christmas." "Yes, Mommy!" Tracy responded, delighted that her Mother finally understood.

MDP, children possess an uncomplicated, but a real, genuine, straight to the heart understanding of the things of God that for some reason we adults, sadly outgrow. "Child like faith" is never cynical, never jaded, never looses its sense of awe and wonder, and is so thankful for the many ways that God reveals Himself in our lives.

The faith of a child is anything but "childish." "Whoever does not accept the Kingdom of God like a child will not enter it," Jesus says in the Gospel today. He is asking us, His followers, to embrace a faith that does not separate our words from our actions; He is asking us to center our faith in God. The power that comes from this kind of faith is its ability to overcome excuses, fears, worries, complications, and demanding agendas. Only in embracing child-like kindness, compassion and forgiveness can we attain greatness in the Kingdom of God. "Whoever does not accept the Kingdom of God like a child will not enter it."

C – LUKE 17:5-10

There's an ancient story about a mouse and a dove having a conversation... The little mouse says, "Tell me the weight of a snowflake." The dove answers, "Why, a snowflake weighs nothing more than nothing." to which the mouse replies, "in that case I must tell you a marvelous story.

"I sat on a fir branch, close to the trunk when it began to snow. It was not a raging storm or blizzard. No, it was just like a quiet dream, without any violence. Since I didn't have anything better to do, I began to count the snowflakes settling on the twigs and needles of my branch. Their number reached exactly 4, 741, 926. And when the next snowflake dropped gently onto the branch weighing, as you said, 'nothing more than nothing,' the branch broke off and fell to the ground.

MDP, nothing in God's creative plan is for nothing. Even a single snowflake weighing more than nothing, counts for something. Even a single snowflake has its rightful place in God's universe. And if that is a perplexing mystery, consider that the top one inch of soil in a single square foot contains an average of 1,356 living creatures, and the microscopic population of a single teaspoon of soil contains as many as 2 billion bacteria, and millions of other life forms.

You heard the Apostles say to the Lord, "Increase our faith." And the Lord replies, "were your faith the size of a mustard seed you could say to this mulberry tree, 'be uprooted and planted in the sea,' and it would obey you." Those first followers of Jesus said, "increase our faith." And we who have joined them in the community of faith gather together today and say the same thing, 'Increase our faith."

MDP, there are times when our best effort to do the right thing, to do a good job of whatever it is we are called to do, seems as difficult and as frustrating as trying to walk on water: trying to be a good mother – or father; trying to get parents to understand; trying not to hold a grudge; trying to cope with the "system" out there; trying to kick some awful habits; trying not to take that first drink or smoke that first cigarette; trying to come to terms with the terrible loneliness and grief that follows the loss of a loved one. Yes sometimes life is like trying to walk on water; we feel nothing solid underfoot. We know that when everything seems to be going our way, the burden is light and we appear to be on solid ground…and our faith comes easy.

But, let me tell you, when things begin to go against us, when the burden becomes heavy, the act of faith really comes hard. The Disciples had to learn that they were never alone. The greatest lesson that Jesus was teaching them was that they were not to fear; they were never abandoned, that fear is deadly and not part of the kingdom.

There is a legend from the Orient about a traveler making his way to the city. One night he meets two other travelers along the road; their names were "fear" and "plague". Plague explains to the traveler that, once they arrive, they are expected to kill 10,000 people in the city. The traveler asks plague if plague would do the killing. "Oh, no. I shall kill only a few hundred. My friend fear will kill the others."

MDP, the words of Jesus in this beautiful Gospel assure us that if we possess just a "mustard seed's" amount of faith, we can face down fear, the fear of failure, the fear of need, the fear to forgive, the fear to love someone. If we really possess just a "mustard seed's" amount of faith, we can "uproot" those things that strangle love, and justice and reconciliation; we can reap great measures of joy and goodness from even the smallest acts of kindness and love. So, the Gospel, the Mass, today calls us to embrace "mustard seed" faith, to really believe that even the most insignificant act of goodness, the smallest act of kindness, the quietest, most hidden stand for justice and mercy has awesome meaning in the reign of God.

TWENTY-EIGHTH SUNDAY IN ORDINARY TIME
A – MATTHEW 22:1-14

Every time I read or listen to the Gospel, I am reminded of an elderly woman named Martha. Martha had always been very active in her parish, and helped the parish in every way she could. Knowing that the end was near, she asked her parish priest if they might talk about her funeral. He came to her home and, over tea, they talked about the readings and the music and other details of the funeral service. Then, as the priest was about to leave, Martha said, "Father, I have one more request, and it's a bit unusual." The priest asked, "And what's that, Martha?" Martha said, "When they put me in the casket, I want my rosary in one hand and a fork in the other." The priest, caught by surprise, stammered a little and said, "I'm sorry, Martha; you want to be buried with a fork?" "Yes; you see, Father, I've been thinking about all the church dinners and banquets I've attended all through the years. I couldn't begin to count them all. But one thing sticks in my mind. At all those wonderful suppers, when the meal was almost finished, a server or hostess would come to the table to collect the dirty dishes. And, at the best dinners, they would say, 'Keep your fork.' Of course, that meant that dessert was coming. And not just a cup of jello or pudding or even a dish of ice cream – you don't need a fork for that. No, it meant the good stuff – like chocolate cake or homemade apple pie. When they said to keep my fork, I knew the best was yet to come!"

"That's exactly what I want people to talk about at my funeral. Oh, they can talk about all the good times we had together. But when they see me in the casket in my beautiful blue dress, I want them to turn to one another and say, 'Why the fork?' And then I want you to tell them that I kept my fork because the best is yet to come!"

MDP, what an incredible statement of faith Martha makes with her fork! She understands that her long life has been a journey to the Messiah's banquet. Sometimes in our busyness, in our getting lost in all kinds of things during our day, in our babysitting, in the care of our spouses and our children, in the demands of our work, we forget this. We are so busy making a living that we fail to make a life; we are so taken up with the nitty gritty of our lives that we overlook the essence of life itself. But this Gospel tells us that God has invited each of us to His Son's banquet, that is, to the fullness of God's life. The only trouble is our inability to hear and accept God's invitation amidst all the noise that consumes our lives.

B – MARK 10:17-30

"Go and sell everything you own and give the money to the poor, and you will have treasure in Heaven..." What a powerful Gospel! Jesus is telling us without hesitating that to be His Disciple demands a heavy price—everything we have; everything we own; everything we are.

There is a first-person story called "Surviving the Ages," in which a rich jeweler tells us about his desert experience. It begins...

"One day I was overtaken by a great storm. It buffeted me and my caravan this way and that until I became completely lost. I had wondered around in circles. Then I realized I had run out of food. I was half dead from starvation and in dire need of nourishment. In a fit of panic, I unloaded every bag on my camel's back, hoping to find a morsel or two tucked away. I searched through every pack, but there was no food. But suddenly, my heart beat with new hope when I came upon a small pouch I had overlooked. My hands were shaking and with trembling fingers I tore open the pouch. And then, my heart sank with great despair, for all it contained were diamonds.

In our Gospel today, Jesus reminds us that we can't eat our diamonds or gold or other riches while we suffer a spiritual hunger that only God can satisfy. The unknown rich young man told Jesus that he was living a good life, but Jesus offered him a 'new' life - "follow Me and you will have treasure in heaven!" And then, "Go and sell what you have, and give to the poor." The young man turned from Jesus and walked away; he did not want to hear this. It would have meant that he had to change his priorities.

You know, I thought about this Gospel all week and tried to think of some images to bring the Gospel right up close to me: a college's star baseball player, for example, went up to the Jesus and asked, "what must I do to inherit eternal life?" Jesus says, "Go to the local playground and help set up an after school program for kids at risk." The baseball star's face fell, and he went away sad, because his focus was on making it to the majors.

The owner of a small business asked Jesus, "what must I do to inherit eternal life?" Jesus said, "Go and create job opportunities for those who have lost their jobs and whose families are struggling." The business owner's face fell, and he went away sad because he was barely keeping his own company going.

A woman who had just buried her daughter who had died of cancer, asked Jesus, "What must I do to inherit eternal life?" With great compassion for her, Jesus said, "Go put aside your grief for your beloved daughter and give some of your time to help raise awareness for cancer research." The woman's face fell, and she went away sad, because the loss of her daughter was just too painful.

Jesus asks a lot from us to be His disciple, but He asks only what we have, not what we don't have! Each of us here has a talent, a skill, a gift given by God to make His kingdom real. But too often we are unable to choose the things of God over the things we own. I often remember an incident on "The Tonight Show" with Johnny Carson: Johnny had the comedian Richard Pryor on. Pryor was critically burned in an accident. He had recovered sufficiently to appear on the "Tonight" Show. In his conversation with Carson, he said he learned that when you are seriously ill, suddenly money isn't that important anymore. Then he added – the line that I remember – "All I could think of was to call on God. I didn't call the Bank of America once."

MDP, we must restructure our days to make time for the things of God, to live our lives in the presence of God. We simply cannot allow ourselves to be possessed by our possessions. We must make a holy effort to distinguish between the things of our world and the things of God. Surely, then, we will be on the road to "follow" Him, and embrace eternity in the time to come.

C – Luke 17:11-19

This beautiful Gospel gives us the chance today to think about gratitude. I often see gratitude as a practice—a powerful way of approaching life. It is to see our life as an ongoing relationship with God. It is grounded in the conviction that God has breathed His life into us for no other reason than His unfathomable love for us. And, our response? It is to stand before Him in quiet and humble gratitude.

I would like to tell you a story on myself! When my battalion of Marines left Vietnam, we were ordered to the Island of Okinawa. I quickly made friends with the local Franciscan missionaries. One day, one of the priests took me to a broken down dilapidated leper colony. When I arrived, one of the leper women offered me a small papaya. It was rare to have fruit at the colony – the usual fare was always a small amount of fish and rice. When I saw her poverty and the poverty of the place, I said to the woman, "No, thank you," thinking that she would enjoy the papaya more than I. Later my priest missionary friend gave me a mild criticism. He explained that one does not refuse an offer. The correct response would have been, he said, to receive the gift no matter the condition of the other person or the gift. He said that in receiving the gift, I would have acknowledged the dignity of the giver.

Gratitude, in the spirit of today's Gospel, is not an expression of thanks for a single act of kindness. Gratitude is seeing every human being as worthy of respect as a child of God; it is an act of humility before all men and women, respecting them as our brothers and sisters in God our Father. Gratitude requires the humility both to give from our poverty and to receive in spite of our wealth. As the Samaritan in the Gospel discovers, each one of us has been given much by God, and realizing this, our spirit of gratitude is the beginning of transforming our lives and being the beautiful persons God wants us to be.

TWENTY-NINTH SUNDAY IN ORDINARY TIME
A – Matthew 23:15-21

A teenage girl left for school wearing one yellow and one orange sock. Her mother, noticing this, headed her off at the front door. The mom asked, "Why are you wearing two different colored socks?" The teenager responded, "I have a right to be different if I want to," and then she added, "Besides, all the kids at school are doing it!"

A man who always wore matching socks had been given cause to wonder whether or not he was a conformist. He said the following: "Today a friend called me eccentric. People have called me all sorts of things through the years, but this was the first time I had been called eccentric. I decided to look up the dictionary definition of the word eccentric. It read, 'an eccentric person deviates from the norm. And eccentric person operates away from the center.' I wasn't sure if my friends had complimented or insulted me. So I did a lot of serious thinking. I wasn't sure that I wanted the label, 'Eccentric,' but the more I thought about it, the more I liked it. If the center is the norm in which the majority of people are living, then I am perfectly satisfied with the label. The truth is that I don't have to be like everyone else. I can be different. The words of my mother linger in my memory: "Don't do it because everyone else is doing it; stand tall, do what you know is right, rather than trying to be like everyone else."

MDP, all of us have the desire to find meaning for our lives. And our blessed Lord made it clear that the only way we could find true meaning for our lives is through God, by living our lives in the presence of God. You know, people talk about God these days. People are trying to understand who He is. We communicate with one another about how God has acted, about how we should pray to God, about what God has to do with war, with earthquakes, and mudslides, and hurricanes, with suffering and death, with human relationships. And so we talk and talk and talk; but the time comes when we need some tangible way of expressing what we are trying to say, what we believe.

In the times of the Bible, people used material things to indicate just where they stood in their relationship with God, like the Pharisees holding up the coin to Jesus in today's Gospel. They knew that if Jesus spoke against the coin, that is the tax, this would please the Jewish zealots, who wanted to gain independence from Rome. They also knew that it would probably result in Jesus' arrest by the Romans. If on the other hand, Jesus spoke for the coin, the tax, he would alienate the Jewish zealots. Either way He would lose. But His answer thwarts the Pharisees and their plot to entrap Him.

It has been said that human beings are like tea bags: you don't know how strong they are until they are in hot water. In our lives as His followers, Jesus calls us to be strong; He calls us to realize that the very gift of our lives is centered in our faith in the God of compassion and forgiveness. He calls us to really believe that God loves us as His sons and daughters. He calls us to feel comfortable with the God who put us here first and foremost to discover His love in the love we have for one another. It is this understanding of our sacred calling as followers of Christ that enables us to make sense of the roles we play as parents, citizens, professionals, workers, students, and to fulfill these roles by "standing tall in Christ, doing what is right, and not just being like everyone else."

B – MARK 10:35-45

This is quite a Gospel! "Can you drink the cup I will drink?" Jesus says.

Our first impulse might be to say, 'No, we cannot." But his question is a challenge. Jesus is asking us to take on a life of humble service; He is challenging us to empty ourselves of our own needs for the sake of others. But, there is a promise in this: That if we try to imitate our Blessed Lord in His compassion, if we seek what is right and good and just, if we are motivated by a generosity and graciousness of heart, then His grace will be with us and we can bring good out of evil, that we can transform the darkness in our world into life!

Allow me to tell you a tender story, which all these years later, still jogs my memory and my spiritual life. After my tour of duty in Southeast Asia, the Navy sent me to be the Chaplain of a new Coast Guard base about 30 miles north of San Francisco. (I was lucky. One can be a Navy Chaplain for 30 years and never have a Coast Guard tour. I had three fantastic years with the Coast Guard.) The base was located in a town called Petaluma, in the midst of miles of chicken farms – almost all run by Italians from the north of Italy. Seeing my last name, the local pastor asked me if I would visit the people who owned these farms. On one visit I met an old woman who was so kind and generous. She had devoted her life to the service of God and her family and friends and people in need. Over the years her hands had become rough and calloused from long hours in the barns, scrubbing pots and pans and tables working in a shelter for the homeless.

She confided to me that as her life was nearing its end, she worried about what she could say to the Lord when she saw Him. She told me that it had never been easy for her to express herself in words. She told me, "I can barely read and write; I won't know what to say or how to say it." I did my best to comfort her and I reminded her that the Lord would be more than pleased to know about all the good work she had done for others. And then, where the words came from I don't know, but I told her, "Don't worry: you won't have to say one word. Just show Him your hands."

I think about this even to this day. What a tribute to a life well lived! And no matter if we spent a lifetime working with our hands, or standing on our feet, Jesus assures us to be ever mindful of His teaching: "In so far as you did it to one of the least of these my brothers or sisters, you did it to Me!"

MDP, the power we have as followers of Jesus grows with use and withers with disuse. There can be no standing still. Either we are moving ahead – as Pope Francis said in New York – "Siempre Adelante", or we are moving back. Either we accept the challenge of Jesus and grow spiritually or we wither spiritually. So, the challenge of the Gospel is "not what's in it for me; but what's in it for God." A single act of kindness can change everything.

C – Luke 18:1-8

The tragedies of the last year have brought us to our knees in prayer. Many of us have been going to that silent, still space within us; we light candles and we wave our flags, trying so hard to gain a wisdom that all of us need. And we listen! We listen to the voice of God that whispers from within, and we ask in prayer, "Lord, what would You have us do to make things right again?"

In a little book about children and prayer, actor Dick Van Dyke tells the story of the little girl who was asked to suggest a prayer for her Sunday school class. She said, "I think we should pray for all the people with the blahs!" An anonymous poet wrote:

I rose one morning early, and rushed into the fray.
With so much to accomplish I had no time to pray.
Troubles tumbled 'round me and heavy was each task.
But where was God to help me?
God said, "You didn't ask."
I tried to see the bright side. But then things turned grey and bleak.
I asked God for the reason, He said, "You didn't seek."

The great scientist, Isaac Newton, was a man rooted in prayer, which is to say, rooted in God. He once said, "I can take my telescope and look millions of miles into space. But I can lay it aside and go into my room, shut the door, get down on my knees and see more of Heaven, and get closer to God than I can assisted by all the telescopes and all the material things on earth."

I think, like Isaac Newton, many of us in our nation are on our knees saying, "Lord, what would you have us do to make our beautiful earth, to make ourselves whole again?"

There is a story about a man who was on a trial for first degree murder. He approached one of the jurors and offered to pay him a large sum of money if he would hold out for a verdict of manslaughter, in which case the sentence would be much less severe than for first degree murder. The juror accepted the bribe. Then the accused man said, "Remember, whatever happens in that jury room, don't be swayed. Hold out for manslaughter." When the trial ended, the jury deliberated and returned its verdict: Manslaughter! Later, outside the courtroom, the convicted man asked the juror, "Did you have a hard time holding out for manslaughter?" The juror replied, "Yes I did. From the beginning all the other jurors wanted to bring in a 'not guilty' verdict.

In today's Gospel Jesus tells the story of a poor widow who sought justice for herself but could not find it. She was really up against it. And to make it worse, she faced a corrupt man who was the judge in her case. But she would not be denied. Her hunger and thirst for justice and her persistence, gave her the strength to "buck" the system and finally, because of the persistence, she won her case. I hope that you noticed how Luke describes Jesus' parable of the corrupt judge and the persistent widow as a lesson on how to "pray continually and never give up, never lose heart."

Although this television program aired before the horror of September 11th, in retrospect I thought that the final episode of The West Wing had something in it of today's Gospel as well as where some of us are today: the fictional President Bartlett's life and presidency are coming apart. His efforts to prevent civil war in Haiti have failed miserably, with the American Embassy under siege. And at home, the nation is about to learn that he has multiple sclerosis – a fact that Bartlett kept from voters at election time. And just when he needs her most, his wise, lifelong counselor, secretary and friend Mrs. Landingham is killed by a drunk driver.

After her funeral, President Bartlett orders the secret service to clear the cathedral and block all the entrances. And here is the most poignant scene which today I could identify with along with so many others. Bartlett is alone with God in the center of the sanctuary. But his "prayer" is not one of praise or petition. Barlett launches into an angry confrontation with God, addressing God with nasty words. He mocks God with a sarcastic Gratias Tibi Ego,

Domine (I thank you, oh Lord") and then blasts God in Latin and English. "Am I really to believe that these are the acts of a loving God? A just God? A wise God? I was your servant here on earth. I spread Your Word and I did Your work. Well, to hell with your punishments and to hell with you!" And in a final act of defiance to almighty God, the President lights a cigarette, takes a drag, and stamps out the butt on the sanctuary floor. He returns to the white house. And packing his notes for what will be a tough press conference, he absentmindedly shouts for Mrs. Landingham as he had done hundreds of times before. Mrs. Landingham dutifully "appears" as the "spirit" of Mrs. Landingham tells President Bartlett to grow up. She says, "God doesn't make cars crash and you know it." "Stop using me as an excuse."

MDP, how many times during this last month did we wonder if God is worth the trouble, worth the investment, the bother. Our efforts to do the right thing are met with resistance and hostility, with pain, ridicule – and often we feel that God is nowhere to be found. And we find ourselves angry and frustrated with God. But Mrs. Landingham and the widow of today's Gospel remind us that there is a cost to be a disciple, that the ways of God often put us on a collision course with the values of the world, that any resurrection in our lives is not won without the cross. But I am here to assure you that God is present even in our darkest nights, in the pit of our deepest despair.

MDP, for me, one of the most touching stories I heard in the aftermath of the terrorist attacks was the story and then words spoken between a husband and wife – words which could have been spoken by the widow in the Gospel. Lysbeth Glick of Hewitt, N.J. spoke on a cell phone with her husband, Jeremy, as his plane was being hijacked. Jeremy was telling his wife that he and some others were going to try to overpower the terrorists. Lyzbeth said, "He was a man who wouldn't let things happen." He was a hero for me because in his final words he told me not to give up, not to be sad."

MDP, we will all go to our deaths with lives lived, with some regrets and with many joys, with sorrows and victories. So what do we say to those we love when our lives are done, when all else is left behind? We look to the widow in today's Gospel whose perseverance in the conviction of what is right and just Jesus honors, and we say to our children and to one another, "Don't give up; don't be sad; persevere, persevere."

THIRTIETH SUNDAY IN ORDINARY TIME
STROKE

A missionary Bishop had to celebrate the Sacrament of Confirmation for a group of severely handicapped children. They were all institutionalized and not one of them was capable of even the simplest kind of school work. The Chaplain of the home told the Bishop not to speak more than two or three minutes; anything more would be beyond the capability of the children to understand.

The Bishop was a little nervous about what he would say. He spoke this message to the children: "Dear children, your mom and dad and brothers and sisters all love you. That's why they gently stroke your head, hair, and cheeks. And that's what happens when you are confirmed. Jesus gently strokes you because He loves you so much. So when I make the sign of the cross on your forehead with the holy oil, our Dear Jesus is stroking and caressing you."

A few minutes later, as he touched the forehead of a child with cerebral palsy, the little boy's face contorted a little and with great difficulty he said the word, 'stroke' while saliva spilled out of his mouth. His mother wiped away the saliva and her tears with the same handkerchief. But the boy had gotten the message that God was stroking him. The Bishop said, "You know, I don't know what the others might think about my theology, but this is what God does. God stroked the people of Israel. The Father stroked the prodigal son. Jesus stroked the children, the lepers; He laid His hand on the eyelids and heads and ears of those who were handicapped and afflicted.

In brief, the Bishop had summed up the message of today's Gospel, of what it means to be a Christian: that God is love, and we need that love and depend on that love if we are to become holy.

A – Matthew 22:34-40

I know a story of a little girl who became an expert at stretching out her night prayers to avoid going to sleep. She developed with some expertise an ever growing list of "Thank you, God" prayers. For example, she would pray for every child she ever knew: "Thank you God for Alice, thank you God for Patty, thank you God for Bobby." Then, she would breathe deeply and run through a list of adults: "Thank you God for our principal, thank you God for Mr. Baker, thank you God for Mrs. Frano, the school librarian," and so on. She had a catch list also that went, "Thank you God for a lady in the shoe store, thank you God for my birthday which comes in eleven weeks." And, of course, "Thank you for Mommy and Daddy."

But there were nights when my little friend was so tired she could hardly keep her eyes opened. She would forget her long list of thank you Gods, and simply say, "Thank you God, for God."

I can think of no better expression of a response to the first great commandment in this morning's Gospel to love. Because God is God, our lives have meaning and purpose. Because God is God, we are going someplace with our lives. "Thank God for God." But if you listened carefully, you noted that Jesus cited the command to love God as part one of a two-part answer to the lawyer's question. The command to love God is followed by the command to love neighbor.

It is more than possible that much of the sickness in our time is the result of our disobedience to the second part of the Great Commandment. The command to love neighbor is the strongest possible affirmation of our having been created for life together: to know one another; to appreciate the uniqueness of one another; to share in one another's joys and sorrows; to enrich one another's life through the gift of self. We are capable of embracing the notion that getting away from it all – getting away from people – is the answer to what's wrong with us.

We remain in families, but without really sharing our lives on any deep level. We are in every day contact with all sorts of people, but how often do we really try to know them on other than a superficial level.

In today's Gospel, Jesus invites us to thank God for God and to thank God for our neighbor. There is a song from an album entitled, "A Song is a Gentle Thing," which contains these haunting lines:

"If I had just 24 hours for living, the things that don't matter could wait

I'd play with the children and hear their stories

I'd tell you I love you before it's too late."

"The Things that Don't Matter," can wait forever, and the thing that does matter has mattered from the beginning. Love is the beginning and the end.

B – MARK 10:46-52

We all know how the paparazzi would chase after Princess Diana. I remember reading once how a woman rode down a hotel elevator. The paparazzi crowded the lobby waiting for Princess Diana to step out of the elevator. The door opened and the woman was greeted by a burst of flashbulbs. The woman instinctively put her head down and her hands over her face. "There she is!" someone shouted. But when she lifted her head up, a photographer said in a loud voice, "Forget it; it's nobody!"

More often than not in our culture, being somebody means being rich or famous; or, at least being athletic or entertaining, or talented or good looking. We all fall into the trap of measuring other people's worth by means of externals – focusing on superficial values.

There was a scene in one of Jerry Seinfield comedy routines when Jerry says that when a man and woman begin to think about each other in terms of a possible lasting relationship. They tend to magnify the externals. Jerry says, for example, that the guy might say to himself something like, "I don't think her eyebrows are even. I can't believe it. Her eyebrows are uneven. Could I even look at uneven eyebrows the rest of my life?" And, at the same time, the girl might be thinking, "What is he staring at? Do I want someone staring at me like that the rest of my life?"

This powerful Gospel this morning of the blind Bartimaeus tells us once again that despite any external evidence to the contrary, all of us are important, and God has entered into an awesome, caring relationship with us. We may not be terribly rich or famous; we may not be witty/ we may not sing very well; we may have uneven eyebrows, but in God's eyes we are so special. We must believe that we are unique masterpieces of God's love and care for us. In all of God's creation there is no other you, no other me – and there never will be.

The blind Bartimaeus cries out, "Jesus have pity on me." The crowd reacts angrily: what arrogance! But Jesus had other ideas about Bartimaeus. This blind beggar asks Jesus to let him see again. Jesus says, "Go, your faith has saved you." His sight is restored immediately and he begins to "follow Jesus."

The message of the blind Bartimaeus is this: That if you carry a hidden burden, you are somebody whom Jesus cares for. If you are worried or have a fear about something, Jesus cares for you. If you are having a hard time coping with your responsibilities to your family, you are somebody to Jesus. If you are carrying a physical illness, you are somebody to Jesus. If you are trying to handle the burdens of a destructive addiction or a destructive relationship, you are somebody to our blessed Lord.

In 1992, Dennis Byrd was a defensive lineman for the New York Jets football team. Dennis suffered a career-ending injury to his spine while still in his 20's. But deep within he continued to believe that he was somebody and that he was the focus of God's loving care. In his autobiography, "Rise and Walk", Dennis Byrd writes: "That's the miracle; that's the magic! It's knowing that all of life is a blessing, that the good Lord is with us no matter how many mistakes we have made."

I know a story of a blind man who was asked by a sympathetic woman, "Doesn't being blind color your life?" The blind man replied, "Yes, but thank God, I can choose the color. And since I am responsible for my life, I'm going to keep on choosing the most beautiful colors I can."

MDP, the miracle in this beautiful Gospel today is that whoever we are, wherever we are in our lives right now, we can color our lives with the knowledge and faith that we are somebody to God – even if our eyebrows are uneven.

C – Luke 18:9-14

MDP, what a powerful prayer we have in the Gospel today: "Oh God, be merciful to me a sinner." I heard someone say once that "the smallest package in the world is a person who is all wrapped up in himself or herself." When personalized automobile license plates were introduced in the State of Illinois, the Department of Motor Vehicles received more than a thousand requests for the number 'One.' The state official whose job it was to approve such requests said, "I'm not about to assign it and disappoint a thousand people." What was his solution? He gave the number to himself!

A little boy and a little girl were riding on one of those mechanical horses in a shopping mall. The little boy, who was riding in front, turned to the little girl and said, "If one of us would get off, there would be more room for me."

And again, there is the story of a conversation between an elderly married couple. The wife says to her husband, "If one of us should die, I'll go and live with my sister."

MDP, in the Bible the story of Adam and Eve in the Garden of Eden, the Devil convinces the couple that he had found a way for them to move God over and become number one. And we still keep looking for ways for us to succeed where Adam and Eve failed.

But Jesus says, "...anyone who wants to be first among you must be a servant to all." He is saying that the weak, the lonely, the helpless, the disenchanted, the dispossessed are His brothers and sisters and ours too.

Leo Tolstoy, the great Russian writer, was walking down the street one day when a man in tattered clothes begged him for money. Tolstoy searched his pockets for a coin, but could find none. He said to the beggar, "I'm sorry, my brother, but I don't have any money on my person." Whereupon the beggar's melancholy expression was transformed into a grateful smile, as he said, "You have given me more than I asked for. You have called me 'brother."

We are all members of the family of God. Our brothers and sisters number in the billions. And whoever aspires to be great among them must be their servant. No one is number one, and everyone is number one.

Often we are like the proud, highly successful business consultant who came to church one Sunday, bowed his head and prayed reverently, "Oh God, you may use me as You will: – and then he added, "only in an advisory capacity."

But we who are in touch with the Gospel of Jesus must bow our heads and pray "Use me in a working capacity; use me in the capacity of a loving, humble servant." Charles Dickens wrote, "No man is useless in this world who lightens the burden of another."

Early on in my priesthood, I had the opportunity to sit on a college's admissions committee to review applications from high school students for the incoming freshmen class. We plowed through one essay after another on why the writer should be admitted to the school. We read about the promise and potential of all of these future presidents, rocket scientists, doctors and lawyers. But there was one student's essay that caught everyone's attention. This essay had no pretense. It read something like this: "I am not a great student nor am I a leader. You could say that I am incredibly average. I work very hard for the grades I get. For the past three summers, I have worked at a camp for children with cancer. At first, I was terrified that I would say something stupid or I would do something that would add to their pain. I was surprised at how much I enjoyed working with these kids. I have been even more surprised at everything I have learned from them about life and death, about coping with illness and disappointment, about what is really important and good. I would like to work with chronically ill and physically challenged children. I would like to pursue a degree in education and psychology so that I might try to give these boys and girls something of what they have given me."

We on the committee immediately put his application into the "admit" pile. I believe the committee felt that we had enough presidents and noble laureates to choose from, we wanted to make sure we had room for one good, dedicated teacher.

MDP, in our own time and place, the parable of the Pharisee and the tax collector in today's Gospel is played out not so much as a lack of humility before God but as a lack of awareness of the needs, hopes and cries for help around us. Sometimes we see ourselves as better than others, who we say have not been as blessed as we have. But if we have grasped the Gospel today we will understand that all we are and will be begins with the life breathed into our souls by our love of God.

Father Thomas Merton wrote that "humility is absolutely necessary if one is to avoid acting like a baby all of one's life. "To grow up," he says, "means to become humble, to throw away the illusion that I am the center of everything and that other people exist to provide me with comfort and pleasure."

Today's Gospel challenges us to embrace the humble, God-centered faith of the tax collector, not the self-centered and self-absorbed claims of the Pharisee. Humility before God demands humility before one another, seeing others as God sees us.

SOLEMNITY OF ALL SAINTS; NOVEMBER 1
(1) – MATTHEW 5:1-12

Today's Solemnity of All Saints honors not just the saints pictured on icons and whose statues grace our churches, but the saints who have walked among us and with us in this time and place of ours.

We honor the 'prophets' who showed us what it means to be the people of God by the example of their selfless commitment and generosity to the victims of poverty, bigotry and injustice.

We honor the "apostles" who taught us about Jesus in parish religious education classes, who prepared us and our children for First Communion, who worked with us and counselled us as we prepared for our marriages, the baptisms of our children, the burials of family members.

We honor the "martyrs" we have known who dedicated their lives to secure our freedom, to suffer with and for the victims of injustice and abuse, to confront political and business leaders on their moral and ethical responsibilities to the common good and paid a heavy price – sometimes the ultimate price for doing so.

We honor the "confessors" and "pastors," all the holy men and women, who have walked with us and guided us and picked us up when we stumbled, and inspired us to realize that spark of the divine that exists within ourselves.

We have all known "saints' whose humble compassion and selfless generosity revealed the love of God in our midst. Today is their day; by their inspiration, may this one day be our day, as well.

CRACKED MARBLE

There is a story about two men, both Italian sculptors and contemporaries, named Donatello and the other Michelangelo. One day Donatello received delivery of a huge block of marble. After examining it carefully, Donatello rejected the marble because it was too flawed and cracked for him to use. Now this was long before forklifts and hydraulic lifts, so the workmen moved the heavy load by using a series of log rollers. Rather than struggle back to the quarry, the quick thinking haulers decided to deliver it down the street to Michelangelo. After all, he was known to be a little absent-minded. He might not realize that he had not ordered a three-on block of marble.

When Michelangelo inspected the marble, he saw the same cracks and flaws, as did Donatello. But he also saw the block as a challenge to his artistic skills. It became a personal challenge he could not pass up. So Michelangelo accepted the block of marble that Donatello had rejected as too flawed and cracked to be of any use. Michelangelo proceeded to carve from that seeming useless block of marble what is considered to be one of the world's greatest art treasures – the statue of "David!"

On the Feast of All Saints, no matter our own personal cracks and flaws, this Gospel of the Beatitudes challenges us to become holy, to become beautiful 'Davids', beautiful saints of God. All of us here have lived among saints, people we know who accepted and lived the challenge of this Gospel.

We remember those who taught us to seek justice and mercy for all. We see among God's saints this day the "pure of heart": those who showed us how to pray not only in words but in deeds, who taught us by the example of their lives how to become the sacrament we receive at the Lord's table.

And we seek this All Saints Day the continued help and wisdom of the "peacemakers" we have known, who always brought comfort, solace and unity to our families, church and communities.

This All Saints Day is to realize the continued presence of these holy men and women in our lives: to give thanks to God for these saints who, in our memories of them, continue to bless and grace our lives with the light of God's compassion and peace as we struggle to become, like them, beautiful 'Davids', people of the Beatitudes.

FEAST OF ALL SOULS; NOVEMBER 2
John 14:1-12

"Do not let your hearts be troubled. Have faith in God and Faith in Me..."

When I read these lines, I thought if someone were looking for a 'mantra' or if there is a line of Scripture that we should memorize immediately; it would be these very lines. All of us worry about something at one time or another. It made me scribble this little doggerel about worry:

Worry never climbed a hill
Worry never paid a bill
Worry never dried a tear.
Worry never calmed a fear.

When I was stationed in Naples a few years ago, a small group of parishioners and myself decided to take the ferry from Brindisi to Greece, and on the way make a stop over on one of the Greek islands. I would like to relate an incident that has remained with me. The waters were pretty choppy as I recall, and the moment we set foot on the dock, we noticed something strange. Everywhere we looked there were Greek men nervously fingering strings of beads – worry beads, they called them. There were old men fingering worry beads, middle aged men fumbling with worry beads, and young men fidgeting with worry beads. We saw them on the coast and we saw them as we moved farther into the island – worry beads were everywhere!

You know, the island was such a beautiful place that not one of us could see what they were all worrying about. Then an interesting thing happened. Some of us wanted to shop and bring something from that island home with us. Well, would you believe that all of us thought the most appropriate souvenir would be worry beads. But the more we thought about it the more some of us began to worry about what kind of beads we ought to get. There were different colors, different sizes, different strings that made different sounds. Strange, we all ended up worrying about worry beads!

Jesus says today, "Do not let your hearts be troubled! (Don't worry) have faith in God and faith in Me." Let me put this Gospel in its setting. Jesus is talking to His Disciples on the evening of Holy Thursday. In this conversation, Jesus tells them that He is about to leave them. He knows that His hour of crucifixion is drawing near. The Disciples are filled with worry. They're fidgeting with their worry beads, so to speak.

In the verses immediately preceding today's reading, Peter tells Jesus that he will follow Him wherever He goes. Jesus answers, "Where I am going you cannot follow Me now". Peter replies, "Lord, why can't I follow You? I will lay down my life for You." And Jesus replies, "You will lay down your life for Me? I tell you, Peter, the cock will not crow till you have denied Me three times." Then, right in the middle of this heavy exchange, Jesus said to the Disciples: "Do not let your hearts be troubled (don't worry), have faith in God and faith in Me."

One of the worst moments in World War II came when the Nazis occupied Warsaw and proceeded to slaughter the Jewish population. There was a very young Jewish girl who managed to escape and hide herself in a cove outside the city. She died there, alone. But before she died, she had scratched on the wall of the cave these words, "I believe in the sun, even when it's not shining. I believe in love, even when feeling it not. I believe in God, even when He is silent."

The Church has us celebrating the Feast of All Souls today to confront us with the inevitability of death and the pain of taking leave of this life and those we love; and she gives us this Gospel so that our faith in the loving providence of the Father will temper our worries about life and death, tempered with trust and hope, that every step we take in the warmth of this earth and every mile we travel through our winter nights will be guided by the words of the risen Lord: "Do not let your hearts be troubled (don't worry), have faith in God and faith in Me."

THIRTY-FIRST SUNDAY IN ORDINARY TIME
A – Matthew 23:1-12

When the Navy stationed me in Naples, Italy, I was fortunate enough to get my sailors and myself involved with Mother Theresa of Calcutta's nuns. They were establishing a convent in Naples, and in my position, I was able to help them a little.

One day the sisters invited me to Rome to meet Mother Theresa at an investiture of some of her nuns. I can't forget that day, especially, in light of this morning's Gospel. I had the chance to talk to one of the sisters who had been working in India in a leprosarium. She told me her story, which has stayed with me until this day. She said that, "As a young university student in Paris, she had taken many courses in philosophy and religion. She said she spent many hours each week in discussion with other students talking about God, about the meaning of life, about some clear purpose for her life. She said it was an exciting and good time for her, but she could not find direction for herself until a young man said something to her that changed her life forever. During one of the discussions, the sister said, "The young man looked right at me and said, 'you will never find God through discussion and debate because He is a God of love. You will find Him only when you love unselfishly.'"

The sister continued, "At that time I was doing research on the life of St. Francis of Assisi. In my research, I came to that moment in the life of Francis which was the turning point in his life. He had given up so much wealth, and felt that God was calling him, but he could not make the breakthrough. It was then, by a sheer act of will, that he forced himself to physically embrace a leper. That was the breakthrough for Francis. I was deeply moved by the episode and when I heard of the need for someone to work at the leprosarium in India, I went, and there I found God."

MDP, Jesus delivers some harsh words to the Pharisees about

their attitude and their approach to others. He came down hard on the values they showed off in church and then discarded these values on the way out of church. He says, "Do not be guided by what they do, since they do not practice what they preach. They tie up heavy burdens and lay them on men's shoulders, but they will not lift a finger to remove them."

MDP, God wants no part of anything we do in church today that does not reflect His love and justice when we leave this church. So anything we do this morning is unacceptable to God unless it is done in the words and actions of a community of persons who really believe that the greatest among us is the one who serves the rest! Jesus put it this way, "Anyone who exalts himself will be humbled; anyone who humbles himself will be exalted."

B – MARK 12:29

The command to love God cannot be fully understood if we merely regard the one that follows: "Love your neighbor," as a separate command. According to the Gospel of Jesus Christ, love of God and love of neighbor are inseparable. We cannot say we love God if, at the same time, we have something against our brother.

MDP, if our concern for one another is shallow, so too is our love for God. And it matters not how often we come to church and offer praise and thanks and love to God. Our words of prayer while we are here will mean nothing unless they indicate a change of heart toward our neighbor.

I read in the magazine "Spirituality and Health" just recently about a fellow named Mike. Mike lived next door to Misuko and her husband. A serious accident left Mike handicapped and dependent on others. Mitsuko was always happy to help Mike anytime he called. Mike came to depend on her for little things: cooking, cleaning, etc. One evening, Mitsuko was out. Her husband, a writer and editor, was working at home on a deadline. Mike called and asked if Mitsuko was home. "Hello Mike," Mitsuko's husband said, shouldering the phone while sending a fax, "Mitsuko is out this evening." "Oh, I see. Well, okay then…" said Mike. There was a pause…"Hmmm," the distracted husband muttered, stalling for time as he read an email. Mike cleared his throat. "Sounds like you're pretty busy." "Yes, I am, Mike. I'm on deadline. Can I help you?" "No, it's okay," said Mike. "No, I'll just wait until Mitsuko gets home." And the call ended.

He may or may not have said goodbye to Mike. Mike would have spoken up if there was a problem, right? The next day Mitsuko told her husband why Mike called: he needed someone to button his shirt. Mike can't manipulate buttons because his fingers are so mangled. Mitsuko's husband took a deep breath and braved the chill running up and down his spine. He thought, "If I don't have two minutes to button a neighbor's shirt, which one of us is disabled?"

MDP, what a different world we would be living in if we realized that there is not greater sacrifice of praise we can make to almighty God for His blessings to us, no greater prayer of thanks we can offer than to honor God in all who have been created in His image. Our love for God is nothing unless it embraces a love for our neighbor. It is in the love and kindness we extend to others that our own humanity most resembles God; it is in the smallest acts of charity and kindness that we make time to participate in the very life of God.

You Never Know

"Heaven and Earth will pass away, but my words will not pass away…"

A little girl sat at her grandmother's feet to listen to the Creation Story from the Book of Genesis. As the wondrous tale unfolded, the grandmother noticed that the child was unusually quiet. "Well, what do you think of it, Dear?" asked the grandmother. "Oh, I love it," the child replied. "You never know what God is going to do next."

MDP, that little girl was making a profound distinction between our preconceived notions of who God is and what He does, and who He really is what He is really doing. It is the difference between being a passive listener to the revealed Word and an actual hearer of the revealed Word. It is the difference between some vague understanding that God has spoken, and an abiding conviction that God is speaking right now to you and to me.

C – LUKE 19:1-10

"TODAY SALVATION HAS COME TO THIS HOUSE..."

The tragedy of September 11th put all of us in touch with the great mysteries we encounter in our everyday human situation. The mystery of life itself; the mystery of love, which is the mystery of God; the mystery of evil, which begs the agonizing question, "Why?" and, of course the mystery of death, which includes the awesome mysteries of afterlife and salvation.

Salvation! That is the question raised in today's Gospel. A question which begins with a man named Zacchaeus who we hear was literally, 'up a tree.' You see, Zacchaeus was a little guy, who had to climb the sycamore tree to get a glimpse of Jesus. People didn't like him because he was a tax collector, and he exploited people. But in the presence of Jesus, we see him filled with remorse; he wanted to make amends; he wanted to make things right; he wanted to repent. No longer would money be his priority; no longer would money get in his way to love other people. And hearing this, Jesus says those beautiful words: "Today salvation has come to this house."

In the midst of our ongoing struggle to deal in a Christlike way with the events and problems of the last few months are sending us 'up a tree,' the Gospel says it is time to climb down, welcome Jesus into our hearts, as Zacchaeus did, adjust our priorities and change that in our lives which needs to be changed.

The great philosopher, "Charlie Brown," of the "Peanuts" cartoons, once made a profound observation that touches on that which we are looking for, "salvation." In the cartoon, Charlie is leaning against a tree, talking to Lucy. She asks, "What do you think security is, Charlie Brown?" Charlie answers, "Security is sleeping in the back seat of a car when you're a little kid, and you've been somewhere with your mom and dad, and it's night. You don't have to worry about anything. Your mom and dad are in the front seat and they are doing all the worrying. They take care of everything." Lucy smiles and says, "That's really neat." Charlie Brown, who never seems to know when to stop, gets a serious look on his face and says, "But it doesn't last. Suddenly you're grown up and it can never be that way again. Suddenly, it's all over, and you'll never get to sleep in the back seat again, never!" Lucy gets a frightened look on her face and asks, "Never?" And Charlie Brown replies, "Never!" As they stand there, sensing the terrible loneliness that goes with growing old and being an adult, Lucy reaches over and says, "Hold my hand, Charlie Brown."

Just maybe in our families, our communities, our great United States today, we need to say just that to one another, "Hold my hand." And in holding one another's hands, in placing ourselves in one another's service, we will experience the presence of Christ's hand in ours, and we will be secure in the knowledge that salvation has come to our house in the form of the love that almighty God has for us, and the loneliness, the fear, the insecurity, will pass away, and we will no longer feel like we are "up a tree" with our lives.

One week after the horrors of September 11, Jay Leno returned to work as host of the NBC's Tonight Show. He opened the show very quietly and reflectively that night, explaining to the audience how difficult it was to begin production of the program so soon after the bombings. Jay Leno then went on to say how irrelevant his job was in light of the horror. He told a story about the time when, as a kid, he was a boy scout and really could do nothing right. The scout master told him not to worry, that he was going to be the scout troop's cheer master. His job was to tell jokes to any of the scouts who seemed to be upset about something. And then Jay said, "I thought, that's a pretty good job. I loved doing that job. And through some bizarre twist of fate, I still have that job. I don't pretend that it's the most important job, but we all can't be at ground zero digging through the rubble – but we can help in some way. We can help one another get on with their lives." "It's amazing," Jay Leno says, "What a small, small country this is when we think of others instead of ourselves."

Mother Teresa often said that God does not call us to be successful but to be faithful!

MDP, whatever it is we do, it is the sincerity of our commitment to bring the love of God into the lives of others! Like Zacchaeus Jesus calls us today to "Come down from the sycamore tree;" Jesus calls us to respond to the love of God in whatever way we can and to enable others to do the same; to hold one another's hand and so transform the darkness that engulfs them, and us, into the light of God's peace and justice.

DEDICATION OF ST. JOHN LATERAN; NOVEMBER 9

JOHN 2:13-22

If you ever have the opportunity to visit Rome, you must visit the Basilica of St. John Lateran; we celebrate the dedication of this great Church today. The Basilica of St. John Lateran is the Cathedral of Rome, and as such, it is the Cathedral of the Pope, who is the Bishop of Rome.

This Church has a long and reverent history. The original Basilica was built in the Fourth Century when Constantine the Great gave to Pope Sylvester I the property owned by the Lateran family, upon which the Basilica was constructed. It was dedicated in 324.

The significance of the Lateran Basilica for us Christians is profound. If you remember, it was Constantine who converted to Christianity and brought an end to an era of systemic persecution of Christians.

To celebrate the dedication of St. John Lateran with a special Sunday celebration is to remember the freedom of the early Christian Church and the freedom of worship wherever it exists today. But, above all, it gives us the opportunity to consider and meditate on our call to be a church, or as St. Paul asks us in the 2nd reading today, "Do you not know that you are God's temple and that God's Spirit dwells in you?"

Please forgive me if what I am about to tell you is a bit simplistic, but the memory of this incident has always said something to me about being God's temple, that is, Church, and how the Spirit of God works and dwells within us. On one of the bases which I served as Chaplain, a parishioner of mine named Frank, was critically ill. I would bring Frank communion at least once a week. The prognosis for Frank was not good. Over the course of the next few months, Frank courageously tackled both his disease and chemotherapy. Frank was a person of prayer and faith, but sometimes it all became too much for him. He would often ask, God, why me? And honestly, sometimes Frank's discouragement would overwhelm him.

At the same time that I was bringing communion to Frank, I began to bring communion to another parishioner. His name was Ben, and he was diagnosed with leukemia. Once I told Frank about Ben's leukemia, actually, the same type that Frank had. Each week when I gave Frank communion, he would pray for Ben and Ben's family. Praying for Ben had an effect on Frank. It gave him a new perspective and a renewed outlook. When I arrived with communion, Frank would immediately ask how Ben was doing. Frank began finding appreciation for all the good things God had given him in his life, and he began to focus on Ben's recovery, even more than his own. And each week when I visited Ben, I would encourage Ben to say a prayer for Frank and his family.

Well, after several months of prayers for each other, I finally got Frank and Ben to meet each other. I so remember that day: Ben ran to greet Frank when he came to the door. The two hugged like old friends. Then Ben took Frank by the hand to show him his room, filled with Tonka trucks, toy model cars and model airplanes. You see, seven year old Ben had much to share with 75 year old Frank – as Frank had already shared so much with his little brother in Christ.

Today's Feast of the Dedication of the Church of St. John Lateran, the mother church of all Christian Churches, is our celebration of the unity we have as Christian Catholics. But sometimes we "Catholics" forget that we belong to every other man, woman and child in this church, in this parish. Through selfless prayer, Frank and Ben came to realize the bond they shared, they came to understand that they were brothers and sisters in Christ and members of a church whose foundation is God Himself, whose framework is the reconciliation of Christ and whose architect is the very Spirit of God.

VETERAN'S DAY; NOVEMBER 11
MATTHEW 25:31-40

I found it interesting that the Church celebrates the Feast Day of Saint Martin of Tours today, the Patron Saint of Soldiers. Saint Martin was a soldier who, after his military duties, became a monk, and then became of Bishop of Tours, where he championed the cause of the poor. He was twenty-three years old when he served in Julian Caesar's army, and at the end of his tour of duty, he told Julian this: "I have served you as a soldier; now let me serve Christ." For all of us Veterans, I thought that we can take Martin's words to heart!

Our great county today wishes us a "Happy Veteran's Day," and many come up to us and say, "Thank you for your service to our country." We receive these wishes with so much gratitude because we know that we have contributed to the great freedoms our country enjoys. All of us veterans know what it is to have placed our lives on the line to protect and defend these precious liberties.

Since the end of World War I, actually on the eleventh hour of the eleventh day of the eleventh month we have celebrated Armistice, or, as we know it now, Veterans Day. With intention, we remember those killed in the line of duty, those still suffering the effects of their generous response, for example, to the recent wars in Iraq and Afghanistan, and, of course, all of us who have retired from active duty. Our annual celebration of Veterans Day helps us to remember the sacrifices so many of fellow soldiers, our shipmates, have made; and many are still making.

Just give me a minute to tell you about the sacrifices of a personal shipmate of mine: his name is Jim Cava and he served with me in Vietnam. Jim was injured badly when his helicopter was shot down. He lost an arm, his legs were crushed and his back was fractured. He spent close to a year in a military hospital. It took four years of therapy before he was able to walk. But he was so determined that he constantly pushed himself. He began jogging and got to the point where he could run in the New York marathon. But Jim did not run for himself. He obtained hundreds of sponsors so he could raise money for other injured vets. He said to me, "I did it so I could do some good for other vets." Jim Cava has a beautiful, spiritual sense about him. He easily talks about Jesus Christ and how Jesus' teaching on love, translates for Jim, into helping others and so making his own life worthwhile.

I know that all of us Veterans can tell hundreds of stories like this, stories about strength of character, that tell of honor and courage at all costs, of holding true to our faith in God, of loving our country. So when someone approaches us and wishes us a "happy Veterans Day" and says "thank you for your service," our response of gratitude contains a humble but powerful spirit of thankfulness first to the good God and His Son, Jesus Christ and then to our fellow and beloved brothers and sisters, citizens of this great country.

Because in the church November 11th is the Feast of St. Martin of Tours, who is the patron of soldiers, I would like to tell you about an incident in his life: on a bitterly cold day, Martin met a poor man, almost naked, trembling in the cold and begging from passersby at the city gate. Martin had nothing but his weapon and his soldier's uniform. He drew his sword, cut his cloak into two pieces, gave one to the beggar and wrapped himself in the other half. Some of the bystanders laughed at his now odd appearance; others were ashamed at not having relieved the poor man's misery. That night in his sleep Martin saw Christ dressed in the half of the garment he had given away, and heard Him say, "Martin, has covered Me with this garment." Yes, the same Martin who said, "I have served as a soldier, now let me serve Christ." Happy Veterans Day!

Veterans Day Prayer

We ask for blessings on all of us who have served their county in the armed forces.

We ask for healing for the veterans who have been wounded, in body and soul, in conflicts around the globe.

We pray especially for the young men and women, in the thousands who are coming home from Iraq with injured bodies and traumatized spirits.

Bring solace to them, O Lord; may we pray for them when they cannot pray.

We ask for, echoing John Paul II, an end to wars and the dawning of a new era of peace, as a way to honor all the veterans of past wars.

Have mercy on all our veterans from World War II, Korea, Vietnam, Iraq, and Afghanistan.

Bring peace to their hearts and peace to the regions they fought in.

Bless all the soldiers who served in non-combative posts...

May their calling to service continue in their lives in many positive ways.

Give us all the creative vision to see a world which, grown weary with fighting...

...moves to affirming the live of every human being and so moves beyond war.

Hear our prayer, O Prince of Peace

THIRTY-SECOND SUNDAY IN ORDINARY TIME
A – MATTHEW 25:1-13

There's some real wisdom in the Gospel this morning! You know, unlike the men and women of the Far East who have made wisdom a supreme human virtue, we in Western Society have little time or are too busy to pursue wisdom through serious, uninterrupted reflection about who we are and what we ought to do with our lives.

I remember reading a story of an American tourist who visited a wise and saintly monk in China. On his arrival at the Monastery to visit the famous monk, the tourist was astonished to discover that the monk lived in one simple room. The walls of the room were lined with books, and a simple table and chair were the only furnishings. "But, Father," the tourist asked, "Where is your furniture?" To which the monk replied, "Where is yours? "Where is mine?" asked the puzzled tourist; "I'm only a visitor here, just passing through." "So am I," answered the monk, "so am I!"

Men, we are crippled in our search for wisdom by a society which describes success as the ability to acquire knowledge and skillfully apply that knowledge for personal gain. We have reached a point of progress wherein our capacity to gather, store, and interpret data is almost limitless. In other words, as a society and as individuals, we are acquiring knowledge at breakneck speed without slowing down, ever, to reflect on how to handle it, what to do with it, how to use it to uplift the human spirit and to better human relationship. As this happens, I believe the need for a deeper devotion to the pursuit of wisdom should become more intense.

There's an old story about a missionary who was making his way through a thick jungle, when suddenly he is face to face with a ferocious lion. "I'm going to have you for lunch," the lion roars, "so you had better prepare for death." Hearing this the missionary immediately gets down on his knees, covers his eyes with his hands and begins to pray with great fervor. And then, hearing nothing further from the lion, he opens his eyes and takes a quick peek through his fingers. He is amazed to see that the lion also is kneeling, with his front paws over his eyes. The missionary breathes a sigh of relief, raises his eyes to heaven, saying, 'Thank you, Lord, for letting my words of prayer melt this wild beast's heart causing him to repent." Whereupon the lion dropped his paws and said, "Quiet please! I'm saying 'grace."

That is the essence of the story Jesus tells us today. He says that true wisdom consists in knowing how and when to prepare for death. The point of the virgins coming prepared with enough oil in their lamps is that foresight is the beginning of wisdom. Living wisely as Christians means looking ahead. Living wisely as Christians means acknowledging that we are "tourists" on God's good earth, only "passing through." Living wisely means pointing ourselves in the direction of almighty God. Living wisely as Christians means acknowledging our dependence on God not only for life but for our way of life. Living wisely as Christians means developing a life style which in itself is an act of faith in God's promise of ultimate fulfillment – even when the tourist season of our life is over.

"Where do you look for God?" "Where do you see God?" Last week in one of the Catholic newspapers that I subscribe to, these questions were put to a group of high school kids. One 11th grader answered poetically: "I find Him in the morning mist/ beyond the shining sun / among the wild flowers / in the city." Another kid answered with deep cynicism: "God is a non-existent security blanket." A 12th grader said he found God "in solitude, in friends, in nature, in other people, in babies, in those over 65."

But possibly the best answer came from a kid who asked simply, "Why, did you lose Him?" Jesus puts it this way, "Keep your eyes open for you know not the day nor the hour."

B – Mark 12:43-44

Once upon a time, there was a piece of iron which was very strong. Many attempts had been made to break it but all had failed. "I'll master it," said the ax; and his blows fell heavily on the iron but every blow made his edge blunter until it ceased to strike. "Leave it to me," said the saw; it worked backward and forward on the iron's surface until its jagged teeth were all worn and broken. Then it fell dull. "Ah!" said the hammer, "I knew you wouldn't succeed. I'll show you the way." But at the first fierce blow, off flew its head and the iron remained as before. "Shall I try?" asked the small, soft flame. "Forget it," everyone else said, "What can you do?" But the small flame curled around the iron, embraced it, and never left it until it melted under its irresistible influence.

As Jesus' Disciples, and the powerful simplicity of the story of the widow in the Gospel, our mission is not to break hearts but to melt hearts—under the irresistible flame of God's infinite love.

We don't like to think about time passing on, that for some of us, much of our life is already past. And sometimes we are a little shaken by questions that come up perhaps during sickness, sadness, or on the occasional night when we can't fall asleep; "What have I done with my life?" "Have I given from my want?" "Have I been an irresistible flame of God's love?" We do our best to avoid the questions because the answers can be disconcerting. Few of us can say that we have done anything great – certainly nothing more than what a handful of people may remember after we are dead.

But the point of today's Gospel is that the pertinent question is not what have we done with our lives, but how have we done it? How have we used the flame, the fire inside each of us. The widow dropping her money into the collection was totally unimportant. But she has now been memorialized for all time in the Gospel. We don't even know her name and she had no notion that her action would make her famous. But people through the centuries have been touched by the power of her little flame.

Jesus tells us that she knew how to live, because she lived generously, openly and trustingly. She did what she could, and she did it without counting the costs, without holding back. If she were asked what she did with her life, she would have answered, "I didn't hold back; I didn't count the costs. I trusted in God.

There's a story about a mother, wishing to encourage her young son's progress on the piano, took the boy to a Paderewski concert. After they were seated, the mother spotted a friend in the audience and walked down the aisle to greet her. Seizing the opportunity to explore the wonders of the concert hall, the little boy rose and eventually made his way through a door marked "no admittance." When the houselights dimmed and the concert was about to begin, the mother returned to her seat and discovered the child was missing. Whereupon, the curtains parted and spotlights focused on the impressive Steinway piano onstage.

To her horror, the mother saw her little boy sitting at the keyboard, innocently picking out "Twinkle, twinkle little star,". At that moment, the great piano master made his entrance, quickly moved to the piano and whispered into the boy's ear, "Don't quit. Keep playing." Then leaning over, Paderewski reached down with his left hand and began filling in a bass part. Soon his right arm reached around to the other side of the child and he added a running obligato. Together, the old master and the young novice transformed an outrageous situation into a wonderful creative experience. And the audience was mesmerized.

Whatever our life situation – however outrageous, however desperate, however mournful, however disappointing the words of Jesus about the widow whisper deep within our soul. "The poor widow contributed more than all the others. She gave from her want!" And He says, "Don't quit. Keep giving from your want. Keep on playing. You are not alone. Your life is secure in My hands. I am still in charge of the world. Together we will transform all the broken patterns into a masterwork of God's creative art. Together, we will mesmerize the world with the irresistible flame of God's infinite love."

C – Luke 20:27-38

The hypothetical situation that the Sadducees pose to Jesus reflects a very limited and negative understanding of God and of His love for humanity. They failed to see that God is a God of 'Yes,' a God of Life, of hope, of joy. All of us at times fear the unknown; we know that change that we can neither control nor anticipate terrifies us. But our belief in a "Loving God" is centered in the constant hope that we live our lives in His presence; that every good Friday, we might experience and our lives be transformed into an Easter Sunday.

This thought made me think of a story I heard long ago. It's a story about the great movie director Cecil B. Demille. The story goes like this:

Demille was canoeing on a lake in Maine when he noticed a horde of water beetles just below the surface of the water. One of the water beetles came to the surface and slowly crawled up the side of the canoe. Finally, struggling to the top, the beetle grasped onto the wood of the canoe and died. Demille forgot about the beetle until a few hours later when he noticed the beetle again. In the hot sun, its shell had become very dry and brittle. As he watched, the shell split open and there emerged a new form, a dragonfly, which took to the air, its magnificent colors illuminated in the sunlight. The dragonfly flew farther in an instant than the water beetle had crawled in days. It circled back and swooped down to the surface of the water. Demille notices its shadow on the water. The water beetles below might have seen it too, but now their companion existed in a state far beyond their comprehension. They were still living in their very small, limited world while their winged cousin had gained for himself all the freedom between earth and sky. When he told friends of what he had seen, Demille concluded with this penetrating question: "Would the great Creator of the universe do that for a water beetle and not for a human being?"

MDP, the Sadducees in the Gospel could not see this. They could not see that in spite of some of the sorrow and disappointments, the situations which worry us, that we can rise to the heights of the life and love that God wants us to have. What the Sadducees did not understand is that God is not about endings but beginnings: He is always calling us to start again, to change some of our old behaviors and to embrace all that is good and affirming about the time we have been given on this earth. To become "sons and daughters of the resurrection" is to live with the real hope of the water beetles, that the love of God transcends all of our worries, our fears, our disappointments so that we can live our lives in the presence of the Easter miracle with a faith that believes the best is yet to come.

THIRTY-THIRD SUNDAY IN ORDINARY TIME
A – Matthew 25:14-30

The parable of the talents focuses on the critical question of not what we possess in terms of talent and ability, but our willingness to use those skills to make the Kingdom of God a reality here and now.

Jesus challenges us to commit whatever talents, strengths, and resources we have, to use whatever wealth we possess, to bring the hope, the peace and the joy of the kingdom of God into our hurting and desperate world. He teaches that our place in His kingdom will depend on how we use the talents God has given us. Are we going to bury them in our fears and selfishness or are we going to use them to tell the world about God in our midst?

There's an older movie called "Harold and Maude." Maude is an eighty-year-old woman who is in love with life. Maude challenges young Harold to a greater sensitivity to the wonders of life around him. In one scene, Harold sees only a field of ordinary daffodils; but Maude asks him to look at the uniqueness of each individual flower. When Harold and Maude drive into the city of Los Angeles, Harold sees tall buildings and lots of cars; but Maude sees a tiny, dying, choking tree and determines to uproot it and plant it where it can grow into the tree it really should become! In the film Maude says many unconventional things which might cause uneasiness. But as the movie goes on, I could not help thinking that perhaps the unconventional Maude has a deeper sense of what it means to be a Christian than many "conventional" Christians.

Our Blessed Lord's call to follow Him is a call to be free, free to become the uniquely beautiful person each of us should become. I believe that this is the point that Jesus is making in this Gospel: He points out that each of the three men is given funds according to his ability. The first two men perform up to their respective capabilities. They invest the money wisely and, in both cases, generate a handsome return. The third man, however, does not perform up to his ability. He is afraid to take a risk to act positively. Consequently, the master uses some vivid language in calling him "worthless."

MDP, our Blessed Lord is telling us that each of us is expected to perform his or her Christian duties according to our abilities. Each of us is given our own unique gifts to do God's will. Each of us is expected to live up to the gifts God has given us. The lesson is clear: the gifts conferred on us grow with use, or they will wither with disuse! There can be no stalling around in God's kingdom on earth. There can be no "I've got it made" attitude. Either we move ahead or we move back! Either we grow spiritually or we wither spiritually.

There is a little story about the great composer Ludwig Van Beethoven. Despite his genius and artistry, he was not a man known for his social grace. He was said to be uncomfortable and gruff with people. One day when the son of a close friend died, Beethoven rushed to the home of his friend to express his grief. He had no words to offer, but for the next half hour, he sat at his friend's piano and expressed his emotions in the most eloquent way he could. When he had finished playing, Beethoven quietly got up and left. His friend later said that no one else's visit meant as much to him and his family.

The great medical missionary, Albert Schweitzer, once said, "The interior joy we feel when we have done a good deed and lent a helping hand, is the nourishment the soul requires." Without those times when one feels part of the spiritual world by her or his actions, the soul decays.

MDP, greatness in the kingdom of God is defined by what we are able to do with the talents and gifts we have been given. We have been given the responsibility of caring for this earth and for one another. And through the life and death and resurrection of our blessed Lord, we have been given the freedom and the power to grow into the beautiful persons God wants each of us to be. And our own beauty is enhanced to the extent that we see one another as also having been chosen by God for fulfillment as uniquely beautiful human beings.

Someone has likened people who remain inside themselves, insensitive to the talents and needs of others to two shipwrecked men sitting together at one end of a life boat, doing nothing. They watch as the people at the other end bail out water furiously, trying to keep the boat afloat. One man then says to the other, "Thank God, that hole isn't in our end of the boat!"

MDP, the gifts and talents God gives us grow with use and wither with disuse. We are all in the boat called life together. We are all moving toward a common destiny in heaven! Our place in heaven will depend on how we use the talents and gifts God gives us to reveal His presence in our midst on this earth.

B – MARK 13:24-32

"Learn a lesson from the fig tree..." What a powerful and chilling Gospel. As followers of Jesus, we all should know where we are going with our lives. Jesus spoke realistically about the end, about his death, about your death and my death, and as you heard in the Gospel, about the end of the world!

But, no matter how you cut it, when you look at our world today, you can easily get the impression that God is not at the center of people's lives, that God is not number one, that He is being moved over, and that more and more people are placing themselves at the center.

It was a little more than a year ago that Lehman Brothers, the International Banking and Securities Firm, collapsed. After years of unchecked spending and trading, Lehman's bankruptcy touched off a global panic that marked the beginning of the worst recession since the depression.

I remember listening to a young executive being interviewed on T.V. He was a former managing director of Lehman Brothers. Today he runs a gas station and a car wash in Florida. He said something like this, "I spent a long time being very angry. Angry for working so hard and doing so much. More importantly, for my family and all the time I was away, the time I put in away from them. Now all the money I earned, the money paid in stock, is gone. I can't go back and remake it."

MDP, I want to ask you and myself a question: what are the wisest things we should invest in? The terrifying images that Jesus talks about in the Gospel confront us with the reality that the things we give our lives to – our careers, our portfolios, our houses, our cars, our celebrity – will one day be no more. He calls us to embrace, not the things of the world, but all the things that are of God!

A priest friend of mine does an interesting thing when he counsels a couple before marriage. He asks the couple to plan each other's funeral. When he first told me this, I said, "How morbid! How depressing! How awful!" But not for him. He finds that the exercise makes the spouses to be think about what kind of person their lover may be years or decades later. The couple start talking about how they might best take care of each other and their marriage right now. By asking how their marriage may end, they discover how it may best begin and be sustained to its end.

MDP, every day we live in the shadow of eternity. In every one of our lives, there is a fig tree and our tree grows and flowers, bears fruit, and then withers. Today Jesus urges us to recognize such "signs" with the eyes and the spirit of faith. He urges us to appreciate what a precious gift our limited time on earth is; to realize that every change we make in our lives, every triumph we have, every pain, and every heartbreak we suffer are opportunities for growth and opportunities to place God at the center of our lives. When we do this, every sign of us getting older, of change, of milestones we pass, we journey with our feet firmly planted on the ground and in the Gospel of Jesus Christ. We journey to the kingdom of heaven.

C – Luke 21:5-11

Those who listened to Jesus' frightening discourse contained in today's Gospel, must have had the feeling that their days were numbered. The fact of the matter is that everyone's days are numbered. And yet, we have Jesus' promise that out of the death of the physical body comes, by the power of Almighty God, the joy of everlasting life, unless, in the midst of life, we do not face up to the fact of death, we are unable to experience the fullness of life. Unless we face honestly the fact of death, we cannot know what in the world is going on in this church, week after week.

You know, we look around at what is happening in our world, and we think of the memorable line in the old movie "Green Pastures" when Gabriel says, "Everything that's fastened down is coming loose." That's the way it seems to be these days. Everything seems to be coming unglued. And all of this seems to be in today's Gospel when Jesus speaks of the coming of "wars and revolutions" and "nations fighting against nations, kingdom against kingdom," "great earthquakes, plagues and great signs from heaven," and "persecutions and imprisonment." In the midst of all of this chaos, Jesus tells His listeners to take heart. "Do not be frightened," He says.

It reminds me of the many times I visited New York City and walked by one of the skyscrapers on Fifth Avenue. In front of this building, I believe it is the RCA building, there stands an imposing statue of the mighty atlas bent over from the weight of the world (a globe) he bears on his giant shoulders. And right across the avenue stands St. Patrick's Cathedral and inside the cathedral, behind the main altar, there stands another statue, a statue of Jesus, about eight or nine years old. And in His hand, He also holds the whole world (a globe) with the greatest of ease. Do not be frightened. The Lord Jesus holds my world and your world, and the whole wide world in His saving hand!

"The days will come when there will not be left a stone upon another stone that will not be thrown down."

A few weeks ago, I remember reading a story in a magazine that touched me. A man's wife had died and he was going through her clothes and things. He opened the bottom drawer of her bureau and lifted out a tissue wrapped package. He unfolded the tissue and handed his wife's sister the package. It contained a beautiful, new slip. The garment was expensive and quite exquisite, handmade of silk and trimmed with intricate lace. The price tag was still attached. The man said to his sister-in-law, "Jan bought this the first time we went to New York, at least eight or nine years ago. She never wore it. She was saving it for a special occasion. Well, I guess this is the occasion."

He took the slip and put it on the bed with the other clothes that they would bring to the funeral home. His hands lingered on the soft material for a moment, then he slammed the drawer shut. He then said something to his sister-in-law that I will never forget. He said, "Don't ever save anything for a special occasion. Everyday you're alive is a special occasion."

His wife's sister remembered those words through the funeral and the difficult days that followed as she helped her brother-in-law and niece attend the sad chores that follow an unexpected death. She thought about the things her sister hadn't seen or heard or done, about all her late sister had done without realizing they were special. The words of her brother-in-law began to have a dramatic impact on her life, and so she wrote:

"Today I am reading more and dusting less. I'm sitting on the deck and admiring the view without fussing about the weeds in the garden. I'm spending more time with my family and friends and less time in committee meetings. I'm not 'saving' anything; we use our good china and crystal for every special event such as losing a pound, getting the sink unstopped, the first camellias blossom. I wear my good blazer to the market. 'Someday" and 'one of these days' are losing their grip on my vocabulary. I'm trying hard not to put off, hold back, or save anything that would add laughter and luster to our lives. And every moment I open my eyes, I tell myself that it is special. Every day, every minute, every breath is a gift of God."

MDP, I believe the Gospel today confronts us with the lessons this woman and her family learned in the unexpected death of her sister: that the time we are given in this life is precious, that God gives us this gift of life to embrace and be embraced by the love that is uniquely of God. Jesus tells us not to be frightened, not to be obsessed with the 'stones' that will one day collapse and become dust, but to seek instead the lasting things of God. We are all called to build the kingdom of God with the lasting stones of compassion, justice, reconciliation, music, beauty, laughter, and appreciation of one another. We are called not to be frightened, not to limit our vision, but with courage and grace to build our world into something sacred, something holy.

A YELLOW SHEET OF PAPER

Jack Finney wrote a short story called "Contents of a Dead Man's Pocket." The main character in the story is a man named Tom Benecke. Tom Benecke has spent months working on a proposal for the supermarket chain he works for. He had copied the results of his research and other critical data on a yellow piece of paper. His ideas could mean a huge promotion and a substantial raise—and his career would take off.

Well, one night, after his wife Clare leaves to go to the movies, Tom stays home in their small apartment to write up his proposal. He left the door of his apartment open, and an unexpected blast of cold air from the hallway blows the yellow piece of paper out a window where it becomes lodged on the ledge just beyond Tom's reach – eleven stories above the street below. Instead of using his common sense, Tom convinces himself that he can retrieve the paper. He carefully makes his way out the apartment window and onto the ledge. Slowly shuffling along the bricks, he manages to grab the yellow paper and stuff it in his jacket pocket. He shuffles back to the window, struggling to keep his balance. But as he begins to move, the old window has slipped closed, and he can't pry it open. He doesn't dare try to break the glass. You see, reaching back to swing at the window will send him falling backwards. So Tom is trapped on the narrow ledge, eleven stories above Lexington Avenue, on a cold New York night. His calls for help are ignored; Clare would not be home for hours. Contemplating his death, Tom is filled with fear and anger as he realizes all that people will find in his pocket will be the yellow sheet of paper. "Contents of a dead man's pocket," he thinks, one sheet of paper bearing penciled notations – incomprehensible.

He thinks of all the hours he had spent away from his beloved Clare, working day and night. He thinks of his crazy ambition and the direction his life has taken. He thinks of the hours he has spent by himself, filling the yellow sheet that has brought him out on the ledge. "Contents of a dead man's pocket", he thinks with sudden, fierce anger, what a wasted life.

THANKSGIVING

There's a wonderful story of a grandmother who went to church on Sunday, aglow with joyful anticipation. Her grandchildren were coming the next day to spend a week with her. She was so happy about it she put five dollars in the collection basket. The very next Sunday, after the grandchildren had just left, she put twenty-five dollars in the collection basket—gratitude—Thanksgiving!

In the process of going through his mid-life evaluation, a man got to thinking about those people whose help had made a difference in his life. He reflected with special gratitude on a teacher who stood out in his memory because she had helped him through a crisis in his youth. Suddenly he realized that he had never thanked her. He tried to contact her at the school, but learned that she had been retired for many years. Consequently, he sent her a letter in which he expressed his gratitude. Shortly thereafter, he received a letter in response. It read as follows:

"My Dear Willie,

I can't tell you how much your note meant to me. I am in my eighties, living alone in a small room, cooking my own meals and, like the last leaf of fall, lingering behind. You will be interested to know that I taught school for fifty years and yours is the first note of appreciation I ever received. It came on a blue, cold morning and it cheered me as nothing has in years."

You heard it this way in this evening's Gospel: "Were not ten made clean? Where are the other nine?"

My dear people, to grow rich in the sight of God, we must not only say "thank you," but we must show our "thank you"—not just in words, but in the things we do. To thank God for His gifts to us, we must use them with this prayer:

- ***Thank you*** *and Your will be done with all the material gifts You have given me.*

- ***Thank you****, O God, and Your will be done with all the spiritual gifts You give me.*

- ***Thank you*** *and Your will be done with the very life you have given me.*

- *Were not ten made clean, where are the other nine?*

THIRTY-FOURTH SUNDAY IN ORDINAY TIME
A – CHRIST THE KING—MATTHEW 25:31-46

When I was stationed in Hawaii, I traveled to one of the outer islands. In a small town on one of these islands, I found three streets named, "This Way," "That way", and "Any way". Then there was a road that ran past a small church, the road was named, "His Way." I thought that this is the road less traveled.

But there was so much meaning in the name of that road. "His Way" is the only sure way to go if we want to experience a joy-filled life. "His Way" is the way we care for someone else; "His Way" is the way we share our lives with someone else; "His Way" is the way of empathy, compassion; understanding. This is the vision that Christ calls us to embrace in the parable of the sheep and the goats.

If we listened carefully to the parable, we would have understood that the vision Christ gives us is the vision of a humanity that sees deeper than the externals of race, nationality, culture and language so as to behold the life of God in every man, woman, child we meet. When we see and feel this, we will understand Jesus when he says, "Come, you have my father's blessing! Inherit the Kingdom prepared for you..." He says, "You have achieved a balance, a holiness in life; you have become the unique and beautiful person I want you to be." He says in effect, you are a caring person, a person sensitive to the needs of others—where you saw hunger, you gave food; where you saw thirst, you gave drink...nakedness, you gave clothing; illness, you gave comfort; loneliness, you gave friendship.

There are husbands and wives, there are children we read about and hear about every day, who are starving for emotional and spiritual support, hungry for acceptance and understanding. There are persons in our family and among our friends, who lack a sense of joy and are trying to discover meaning in their lives. We must be Christ and exercise His ministry of love to these and to those closest to us!

When Albert Einstein was on the lecture circuit, giving talks on his "theory of relativity", he ordinarily traveled with a driver. One day while on the road, Einstein's driver said to him, "Doctor Einstein, I have heard you deliver that lecture on relativity dozens of times; I've memorized it and I'll wager I could deliver it myself." Einstein replied, "very well, I'll give you that opportunity. The people at the university where I am to lecture next have never met me. Before we get there, I'll put on your cap and you will introduce me as your chauffeur and you yourself as me. Then, you will give the lecture." For a while, all went according to plan. The chauffeur delivered the lecture flawlessly. But as the lecture concluded, a professor in the audience rose and asked a complex question involving mathematical equations and formulas. The quick-thinking chauffeur replied, "The solution to that problem is so simple I'm really surprised you have asked me to give it to you. Indeed, to prove to you how simple it is, I am going to ask my chauffeur to step forward and answer it!"

MDP, we must live a balanced life, a wholesome life. Herein lies holiness! How do we do this? The answer is so simple that you may not believe me. So I am going to let Jesus, the Christ and King, answer the question: feed the hungry, give drink to the thirsty, love one another as I have loved you. And you will be the uniquely beautiful persons I want you to be.

For the least of my brothers

There is a story during the horrible days of Hitler about a young German soldier named Joseph Schultz.

Shultz was sent to Yugoslavia shortly after the invasion. He was a loyal, young German soldier on patrol. One day the sergeant called out eight names, his among them. They thought they were going on a routine patrol. As they hitched up their rifles, they came over a hill, still not knowing what their mission was. There were eight Yugoslavians there, standing on the brow of the hill, five men and three women. It was only when they got about fifty feet away from them, where any marksman could shoot out an eye of a pheasant, that the solders realized what their mission was.

The eight soldiers were lined up. The sergeant barked out "Ready!" and they lifted up their rifles. "Aim!" and they got their sights. And suddenly in the silence that prevailed, there was a thud of a rifle butt against the ground. The sergeant, the seven other soldiers, and those eight Yugoslavians stopped and looked. Private Joseph Schultz walked toward the Yugoslavians. His sergeant called after him and ordered him to come back, but he pretended not to hear him. Instead, he walked fifty feet to the mound of the hill and joined hands with the eight Yugoslavians. There was moment of silence; then the sergeant yelled, "Fire!" And Private Joseph Schultz died, mingling his blood with that of those innocent men and women.

In the pocket of his uniform was a piece of paper with the words from today's powerful Gospel, "Whatever you did for one of the least of my brothers, you did for Me…"

B – Christ the King—John 18:33-37

This is the last Sunday of the liturgical year. Next Sunday we begin our celebration of Advent. Today is also the Sunday before Thanksgiving.

As we see Jesus standing before Pilate, we thankfully realize that He has come to reveal God's love for us.

I would like to share a story with you that I have been carrying for years. It is a story of thanksgiving and concerns two close friends who served with me in the Navy. Their names are Dede and Wil; they are married and now live in California. (I called them this week and asked if I could share their "Thanksgiving" story with you.)

Many years ago, Dede and Wil were celebrating their first New Year's together as husband and wife. Married just a few months before, they were caught up with the struggles every couple experiences in the first years: creating a home, balancing careers and marriage, trying to keep up with their student and car loans, etc.

That New Year's Eve, they decided to stay home. Wil comes home from work and sees Dede on an easy chair in the living room writing in a new note book. "What are you doing?" he asks. "Oh, nothing. Just writing down all that's happened this year." "Can I take a look?" Wil takes the journal and starts to read:

"A beautiful wedding with family and friends. Our honeymoon in Bermuda. Mom and Dad's help to buy our first place. My wonderful husband."

Then he took the pen and added: "My brother's help in fixing up our house. A tough but good year at my practice which shows promise. My lovely, caring wife."

She wrote at the end of the list: "We have much to be thankful for!"

And so began a tradition. Every New Year's, they would open the notebook and list the blessings of the year past. In those early years, the list was long:

"The birth of Beth, their first daughter, her promotion at school; the launch of a new practice."

Some years the list was short and almost terse: (for example) "Managed to keep it together during a bad year. Survived her cancer surgery. A stormy year with our teenager, Francis. But we all made it."

And every year's pages end with the words, "We have much to be thankful for."

Their journal now runs forty plus pages. Recent entries include the blessings of grandchildren. Pasted inside are prayer cards remembering loved ones and old friends who have gone on to God.

Dede and Wil keep the journal on the top of a dresser where they can't help but see it every day. Its very presence throughout the year reminds them, in good times and bad, in moments of sadness and crisis, "we have much to be thankful for."

MDP, we are loved by God to a degree we cannot begin to even imagine. We are loved by a God who refuses to give up on us, no matter what we have done in our lives. We are loved by a God who humbles Himself to become one of us so that we might become something of Him.

We have so much to be grateful for. May we find fulfillment and purpose, and consolation and grace in our own personal gratefulness journals, and may we realize that Christ the King has come to reveal the truth of the love of God for each of us.

C (1) – Luke 23:35-43

This is the last Sunday of the liturgical year—next Sunday is the first Sunday of Advent. It is also the Sunday before Thanksgiving. I have always loved this Gospel and so often, I think of it, and I hope you will, especially the words of the good thief: "Remember me when you come into Your Kingdom," and then the promise that has rung through the centuries: "Today you will be with Me in paradise." The good thief knew that Jesus came to reveal God's love for us.

But, the other thief—a lot like us—is yelling, "Are you not the Christ? Save yourself and us." Like this thief, we often see our personal experiences of the cross in lives through the perspective of this thief. It's all about saving ourselves; that our survival blinds us to the crosses of others, that we are the victims, and we think it is never our fault or responsibility.

I would like to share a story with you about two Navy friends of mine – husband and wife. I met them in my tour in Hawaii. My friend was diagnosed with cancer and had a double lung transplant, and she threatened to leave him. It goes like this: he had been sick for awhile and a transplant was his only hope. They left Hawaii for a hospital in Palo Alto, California. She was right there the whole time, supervising the diet, dealing with his mood swings, cheering him up when all seemed lost. She knew how radically life-altering a transplant process is and how exasperated one becomes while waiting and wasting away.

Then one day she said to my friend, her husband, "I don't think I can do this anymore." She already bought a plane ticket back to Hawaii. His mother flew in to help. I remember how angry he was for the next week or two. He ranted, "How could she?" "Who does something like this/" They didn't talk much while she was away. Then, he had an epiphany. He explained it to me like this: "Once I knew she was coming back, I began deciding what I was going to say to her, how I was going to explain how hurt and upset I was that she would simply abandon me after everything I had gone through. And there it was. I hadn't gone through anything. We had, together!

Every problem my health presented had to be handled twice over, worrying about me and worrying about her life after me if it all went sideways. She had to deal with the information, acting as nurse, housekeeper, chauffeur, and lawyer for me. The man who was supposed to share her life and not consume her life. When she said, "I don't think I can do this anymore," I got angry, but I was wrong. Her retreat didn't mean that she was done with me. It meant that she was as broken as I was."

MDP, there it is – the first thief! Saving himself and not seeing the Christ suffering on the cross next to him! The Kingdom of Christ begins with humility, with compassion, with understanding. At the heart of His Kingdom is the realization that God is with us in the love we have for our family, in the care and kindness we show our friends. The Kingdom of Christ that we celebrate today, this last Sunday of the liturgical year, is founded on the power of forgiveness, of compassion, of graciousness, of a vision that we are one family under the providence of this great God.

C–(2) LUKE 23:35-43

A few weeks ago, I told you about the Navy, after my tour in Southeast Asia and the Far East, sent me to a Coast Guard tour in Petaluma, California—beautiful, acres of farm land, and very close to Bodega Bay, where Alfred Hitchcock filmed "The Birds." There was a family that came to my Mass on the base—Reggie and Margaret Green. We became friends, and I will never forget them. On this Feast of Christ the King, the words of the Gospel, "For this I was born, and for this I came into the world, to testify to the truth..." prompted me to tell you their story.

Reggie and Margaret had two beautiful children, Nicholas, age seven, and Eleanor, age four. They decided to vacation in Italy. They were driving on a highway near Salerno when a small car came up behind them. Suddenly, masked gunmen in the small car opened fire on them. Reggie managed to speed away and elude the bandits. Only after he was able to stop the car did he and Margaret discover that Nicolas, who was sleeping in the back seat, had been shot in the head. Nicholas was declared brain dead the following day.

Reggie and Margaret did an extraordinary thing. They donated their son's organs to five Italian children waiting for such transplants. Rather than show rage or vengeance, they said many times during their ordeal, that Italians were not to blame for what happened. Rather than say they wanted nothing more to do with Italy, they made a point of saying that the transplants of their little boy's organs to other Italian children would lessen their pain.

Reggie said, "I would have liked Nicholas to live a long time, and now I wish the same thing for his heart." Their extraordinary charity affected the people of Italy. Reggie shared one editorial with me. It read, "Perhaps the Green family does not realize how rare their gesture is in our country. With us violence is an ancient evil, and marks many destinies. This land, famous for history and beauty and art, suffers from invincible cruelty which hides behind the oleanders and the sycamores and the ancient ruins. I must, I want to thank you not only for the transplants, but for the lesson of generosity, composure and faith."

MDP, confronted by death, the Green family proclaimed life; challenged by anger and hatred, they championed hope and love. This Feast of Christ the King confronts all of us with the beliefs that rule our hearts and minds and the values that govern all of our decisions. The Jesus on the Cross in this beautiful Gospel gives us reason to seek what is right and good in all things, to embrace the truth of His love and compassion without any second guessing, and to hope in the fulfillment of God's reign in our own personal circumstances, in our time and place.